T0258875

Advances on Mathematical Modeling and Optimization with Its Applications

Advances on Mathematical Modeling and Optimization with its Applications discusses optimization, equality, and inequality constraints and their application in the versatile optimizing domain. It further covers nonlinear optimization methods such as global optimization, and gradient-based nonlinear optimization, and their applications.

Key Highlights:

- Discusses important topics including multi-component differential equations, geometric partial differential equations, and computational neural systems.
- Covers linear integer programming and network design problems, along with an application of mixed integer problems.
- Discusses constrained and unconstrained optimization, equality, and inequality constraints, and their application in the versatile optimizing domain.
- Elucidates the application of statistical models, probability models, and transfer learning concepts.
- Showcases the importance of multi-attribute decision modeling in the domain of image processing and soft computing.

The text is primarily for senior undergraduate and graduate students, and academic researchers in the fields of mathematics, statistics, and computer science.

Emerging Technologies

Research and Practical Applications

Series Editors: Aryan Chaudhary, Chief Scientific Advisor, Bio Tech Sphere Research, India
Raman Chadha, Chandigarh University, Punjab

ABOUT THE SERIES

The series offers a comprehensive exploration of frameworks and models that harness information and knowledge from diverse perspectives. It delves into the application of these insights to address global issues in industries, the environment, and communities. The focus is on knowledge transfer systems and innovative techniques that facilitate effective implementation. This amalgamation of intelligent systems and various applications necessitates collaboration across disciplines such as science, technology, business, and humanities.

Covering a wide range of cutting-edge topics, the series includes books on Artificial Intelligence, Big Data Analytics, Cloud Computing Technologies, Design Automation, Digital Signal Processing, IoTs, Internet of Medical Things, Machine Learning, Natural Language Processing, Robotics and Automation, Signal Processing, Healthcare applications, Convolutional neural organization, Medical Imaging, Voice Biomarker (Voice Tech in Health), Image Recognition, and more.

FORTHCOMING BOOKS

Artificial Intelligence and Society 5.0
Issues, Opportunities, and Challenges
Edited by Vikas Khullar, Vrajesh Sharma, Mohit Angurala, and Nipun Chhabra

Advances on Mathematical Modeling and Optimization with Its Applications
Edited by Gunjan Mukherjee, Biswadip Basu Mallik, Rahul Kar, and Aryan Chaudhary

For more information about the series, please visit: https://www.routledge.com/ Emerging-Technologies/book-series/CRCCHETRPA

Advances on Mathematical Modeling and Optimization with Its Applications

Edited by
Gunjan Mukherjee, Biswadip Basu Mallik,
Rahul Kar, and Aryan Chaudhary

CRC Press
Taylor & Francis Group
Boca Raton London New York

CRC Press is an imprint of the
Taylor & Francis Group, an **informa** business

First edition published 2024
by CRC Press
2385 NW Executive Center Drive, Suite 320, Boca Raton FL 33431

and by CRC Press
4 Park Square, Milton Park, Abingdon, Oxon, OX14 4RN

CRC Press is an imprint of Taylor & Francis Group, LLC

© 2024 selection and editorial matter, Gunjan Mukherjee, Biswadip Basu Mallik, Rahul Kar, and Aryan Chaudhary; individual chapters, the contributors

Reasonable efforts have been made to publish reliable data and information, but the author and publisher cannot assume responsibility for the validity of all materials or the consequences of their use. The authors and publishers have attempted to trace the copyright holders of all material reproduced in this publication and apologize to copyright holders if permission to publish in this form has not been obtained. If any copyright material has not been acknowledged please write and let us know so we may rectify in any future reprint.

Except as permitted under U.S. Copyright Law, no part of this book may be reprinted, reproduced, transmitted, or utilized in any form by any electronic, mechanical, or other means, now known or hereafter invented, including photocopying, microfilming, and recording, or in any information storage or retrieval system, without written permission from the publishers.

For permission to photocopy or use material electronically from this work, access www.copyright.com or contact the Copyright Clearance Center, Inc. (CCC), 222 Rosewood Drive, Danvers, MA 01923, 978-750-8400. For works that are not available on CCC please contact mpkbookspermissions@tandf.co.uk

Trademark notice: Product or corporate names may be trademarks or registered trademarks and are used only for identification and explanation without intent to infringe.

ISBN: 9781032479613 (hbk)
ISBN: 9781032481104 (pbk)
ISBN: 9781003387459 (ebk)

DOI: 10.1201/9781003387459

Typeset in Times
by codeMantra

Contents

Preface..x
Editors...xii
Contributors xiv

Chapter 1 Mathematical Modeling and Analysis of a Marine Ecosystem:
A Deterministic and Stochastic Process 1

Anal Chatterjee

1.1 Introduction 1
1.2 The Mathematical Model 2
1.3 Some Preliminary Results..3
1.4 Optimal Harvesting Policy...6
1.5 The Stochastic Model 9
1.6 Numerical Simulations 12
1.7 Discussion...17
References 20

Chapter 2 Multi-criteria Optimisation and Compromise Solution to Select Financially
Efficient NIFTY IT Companies Pre and During COVID-19 Pandemic...................21

*Subrata Jana, Bibhas Chandra Giri, Anirban Sarkar,
and Biswadip Basu Mallik*

2.1 Introduction 21
2.2 Literature Review 23
2.3 Research Objectives 25
2.4 Research Methodology 25
2.5 Data and Findings...29
2.6 Suggestions for Compromise Solution 40
2.7 Conclusions...41
2.8 Limitations..42
2.9 Future Scope of Study 42
References 42

Chapter 3 Conjoint Analysis: A Heuristic Decision-Making Model of
Product Selection..43

Sweety Mukherjee, Ayushman Malakar, and Arnab Roy

3.1 Introduction 43
3.2 Historical Background of Conjoint Analysis..........................44
3.3 Statistical Modeling of Conjoint Analysis.............................44
3.4 Steps of Conjoint Analysis 46
3.5 Application of Conjoint Analysis for Market Researchers.............48
3.6 An Illustration of Conjoint Analysis with the Application of Software.............48
3.7 Merits and Demerits of Conjoint Analysis 51
3.8 Conclusion 52
References 53

Chapter 4   Ranking of Wear Behavior Characteristics in Al6061 Reinforced with
                Industrial Waste Materials Using PROMETHEE and MOORA Methods.................55

*Sibabrata Mohanty, Amit Jain Biswal, Niyati Naik, Debesh Mishra,
and Ajay Soni*

4.1   Introduction 55
4.2   Material and Methods 56
4.3   Experimental Procedure...59
4.4   Result Analysis...60
4.5   Conclusion 65
References 65

Chapter 5   Aqueous Humor Flow in the Schlemm's Canal via Rectangular Channel:
                Mathematical Modeling for Analytical Results, Numerical Experiments,
                and Implications for Treatments...66

Shabab Akbar, Sapna Ratan Shah, and Sardar M. N. Islam

5.1   Introduction 66
5.2   Model Description...69
5.3   Governing Equation 69
5.4   Boundary Conditions...70
5.5   Problem Formulation...70
5.6   Results and Discussion 71
5.7   Conclusion 74
References 74

Chapter 6   Solving Fuzzy Nonlinear Optimization Problems Using
                Evolutionary Algorithms...76

Yogeesh N.

6.1   Introduction 76
6.2   Literature Review 79
6.3   Methodology..81
6.4   Discussion of Strengths and Limitations of Existing Approaches.................83
6.5   EAs for Fuzzy Nonlinear Optimization 84
6.6   Case Studies..87
6.7   Comparison with Other Methods 90
6.8   Conclusion and Future Directions...92
References 93

Chapter 7   Mathematical Modelling Techniques and Applications of Wireless
                Communication Using Fuzzy Logic 96

Yogeesh N., Girija D. K., Rashmi M., and Shilpa H. K.

7.1   Introduction 96
7.2   Fuzzy Logic Control Overview and Classification 97
7.3   The Benefits and Capabilities of Fuzzy Logic Techniques 101
7.4   Wireless Sensor Network's Features (WSN)..............................102

7.5 Wireless Sensor Network Difficulties 104
7.6 List of Various Techniques and Applications of Wireless
     Communication Using Fuzzy Logic... 106
7.7 Key Findings and Results of the Research Chapter 112
7.8 Summary and Future Study 113
7.9 Conclusion 114
References 115

Chapter 8   Availability Optimization of Poly-Ethylene Terephthalate Bottle
               Hot Drink Filling System Using Particle Swarm and
               Grey Wolf Optimizers 117

Parul Punia, Amit Raj, and Pawan Kumar

8.1 Introduction 117
8.2 System Description, Notations, and Assumptions 118
8.3 Mathematical Modeling of the System in Steady State 119
8.4 Evolutionary Algorithms 123
8.5 Results and Discussion 124
8.6 Conclusion 126
References 127

Chapter 9   Optimisation of Drilling Parameters on Glass Fibre Reinforced
               Polymer Composites with Stainless Steel Mesh using Taguchi and
               Grey Fuzzy Relation Method 128

M. Sakthivel and P. Raja

9.1 Introduction 128
9.2 Experimental Method.. 129
9.3 Results and Discussion 132
9.4 Conclusion 137
References 138

Chapter 10 A Comprehensive Mathematical Framework for Diabetes
               and Its Complications in Crisp and Fuzzy Settings 140

Purnima Pandit, Payal Singh, and Sujata Panda

10.1 Introduction 140
10.2 Fuzzy Differential Equations 140
10.3 Basic Concepts 141
10.4 Predictive Mathematical Model of Diabetes in a Crisp Environment 143
10.5 Mathematical Modelling of Diabetes in Fuzzy Environment...................... 145
10.6 Stability Analysis.. 148
10.7 Numerical Illustration 148
10.8 Results and Discussion 149
10.9 Conclusion 150
References 150

Chapter 11 Applications of Mathematical Techniques to Artificial Intelligence: Mathematical Methods, Algorithms, Computer Programming and Applications 152

Rashmi Singh, Neha Bhardwaj, and Sardar M. N. Islam

11.1   Introduction: Background and Driving Forces............................. 152
11.2   Linear Algebra... 153
11.3   Applications of Statistics in Data Science through Machine Learning Algorithms.. 155
11.4   Some Other Statistical Methods.. 159
11.5   Calculus 161
11.6   Optimization or Operation Research.. 165
11.7   Computer Programs.. 167
11.8   AI Applications.. 167
11.9   Concluding Remarks 168
References 168

Chapter 12 Prediction of Winning Team in Soccer Game: A Supervised Machine Learning-Based Approach 170

Sanjay Chakraborty, Lopamudra Dey, Saikat Maity, and Animesh Kairi

12.1   Introduction 170
12.2   Literature Survey 171
12.3   Background.. 172
12.4   Result Analysis.. 176
12.5   Conclusions and Future Works.. 179
Conflict of Interest... 184
Funding.. 184
References 184

Chapter 13 Asset Liability Management Model Based on Duration and Convexity for Commercial Banks 187

Sahidul Islam

13.1   Introduction 187
13.2   Prerequisite Terms... 189
13.3   Mathematical Model.. 192
13.4   Mathematical Analysis.. 196
13.5   Numerical Illustrations.. 199
13.6   Conclusions..203
References 203

Chapter 14 A Qualitative Mathematical Analysis of Pandemic SARS-Cov-2 with Special Emphasis on Uncertain Environments................................205

Kalyan Das, M. N. Srinivas, Md Humayun Kabir, Md Osman Gani, and Md Haider Ali Biswas

14.1   Introduction 205
14.2   Model of SARS-Cov-2 with Time Delay 206
14.3   Mathematical Analysis of System (14.2) without Time Delay 207

14.4 Investigation of the Ideal's Stability at Steadiness
without Time Delay 210
14.5 Analysis of the Delayed NVIR Model 212
14.6 Numerical Simulations 214
14.7 Discussion and Concluding Remarks 228
Contributions of Authors 232
Conflict of Interest 232
Acknowledgment 232
References 232

Chapter 15 A Game Theory Model to Analyze Business Strategies
for Increasing Profits: Analytical and Computational Approaches 235

Wong Wai Peng, Sardar M N Islam, and Daniel Christopher Schoch

15.1 Introduction: Background and Driving Forces 235
15.2 The Company Context 236
15.3 Game Theory as an Analytical Approach 237
15.4 The Game Model 237
15.5 Value of Fuels and Lignocellulose as Raw Material 241
15.6 Recommendations 244
15.7 Implications and Conclusion 244
Acknowledgment 245
References 245

Chapter 16 An Efficient Course Assignment Technique Based on Teachers Rating
to Support Higher Education Systems 246

*Chittaranjan Mallick, Sourav Kumar Bhoi, Kalyan Kumar Jena,
and Debasis Mohapatra*

16.1 Introduction 246
16.2 Related Works 247
16.3 Materials and Methods 247
16.4 Proposed Method of Assignment for Course Assignment 248
16.5 Case Study 249
16.6 Results 250
16.7 Conclusion 259
References 259

Index 261

Preface

Science and engineering has become the more valuable hotbed in the research domain at present. Computing has become the most demanding topic of such domain in the fields of science and engineering. There are many innumerable problems found in the mathematics and sciences. These problems can take a big shape even in the fields of technology as the evolution of the same requires concrete knowledge in native fields. The main objective of such an approach has become concerned with grasping and solving such problems. Modern technology is entirely dependent on the data-driven approach, which needs mathematical aid, especially in the fields of symbolic computation dealing with the real world issues. With the passing days and gradual escalation of research and its outcomes, Artificial Intelligence and Machine learning have gained much momentum in the research fields. Such improvement of technological fields could not be possible without the mathematical concept. The wide scope of application has the wide scope of application in various areas of development and can be implemented in its own area of interest. The core of AI and machine learning has become immensely dependent on the statistics and application of statistical models. Significant light has been shed on the solution and interpretation of fundamental relationships between the models and their behavior thanks to the complex mathematical foundation and its built-in equation base. the statistical procedures, such as data variable correlations. Samples, populations, and hypotheses are all used in statistical modeling.

Math has become a part of our everyday life. From the minute we wake up to the moment we go to bed, we use mathematics in every aspect of our lives. The exhaustive contribution of mathematical aspects and applicative knowledge has become research worthy due to the invention and discoveries of many advanced sorts of theorems, Whether a person is Data Scientist, Data Analyst, or Machine Learning Engineer, "Mathematics" should be a key focus of the studies. Whatever the fields of research in science and technology are, it is inevitable to think about various streams with the application of mathematics. Mathematics has become the bedrock of many new kinds of inventions in the aforementioned fields. All real world business and data-driven applications require mathematics as a fundamental building block. From analyzing corporate transactions to figuring out how to expand in the day-to-day market, from calculating future stock estimates to estimating future sales, math is used in almost every facet of business. In a range of industries, such as retail, manufacturing, and information technology, math applications are used to offer a solid perspective in terms of sales, production, product intake, compensation paid, and market predictions, among other things. Therefore, mathematics has a real grasp on all sorts of technological fields to set up a relational bridge with the allied attributes of such technological overgrowths.

Artificial intelligence (AI) and machine learning (ML) are hot topics in the computer world, and for good reason. They help companies streamline operations and unearth data so that they can make better business decisions. The business growth is directly or indirectly managed by the proper trend analysis and the predictive approach of growth to the ultimate level of development. They're boosting almost every industry by allowing employees to work more effectively, and they're fast becoming a critical piece of technology for businesses to remain competitive with others. The gradual advancement of technology and its influence on overall business growth has led to a new path toward the stability of the modern economy.

Other core technologies such as face recognition on smartphones, personalized online shopping experiences, virtual assistants in homes, and even sickness diagnosis are all feasible due to extensive research works in these fields of technology. The demand for these technologies, as well as experts who are familiar with them, is on the rise with continuous and consistent research works and many innovations. The average number of AI projects in place at a business is likely to be more than treble over the next two years, according to a report by research firm Gartner. Organizations face challenges as a result of this exponential expansion. They cite a lack of expertise, difficulties in understanding AI use cases, and worries about data scope or quality as their top issues with these technologies. AI and ML, which were once the stuff of science fiction, are now becoming ubiquitous in enterprises. While these technologies are closely linked, there are significant distinctions between them. Here's a closer look at AI and ML, as well as some of the most popular vocations and talents, and how you can get started. Once again the startup policies of technology are being backed up by consistent persuasion in research along with the fruitful benefits of such a notion.

Computing time reduction is a difficult problem to overcome. The complexity of any problem in any domain is based on the interrelationships among its involved entities and the effects due to its interactions with others even lying outside the defined peripheries. For example, driving to a train station, taking the train to the best stop, and then walking or taking a ride-share service from that stop to the final destination considering all types of likely hazards. All such emancipation of problems can be mitigated by means of mathematics and different allied tools. This book provides us with enough insights into optimization and its mathematical connections through the research-oriented approach toward the better goal to achieve.

Editors

Dr. Gunjan Mukherjee is currently an associate professor in the Department of Computational Sciences at Brainware University. He completed his BSc in Physics from Calcutta University, MCA from IGNOU, MTech from Calcutta University and earned his PhD in Engineering from Jadavpur University. His areas of research interests include computer vision, machine learning, soft computing, image processing, etc. He is a life member of CSI, ISOC, and IAENG and has published a number of papers in journals and international conferences of repute. Dr. Mukherjee guided many students of BTech and MCA in their projects and research works. He has solely authored the school computer book series (classes 3–10), a textbook on IT systems theory for engineering students, and is presently writing a book on Python technology. He is currently attached to a reputed publishing house for publication of question/answer-based books for diploma and engineering level students. He has acted as a reviewer for many technical books. Dr. Gunjan was an assistant teacher at the Sree Aurobindo Institute of Education, an education officer in CSI, Kolkata chapter, a senior faculty in NIT Ltd, and a lecturer at Calcutta Institute of Technology. He also served as a visiting faculty in Aliha University, Techno India College and JIS College.

Dr. Biswadip Basu Mallik is presently an Associate Professor of Mathematics in the Department of Basic Sciences and Humanities at Institute of Engineering & Management, Kolkata, India. He has been involved in teaching and research for almost 22 years and has published several research papers and book chapters in various scientific journals and with reputed publishers. He has authored five books at undergraduate levels in the areas of Engineering Mathematics, Quantitative Methods and Computational Intelligence. He has also published five Indian patents along with thirteen edited books. His fields of research work are Computational Fluid Dynamics, Mathematical Modelling, Machine Learning, and Optimization. Dr. Basu Mallik is a series Editor of the Book series titled "Mathematics and Computer Science" from Wiley-Scrivener, USA and a Managing editor of Journal of Mathematical Sciences & Computational Mathematics (JMSCM), USA. He is also an Editorial board member and reviewer of several scientific journals. He is a senior life member of Operational Research Society of India (ORSI) and a life member of Calcutta Mathematical Society (CMS), Indian Statistical Institute (ISI), Indian Science Congress Association (ISCA), and International Association of Engineers (IAENG).

Rahul Kar has an M.Sc. in Pure Mathematics and is pursuing his PhD from Bankura University. He currently works as a Faculty of Mathematics at Kalyani Mahavidyalaya, Kalyani, Nadia, West Bengal. He has served as a guest faculty of the Gurunanak Institute of Technology and two other colleges. In total, he has 7 years of teaching experience. Rahul has published many research papers with the Scopus index and is an editor of four national and international journals and a reviewer of five international journals. He has been an editor for ten mathematics/computer books and is an annual member of the Indian Mathematical Society as well as an honorary member of Carmels Research Institute, Dakar, Senegal.

Aryan Chaudhary is the Chief Scientific Advisor at BioTech Sphere Research, India, having served as the Research Head at Nijji HealthCare Pvt Ltd, Head of Research, Nuvem Resources, and other invited positions. He has demonstrated his expertise in leveraging revolutionary technologies such as artificial intelligence, deep learning, IoT, cognitive technology, and blockchain to revolutionize the healthcare landscape. His relentless pursuit of excellence and innovation has earned him recognition as a thought leader in the industry. His dedication to advancing healthcare is evident through his vast bodies of work. He has authored several influential academic papers on public health and digital health, published in prestigious international journals. His research primarily focuses on integrating IoT and sensor technology for efficient data collection through one-time and ambulatory monitoring. As a testament to his expertise and leadership, he is not only a keynote speaker at numerous international and national conferences but also serves as the Series Editor of a CRC book series and is the editor of several books on biomedical science. His commitment to the advancement of scientific knowledge extends further, as he acts as a guest editor for special issues in renowned journals. Recognized for his significant contributions, he has received prestigious accolades, including the "Most Inspiring Young Leader in Healthtech Space 2022" by Business Connect, and the title of the best project leader at Global Education and Corporate Leadership. Moreover, he holds senior memberships in various international science associations, reflecting his influence and impact in the field. Adding to his accomplishments, Aryan Chaudhary is currently serving as a Guest Editor for a special issue in the highly regarded Journal: *EAI Endorsed Transactions on AI and Robotics*, and he has joined the Editorial Board of Biomedical Science and Clinical Research (BSCR). Additionally, he is a respected professional member of the Association for Computing Machinery (ACM). Recently, he has been elected as Chair for the ACM Professional Chapter.

Contributors

Shabab Akbar
School of Computational and Integrative
    Sciences
Jawaharlal Nehru University
New Delhi, India

Neha Bhardwaj
School of Basic Sciences and Research
Sharda University
Greater Noida, India

Sourav Kumar Bhoi
Department of Computer Science and
    Engineering
Parala Maharaja Engineering College (Govt.)
Berhampur, India

Amit Jain Biswal
GIET Ghangapatna, Affiliated to Biju Patnaik
    University of Technology (BPUT)
Rourkela, Odisha, India

Md Haider Ali Biswas
Mathematics Discipline
Khulna University
Khulna, Bangladesh

Sanjay Chakraborty
CSE Department
Techno International New Town
Kolkata, India

Anal Chatterjee
Department of Mathematics
Barrackpore Rastraguru Surendranath College
Barrackpore, India

Kalyan Das
Department of Basic and Applied Sciences
National Institute of Food Technology
    Entrepreneurship and Management
Kundli, India

Lopamudra Dey
CSE Department
Heritage Institute of Technology
Kolkata, India

Md Osman. Gani
Department of Mathematics
Jahangirnagar University
Dhaka, Bangladesh

Bibhas Chandra Giri
Department of Mathematics
Jadavpur University, Kolkata, India

D. K. Girija
Department of Computer Science
Government First Grade College
Madhugiri, India

Sahidul Islam
Department of Mathematics
University of Kalyani
Kalyani, India

Sardar M. N. Islam
ISILC, Victoria University
Melbourne, Australia

Subrata Jana
Department of Mathematics
Jadavpur University
Jadavpur, India

Kalyan Kumar Jena
Department of Computer Science and
    Engineering
Parala Maharaja Engineering College (Govt.)
Berhampur, India

Md Humayun Kabir
Department of Mathematics
Jahangirnagar University
Dhaka, Bangladesh

Animesh Kairi
Institute of Engineering and Management
Kolkata, India

Pawan Kumar
Department of Mathematics
Central University of Haryana
Jant-Pali, India

Saikat Maity
CSE Department
Sister Nivedita University
Kolkata, India

Ayushman Malakar
Genetics and Tree Improvement Division
ICFRE-Institute of Forest Productivity
Ranchi, India

Chittaranjan Mallick
Department of Basic Science (Mathematics)
Parala Maharaja Engineering College (Govt.)
Berhampur, India

Biswadip Basu Mallik
Department of Basic Science and Humanities
Institute of Engineering & Management
Kolkata, India

Debesh Mishra
Mechanical Engineering
IES University
Bhopal, India

Sibabrata Mohanty
GIET Ghangapatna, Affiliated to Biju Patnaik
    University of Technology (BPUT)
Rourkela, Odisha, India

Debasis Mohapatra
Department of Computer Science and
    Engineering
Parala Maharaja Engineering College (Govt.)
Berhampur, India

Sweety Mukherjee
Division of Agricultural Extension
ICAR-Indian Agricultural Research Institute
New Delhi, India

Niyati Naik
GIET Ghangapatna, Affiliated to Biju Patnaik
    University of
Technology (BPUT), Rourkela, Odisha, India

Sujata Panda
Department of Applied Sciences, Faculty of
    Engineering & Technology
Parul University
Vadodara, India

Purnima Pandit
M. S. University of Baroda
Vadodara, India

Wong Wai Peng
Monash University, Malaysia Campus,
    Malaysia

Parul Punia
Department of Mathematics
Central University of Haryana
Jant-Pali, Mahendergarh, India

Amit Raj
Department of Mathematics,
Central University of Haryana
Jant-Pali, Mahendergarh, India

P. Raja
Department of Mechanical Engineering
Prathyusha Engineering College
Chennai, India

M. Rashmi
Faculty in Computer Science
GFGC, Vijayanagar
Bengaluru, India

Arnab Roy
Sericultural Economics and Extension Division
Central Tasar Research and Training Institute
Ranchi, India

M. Sakthivel
Department of Mechanical Engineering
Adhiyamaan College of Engineering
Hosur, India

Anirban Sarkar
Department of Management and Marketing
West Bengal State University
Barasat, India

Daniel Christopher Schoch
American University of Ras Al Khaimah, UAE

Sapna Ratan Shah
School of Computational and Integrative
    Sciences
Jawaharlal Nehru University, New Delhi, India

H. K. Shilpa
Faculty in Computer Science
Mandya University
Mandya, India

Payal Singh
Department of Applied Sciences, Faculty of
    Engineering & Technology
Parul University
Vadodara, India

Rashmi Singh
Amity Institute of Applied Sciences
AUUP

Ajay Soni
Mathematics
IES College of Technology
Bhopal, India

M. N. Srinivas
Department of Mathematics
Vellore Institute of Technology
Vellore, India

N. Yogeesh
Department of Mathematics, Government First
    Grade College, Tumkur-572102, Karnataka,
    India

1 Mathematical Modeling and Analysis of a Marine Ecosystem
A Deterministic and Stochastic Process

Anal Chatterjee
Barrackpore Rastraguru Surendranath College,
West Bengal State University, West Bengal, India

1.1 INTRODUCTION

Plankton, consisting of phytoplankton and zooplankton, play an indispensable role in the marine ecosystem, which is widely acknowledged. Fish, being closely connected with the physical, chemical, and biological aspects of their environment, are also essential components of this ecosystem. As a result, researchers have dedicated considerable attention to studying the biomass of both fish and plankton and their impacts on the ecosystem.

Research on the dynamics of plankton and fish has examined the top-down and bottom-up effects, as detailed in [1,2]. When fish densities are high, the findings from these investigations demonstrate that predation regulates zooplankton populations, while the growth of algal biomass is limited by light or nutrient availability. In contrast, when fish densities are low, zooplankton experiences a limitation in food availability, while the density of phytoplankton is controlled by grazing. Furthermore, isocline analysis and simulations, as presented in [3], have explored how changes in fish predation influence plankton dynamics and the emergence of bifurcations. The influence of gestation delay under stochastic fluctuations in the plankton–fish system has been investigated as well, as outlined in references [4,5].

In [6], realistic patchiness patterns in plankton–fish dynamics were investigated using reaction-diffusion models. The study of food sources for fish larvae, which rely on zooplankton dynamics, was conducted in [7]. Furthermore, a conceptual mathematical model was formulated and analyzed in [8], which focuses on the populations of fish and zooplankton in lakes Naroch and Myastro.

Different aspects of two-species fisheries have been investigated in prior research, including the examination of discrete time delay in the combined harvesting model as presented in [9] as well as the exploration of the impacts of toxicity on the harvesting of two competing fish species discussed in [10]. In [11], the researchers explored the impact of adjusting harvest effort as a means to control bifurcations and restore system stability in situations where positive economic profit exists. In addition, the chaotic nature and bifurcation analysis of plankton–fish models have been explored in [12–14]. A recent study [15] explored the stability and bifurcation characteristics of a mathematical model that depicts the interactions among three essential species in a marine ecosystem: phytoplankton, zooplankton, and fish. The model accounts for the impact of fear on zooplankton behavior and the effects of fish harvesting on the system. The study examines how changes in the model parameters can affect the equilibrium points as well as the presence of limit cycles and bifurcations. This finding could have profound consequences for the long-term dynamics of the ecosystem.

DOI: 10.1201/9781003387459-1

Deterministic models in ecology have certain limitations as they fail to consider random parameter variations leading to environmental fluctuations [16]. Therefore, it is important to consider stochastic models to provide a more realistic description of natural systems. In a recent study [17], deterministic and stochastic models of nutrient-plankton interactions were examined, highlighting that elevated toxin production rates can induce chaotic dynamics. The significance of incorporating deterministic and stochastic approaches is underscored by these findings to gain a clearer understanding of ecological systems.

In contrast, in our present context, we widely focus on both deterministic and stochastic systems and examine the impact of top-down effects to study the system's dynamic behavior. Examining the combined effects of the harvesting rate and mortality rate of fish population, conversion rate and competition coefficient of fish population is the aim of this study. Based on the aforementioned assumptions, a mathematical model is developed, and the system's equilibrium point and stability are investigated. The main contributions can be summarized as follows:

- Our study examines how the harvesting and mortality rates of fish impact the plankton–fish ecosystem, and assesses the combined effects of these factors on the population dynamics.
- We establish that the rate of competition coefficient and conversion rate of fish population are vital in stabilizing the system.
- We compare the deterministic and stochastic models and derive the conditions needed to keep the model system stable.

This study examines the dynamics of a three-component open system consisting of phytoplankton, zooplankton, and planktivorous fish. A mathematical model that describes the interactions among these components is presented, and the stability analysis is conducted at each possible equilibrium point. This study specifically examines the conditions that lead to system instability and Hopf bifurcation around the coexistence equilibrium. Furthermore, this study discusses an optimal harvesting policy by employing Pontryagin's maximum principle. Numerical simulations are carried out across a range of parameter values to provide support for the analytical findings. Finally, the discussion section provides a summary of the main findings of the analysis.

1.2   THE MATHEMATICAL MODEL

In a given system, there are three populations whose concentrations are denoted by $x(t)$, $y(t)$, and $z(t)$. $x(t)$ represents the concentration of phytoplankton, which has a constant intrinsic growth rate of r and a carrying capacity of K. $y(t)$ represents the concentration of zooplankton biomass, whereas $z(t)$ represents the concentration of planktivorous fish biomass.

The grazing and conversion phenomena in the system are described by several parameters. The maximal ingestion rate of zooplankton is denoted by α_1, while the maximal conversion rate for zooplankton growth is represented by α_2 ($\alpha_2 \leq \alpha_1$). Similarly, the growth of planktivorous fish is influenced by the maximal ingestion rate (γ_1) and maximal conversion rate (γ_2) with the condition ($\gamma_2 \leq \gamma_1$), respectively. Here, μ_2 and μ_3 are the respective representations for the mortality rates of zooplankton and planktivorous fish biomass, respectively. The parameter h_1 is used to represent the harvesting rate of the planktivorous fish population and δ is the competition coefficient of fish population. The grazing phenomena are modeled using Holling type II and Holling III functional forms, with half saturation constants K_1 and K_2.

The system's fundamental equations are defined by incorporating all the parameters described earlier.

$$\left.\begin{array}{l} \dfrac{dx}{dt} = rx\left(1-\dfrac{x}{K}\right)-\dfrac{\alpha_1 xy}{K_1+x} \equiv J_1(x,y,z) \\[3mm] \dfrac{dy}{dt} = \dfrac{\alpha_2 xy}{K_1+x}-\dfrac{\gamma_1 y^2 z}{K_2+y^2}-\mu_2 y \equiv J_2(x,y,z) \\[3mm] \dfrac{dz}{dt} = \dfrac{\gamma_2 y^2 z}{K_2+y^2}-(\mu_3+h_1)z-\delta z^2 \equiv J_3(x,y,z). \end{array}\right\} \qquad (1.1)$$

Set $X = (x,\ y,\ z)^T \in \mathbf{R}_+^3$ and $J(X) = [J_1(X),\ J_2(X),\ J_3(X)]^T$, with $J : \mathbf{R}_+^3 \to \mathbf{R}^3$. The compact representation of the system (1.1) is expressed as $\dot{X} = J(X)$. Its Jacobian is

$$\bar{V} = \begin{bmatrix} r-\dfrac{2r\bar{x}}{K}-\dfrac{\alpha_1 K_1 \bar{y}}{(K_1+\bar{x})^2} & -\dfrac{\alpha_1 \bar{x}}{K_1+\bar{x}} & 0 \\[4mm] \dfrac{\alpha_2 K_1 \bar{y}}{(K_1+\bar{x})^2} & \dfrac{\alpha_2 \bar{x}}{K_1+\bar{x}}-\dfrac{2\gamma_1 K_2 \bar{y}\bar{z}}{(K_2+\bar{y}^2)^2}-\mu_2 & -\dfrac{\gamma_1 \bar{y}^2}{K_2+\bar{y}^2} \\[4mm] 0 & \dfrac{2\gamma_2 K_2 \bar{y}\bar{z}}{(K_2+\bar{y}^2)^2} & \dfrac{\gamma_2 \bar{y}^2}{K_2+\bar{y}^2}-\mu_3-h_1-2\delta\bar{z} \end{bmatrix} \qquad (1.2)$$

1.3   SOME PRELIMINARY RESULTS

1.3.1   POSITIVE INVARIANCE

Although the system (1.1) is not homogeneous, it possesses a biological well-posedness property. Specifically, if the initial values of $X(0)$ are chosen such that $X_i = 0$ for $i = 1,2,3$, then the corresponding Jacobian matrix $J_i(X)$ is non-negative. This characteristic guarantees that the system's solution remains confined to the positive orthant, which means that all populations remain positive. Therefore, the system ensures the biological well-posedness.

1.3.2   BOUNDEDNESS OF THE SYSTEM

Proposition 1.1

All solutions of equation (1.1) exhibit bounded behavior.
Proof. Let us establish a function

$w = x+y+z$.
We have $\dfrac{dx}{dt} \le rx\left(1-\dfrac{r}{K}\right)$ which indicates $x \le \dfrac{c_1 K}{c_1+e^{-rt}} \to K$ as $t \to \infty$, in which c_1 is constant.

When t becomes sufficiently large, we observe that $\dfrac{dw}{dt} \le rx-D_0 w$,

where $D_0 = \min\{\mu_2,(\mu_3+h_1)\}$.

Let $\hat{x}(t)$ be the solution of $\dfrac{d\hat{x}}{dt}+\hat{x}D_0 = rK$, satisfying $\hat{x}(0) = w(0)$.

Therefore, $\hat{x}(t) = \dfrac{rK}{D_0}+\left(w(0)-\dfrac{rK}{D_0}\right)e^{-D_0 t} \to \dfrac{rK}{D_0}$ as $t \to \infty$. By comparison, it follows that $\lim$

$\sup_{t\to\infty}[x(t)+y(t)+z(t)] \le \dfrac{rK}{D_0}$, proving the theorem.

1.3.3   Equilibria

Equation (1.1) describes a system with four distinct equilibrium states. The equilibrium $E_0 = (0,0,0)$ signifies the absence of plankton, while the equilibrium $E_{01} = (K,0,0)$ represents the absence of zooplankton but a high concentration of phytoplankton equal to K. The third equilibrium, $E_1 = (x_1, y_1, 0)$, represents a state where planktivorous fish are absent, but both phytoplankton and zooplankton are present in concentrations x_1 and y_1, respectively. The fourth equilibrium, $E^* = (x^*, y^*, z^*)$, represents a state of coexistence where all three populations exist with concentrations x^*, y^*, and z^*, respectively.

1.3.4   Plankton Free Equilibrium

The equilibrium point $E_0 (0,0,0)$ is consistently feasible, and upon evaluating the Jacobian (1.2) at this equilibrium, we find the eigenvalues to be $-\mu_2 < 0$, $-\mu_3 < 0$, and $r > 0$. It is evident that E_0 is inherently unstable in all cases.

1.3.5   Zooplankton Free Equilibrium

At the equilibrium point E_{01}, the Jacobian (1.2) factorizes, resulting in three distinct eigenvalues: $-r < 0$, $-\mu_3 < 0$ and $\mu_2 (R_0 - 1)$ where R_0 is defined below. Consequently, E_{01} is locally asymptotically stable (LAS) iff

$$R_0 = \frac{\alpha_2 K}{\mu_2 (K_1 + K)} < 1. \tag{1.3}$$

1.3.6   Planktivorous Fish-Free Equilibrium

The population levels at E_1 are given by

$$x_1 = \frac{\mu_2 K_1}{\alpha_2 - \mu_2}, \ y_1 = \frac{\alpha_2 K_1 r \left[K(\alpha_2 - \mu_2) - \mu_2 K_1 \right]}{\alpha_1 K (\alpha_2 - \mu_2)^2}.$$

The feasibility of E_1 is determined by the condition

$$\alpha_2 > \max \left\{ \mu_2, \mu_2 \left[\frac{K_1}{K} + 1 \right] \right\}. \tag{1.4}$$

At E_1, the Jacobian (1.2) factorizes, resulting in one explicit eigenvalue given $\gamma_2 y_1^2 (K_2 + y_1^2)^{-1} - \mu_3 - h_1$ and the quadratic $\lambda^2 + \left(\frac{r x_1}{K} - \frac{x_1 \alpha_1 y_1}{(K_1 + x_1)^2} \right) \lambda + \frac{\alpha_1 \alpha_2 K_1 x_1 y_1}{(K_1 + x_1)^3} = 0$. Routh–Hurwitz conditions for the latter are satisfied only when condition (1.4) is satisfied. Consequently, the stability of E_1 is guaranteed by the condition

$$R_1 = \frac{\alpha_2 K_1 r (\gamma_2 - \mu_3 - h_1) \left[K(\alpha_2 - \mu_2) - K_1 \mu_2 \right]}{\alpha_1^2 K^2 K_2 \mu_3 (\alpha_2 - \mu_2)^4} < 1. \tag{1.5}$$

1.3.7   The Coexistence Equilibrium

It is not possible to obtain an explicit expression for the coexistence equilibrium, $E^* = (x^*, y^*, z^*)$, since $y^* = \frac{r}{\alpha_1} \left(1 - \frac{x^*}{K} \right) (K_1 + x^*) = A (say)$, $z^* = \left[\frac{\gamma_2 A^2}{K_2 + A^2} - (\mu_3 + h_1) \right] \frac{1}{\delta}$. Therefore, solving the second equation by substituting the values y^* and z^* of system (1.1) we get x^*. Therefore, $E^*\left(x^*,\,y^*,z^*\right)$ exists if the condition $x^* > 0$, $y^* > 0$, $z^* > 0$ are satisfied.

1.3.7.1 Analyzing the Stability of the Coexistence Equilibrium in System (1.1)

The Jacobian matrix, denoted as V^*, of system (1.1) around $E^* = \left(x^*,y^*,z^*\right)$ is

$$V^* = \begin{bmatrix} n_{11} & n_{12} & 0 \\ n_{21} & n_{22} & n_{23} \\ 0 & n_{32} & n_{33} \end{bmatrix},$$

where $\quad n_{11} = \dfrac{\alpha_1 x^* y^*}{(K_1 + x^*)^2} - \dfrac{r x^*}{K}, \quad n_{12} = -\dfrac{\alpha_1 x^*}{K_1 + x^*}\Big\langle 0, \; n_{21} = \dfrac{K_1 \alpha_2 y^*}{(K_1 + x^*)^2}\Big\rangle 0, \quad n_{22} = \dfrac{\gamma_1 y^* z^*\left[y^{*2} - K_2\right]}{(K_2 + y^{*2})^2},$

$n_{23} = -\dfrac{\gamma_1 y^{*2}}{K_2 + y^{*2}} < 0, \; n_{32} = \dfrac{2K_2 \gamma_2 y^* z^*}{(K_2 + y^{*2})^2} > 0, \; n_{33} = -\delta z^*.$

The characteristic equation is

$Q^3 + B_1 Q^2 + B_2 Q + B_3 = 0,$

where $B_1 = -\left(n_{11} + n_{22} + n_{33}\right)$, $B_2 = n_{22}n_{33} + n_{33}n_{11} + n_{11}n_{22} - n_{12}n_{21} - n_{32}n_{23}$,

$B_3 = n_{11}n_{32}n_{23} + n_{12}n_{21}n_{33} - n_{11}n_{22}n_{33}.$

Case 1.1: If $n_{11} > 0$ then $\dfrac{r x^*}{K} + \delta z^* > \dfrac{\alpha_1 x^* y^*}{(K_1 + x^*)^2} + \dfrac{\gamma_1 y^* z^*\left(y^{*2} - K_2\right)}{(K_2 + y^{*2})^2}$ implies $B_1 > 0$.

In this case, $-n_{12}n_{21} - n_{32}n_{23} > -n_{11}n_{33} - n_{22}n_{33} - n_{11}n_{22}$ implies $B_2 > 0$.

Also, $B_3 > 0$ if $n_{12}n_{21}n_{33} > n_{11}n_{22}n_{33} - n_{11}n_{32}n_{23}$.

Case 1.2: If $n_{11} < 0$ in which $B_1 > 0$ if $-\left(n_{11} + n_{33}\right) > n_{22}$

Also $B_2 > 0$ if $n_{33}n_{11} - n_{12}n_{21} - n_{32}n_{23} > -\left(n_{11}n_{22} + n_{22}n_{33}\right)$ where $n_{23}n_{32} < 0$, $n_{12}n_{21} < 0$ when $n_{11}n_{22}$ and $n_{22}n_{33}$ are positive or negative. So, $B_1 B_2 - B_3 > 0$ if $B_1 B_2 > B_3$.

The application of the Routh–Hurwitz criteria to the cubic equation linked to the described system enables us to ascertain the LAS of the system around E^*.

The system is LAS around E^* if the cubic equation's roots have negative real parts and meet the conditions $B_i > 0$, $i = 1, 2, 3$, and $B_1 B_2 - B_3 > 0$.

The system's stability can vary based on the parameter values, potentially resulting in stable or unstable behavior in different conditions.

Table 1.1 provides a summary of the analytical results obtained from the analysis of the system described in the previous sections.

1.3.8 Hopf Bifurcation at Coexistence

Proposition 1.2

When the harvesting rate of planktivorous fish, represented by h_1, surpasses a critical threshold h_1^*, a Hopf bifurcation occurs in the system described by equation (1.1) in proximity to the coexistence

TABLE 1.1
Thresholds and Stability Analysis of Steady States

Thresholds (R_0, R_1)	$E_0(0,0,0)$	$E_{01}(K,0,0)$	$E_1(x_1, y_1, 0)$	$E^*(x^*, y^*, z^*)$
$R_0 < 1$	Unstable	Asymptotically stable	Not feasible	Not feasible
$R_0 > 1$, $R_1 < 1$	Unstable	Unstable	Asymptotically stable	Not feasible
$R_1 > 1$	Unstable	Unstable	Unstable	Asymptotically stable

equilibrium point. This bifurcation triggers persistent oscillations in the population dynamics, resulting in substantial alterations to the system's behavior.

Proof. In order for a Hopf bifurcation to occur in the system described by equation (1.1) at $h_1 = h_{1_*}^*$ it is essential to fulfill a set of necessary and sufficient conditions, which can be summarized as follows: (i) the coefficients $B_i\left(h_1^*\right) > 0$; $i = 1,2,3$, (ii) $B_1\left(h_1^*\right)B_2\left(h_1^*\right) > B_3\left(h_1^*\right) = 0$; and (iii) $B_{1'}\left(h_1^*\right)B_2\left(h_1^*\right) + B_1\left(h_1^*\right)B_{2'}\left(h_1^*\right) - B_{3'}\left(h_1^*\right) \neq 0$. The third condition is known as the transversality condition, which ensures that the eigenvalues of the characteristic equation, denoted by $\chi_i = u_i + iv_i$, satisfy the condition $\left.\dfrac{du_i}{dh_1}\right|_{h_1 = h_1^*} \neq 0$, where h_1 denotes the bifurcation parameter. This condition is important for ensuring that the Hopf bifurcation is transverse, and that the system behavior changes smoothly as the parameter h_1 crosses the critical value h_1^*.

Next, we proceed to confirm the fulfillment of Hopf-bifurcation condition (iii) by substituting $\chi = u + iv$ into the characteristic equation, yielding the following expression

$$(u + iv)^3 + B_1(u + iv)^2 + B_2(u + iv) + B_3 = 0, \tag{1.6}$$

By separating the real and imaginary components and eliminating v, the resulting expression is as follows:

$$8u^3 + 8B_1u^2 + 2u\left(B_1^2 + B_2\right) + B_1B_2 - B_3 = 0. \tag{1.7}$$

From the aforementioned analysis, it is evident that $u\left(h_1^*\right) = 0$ if the condition $B_1\left(h_1^*\right)B_2\left(h_1^*\right) - B_3\left(h_1^*\right) = 0$ holds true. Moreover, when $h_1 = h_1^*$, $u\left(h_1^*\right)$ corresponds to the unique root since the discriminant of $8u^2 + 8B_1u + 2\left(B_1^2 + B_2\right) = 0$ only becomes negative if $64B_1^2 - 64\left(B_1^2 + B_2\right) < 0$. Taking the derivative of equation (1.7) with respect to h_1, yields the following:

$$24u^2\frac{du}{dh_1} + 16B_1u\frac{du}{dh_1} + 2\left(B_1^2 + B_2\right)\frac{du}{dh_1} + 2u\left[2B_1\frac{dB_1}{dh_1} + \frac{dB_2}{dh_1}\right] + \frac{dS}{dh_1} = 0$$

where $S = B_1B_2 - B_3$.

At $h_1 = h_1^*$, we have $u\left(h_1^*\right) = 0$, so that the aforementioned equation becomes

$$\left[\frac{du}{dh_1}\right]_{h_1 = h_1^*} = \frac{-\dfrac{dS}{dh_1}}{2\left(B_1^2 + B_2\right)} \neq 0 \text{ providing the third condition (iii).}$$

A Hopf bifurcation occurs near E^* in the system, as guaranteed by the conditions discussed.

1.4 OPTIMAL HARVESTING POLICY

The objective of this section is to examine an optimal harvesting strategy for system (1.1) within an unrestricted area. To do so, we substitute $h_1 = qE$ into the mathematical model (1.1). In the context of the unreserved zone, the catchability coefficient of the planktivorous fish is denoted by q, while E represents the level of effort exerted for harvesting the fish species. In addition, we incorporate two additional parameters into the analysis: c, which represents the cost incurred per unit effort for harvesting the fish species, and p, which denotes the price per unit biomass of the fish species. By employing Pontryagin's maximum principle, we determine the trajectory of the optimal harvesting policy. Specifically, we examine the present value J associated with a continuous time series and apply the principle to derive the optimal policy. These ideas are adapted from the works of Chatterjee and Pal [18] and Toaha [19].

$$J = \int_0^\infty L(x, y, z, E, t) e^{-\delta_1 t} dt, \qquad (1.8)$$

where L is the net revenue given by

$$L(x, y, z, E, t) = (pqz - c)E, \qquad (1.9)$$

Here, the objective is to maximize the present value J, taking into account the three equations of system (1.1) while considering δ_1 as the instantaneous annual rate of discount.

First, we construct the following Hamiltonian function

$$H = e^{-\delta_1 t} \left[[pqz - c] E \right] + \lambda_1 \left[rx \left(1 - \frac{x}{K} \right) - \frac{\alpha_1 xy}{K_1 + x} \right]$$

$$+ \lambda_2 \left[\frac{\alpha_2 xy}{K_1 + x} - \frac{\gamma_1 y^2 z}{K_2 + y^2} - \mu_2 y \right] \qquad (1.10)$$

$$+ \lambda_3 \left[\frac{\gamma_1 y^2 z}{K_2 + y^2} - \mu_3 z - qEz - \delta z^2 \right].$$

In addition, the adjoint variables λ_1, λ_2 and λ_3 are introduced as unknown functions within the system. The control variable E is subject to the constraint $0 \le E \le (E)_{max}$ and the switching function $e^{-\delta_1 t}(pz - c) - \lambda_3 qz$ is defined accordingly.

The objective is to identify an optimal equilibrium $((x)_{\delta_1}, (y)_{\delta_1}, (z)_{\delta_1}, (E)_{\delta_1})$ that maximizes the Hamiltonian H.

Due to the linearity of the Hamiltonian H with respect to the control variables E, the optimal control may involve extreme controls or the singular control, resulting in the following considerations:
$E = (E)_{max}$, when $\phi_1(t) > 0$ i.e., when $\lambda_3(t)e^{\delta_1 t} < p - \dfrac{c}{qz}$; $E = 0$, when $\phi_1(t) < 0$ i.e., when

$\lambda_3(t)e^{\delta_1 t} > p - \dfrac{c}{qz}$;

when $\phi_1(t) = 0$, $\lambda_3(t)e^{\delta_1 t} = p - \dfrac{c}{qz}$ or

$$\frac{\partial H}{\partial E} = 0, \qquad (1.11)$$

The optimal control in this scenario is referred to as the singular control, and the conditions presented in (1.11) are necessary for maximizing the Hamiltonian H. The adjoint equations, derived from Pontryagin's maximum principle, are given by:

$$\frac{d\lambda_1}{dt} = -\frac{\partial H}{\partial x} = -\left[\lambda_1 \left(r - \frac{2xr}{K} - \frac{K_1 \alpha_1 y}{(K_1 + x)^2} \right) + \lambda_2 \left(\frac{K_1 \alpha_2 y}{(K_1 + x)^2} \right) \right], \qquad (1.12)$$

$$\frac{d\lambda_2}{dt} = -\frac{\partial H}{\partial y} = -\left[\lambda_1 \left(-\frac{\alpha_1 x}{K_1 + x} \right) + \lambda_2 \left(\frac{\alpha_2 x}{K_1 + x} - \frac{2\gamma_1 K_2 yz}{(K_2 + y^2)^2} - \mu_2 \right) + \lambda_3 \left[\frac{2\gamma_2 K_2 yz}{(K_2 + y^2)^2} \right] \right], \qquad (1.13)$$

$$\frac{d\lambda_3}{dt} = -\frac{\partial H}{\partial z} = -\left[e^{-\delta_1 t} pqE + \lambda_2 \left(\frac{-\gamma_1 y^2}{K_2 + y^2} \right) + \lambda_3 \left(\frac{\gamma_2 y^2}{K_2 + y^2} - \mu_3 - qE - 2\delta z \right) \right]. \tag{1.14}$$

Considering the interior equilibrium $E^* \left(x^*, y^*, z^* \right)$ and substituting the value of λ_2 from (1.11) in (1.14), we get

$$\lambda_2 = \frac{e^{-\delta_1 t} \left[pqE - \delta_1 \left(p - \frac{c}{qz^*} \right) - \left(p - \frac{c}{qz^*} \right) \delta z^* \right]}{\frac{\gamma_1 y^{*2}}{K_2 + y^{*2}}}. \tag{1.15}$$

Now using (1.15) in (1.12) we get

$$\frac{d\lambda_1}{dt} - \lambda_1 A_1 = -A_2 e^{-\delta_1 t},$$

where $A_1 = \frac{rx^*}{K} - \frac{\alpha_1 x^* y^*}{(K_1 + x^*)^2}$, $A_2 = \frac{\left[-\delta_1 \left(p - \frac{c}{qz^*} \right) - \left(p - \frac{c}{qz^*} \right) \delta z^* + pqE \right]}{\frac{\gamma_1 y^{*2}}{K_2 + y^{*2}}} \frac{K_1 \alpha_2 y^*}{(K_1 + x^*)^2}$.

We can calculate that

$$\lambda_1 = \frac{A_2}{A_1 + \delta_1} e^{-\delta_1 t}. \tag{1.16}$$

Again considering the interior equilibrium $E^* \left(x^*, y^*, z^* \right)$ and substituting the value of λ_1 and λ_3 from (1.16) and (1.11) in (1.13), we get

$$\frac{d\lambda_2}{dt} - \lambda_2 A_3 = -A_4 e^{-\delta_1 t},$$

where $A_3 = \frac{\gamma_1 K_2 y^* z^* - \gamma_1 y^{*3} z^*}{\left(K_2 + y^{*2} \right)}$, $A_4 = \left(p - \frac{c}{qz^*} \right) \frac{2\gamma_2 K_2 y^* z^*}{K_2 + y^{*2})^2} - \frac{A_2}{A_1 + \delta_1} \frac{\alpha_1 x^*}{K_1 + x^*}$.

We can calculate that

$$\lambda_2 = \frac{A_4}{A_3 + \delta_1} e^{-\delta_1 t}. \tag{1.17}$$

Similarly, by considering the interior equilibrium $E^* \left(x^*, y^*, z^* \right)$ and substituting the value of λ_2 from (1.17) in (1.14), we get

$$\frac{d\lambda_3}{dt} = -A_5 e^{-\delta_1 t},$$

where $A_5 = pqE - \frac{A_4}{A_3 + \delta} \frac{\gamma_1 y^{*2}}{K_2 + y^{*2}} - \left(p - \frac{c}{qz^*} \right) \delta_1 z^*$. We can calculate that

$$\lambda_3 = \frac{A_5}{\delta_1} e^{-\delta_1 t}. \tag{1.18}$$

It is obvious that $\lambda_1(t)$, $\lambda_2(t)$, and $\lambda_3(t)$ are bounded as $t \to \infty$.

By substituting (1.11) and (1.18), we subsist a singular path

$$p - \frac{c}{qz^*} = \frac{A_5}{\delta_1}. \tag{1.19}$$

Using x^*, y^*, and z^* we get the value of A_1, A_2, A_3, A_4, and A_5. Consequently, by rearranging equation (1.19), we can express it as follows:

$$G_1\left(z^*\right) = \left(p - \frac{c}{qz^*}\right) - \frac{A_5}{\delta_1}.$$

Under the conditions where $G_1(0) < 0$, $G_1(\mathbf{x}_1) > 0$, and $G_1'\left(z^*\right) > 0$ for $z^* > 0$, there exists a single positive root $z^* = (z^*)_{\delta_1}$ of $G_1\left(z^*\right) = 0$ within the interval $0 < z^* < \mathbf{x}_1$.

As a result, we obtain the optimal values $x^* = (x^*)_{\delta_1}$, $y^* = (y^*)_{\delta_1}$, $z^* = (z^*)_{\delta_1}$,

$$(E)_\delta = \frac{1}{q}\left[\frac{\gamma_2(y^2)_\delta}{K_2 + (y^2)_\delta} - \mu_3\right].$$

Once the optimal equilibrium $\left((x)\delta_1, (y)\delta_1, (z)\delta_1\right)$ is established, the corresponding optimal harvesting effort $(E)\delta_1$ can be determined. Based on the conditions presented in (1.11), (1.15)–(1.18), it is observed that, in the optimal equilibrium, $\lambda_i(t)$, where $i = 1, 2, 3$, remain constant over time. Therefore, as t approaches infinity, these parameters remain bounded.

1.5 THE STOCHASTIC MODEL

Despite any alterations or fluctuations in the environment, the preceding discussion assumes a constant state of the environmental parameters within the model. In light of environmental fluctuations, it is essential to consider their impact on the system and analyze the stochastic stability of the coexistence equilibrium.

Two approaches exist for constructing a stochastic model based on an established deterministic system. The first method involves replacing the deterministic model's environmental parameters with random parameters. As an example, one possible modification involves substituting the growth rate parameter 'r' with '$r_0 + \epsilon\gamma(t)$', wherein 'r_0' denotes the average growth rate, '$\gamma(t)$' represents the noise function, and 'ϵ' signifies the intensity of fluctuation.

The second approach entails introducing a random fluctuating driving force directly into the deterministic dynamic equations, without making any changes to specific parameters, as suggested by [20]. In this study, we opted for the latter method. Our assumption in this study was that the stochastic perturbations of the state variables, around their steady-state values 'E^*', conform to a Gaussian white noise pattern. This modeling approach proves to be highly effective in capturing rapidly fluctuating phenomena. Consequently, it can be inferred that the stochastic perturbations are proportional to the deviations of each population from its respective equilibrium value as explained in [21].

Therefore, the stochastic model can be derived from the deterministic system (1.1) as follows:

$$dx = F_1\left(x, y, z\right)dt + \sigma_1\left(x - x^*\right)d\xi_t^1,$$

$$dy = F_2\left(x, y, z\right)dt + \sigma_2\left(y - y^*\right)d\xi_t^2, \tag{1.20}$$

$$dz = F_3\left(x, y, z\right)dt + \sigma_3\left(z - z^*\right)d\xi_t^3,$$

where the real constants $\sigma_1, \sigma_2,$ and σ_3 denote the intensities of environmental fluctuations in the stochastic model. Meanwhile, $\xi_t^i = \xi_i(t)$, where $i = 1, 2, 3$, represents independent standard Wiener processes.

Equation (1.20) is regarded as a stochastic differential system (SDE) of the Itō type in our analysis. Therefore,

$$dX_t = F(t, X_t)dt + g(t, X_t)d\xi_t, \quad X_{t_0} = X_0. \tag{1.21}$$

The solution to this system, denoted by $X_t = (x, y, z)^T$, is an Itō process. In this context, the symbol F denotes the slowly varying continuous component, also known as the drift coefficient, whereas the diagonal matrix g represents the rapidly varying continuous random component, referred to as the diffusion coefficient. Here, g is given by $diag\left[\sigma_1\left(x - x^*\right), \sigma_2\left(y - y^*\right), \sigma_3\left(z - z^*\right)\right]$, where $\sigma_1, \sigma_2,$ and σ_3 are constants and $x^*, y^*,$ and z^* are fixed points. The stochastic process $\xi_t = (\xi_t^1, \xi_t^2, \xi_t^3)^T$ is a three-dimensional process consisting of scalar components of Wiener processes. Each component's increments, denoted as $\Delta\xi_t^j$, are independent Gaussian random variables with a mean of 0 and a standard deviation of $\sqrt{(\Delta t)}$.

The system is characterized as having multiplicative noise because the diffusion matrix g is dependent on the solution of X_t.

1.5.1 Analysis of the Steady State of Coexistence under Stochastic Factor

To align the SDE (1.20) with its coexistence equilibrium, E^*, the system needs to be centered and it is possible to introduce a perturbation vector $U(t) = (u_1(t), u_2(t), u_3(t))^T$, where $u_1 = x - x^*$, $u_2 = y - y^*$, and $u_3 = z - z^*$. One approach to achieve asymptotic stability in the mean square sense is by utilizing Lyapunov functions with the complete nonlinear equations (1.20).

To simplify the analysis, we will focus on the SDEs obtained by linearizing equation (1.20) around E^*. The linearized form equation of (1.21) around E^* is represented by

$$dU(t) = F_L\left(U(t)\right)dt + g\left(U(t)\right)d\xi(t), \tag{1.22}$$

where now $g\left(U(t)\right) = diag\left[\sigma_1 u_1, \sigma_2 u_2, \sigma_3 u_3\right]$ and

$$F_L\left(U(t)\right) = \begin{bmatrix} n_{11}u_1 + n_{12}u_2 + n_{13}u_3 \\ n_{21}u_1 + n_{22}u_2 + n_{23}u_3 \\ n_{31}u_1 + n_{32}u_2 + n_{33}u_3 \end{bmatrix} = V^*U,$$

and E^*, which now corresponds to the origin $(u_1, u_2, u_3) = (0, 0, 0)$. Let $\Omega = \left[(t \geq t_0) \times R^3, t_0 \in R^+\right]$ and let $\Theta(t, X) \in C^{(1,2)}(\Omega)$ be a differentiable function of time t and twice differentiable function of X.

Consider the domain $\Omega = [(t \geq t_0) \times \mathbb{R}^3, t_0 \in \mathbb{R}^+]$, where t is time and X is a differentiable function of time t and twice a differentiable function of X, denoted as $\Theta(t, X) \in C^{(1,2)}(\Omega)$.

Let can further define the function

$$L_\Theta(t, u) = \frac{\partial\Theta(t, u(t))}{\partial t} + f^T\left(u(t)\right)\frac{\partial\Theta(t, u)}{\partial u} + \frac{1}{2}tr\left[g^T\left(u(t)\right)\frac{\partial^2\Theta(t, u)}{\partial u^2}g\left(u(t)\right)\right] \tag{1.23}$$

where

$$\frac{\partial\Theta}{\partial u} = \left(\frac{\partial\Theta}{\partial u_1}, \frac{\partial\Theta}{\partial u_2}, \frac{\partial\Theta}{\partial u_3}\right)^T, \quad \frac{\partial^2\Theta(t, u)}{\partial u^2} = \left(\frac{\partial^2\Theta}{\partial u_j \partial u_i}\right)_{i,j=1,2,3}.$$

Given the aforementioned positions, we now bring to mind the following result, as stated in reference [23].

Proposition 1.3

Under the assumptions that the functions $\Theta(U,t) \leq r_2$ belong to $C_3(\Omega)$ and L_Θ satisfies the inequalities

$$r_1|U|^\alpha \leq \Theta(U,t) \leq r_2|U|^\alpha, \tag{1.24}$$

where r_1, r_2 are positive constants and α is a real number, it holds true.

$$L_\Theta(U,t) \leq -r_3|U|, \quad r_i\rangle 0, \quad i = 1,2,3, \quad \alpha > 0. \tag{1.25}$$

Consequently, the trivial solution of equation (1.22) exhibits exponential α-stability for all time $t \geq 0$.

Remark 1.1

As per [23], for $\alpha = 2$ in equations (1.24) and (1.25), the trivial solution of equation (1.22) is both exponentially mean square stable as well as globally asymptotically stable (GAS) in probability.

Proposition 1.4

Let $n_{ij} < 0$, $i,j = 1,2,3$, and suppose there exist positive real values of ω_k, for $k = 1,2$, such that the following inequality holds

$$\left[2(1+\omega_2)n_{22} + 2n_{32}\omega_2 + (1+\omega_2)\sigma_2^2\right]\left[2n_{23}\omega_1 + 2n_{33}(\omega_1+\omega_2)\right.$$
$$\left. + (\omega_1+\omega_2)\sigma_3^2\right] > \left[n_{12}\omega_1 + n_{22}\omega_2 + n_{23}(1+\omega_2) + n_{32}(\omega_1+\omega_2) + n_{33}\omega_2\right]^2. \tag{1.26}$$

Then it follows that

$$\sigma_1^2 < -2n_{11}, \quad \sigma_2^2 < -\frac{2n_{22}(1+\omega_2) + 2n_{32}\omega_2}{1+\omega_2}, \quad \sigma_3^2 < -\frac{2n_{23}\omega_1 + 2n_{33}(\omega_1+\omega_2)}{\omega_1+\omega_2}, \tag{1.27}$$

$$\omega_1^* = \frac{n_{21}}{n_{11} + n_{33} - n_{12} - n_{32}}, \quad \omega_2^* = \frac{n_{11} + n_{33}}{n_{12} - (n_{11} + n_{33}) + n_{32}}, \tag{1.28}$$

and the system (1.20) has a zero solution that is asymptotically mean square stable.

Proof. Let's examine the Lyapunov function denoted as

$$\Theta(u(t)) = \frac{1}{2}\left[\omega_1(u_1+u_3)^2 + u_2^2 + \omega_2(u_2+u_3)^2\right],$$

where the positive real constants ω_k will be determined at a later stage.

Verifying the validity of inequalities (1.24) for $\alpha = 2$ is a straightforward task. Furthermore,

$$L_\Theta(u(t)) = \left[n_{22}(1+\omega_2) + n_{32}\omega_2\right]u_2^2 + \left[n_{23}\omega_2 + n_{33}(\omega_1+\omega_2)\right]u_3^2$$
$$+ u_1u_2\left[n_{12}\omega_1 + n_{21}(1+\omega_2) + n_{32}\omega_1\right] + u_2u_3\left[n_{12}\omega_1 + n_{22}\omega_2 + n_{23}(1+\omega_2)\right.$$
$$+ n_{32}(\omega_1+\omega_2) + n_{33}\omega_2\right] + u_3u_1\left[n_{11}\omega_1 + n_{21}\omega_2 + n_{33}\omega_1\right]$$
$$+ n_{11}\omega_1u_1^2 + \frac{1}{2}tr\left[g^T(u(t))\frac{\partial^2\Theta}{\partial u^2}g(u(t))\right].$$

Now observe that

$$\frac{\partial^2 \Theta}{\partial u^2} = \begin{vmatrix} \omega_1 & 0 & \omega_1 \\ 0 & 1+\omega_2 & \omega_2 \\ \omega_1 & \omega_2 & \omega_1+\omega_2 \end{vmatrix}.$$

Consequently, we can compute the trace term in the following manner.

$$tr\left[g^T\big(u(t)\big)\frac{\partial^2 \Theta}{\partial u^2} g\big(u(t)\big)\right] = \omega_1\sigma_1^2 u_1^2 + (1+\omega_2)\sigma_2^2 u_2^2 + (\omega_1+\omega_2)\sigma_3^2 u_3^2.$$

Using then (1.28), the Lyapunov function becomes $L_\Theta\big(u(t)\big) = -u^T Q u$, with the real symmetric matrix

$$Q = \begin{vmatrix} -n_{11}\omega_1 - \dfrac{1}{2}\omega_1\sigma_1^2 & 0 & 0 \\ 0 & -(1+\omega_2)n_{22} - \omega_2 n_{32} - \dfrac{1}{2}(1+\omega_2)\sigma_2^2 & Q_{23} \\ 0 & Q_{23} & Q_{33} \end{vmatrix},$$

where

$$Q_{23} = -\frac{n_{12}\omega_1 + n_{22}\omega_2 + n_{23}(1+\omega_2) + n_{32}(\omega_1+\omega_2) + n_{33}\omega_2}{2}$$

and $Q_{33} = -n_{13}\omega_1 - n_{23}\omega_2 - n_{33}(\omega_1+\omega_2) - \dfrac{1}{2}(\omega_1+\omega_2)\sigma_3^2$. Easily, the inequality $L_\Theta\big(u(t)\big) \le -u^T Q u$ holds. Alternatively, from equations (1.26) and (1.27), we can conclude that the matrix Q is positive definite, leading to the fact that all its eigenvalues, denoted as $\lambda_i(Q)$, $i = 1,2,3$, are positive real values. Let, $\lambda_m = min\{\lambda_i(Q), i = 1,2,3\} > 0$. By applying the aforementioned inequality to $L_\Theta\big(u(t)\big)$, we obtain the expression

$$L_\Theta\big(u(t)\big) \le -\lambda_m |u(t)|^2,$$

thereby concluding the proof.

Remark 1.2

Based on reference [16], Proposition 1.4 presents the fundamental conditions necessary to establish the stochastic stability of E^* when confronted with environmental fluctuations. Hence, it can be inferred that the stability of the stochastic system relies significantly on both the internal parameters of the model and the magnitude of the environmental fluctuations.

1.6 NUMERICAL SIMULATIONS

The purpose of this section is to investigate the causes and cessation of oscillations observed in the populations of plankton and fish, specifically emphasizing the parameter values of $r = 8$, $K = 1.5$, $\alpha_1 = 2$, $\alpha_2 = 1.5$, $\gamma_1 = 1$, $\gamma_2 = 0.8$, $\mu_2 = 0.3$, $\mu_3 = 0.36$, $K_1 = 0.5$, $K_2 = 1$, $h_1 = 0.025$, and $\delta = 0.02$ as

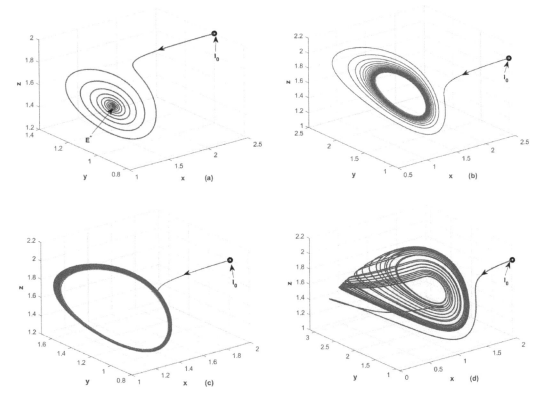

FIGURE 1.1 (a) For the parameter values specified in this chapter, E^* is characterized as stable. (b–d) The Figures demonstrate the occurrence of oscillatory patterns around E^* in each scenario, as the values of δ decrease from 0.02 to 0.1, μ_3 increase from 0.36 to 0.4, and h_1 increase from 0.025 to 0.2, respectively.

reported in reference [5]. The coexistence equilibrium point $E^* = (1.28, 1.04, 1.56)$, exhibits local asymptotic stability and takes the form of a stable focus, as illustrated in Figure 1.1a.

1.6.1 EFFECT OF δ

The system described by the mathematical model (1.1) demonstrates oscillatory behavior around the coexistence equilibrium E^* when the value of δ is increased from 0.02 to 0.09 while keeping other parameters constant, as shown in (cf. Figure 1.1b). To depict the steady-state behavior of each population, we have plotted Figure 1.2a–d in $\delta - y - z$ plane, over a range of parameter values for δ. These plots indicate the existence of three Hopf points, identified with red stars (H), occurring at $\delta = 0.083$, 0.125, and 0.209, respectively. The corresponding first Lyapunov coefficients for these Hopf points are -0.006, -0.139, and -1.345.

1.6.2 EFFECTS OF μ_3

The system described by the mathematical model (1.1) exhibits oscillatory behavior around the coexistence equilibrium E^* when the value of μ_3 is increased from 0.36 to 0.4 while keeping the other parameters constant (cf. Figure 1.1c). We illustrate the steady-state behavior of each population by plotting Figure 1.3a–d in $\mu_3 - y - z$ plane for a range of values of the parameter μ_3. The plots reveal three Hopf points, marked with red stars (H), at $\mu_3 = 0.394$, 0.608, and 0.645, respectively. The corresponding first Lyapunov coefficients for these Hopf points are -0.0382, -1.21, and 5.89.

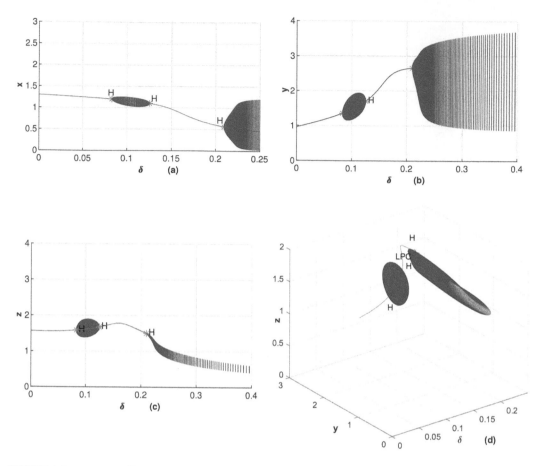

FIGURE 1.2 (a–c) For δ, the trajectory illustrates the various dynamical behaviors of phytoplankton, zooplankton and fish population, respectively. (d) The trajectory illustrates the various dynamical behaviors of all the populations in $\delta - y - z$ plane.

Negative (positive) sign of the first Lyapunov coefficient indicates the emergence of a stable (unstable) limit cycle, leading to a loss of stability for the system (1.1). The plots also show a Branch point (BP) and a Limit point (LP) at $\mu_3 = 0.653$ and 0.647, respectively. Furthermore, the plots reveal a fold bifurcation (LPC) of the cycle, Neimark–Sacker (NS), and Period doubling (PD) bifurcations generated from the Hopf point (H). PD bifurcation is a type of bifurcation in dynamical systems theory, where a stable fixed point transitions to chaotic behavior by undergoing it. The NS bifurcation is closely related to the Hopf bifurcation, which arises when a stable fixed point becomes unstable and gives rise to the birth of a stable periodic orbit.

1.6.3   Effects of h_1

In Figure 1.1d, it can be observed that the system displays chaotic dynamics when h_1 is set to 0.2 while keeping all other parameters constant. The steady-state behavior of each population in the mathematical model (1.1) is shown in Figure 1.4a–d, where a range of values of the parameter h_1 is plotted in $h_1 - y - z$ plane. These plots reveal the existence of three Hopf points, denoted by red stars (H), located at $h_1^* = 0.059$, 0.274, and 0.310, respectively. The corresponding first Lyapunov coefficients for these Hopf points are -0.0382, -1.21, and 5.89. Furthermore, the plots show the

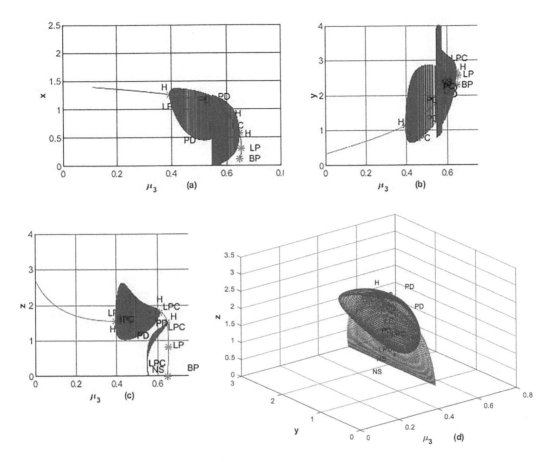

FIGURE 1.3 (a-c) For μ_3, the trajectory illustrates the various dynamical behaviors of phytoplankton, zooplankton and fish population, respectively. (d) The trajectory illustrates the various dynamical behaviors of all the populations in $\mu_3 - y - z$ plane.

presence of one BP and one LP located at $h_1 = 0.3120$ and 0.3186, respectively. In addition to the previously mentioned Hopf points, the plots also reveal the presence of other types of bifurcations. Specifically, fold bifurcation (LPC) of the cycle, NS, and PD bifurcations can be observed, all of which are generated from the Hopf points (H).

1.6.4 Effect of γ_2

The behavior of a system described by equation (1.1) is studied as the value of parameter γ_2 varies. To demonstrate the distinct steady-state dynamics exhibited by each population under varying values of γ_2, Figure 1.5a–d in $\gamma_2 - y - z$ plane are presented. The plots depict three Hopf points at $\gamma_2 = 0.7382$, 0.5031 and 0.4740 (marked with a red star (H)), with first Lyapunov coefficients of $-0.004, -1.28$ and 3.53, respectively. In addition, there are one BP and one LP located at $\gamma_2 = 0.4583$ and 0.4582, respectively. As γ_2 crosses the value of 0.4583, the fish population goes to extinction, and the system exhibits transcritical bifurcations. Moreover, the plots show a BP and an LP at $\mu_3 = 0.653$ and 0.647, respectively. At an LP, the stability of a specific equilibrium point within the system is relinquished, leading to the emergence of either a new equilibrium point or a limit cycle. In addition, the plots reveal fold bifurcation (LPC) of the cycle, NS, and PD bifurcations generated from the Hopf point (H).

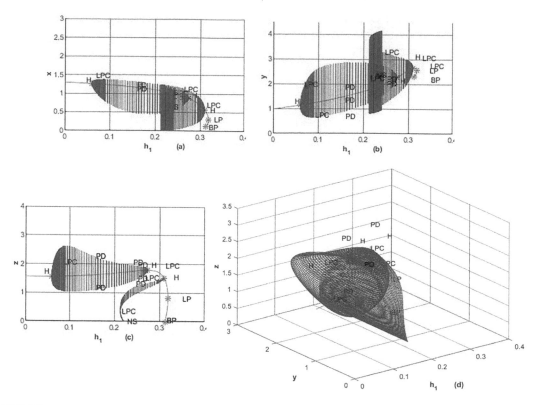

FIGURE 1.4 (a–c) For h_1, the trajectory illustrates the various dynamical behaviors of phytoplankton, zooplankton and fish population, respectively. (d) The trajectory illustrates the various dynamical behaviors of all the populations in $h_1 - y - z$ plane.

1.6.5 Hopf-bifurcation

A bifurcation diagram (cf. Figure 1.6a) has been created to improve the understanding of how variations in the competition coefficient (δ) of planktivorous fish influence the system's dynamics. In addition, three separate bifurcation diagrams have been produced for μ_3, h_1, and γ_2, as demonstrated in Figure 1.6b–d, each depicting the effect of one parameter while holding the others constant.

The stability of the proposed plankton–fish system was investigated through a two-parameter bifurcation analysis, using $h_1 - \mu_3$ and $h_1 - \gamma_2$ as the bifurcation parameters, along with three other species. A bifurcation diagram was plotted, as illustrated in Figure 1.7a and b, to identify the stable and unstable regions of the system. The key findings of the study, which outline the properties of the equilibrium points within the mathematical model representing the interactions among phytoplankton, zooplankton, and fish populations, are condensed in Table 1.2.

1.6.6 Environmental Fluctuations

Within this section, we delve into the examination of the system's reaction to environmental disturbances. To model this situation, we utilize MATLAB software and employ the Euler–Maruyama method to simulate the stochastic differential equation (1.20). By employing a suitable function [22], we have derived the condition for the mean square asymptotic stability of the coexistence equilibrium point E^*. The dependence of these conditions on $\sigma_1, \sigma_2, \sigma_3$, and the parameters of the model (1.20) should be taken into account. By utilizing the reference values from Table 1.2 and setting the environmental perturbations' intensities as $\sigma_1 = 0.03$, $\sigma_2 = 0.04$, $\sigma_3 = 0.01$ which fulfill condition

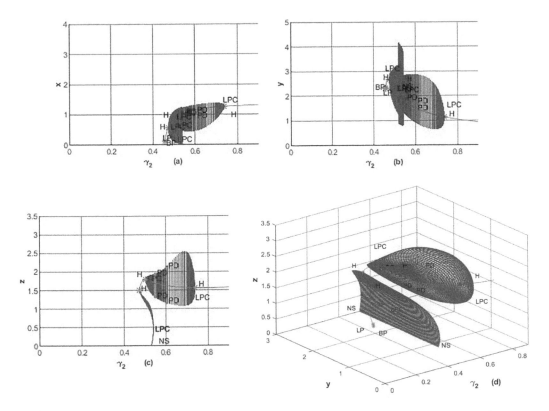

FIGURE 1.5 (a–c) For γ_2, the trajectory illustrates the various dynamical behaviors of phytoplankton, zooplankton and fish population, respectively. (d) The trajectory illustrates the various dynamical behaviors of all the populations in $\gamma_2 - y - z$ plane.

(1.27), the system demonstrates stochastic stability, resulting in the coexistence of all three species as shown in Figure 1.8a on the left.

Upon increasing the perturbation magnitudes to $\sigma_1 = 0.2$, $\sigma_2 = 0.2$, $\sigma_3 = 0.1$, the fluctuations amplify, indicating instability of the coexistence equilibrium. This is illustrated in Figure 1.8b on the right.

1.7 DISCUSSION

The study of the relationship between plankton and fish is crucial in ecology. To better understand this relationship, we propose and analyze a phytoplankton-zooplankton-planktivorous fish interaction model. Table 1.1 presents the determined conditions for the existence and stability of different steady states based on our study of the model. Interestingly, we observe that high harvesting rates of planktivorous fish can lead to population fluctuations.

Moreover, low conversion rates of planktivorous fish can result in oscillations around the coexistence equilibrium. In addition, we utilize Pantryagin's maximum principle to derive an optimal harvesting policy. Our analysis focuses on identifying effective control measures that promote the stable coexistence of all species. Our findings indicate that achieving a balance between the maximal planktivorous fish conversion rate, mortality rate, and harvesting rate is crucial in controlling population fluctuations and ensuring stability at the coexistence equilibrium.

Based on our findings, it may be concluded that planktivorous fish can serve as a bio-control agent to mitigate algal bloom problems.

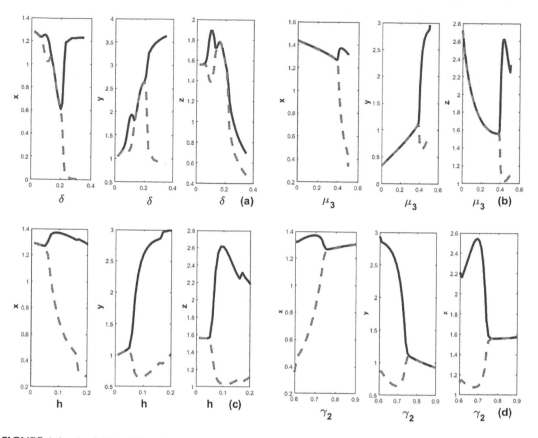

FIGURE 1.6   (a–d) The bifurcation diagram displays the behavior of each population with δ, μ_3, h_1, and γ_2 serving as the respective bifurcation parameters.

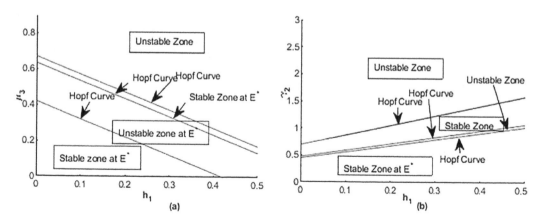

FIGURE 1.7   (a–b) The bifurcation diagram in the h_1-μ_3 and h_1-γ_2 planes showcase the dynamics of two parameters respectively.

TABLE 1.2
Characteristics Associated with Equilibrium Points

Parameters	Values	Eigenvalues	Equilibrium Points
μ_3	0.394	$(-5.71, \pm 0.55i)$	Hopf (H)
	0.608	$(-2.24, \pm 0.41i)$	Hopf (H)
	0.645	$(-0.04, \pm 1.33i)$	Hopf (H)
	0.653	$(0, 0.48 \pm 1.28)$	Limit point (LP)
	0.647	$(0, 0.4 \pm 1.26)$	Branch point (BP)
h_1	0.059	$(-5.71, \pm 0.55i)$	Hopf (H)
	0.270	$(-2.24, \pm 0.41i)$	Hopf (H)
	0.310	$(-.04, \pm 1.48i)$	Hopf (H)
	0.317	$(0, 0.48 \pm 1.48)$	Limit point (LP)
	0.312	$(0, 0.4 \pm 1.26)$	Branch point (BP)
δ	0.083	$(-5.19, \pm 0.51i)$	Hopf (H)
	0.120	$(-4.26 \pm 0.43i)$	Hopf (H)
	0.200	$(-0.31, \pm 1.34i)$	Hopf (H)
γ_2	0.738	$(-5.71, \pm 0.53i)$	Hopf (H)
	0.503	$(-2.26, \pm 0.32i)$	Hopf (H)
	0.474	$(-0.04, \pm 1.32i)$	Hopf (H)
	0.4582	$(0, 0.418 \pm 1.28)$	Limit point (LP)
	0.4583	$(0, 0.3769 \pm 1.23)$	Branch point (BP)

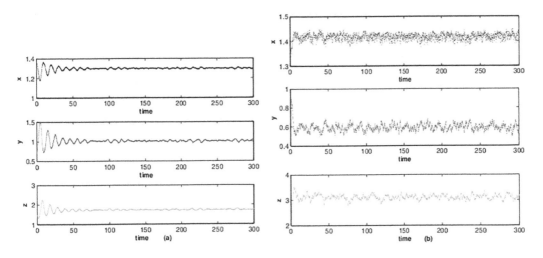

FIGURE 1.8 (a, b) Effects of environmental fluctuations. Left: $\sigma_1 = 0.03, \sigma_2 = 0.04$, and $\sigma_3 = 0.01$; Right: $\sigma_1 = 0.1, \sigma_2 = 0.2$, and $\sigma_3 = 0.2$.

REFERENCES

[1] Scheffer, M. "Fish and nutrients interplay determines algal biomass: a minimal model." *Oikos* 62 (1991): 271–282.

[2] Pal, S., and A. Chatterjee. "Role of constant nutrient input and mortality rate of planktivorous fish in plankton community ecosystem with instantaneous nutrient recycling." *Canadian Applied Mathematics Quarterly* 20 (2012): 179–207.

[3] Scheffer, M., S. Rinaldi, and Y. A. Kuznetsov. "Effects of fish on plankton dynamics: a theoretical analysis." *Canadian Journal of Fisheries and Aquatic Sciences* 57, no. 6 (2000): 1208–1219.

[4] Mukhopadhyay, B., and R. Bhattacharyya. "Role of gestation delay in a plankton-fish model under stochastic fluctuations." *Mathematical Biosciences* 215, no. 1 (2008): 26–34.

[5] Pal, S., and A. Chatterjee. "Dynamics of the interaction of plankton and planktivorous fish with delay." *Cogent Mathematics* 2, no. 1 (2015): 1074337.

[6] Upadhyay, R. K., N. Kumari, and V. Rai. "Wave of chaos in a diffusive system: Generating realistic patterns of patchiness in plankton-fish dynamics." *Chaos, Solitons & Fractals* 40, no. 1 (2009): 262–276.

[7] Biktashev, V. N., J. Brindley, and J. W. Horwood. "Phytoplankton blooms and fish recruitment rate." *Journal of plankton Research* 25, no. 1 (2003): 21–33.

[8] Medvinskiĭ, A. B., A. V. Rusakov, A. E. Bobyrev, V. A. Burmenskiĭ, A. E. Kriksunov, N. I. Nurieva, and M. M. Gonik. "A conceptual mathematical model of aquatic communities in lakes Naroch and Myastro (Belarus)." *Biofizika* 54, no. 1 (2009): 120–125.

[9] Mukhopadhyay, A., J. Chattopadhyay, and P. K. Tapaswi. "Selective harvesting in a two species fishery model." *Ecological Modelling* 94, no. 2–3 (1997): 243–253.

[10] Kar, T. K., and K. S. Chaudhuri. "On non-selective harvesting of two competing fish species in the presence of toxicity." *Ecological Modelling* 161, no. 1–2 (2003): 125–137.

[11] Zhao, H., X. Huang, and X. Zhang. "Hopf bifurcation and harvesting control of a bioeconomic plankton model with delay and diffusion terms." *Physica A: Statistical Mechanics and Its Applications* 421 (2015): 300–315.

[12] Dubey, B., A. Patra, and R. K. Upadhyay. "Dynamics of phytoplankton, zooplankton and fishery resource model." *Applications and Applied Mathematics: An International Journal (AAM)* 9, no. 1 (2014): 14.

[13] Sajan, S., S. K. Sasmal, and B. Dubey. "A phytoplankton-zooplankton-fish model with chaos control: In the presence of fear effect and an additional food." *Chaos: An Interdisciplinary Journal of Nonlinear Science* 32, no. 1 (2022): 013114.

[14] Chatterjee, A. "Impact of planktivorous fish on delay-induced plankton fish ecosystem model." *Nonlinear Studies* 29 (2022): 1063–1078.

[15] Panja, P., T. Kar, and D. K. Jana. "Stability and bifurcation analysis of a phytoplankton-zooplankton-fish model involving fear in zooplankton species and fish harvesting." *International Journal of Modelling and Simulation* 43 (2022): 1–16.

[16] Bandyopadhyay, M., and J. Chattopadhyay. "Ratio-dependent predator-prey model: Effect of environmental fluctuation and stability." *Nonlinearity* 18, no. 2 (2005): 913.

[17] Jang, S. R.-J., and E. J. Allen. "Deterministic and stochastic nutrient-phytoplankton-zooplankton models with periodic toxin producing phytoplankton." *Applied Mathematics and Computation* 271 (2015): 52–67.

[18] Chatterjee, A., and S. Pal. "A predator-prey model for the optimal control of fish harvesting through the imposition of a tax." *An International Journal of Optimization and Control: Theories & Applications (IJOCTA)* 13, no. 1 (2023): 68–80.

[19] Bahri, M. "Stability analysis and optimal harvesting policy of prey-predator model with stage structure for predator." *Applied Mathematical Sciences* 8, no. 159 (2014): 7923–7934.

[20] Tapaswi, P. K., and A. Mukhopadhyay. "Effects of environmental fluctuation on plankton allelopathy." *Journal of Mathematical Biology* 39 (1999): 39–58.

[21] Beretta, E., V. Kolmanovskii, and L. Shaikhet. "Stability of epidemic model with time delays influenced by stochastic perturbations." *Mathematics and Computers in Simulation* 45, no. 3–4 (1998): 269–277.

[22] Afanas'ev, V. N., V. B. Kolmanowskii, and V. R. Nosov. 1996, "*Mathematical Theory of Control Systems Design.*" Kluwer Academic, Dordrecht.

[23] Chatterjee, S., M. Isaia, F. Bona, G. Badino, and E. Venturino. "Modelling environmental influences on wanderer spiders in the Langhe region (Piemonte-NW Italy)." *Journal of Numerical Analysis, Industrial and Applied Mathematics* 3, no. 3–4 (2008): 193–209.

2 Multi-criteria Optimisation and Compromise Solution to Select Financially Efficient NIFTY IT Companies Pre and During COVID-19 Pandemic

Subrata Jana and Bibhas Chandra Giri
Jadavpur University

Anirban Sarkar
West Bengal State University

Biswadip Basu Mallik
Department of Basic Science and Humanities,
Institute of Engineering & Management

2.1 INTRODUCTION

Computers and any kind of communication system capable of storing, analysing, retrieving, transmitting, manipulating, and sending data are at the heart of information technology (IT). As per people's requirement to do the major functions and implement them on a constant basis, IT depends on a collation of software and hardware. It's making formerly difficult forms of communication simple, quick, and inexpensive. In addition, the enhancement of communication made possible by IT is crucial to the success of many firms. Companies in the telecommunications and contact centre industries are good examples. IT is used in nearly every aspect of modern life. Almost every sector is beginning to recognise the significance of IT. Some of the areas of society that absolutely require IT are listed below. You can walk into any company and guarantee that they use managed IT services. These days, businesses can't function without their reliance on IT infrastructure. Education is currently monitoring how IT may be a crucial instrument for academic performance due to the prevalence of distant learning across the world, especially after 2020. There are many places to get excellent resources for personal growth and development online. The trend has spread to colleges and institutions recently. IT enables a variety of transactions, including online shopping, online banking, and internal business deals. Therefore, IT is essential for the financial sector as a whole. Paper records are giving way to electronic health records. Nowadays, computers help medical professionals manage patient information, treatment plans, hospital bills, consultations, and charting. Due to the ability to store massive volumes of data indefinitely, IT is both quicker and more trustworthy than paper files. A patient's medical history, from birth to death, may be stored in one place, so doctors and other caregivers can quickly and easily retrieve it and consult it as needed. There is

DOI: 10.1201/9781003387459-2

no denying the crucial role that IT plays in today's environment. Despite the fact that we take it for granted more and more frequently as time goes on. It's quite evident every time we have IT performance issues, including hardware failures or power outages. Thus, we live in the modern age, when the introduction of a new piece of technology can either improve existing procedures or completely upend them.

Several parts of IT industries are IT Hardware, IT Software, BPOs, IT Education, etc. Figure 2.1 shows segment wise market share.

Figure 2.1 shows segment wise market share of IT industry in India.

Due to the rising demand for skills and expertise, the top three Indian IT giants, TCS, Wipro, and Infosys, are forecast to create 1.05 lakh new jobs in FY22. By 2025, the Indian IT and business services industry are expected to be worth US$ 19.93 billion. IT expenditures in India were predicted by Gartner to reach US$ 81.89 billion in 2021 and rise to US$ 101.8 billion" in 2022.

Figure 2.2 shows market size of IT industry in India.

However, in today's day and age, we cannot do away with technology, and this is why IT companies mostly see a rise in their values year on year (y-o-y). During the COVID-19 pandemic, the entire world was dependent on two sectors. One is pharmaceutical sector and another is IT industry. So it is very pertinent to find out the financial efficiency of IT companies during and pre COVID-19 pandemic. To find out which company is efficient and superior, this study took into consideration the financial ratios of the companies and then concluded with ranking for pre and during the COVID-19 pandemic. Several financial ratios, such as net profit, total income, and net profit margin, play a pivotal role in measuring the companies' earnings. Net worth and return on net worth throw light as the intrinsic indicators of the value of the company, and dividends and bonuses earned from the company act as the crowd pullers.

Multi-Criteria Decision-Making (MCDM) techniques are used in problem solving, which involves selection from a finite number of alternatives. It can be applied in psychometrics, applied statistics, decision theory, and many more. This study used "Multi-criteria Optimization and Compromise Solution" i.e. VIKOR (VIseKriterijumskaOptimizacija I KompromisnoResenje) for finding out the efficiency score and rank of Indian IT companies, which is listed in NIFTY using financial ratios. There has been a lot of research on the uses of "Multi-criteria Optimization and Compromise Solution" VIKOR and the ranking of companies, but to the best of our knowledge, this is the novel initiation on the Indian IT companies being ranked according to the performance score pre and during COVID-19 pandemic.

Segment Wise Market Share

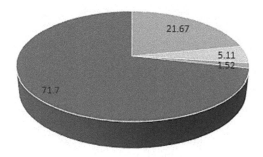

IT Hardware   BPO ITeS   IT Education   IT Software

FIGURE 2.1   Segment wise market share.

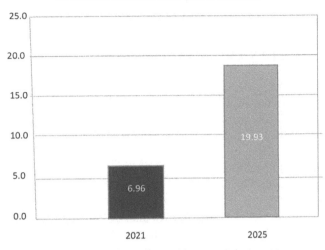

Indian IT Market Size (US $ Billion)

■ **Indian IT and Service Market Size**

FIGURE 2.2 IT market size of India.

2.2 LITERATURE REVIEW

The financial market has seen a large quantity of studies based on financial ratio analysis, which is used to evaluate business success. The entropy approach was utilised by Deng, Yeh, and Willis (2000) to calculate the objective weight, and the TOPSIS method was used to rank the possible solutions. Each of the seven textile firms had their performance graded based on their ratios of debt to equity, efficiency to market share, market share to profitability, and other such metrics. The VIKOR and TOPSIS techniques of MCDM developed by Opricovic and Tzeng (2004) use an aggregating function reflecting "closeness to the ideal" that has its roots in the compromise programming approach. The elimination of criteria function unit usage is accomplished by vector normalisation in TOPSIS and linear normalisation in VIKOR. The VIKOR technique of compromise ranking finds an agreement that will satisfy the "majority" with the most "group utility" while leaving the "opponent" with the least amount of regret. Without taking into account the relative importance of these distances, the TOPSIS technique finds a solution that is the farthest from the ideal solution and the closest to the negative ideal solution. A numerical example is used to compare and contrast the two approaches and highlight their shared features and distinct characteristics. Assuming that compromising is acceptable for conflict resolution, that the decision maker wants a solution that is the closest to the ideal, and that the alternatives are evaluated according to all established criteria, Opricovic and Tzeng (2007) developed the VIKOR method to solve MCDM problems with conflicting and noncommensurable (different units) criteria. In the face of competing criteria, this technique prioritises the identification, evaluation, and recommendation of compromise solution(s). Stability analysis, which establishes the weight stability intervals, and trade-off analysis are added to the VIKOR approach. Three more multi-criteria decision-making (MCDM) approaches—TOPSIS, PROMETHEE, and ELECTRE—are compared to the expanded VIKOR technique. Using a numerical example, we compare the outcomes from the four different approaches and show how the VIKOR method might be useful. Wang (2008) ranked the airlines using the fuzzy TOPSIS approach. Based on their financial results, the research ranked Taiwanese domestic carriers. Five key financial indicators and the VIKOR (VIseKriterijumskaOptimizacija I KompromisnoResenje) technique were utilised by Lin, Chang, and Wu (2009) to evaluate 100 publicly traded corporations. Benford's law analyses the correlation between deals between affiliated businesses and overall revenue. The combination of VIKOR and Benford's law was shown to be more effective than either method alone in detecting the manipulation of monthly sales figures in corporations. The VIKOR approach was created by Sayadi, Heydari, and Shahanaghi (2009). It is used for multi-criteria optimisation of complex systems. With the original (provided) weights, it determines the compromise ranking list and the compromise solution. This strategy is used when making a decision among many options that don't all satisfy the same set of criteria. The multi-criteria ranking index is introduced, which is based on a specific measure of "closeness" to the "ideal" answer. The purpose of this study is to adapt the VIKOR approach to interval-based decision-making situations. We add as an optimism level decision maker to facilitate comparisons between intervals, which is how the expanded VIKOR technique determines its rankings. The study concludes with a numerical example that serves to demonstrate and clarify the research's key findings. To address the fuzzy multi-criteria problem with competing and noncommensurable (different units) criteria, Opricovic (2011) created the fuzzy VIKOR approach. This technique is useful for situations in which the criteria and/ or weights are themselves fuzzy sets. For approximate calculations, we turn to the triangular fuzzy numbers. The distance from the ideal answer to each alternative is represented by the fuzzy merit that is aggregated in fuzzy VIKOR. The fuzzy VIKOR algorithm was created with the use of fuzzy operations and methods for sorting fuzzy integers. In the presence of competing criteria, the VIKOR method prioritises and selects" among options while also suggesting a compromise solution (or solutions). A cost-benefit analysis is added to it. The offered technique is applied to water resources planning by analysing the creation of a reservoir system to store the surface flows of the Mlava River and its tributaries for regional water supply, and a numerical example is provided to illustrate this. Fuzzy VIKOR's findings are compared to those obtained using a number of other methods. The financial performance of the four chosen firms from 1999 to 2009 was evaluated using two different approaches by Lee, Lin, and Shin (2012). Grey connection analysis was used to rank the firms during the time period after entropy was used to determine the relative importance of each company's financial ratio. These findings have important policy implications for businesses looking to lessen the blow of global financial instability on the shipping industry. The rankings were made by industry using the TOPSIS and VIKOR techniques, and the weights were determined using the fuzzy analytic hierarchy process (FAHP) by Yalcin, Bayrakdaroglu, and Kahraman (2012). Results reveal that the company rankings generated using these methodologies are consistent with the firms' standings within their respective industries. Using ten financial ratios in the entropy method, Bulgurcu (2013) analysed the financial performance of ten automotive companies listed on the Istanbul Stock Exchange Market (ISEM) between 2009 and 2013 and then used the TOPSIS method to determine the objective weight of each criterion. According to the results, the F-M Izmit Piston company maintained its top financial performance ranking during a four-year period. A hybrid method combining accounting and economic value metrics was suggested by Safaei Ghadikolaei, Khalili Esbouei, and Antucheviciene (2014). This method was then applied to the stock market performance of automobile businesses listed on the Tehran Stock Exchange. Fuzzy Additive Ratio Assessment (ARAS-F), Fuzzy Complex Proportional Assessment (fuzzy COPRAS), and fuzzy VIKOR (in Serbian) were all used in concert to rank the companies. The mean ranks were used to aggregate the outcomes of three different outranking strategies. The ranking of six firms revealed that economic value criteria are accorded greater weight than accounting metrics when assessing financial success. Gündoğdu (2015) investigated the financial performance during 2003–2013 of the foreign banks in Turkey by picking 10 banks and used 16 criteria for TOPSIS method evaluation from 2003 to 2013, Deutsche Bank came out on top in terms of financial performance, while Burgan Bank and Turkland Bank ranked last. In 2015, Shen and Tzeng (2015) integrated formal concept analysis (FCA), dominance-based rough set approach (DRSA), and decision-making trial and evaluation laboratory technique (DEMATEL) to create a soft computing model that addressed the value stock selection issue. This solved the value stock picking problem in its entirety. Using fuzzy-based multi-criteria decision-making (MCDM), Visalakshmi, Lakshmi, Shama, and Vijayakumar (2015) selected 14 GREENEX businesses from various Indian manufacturing sectors. Fuzzy decision-making trial and evaluation laboratory (DEMATEL) methodology were used to assign weights to criteria and sub-criteria, and Technique for order performance by similarity to ideal solution (TOPSIS) methodology was used to rank enterprises in the GREENEX sector. The empirical findings indicate that the financial ratios would contribute to a more thorough performance evaluation and ranking if they were included in the MCDM problem.

2.3 RESEARCH OBJECTIVES

The prime aim of this research is to evaluate the performance of NIFTY IT companies listed in NSE, India on 08.09.2022 with the use of "Multi-criteria Optimization and Compromise Solution" i.e. VIKOR method which is a MCDM technique.

    I. What is the ranking of each IT company pre and during COVID-19?
    II. What are the best IT companies pre and during COVID-19?
    III. What is the relative efficiency of each IT company pre and during COVID-19?

2.4 RESEARCH METHODOLOGY

The financial ratios of NIFTY IT companies listed in NSE & BSE, India on 08.09.2022 have been taken for four financial years, i.e. FY 2018–2019, FY 2019–2020, FY 2020–2021, and FY 2021–2022.

Table 2.1 shows that NIFTY IT companies which are considered as alternatives in this study.

The study has been considered 13 financial ratios. The ten beneficiary criteria's have been taken as current ratio, quick ratio, current assets turnover, fixed assets turnover, net profit margin, return on equity, working capital turnover, return on assets, interest coverage ratio, and price to book ratio. The three non-beneficiary criteria taken are the debt-equity ratio, price earnings ratio, and price sales ratio.

Table 2.2 represents the 13 financial ratios which are taken as criteria for this study.

- Sources of data: NSE website
- Type of data: secondary data
- Period of study: four years (FY 2018–2019 to FY 2021–2022)
- Technique used: "Multi-criteria Optimization and Compromise Solution" i.e. VIKOR method"

TABLE 2.1
NIFTY IT Companies (Alternatives)

Code for Alternatives	Companies' Name	NSE	BSE	ISIN Code
A01	Coforge Ltd.	COFORGE	532,541	INE591G01017
A02	HCL Tech	HCLTECH	532,281	INE860A01027
A03	Infosys	INFY	500,209	INE009A01021
A04	L & T Infotech	LTI	540,005	INE214T01019
A05	L & T Technology	LTTS540115	540,115	INE010V01017
A06	Mindtree	MINDTREE	532,819	INE018I01017
A07	Mphasis	MPHASIS	526299	INE356A01018
A08	TCS	TCS	532,540	INE467B01029
A09	Tech Mahindra	TECHM	532,755	INE669C01036
A10	Wipro	WIPRO	507,685	INE075A01022

TABLE 2.2
Financial Ratios (Criteria)

Code for Criteria	Ratios	Formula	Criteria Type
C01	Current ratio	$\text{Current Ratio} = \dfrac{\text{Current Assets}}{\text{Current Liabilities}}$	Beneficiary
C02	Acid test ratio or quick ratio	$\text{Acid Test Ratio} = \dfrac{\text{Current Assets-Inventories}}{\text{Current Liabilities}}$	Beneficiary
C03	Debt-to-equity ratio	$\text{Debt Equity Ratio} = \dfrac{\text{Total Debt or Total Liabilities}}{\text{Total Shareholder's Equity}}$	Non-beneficiary
C04	Current assets turnover	$\text{Current Assets Turnover} = \dfrac{\text{Sales}}{\text{Average Current Assets}}$	Beneficiary
C05	Fixed assets turnover	$\text{Fixed Assets Turnover} = \dfrac{\text{Net Revenue}}{\text{Average Fixed Assets}}$	Beneficiary
C06	Net profit margin	$\text{Net Profit Margin} = \dfrac{\text{Revenue-Cost}}{\text{Revenue}}$	Beneficiary
C07	Return on equity	$\text{Return on Equity} = \dfrac{\text{Net Profit}}{\text{Total Shareholder's Equity}}$	Beneficiary
C08	Working capital turnover	$\text{Working Capital Turnover} = \dfrac{\text{Net Sales}}{\text{Netr Working Capital}}$	Beneficiary
C09	Return on assets	$\text{Return on Assets} = \dfrac{\text{Net Profit}}{\text{Total Assets}}$	Beneficiary
C10	Interest coverage ratio	$\text{Interest Coverage Ratio} = \dfrac{\text{EBIT}}{\text{Interst Expense}}$	Beneficiary
C11	Price earnings ratio	$\text{Price Earnings Ratio} = \dfrac{\text{Market Price Per Share}}{\text{Earnings Per Share}}$	Non-beneficiary
C12	Price to book ratio	$\text{Price to Book Ratio} = \dfrac{\text{Market Price Per Share}}{\text{Book Value Per Share}}$	Beneficiary
C13	Price sales ratio	$\text{Price Sales Ratio} = \dfrac{\text{Market Capitalization}}{\text{Annual Sales}}$	Non-beneficiary

The arithmetic mean of these 13 ratios for two pre COVID-19 years and two during COVID-19 years have been calculated and used to prepare the two original data matrix of order 10 * 13. Equal weights are given to all 13 criteria and no lingual variables are used. The sum of total weights must be equal to 1. Therefore, weights for each criterion would be 0.077. Finally, the "Multi-criteria Optimization and Compromise Solution" i.e. VIKOR method has been used to rank the firms based on their financial performance.

MCDM and multi-criteria decision analysis (MCDA) techniques like the "Multi-criteria Optimisation and Compromise Solution" (VIKOR) approach are widely used nowadays. It was created by Serafim Opricovic to help with decision-making when there are competing and non-commensurable (measured in different ways) criteria involved, with the caveats that a middle ground is acceptable for resolving conflicts, the decision maker seeks the best possible outcome, and all feasible options are considered. As part of its "Multi-criteria Optimisation and Compromise Solution" feature, VIKOR evaluates possible solutions based on how close they get to meeting all of the criteria in question. When two parties come to an understanding through compromise, they each make some concessions. It's essentially a distance-based strategy.

In MCDM, Po-Lung Yu and Milan Zeleny established the concept of a compromise solution in 1973. In his 1979 Ph.D. dissertation, S. Opricovic outlined the foundational principles for what would become "Multi-criteria Optimisation and Compromise Solution," or VIKOR; a subsequent application was published in 1980. Its name, VIseKriterijumska Optimizacija I Kompromisno Resenje (pronounced vikor), comes from the Serbian for "Multicriteria Optimisation and Compromise Solution" and first appeared in 1990. In 1998, the apps were shown to be functional. The 2004 publication helped bring the "Multi-criteria Optimisation and Compromise Solution," often known as the VIKOR approach, to the attention of researchers throughout the world. VIKOR's fundamental principle is comparable to TOPSIS.

By ranking alternatives and identifying the compromise solution that is the closest to the ideal, the "Multi-criteria Optimisation and Compromise Solution" (VIKOR) technique implies that compromise is acceptable for conflict resolution. Ranking in VIKOR may be done with varying criterion weights. It's especially helpful when the decision maker is unable to voice a choice during the early stages of system design.

VIKOR is the multi-criteria measure for compromise ranking is developed from "$L_p - metric$" which is used as an aggregating function in a compromise programming method. It is defined as:

$$L_{p,i} = \left[\sum_{j=1}^{m} \left\{ W_j * \frac{X_i^+ - X_{ij}}{X_i^+ - X_i^-} \right\}^p \right]^{\frac{1}{p}}, \quad \text{where} \quad 1 \le p \le \infty \tag{2.1}$$

$L_{p,i}$ represents the distance of the alternative a_k to the ideal solution.

Here, i=alternatives, $i=1, 2, …, n$

j=criteria, $j=1, 2, …, m$

W_j is the weight of the criterion.

X_i^+ is the best score w.r.t criteria

X_i^- is the worst score w.r.t criteria

X_{ij} is the score of i-th row/alternative w.r.t j-th column/criteria

By putting $p = 1$ in "L_p-metric", we can get

$$\text{Unity Measure} = L_{1,i} = S_i = \sum_{j=1}^{m} \left(W_j * \frac{X_i^+ - X_{ij}}{X_i^+ - X_i^-} \right) \tag{2.2}$$

By putting $p = \infty$ in "L_p-metric", we can get

$$\text{Individual Regret} = L_{\infty,i} = R_i = \max_j \left(W_j * \frac{X_i^+ - X_{ij}}{X_i^+ - X_i^-} \right) \tag{2.3}$$

Here the S_i and R_i are used as boundary measures to formulate the ranking measure.

Steps of "Multi-criteria Optimization and Compromise Solution" i.e. VIKOR method:

- **Step 1:** Formation of aggregated Decision Matrix
  To get Decision Matrix" aggregate the data by Arithmetic Mean.
- **Step 2:** Calculation of the best values (X_i^+) and worst values (X_i^-) for all criteria

$$X_i^+ = \max_i \left(a_{ij} \right) \tag{2.4}$$

$$X_i^- = \min_i \left(a_{ij} \right) \tag{2.5}$$

where a_{ij} stands for elements of decision matrix, i=Criteria, j=Alternatives
- **Step 3:** Calculation of relative matrix (R_{ij})

$$R_{ij} = \frac{X_i^+ - X_{ij}}{X_i^+ - X_i^-} \tag{2.6}$$

- **Step 4:** Calculation of weighted normalised decision matrix
  Cell value can be obtained with help the formula

$$W_{ij} = W_j * R_{ij} = W_j * \frac{X_i^+ - X_{ij}}{X_i^+ - X_i^-} \tag{2.7}$$

- **Step 5:** Calculation of the values of S_i and R_i for all the alternatives

$$\text{Unity Measure} = S_i = \sum_{j=1}^{m} \left(W_j * \frac{X_i^+ - X_{ij}}{X_i^+ - X_i^-} \right) \tag{2.8}$$

$$\text{Individual Regret} = R_i = \max_j \left(W_j * \frac{X_i^+ - X_{ij}}{X_i^+ - X_i^-} \right) \tag{2.9}$$

- **Step 6:** Calculation of S^*, S^-, R^* and R^-

$$S^* = \min_i S_i \tag{2.10}$$

$$S^- = \max_i S_i \tag{2.11}$$

$$R^* = \min_i R_i \tag{2.12}$$

$$R^- = \max_i R_i \tag{2.13}$$

- **Step 7:** Calculation of Q_i for all alternatives

$$Q_i = v * \frac{S_i - S^*}{S^- - S^*} + (1 - v) * \frac{R_i - R^*}{R^- - R^*} \tag{2.14}$$

where, v is introduced as weight for the strategy of maximum group utility. (Generally, $v = 0.5$)
- **Step 8:** Ranking of the alternatives by sorting the values of S_i, R_i, and Q_i
  Based on the Q_i value the ranking of the alternatives can be obtained.
- **Step 9:** Propose a Compromise Solution

In VIKOR, a compromise solution is proposed for which we check two conditions:

  i. Condition 1: Acceptable advantage
     Let's check the first condition that is Acceptable advantage.

$$Q(A^2) - Q(A^1) \geq DQ, \quad \text{where} \quad DQ = \frac{1}{j-1}, \quad j \text{ is the number of alternatives} \quad (2.15)$$

If condition 1 is not fulfilled, then proceed for condition 2.
ii. Condition 2: Acceptable stability in decision-making

Based on those two conditions, a compromise solution is proposed which consists of
A^1 and A^2 if only condition 2 is not satisfied, or
A^1, A^2,..., A^M if condition 1 is not satisfied; and

$$A^M \text{ is determined by the relation} \quad Q(A^M) - Q(A^1) \leq DQ \quad (2.16)$$

Remember that A^1, A^2,..., $A^{M''}$ are the members of the compromise group.

2.5 DATA AND FINDINGS

2.5.1 PRE COVID

In Table 2.3, the arithmetic mean of 13 financial ratios of 10 NIFTY IT companies for two years of pre COVID has been calculated by simply adding them and dividing by 2.

$$\text{Arithmetic Mean} = \frac{\sum x}{n}$$

So the original data matrix has order 10 * 13, i.e. the matrix has 130 junctions.
No linguistic variables are used. So the value of each and every junction is numeric.
Table 2.4 shows the best and worst values of each criteria.
The best and the worst value should be the maximum and minimum value of the respective columns for beneficiary criteria. In the aforementioned table, C01, C02, C04, C05, C06, C07, C08, C09, C010, and C12 are beneficiary criteria.
The best and the worst value should be the minimum and maximum value of the respective columns for non-beneficiary criteria.
In the aforementioned table, C03, C11, and C13 are non-beneficiary criteria.

TABLE 2.3
Aggregated Decision Matrix by Arithmetic Mean

	C01	C02	C03	C04	C05	C06	C07	C08	C09	C10	C11	C12	C13
A01	7.21	7.21	0.01	0.86	0.39	33.88	38.93	0.62	33.05	102.61	36.33	6.94	3.95
A02	4.62	4.62	0.18	1.44	1.14	58.96	60.84	0.76	38.6	102.22	18.1	5.87	4.12
A03	5.88	5.88	0	1.15	0.33	39.77	62.66	0.75	37.77	130.45	37.45	9.11	6.89
A04	6.14	6.14	0.01	1.11	0.16	31.8	60.97	0.8	42.35	217.55	35.76	10.6	5.39
A05	5.73	5.73	0.04	0.82	0.31	30.09	73.74	0.3	41.05	574.98	36.01	10.98	5.38
A06	5.69	5.69	0	0.81	0.32	18.85	52.77	0.52	30.27	357.95	42.17	9.01	3.97
A07	4.22	4.22	0.2	1.16	0.15	50.12	62.97	0.65	39.84	101.69	28.13	5.64	3.78
A08	7.48	7.48	0	1.25	0.2	49.73	82.82	0.89	61.89	257.63	45.29	16.52	9.48
A09	5.44	5.44	0.18	1.27	0.22	31.6	41.56	0.85	29.38	70.5	28.25	5.66	3.32
A10	5.74	5.71	0.28	1.9	0.31	27.81	34.54	1.2	24.65	34.38	28.8	4.75	4.44

TABLE 2.4

Best Values and Worst Values

	B	B	NB	B	B	B	B	B	B	B	NB	B	NB
Criteria Type	C01	C02	C03	C04	C05	C06	C07	C08	C09	C10	C11	C12	C13
A01	7.21	7.21	0.01	0.86	0.39	33.88	38.93	0.62	33.05	102.61	36.33	6.94	3.95
A02	4.62	4.62	0.18	1.44	1.14	58.96	60.84	0.76	38.6	102.22	18.1	5.87	4.12
A03	5.88	5.88	0	1.15	0.33	39.77	62.66	0.75	37.77	130.45	37.45	9.11	6.89
A04	6.14	6.14	0.01	1.11	0.16	31.8	60.97	0.8	42.35	217.55	35.76	10.6	5.39
A05	5.73	5.73	0.04	0.82	0.31	30.09	73.74	0.3	41.05	574.98	36.01	10.98	5.38
A06	5.69	5.69	0	0.81	0.32	18.85	52.77	0.52	30.27	357.95	42.17	9.01	3.97
A07	4.22	4.22	0.2	1.16	0.15	50.12	62.97	0.65	39.84	101.69	28.13	5.64	3.78
A08	7.48	7.48	0	1.25	0.2	49.73	82.82	0.89	61.89	257.63	45.29	16.52	9.48
A09	5.44	5.44	0.18	1.27	0.22	31.6	41.56	0.85	29.38	70.5	28.25	5.66	3.32
A10	5.74	5.71	0.28	1.9	0.31	27.81	34.54	1.2	24.65	34.38	28.8	4.75	4.44
Best value	7.48	7.48	0	1.9	1.14	58.96	82.82	1.2	61.89	574.98	18.1	16.52	3.32
Worst value	4.22	4.22	0.28	0.81	0.15	18.85	34.54	0.3	24.65	34.38	45.29	4.75	9.48

Table 2.5 calculate relative matrix.

For the (1,1) junction of Table 2.5, the value of relative matrix should be

$$R_{11} = \frac{X_1^+ - X_{11}}{X_1^+ - X_1^-} = \frac{7.48 - 7.21}{7.48 - 4.22} = 0.08282$$

Table 2.6 calculate weighted normalised decision matrix.

Total weight assumed to be 1 for all criteria. There are 13 criteria. So weightage of each criteria is $\frac{1}{13} = 0.077$.

To get weighted normalised decision matrix, each value of relative matrix should be multiplied by 0.077.

Table 2.7 calculate the value of S_i and R_i.

S_i is nothing but the summation of each rows weighted normalised decision matrix and R_i is the maximum value of each rows weighted normalised decision matrix.

Table 2.8 detects the value of S^*, S^-, R^* and R^-. Here S^* and S^- are the minimum and maximum values of S_i. Also R^* and R^- are the minimum and maximum values of R_i.

Table 2.9 calculates the value of Q_i by the formula

$$Q_i = v * \frac{S_i - S^*}{S^- - S^*} + (1 - v) * \frac{R_i - R^*}{R^- - R^*}$$

where v is introduced as weight for the strategy of maximum group utility. (Generally, $v = 0.5$) and the aforementioned table also shows the final ranking of alternatives according to the values of Q_i. Minimum value Q_i is more efficient alternatives.

Figure 2.3 shows that pre COVID ranking of IT companies.

2.5.2 During COVID

In Table 2.10, the arithmetic mean of 13 financial ratios of 10 NIFTY IT companies for two years of during COVID has been calculated by simply adding them and dividing by 2.

$$\text{Arithmetic Mean} = \frac{\sum x}{n}$$

So the original data matrix has order 10 * 13 i.e. the matrix has 130 junctions.

No linguistic variables are used. So the value of each and every junction is numeric.

TABLE 2.5

Calculation of Relative Matrix

	C01	C02	C03	C04	C05	C06	C07	C08	C09	C10	C11	C12	C13
A01	0.082822086	0.082822086	0.035714286	0.954128	0.757576	0.62528	0.909072	0.644444	0.774436	0.873788	0.670467	0.813934	0.102273
A02	0.877300613	0.877300613	0.642857143	0.422018	0	0	0.455261	0.488889	0.625403	0.87451	0	0.904843	0.12987
A03	0.490797546	0.490797546	0	0.688073	0.818182	0.478434	0.417564	0.5	0.64769	0.82229	0.711659	0.629567	0.579545
A04	0.411042945	0.411042945	0.035714286	0.724771	0.989899	0.677138	0.452568	0.444444	0.524705	0.661173	0.649503	0.502974	0.336039
A05	0.536809816	0.536809816	0.142857143	0.990826	0.838384	0.719771	0.18807	1	0.559613	0	0.658698	0.470688	0.33416
A06	0.549079755	0.549079755	0	1	0.828283	1	0.622411	0.755556	0.849087	0.401461	0.885252	0.638063	0.105519
A07	1	1	0.714285714	0.678899	1	0.220394	0.411143	0.611111	0.592105	0.87549	0.368886	0.924384	0.074675
A08	0	0	0	0.59633	0.949495	0.230117	0	0.344444	0	0.587033	1	0	1
A09	0.625766871	0.625766871	0.642857143	0.577982	0.929293	0.682124	0.854598	0.388889	0.872986	0.933185	0.373299	0.922685	0
A10	0.533742331	0.542944785	1	0	0.838384	0.776614	1	0	1	1	0.393527	1	0.181818

TABLE 2.6
Calculation of weighted normalized decision matrix

	C01	C02	C03	C04	C05	C06	C07	C08	C09	C10	C11	C12	C13
Weightage	0.077	0.077	0.077	0.077	0.077	0.077	0.077	0.077	0.077	0.077	0.077	0.077	0.077
A01	0.006377301	0.006377301	0.00275	0.073468	0.058333	0.048147	0.069999	0.049622	0.059632	0.067282	0.051626	0.062673	0.007875
A02	0.067552147	0.067552147	0.0495	0.032495	0	0	0.035055	0.037644	0.048156	0.067337	0	0.069673	0.01
A03	0.037791411	0.037791411	0	0.052982	0.063	0.036839	0.032152	0.0385	0.049872	0.063316	0.054798	0.048477	0.044625
A04	0.031650307	0.031650307	0.00275	0.055807	0.076222	0.05214	0.034848	0.034222	0.040402	0.05091	0.050012	0.038729	0.025875
A05	0.041334356	0.041334356	0.011	0.076294	0.064556	0.055422	0.014481	0.077	0.04309	0	0.05072	0.036243	0.02575
A06	0.042279141	0.042279141	0	0.077	0.063778	0.077	0.047926	0.058178	0.06538	0.030913	0.068164	0.049131	0.008125
A07	0.077	0.077	0.055	0.052275	0.077	0.01697	0.031658	0.047056	0.045592	0.067413	0.028404	0.071178	0.00575
A08	0	0	0	0.045917	0.073111	0.017719	0	0.026522	0	0.045202	0.077	0	0.077
A09	0.048184049	0.048184049	0.0495	0.044505	0.071556	0.052524	0.065804	0.029944	0.06722	0.071855	0.028744	0.071047	0
A10	0.04109816	0.041806748	0.077	0	0.064556	0.059799	0.077	0	0.077	0.077	0.030302	0.077	0.014

TABLE 2.7

Calculation of the values of S_i and R_i for all the alternatives

	C01	C02	C03	C04	C05	C06	C07	C08	C09	C10	C11	C12	C13	S_i	R_i
A01	0.006377301	0.006377301	0.00275	0.073468	0.058333	0.048147	0.069999	0.049622	0.059632	0.067282	0.051626	0.062673	0.007875	0.56416	0.073468
A02	0.067552147	0.067552147	0.0495	0.032495	0	0	0.035055	0.037644	0.048156	0.067337	0	0.069673	0.01	0.484965	0.069673
A03	0.037791411	0.037791411	0	0.052982	0.063	0.036839	0.032152	0.0385	0.049872	0.063316	0.054798	0.048477	0.044625	0.560144	0.063316
A04	0.031650307	0.031650307	0.00275	0.055807	0.076222	0.05214	0.034848	0.034222	0.040402	0.05091	0.050012	0.038729	0.025875	0.525218	0.076222
A05	0.041334356	0.041334356	0.011	0.076294	0.064556	0.055422	0.014481	0.077	0.04309	0	0.05072	0.036243	0.02575	0.537225	0.077
A06	0.042279141	0.042279141	0	0.077	0.063778	0.077	0.047926	0.058178	0.06538	0.030913	0.068164	0.049131	0.008125	0.630152	0.077
A07	0.077	0.077	0.055	0.052275	0.077	0.01697	0.031658	0.047056	0.045592	0.067413	0.028404	0.071178	0.00575	0.652296	0.077
A08	0	0	0	0.045917	0.073111	0.017719	0	0.026522	0	0.045202	0.077	0	0.077	0.362471	0.077
A09	0.048184049	0.048184049	0.0495	0.044505	0.071556	0.052524	0.065804	0.029944	0.06722	0.071855	0.028744	0.071047	0	0.649066	0.071855
A10	0.04109816	0.041806748	0.077	0	0.064556	0.059799	0.077	0	0.077	0.077	0.030302	0.077	0.014	0.636561	0.077

TABLE 2.8

Calculation of S^*, S^-, R^* and R^-

	S_i	R_i
A01	0.564160341	0.07346789
A02	0.484965414	0.069672897
A03	0.560144228	0.063316334
A04	0.525218076	0.076222222
A05	0.537224509	0.077
A06	0.630151942	0.077
A07	0.652295766	0.077
A08	0.362471323	0.077
A09	0.649066254	0.071855272
A10	0.636561347	0.077
	$S^*=0.362471323$	$R^*=0.063316334$
	$S^-=0.652295766$	$R^-=0.077$

TABLE 2.9

Calculation of Q_i for all Alternatives and Ranking

	S_i	R_i	Q_i	Rank
A01	0.564160341	0.07346789	0.71888732	4
A02	0.484965414	0.069672897	0.443592921	2
A03	0.560144228	0.063316334	0.341021787	1
A04	0.525218076	0.076222222	0.752347885	5
A05	0.537224509	0.077	0.801481103	6
A06	0.630151942	0.077	0.961797867	8
A07	0.652295766	0.077	1	10
A08	0.362471323	0.077	0.499999999	3
A09	0.649066254	0.071855272	0.806440574	7
A10	0.636561347	0.077	0.972855259	9
	$S^*=0.362471323$	$R^*=0.063316334$		
	$S^-=0.652295766$	$R^-=0.077$		

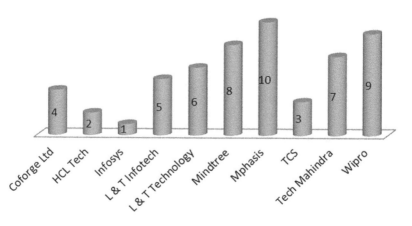

FIGURE 2.3 Pre COVID Rankings of IT companies.

TABLE 2.10

Aggregated Decision Matrix by Arithmetic Mean

	C01	C02	C03	C04	C05	C06	C07	C08	C09	C10	C11	C12	C13
A01	3.37	3.37	0.13	0.54	0.28	29.39	42.5	0.21	30.54	61.7	80.08	17.12	8.23
A02	5.94	5.73	0.12	1.44	1.07	51.25	43.6	0.94	36.14	99.72	47.31	9.56	7.23
A03	4.84	4.84	0	1.04	0.32	41.43	55.86	0.61	40.57	306.48	66.3	18.23	12.36
A04	6.46	6.46	0.1	1.24	0.2	31.15	52.66	0.85	37.21	86.48	83.45	21.92	12.61
A05	6.55	6.56	0	1.14	0.38	29.18	53.44	0.72	30.05	56.58	98.06	20.96	13.31
A06	5.63	5.63	0	1.15	0.29	29.63	70.42	0.74	37.71	85.74	73.8	20.9	11.05
A07	4.73	4.73	0.16	1.07	0.19	36.67	64.84	0.61	36.53	57.33	71.47	14.24	8.73
A08	5.41	5.4	0	1.2	0.17	45.95	90.87	0.75	59.52	150.79	72.74	28.95	14.3
A09	5.92	5.92	0.13	1.17	0.2	28.44	35.94	0.77	26.73	99.74	43.26	8.37	5.24
A10	4.73	4.73	0.35	1.76	0.34	40.5	44.55	1.02	30.39	68.93	48.13	9.09	7.75

TABLE 2.11

Best Values and Worst Values

	B	B	NB	B	B	B	B	B	B	B	NB	B	NB
Criteria Type	C01	C02	C03	C04	C05	C06	C07	C08	C09	C10	C11	C12	C13
A01	3.37	3.37	0.13	0.54	0.28	29.39	42.5	0.21	30.54	61.7	80.08	17.12	8.23
A02	5.94	5.73	0.12	1.44	1.07	51.25	43.6	0.94	36.14	99.72	47.31	9.56	7.23
A03	4.84	4.84	0	1.04	0.32	41.43	55.86	0.61	40.57	306.48	66.3	18.23	12.36
A04	6.46	6.46	0.1	1.24	0.2	31.15	52.66	0.85	37.21	86.48	83.45	21.92	12.61
A05	6.55	6.56	0	1.14	0.38	29.18	53.44	0.72	30.05	56.58	98.06	20.96	13.31
A06	5.63	5.63	0	1.15	0.29	29.63	70.42	0.74	37.71	85.74	73.8	20.9	11.05
A07	4.73	4.73	0.16	1.07	0.19	36.67	64.84	0.61	36.53	57.33	71.47	14.24	8.73
A08	5.41	5.4	0	1.2	0.17	45.95	90.87	0.75	59.52	150.79	72.74	28.95	14.3
A09	5.92	5.92	0.13	1.17	0.2	28.44	35.94	0.77	26.73	99.74	43.26	8.37	5.24
A10	4.73	4.73	0.35	1.76	0.34	40.5	44.55	1.02	30.39	68.93	48.13	9.09	7.75
Best value	6.55	6.56	0	1.76	1.07	51.25	90.87	1.02	59.52	306.48	43.26	28.95	5.24
Worst value	3.37	3.37	0.35	0.54	0.17	28.44	35.94	0.21	26.73	56.58	98.06	8.37	13.31

Table 2.11 shows the best and worst values of each criteria.

The best and the worst value should be the maximum and minimum value of the respective columns for beneficiary criteria. In the aforementioned table, C01, C02, C04, C05, C06, C07, C08, C09, C010, and C12 are beneficiary criteria.

The best and the worst value should be the minimum and maximum value of the respective columns for non-beneficiary criteria.

In the aforementioned table, C03, C11, and C13 are non-beneficiary criteria.

Table 2.12 calculate relative matrix.

For the (1,1) junction of Table 2.12, the value of relative matrix should be

$$R_{11} = \frac{X_1^+ - X_{11}}{X_1^+ - X_1^-} = \frac{6.55 - 3.37}{6.55 - 3.37} = 0.191824$$

Table 2.13 calculates weighted normalised decision matrix.

Total weight assumed to be 1 for all criteria. There are 13 criteria. So weightage of each criterion is $\frac{1}{13} = 0.077$.

To get weighted normalised decision matrix, each value of relative matrix should be multiplied by 0.077.

Table 2.14 calculates the value of S_i and R_i.

TABLE 2.12
Calculation of Relative Matrix

	C01	C02	C03	C04	C05	C06	C07	C08	C09	C10	C11	C12	C13
A01	1	1	0.371428571	1	0.877778	0.958352	0.880575	1	0.883806	0.979512	0.671898	0.57483	0.370508
A02	0.191823899	0.260188088	0.342857143	0.262295	0	0	0.86055	0.098765	0.713022	0.827371	0.073905	0.942177	0.246592
A03	0.537735849	0.539184953	0	0.590164	0.833333	0.430513	0.637357	0.506173	0.57792	0	0.420438	0.520894	0.88228
A04	0.028301887	0.031347962	0.285714286	0.42623	0.966667	0.881192	0.695613	0.209877	0.68039	0.880352	0.733394	0.341594	0.913259
A05	0	0	0	0.508197	0.766667	0.967558	0.681413	0.37037	0.89875	1	1	0.388241	1
A06	0.289308176	0.29153605	0	0.5	0.866667	0.94783	0.372292	0.345679	0.665142	0.883313	0.557299	0.391156	0.71995
A07	0.572327044	0.573667712	0.457142857	0.565574	0.977778	0.639193	0.473876	0.506173	0.701128	0.996999	0.514781	0.714772	0.432466
A08	0.358490566	0.363636364	0	0.459016	1	0.232354	0	0.333333	0	0.623009	0.537956	0	1.122677
A09	0.198113208	0.200626959	0.371428571	0.483607	0.966667	1	1	0.308642	1	0.827291	0	1	0
A10	0.572327044	0.573667712	1	0	0.811111	0.471285	0.843255	0	0.888381	0.95058	0.088869	0.965015	0.311029

TABLE 2.13

Calculation of weighted normalised decision matrix

Weightage	C01	C02	C03	C04	CO5	C06	C07	C08	C09	C10	C11	C12	C13
	0.077	0.077	0.077	0.077	0.077	0.077	0.077	0.077	0.077	0.077	0.077	0.077	0.077
A01	0.077	0.077	0.0286	0.077	0.067589	0.073793	0.067804	0.077	0.068053	0.075422	0.051736	0.044262	0.028529
A02	0.01477044	0.020034483	0.0264	0.020197	0	0	0.066262	0.007605	0.054903	0.063708	0.005691	0.072548	0.018988
A03	0.04140566	0.041517241	0	0.045443	0.064167	0.033149	0.049076	0.038975	0.0445	0	0.032374	0.040109	0.067936
A04	0.002179245	0.002413793	0.022	0.03282	0.074433	0.067852	0.053562	0.01616	0.05239	0.067787	0.056471	0.026303	0.070321
A05	0	0	0	0.039131	0.059033	0.074502	0.052469	0.028519	0.069204	0.077	0.077	0.029895	0.077
A06	0.02227673	0.022448276	0	0.0385	0.066733	0.072983	0.028666	0.026617	0.051216	0.068015	0.042912	0.030119	0.055436
A07	0.044069182	0.044172414	0.0352	0.043549	0.075289	0.049218	0.036488	0.038975	0.053987	0.076769	0.039638	0.055037	0.0333
A08	0.027603774	0.028	0	0.035344	0.077	0.017891	0	0.025667	0	0.047972	0.041423	0	0.086446
A09	0.015254717	0.015448276	0.0286	0.037238	0.074433	0.077	0.077	0.023765	0.077	0.063701	0	0.077	0
A10	0.044069182	0.044172414	0.077	0	0.062456	0.036289	0.064931	0	0.068405	0.073195	0.006843	0.074306	0.023949

TABLE 2.14

Calculation of the values of S_i and R_i for all the alternatives

	C01	C02	C03	C04	C05	C06	C07	C08	C09	C10	C11	C12	C13	S_i	R_i
A01	0.077	0.077	0.0286	0.077	0.067589	0.073793	0.067804	0.077	0.068053	0.075422	0.051736	0.044262	0.028529	0.813789	0.077
A02	0.01477044	0.020034483	0.0264	0.020197	0	0	0.066262	0.007605	0.054903	0.063708	0.005691	0.072548	0.018988	0.371105	0.072548
A03	0.04140566	0.041517241	0	0.045443	0.064167	0.033149	0.049076	0.038975	0.0445	0	0.032374	0.040109	0.067936	0.498651	0.067936
A04	0.002179245	0.002413793	0.022	0.03282	0.074433	0.067852	0.053562	0.01616	0.05239	0.067787	0.056471	0.026303	0.070321	0.544693	0.074433
A05	0	0	0	0.039131	0.059033	0.074502	0.052469	0.028519	0.069204	0.077	0.077	0.029895	0.077	0.583752	0.077
A06	0.02227673	0.022448276	0	0.0385	0.066733	0.072983	0.028666	0.026617	0.051216	0.068015	0.042912	0.030119	0.055436	0.525923	0.072983
A07	0.044069182	0.044172414	0.0352	0.043549	0.075289	0.049218	0.036488	0.038975	0.053987	0.076769	0.039638	0.055037	0.0333	0.625693	0.076769
A08	0.027603774	0.028	0	0.035344	0.077	0.017891	0	0.025667	0	0.047972	0.041423	0	0.086446	0.387346	0.086446
A09	0.015254717	0.015448276	0.0286	0.037238	0.074433	0.077	0.077	0.023765	0.077	0.063701	0	0.077	0	0.566441	0.077
A10	0.044069182	0.044172414	0.077	0	0.062456	0.036289	0.064931	0	0.068405	0.073195	0.006843	0.074306	0.023949	0.575615	0.077

S_i is nothing, but the summation of each rows weighted normalised decision matrix and R_i is the maximum value of each rows weighted normalised decision matrix.

Table 2.15 detects the value of S^*, S^-, R^* and R^-.

Here S^* and S^- are the minimum and maximum values of S_i. Also R^* and R^- are the minimum and maximum values of R_i.

Table 2.16 calculates the value of Q_i by the formula

$$Q_i = v * \frac{S_i - S^*}{S^- - S^*} + (1 - v) * \frac{R_i - R^*}{R^- - R^*}$$

where v is introduced as weight for the strategy of maximum group utility. (Generally, $v = 0.5$) and the aforementioned table also shows the final ranking of alternatives according to the values of Q_i. Minimum value Q_i is more efficient alternatives.

Figure 2.4 shows the rankings of IT companies in India during COVID.

TABLE 2.15
Calculation of S^*, S^-, R^* & R^-

	S_i	R_i
A01	0.813788889	0.077
A02	0.371105115	0.072547619
A03	0.498651434	0.067935564
A04	0.544692713	0.074433333
A05	0.583752029	0.077
A06	0.52592333	0.072982902
A07	0.625692524	0.076768908
A08	0.387346411	0.086446097
A09	0.566440864	0.077
A10	0.575614884	0.077
	$S^* = 0.371105115$	$R^* = 0.067935564$
	$S^- = 0.813788889$	$R^- = 0.086446096$

TABLE 2.16
Calculation of Q_i for all alternatives and Ranking

	S_i	R_i	Q_i	Rank
A01	0.813788889	0.077	0.744845361	10
A02	0.371105115	0.072547619	0.124579213	1
A03	0.498651434	0.067935564	0.144060306	2
A04	0.544692713	0.074433333	0.371578216	4
A05	0.583752029	0.077	0.485024612	7
A06	0.52592333	0.072982902	0.311200144	3
A07	0.625692524	0.076768908	0.526153141	9
A08	0.387346411	0.086446097	0.518344129	8
A09	0.566440864	0.077	0.465472093	5
A10	0.575614884	0.077	0.475833914	6
	0.371105115	**0.067935564**		
	0.813788889	**0.086446097**		

Ranking (During Covid)

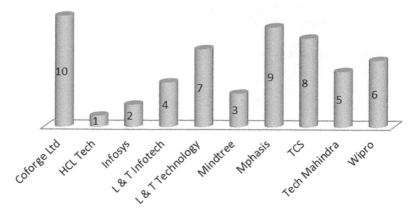

FIGURE 2.4   During COVID Rankings of IT companies.

2.6   SUGGESTIONS FOR COMPROMISE SOLUTION

2.6.1   PRE COVID

In VIKOR, a compromise solution is proposed for which we check two conditions:

i. Condition 1: Acceptable advantage
   Let's check the first condition that is acceptable advantage.

$$Q(A02) - Q(A03) \geq DQ, \quad \text{where} \quad DQ = \frac{1}{j-1}, \; j \text{ is the number of alternatives}$$

Now, $Q(A02) - Q(A03) = 0.443592921 - 0.341021787 = 0.102571134$

$$DQ = \frac{1}{j-1} = \frac{1}{10-1} = \frac{1}{9} = 0.111111111$$

Since $0.102571134 < 0.111111111$
   Therefore, $Q(A02) - Q(A03) < DQ$
   So condition 1 is not fulfilled, then proceed for condition 2.
ii. Condition 2: Acceptable stability in decision making
   Alternative which is ranked 1 by Q_i should also be ranked 1 by S_i or R_i.
   From the Table 2.9, based on R_i, A03 is ranked 1.
   So Condition 2 is satisfied.

$$Q(A02) - Q(A03) = 0.443592921 - 0.341021787 = 0.102571134 < DQ$$

$$Q(A08) - Q(A03) = 0.499999999 - 0.341021787 = 0.158978212 > DQ$$

So A02 and A03 are the members of the compromise group, but we can't take A08 in the compromise group because the value of DQ i.e. 0.111111 is smaller than the value of $Q(A08) - Q(A03)$.

2.6.2 DURING COVID

In VIKOR, a compromise solution is proposed for which we check two conditions:

  i. Condition 1: Acceptable advantage
     Let's check the first condition that is acceptable advantage.

$$Q(A03) - Q(A02) \geq DQ, \text{ where } DQ = \frac{1}{j-1}, j \text{ is the number of alternatives}$$

    Now, $Q(A03) - Q(A02) = 0.14406 - 0.12458 = 0.01948$

$$DQ = \frac{1}{j-1} = \frac{1}{10-1} = \frac{1}{9} = 0.111111111$$

    Since $0.01948 < 0.111111111$

    Therefore, $Q(A03) - Q(A02) < DQ$
    So Condition 1 is not fulfilled, then proceed for condition 2.
  ii. Condition 2: Acceptable stability in decision-making
     Alternative which is ranked 1 by Q_i should also be ranked 1 by S_i or R_i.
     From the Table 2.16, based on S_i, A02 is ranked 1.
     So Condition 2 is satisfied.

$$Q(A03) - Q(A02) = 0.14406 - 0.12458 = 0.01948 < DQ$$

$$Q(A06) - Q(A02) = 0.52592 - 0.12458 = 0.40134 > DQ$$

So A03 and A02 are the members of the compromise group but we can't take A06 in the compromise group because the value of DQ i.e. 0.111111 is smaller than the value of $Q(A06) - Q(A02)$.

2.7 CONCLUSIONS

To assure the success of an organisation, it is an important task to assess the performance on a regular basis. To comprehend the financial strength and weakness, the analysis of financial conditions of that organisation is very much required. Financial ratios are vital tools for quantitative data analysis. Financial ratios take information contained in the financial statement. Financial ratios provide information that encompasses the operations and profit activities of a firm running under any industry. To ascertain and understand, how competitive a firm is and evaluating the financial performance of such firms, financial ratio analysis plays a significant role. This analysis helps investor and leaders to understand what changes need to be made timely.

The study shows that in the pre-COVID-19 duration of two years, Infosys was ranked No. 1 IT company in India because of its high values of fxed assets turnover and working capital turnover and lower value of debt-to-equity ratio. Also HCL Tech is the second-ranked IT company since it has high values of current assets turnover, fixed assets turnover, and net profit margin and the lower values of price earning ratio and price sales ratio. On the other hand, Mphasis has the worst rank because of its lower values of current ratio, quick ratio, and fixed assets turnover.

During COVID-19, HCL Tech was ranked No. 1 IT company because of its higher values of current assets turnover, fixed assets turnover, net profit margin and working capital turnover, and low values of price earning ratio and price sales ratio. Infosys stand second in the list since it has the ratios such as fixed assets turnover, net profit margin, return on assets, and interest coverage ratio that have higher values. Coforge Ltd. has the ratios such as current ratio, quick ratio, current assets turnover, net profit margin, return on equity, working capital turnover, and interest coverage ratio are performed continuously poorly, which is one of the major reasons for it falling lowest in the ranking calendar.

In the investment point of view in the Indian financial market, an investor can choose Infosys and HCL Tech in the IT sector for investment as these two key players have continuously performed better than others in the past four years of analysis.

2.8   LIMITATIONS

I. This study is limited to ten NIFTY IT companies only.
II. The study also limited to only four Financial Years.

2.9   FUTURE SCOPE OF STUDY

Other MCDM methods such as TOPSIS, SAW, COPRAS, ELECTRE, and PROMETHEE can be used to give a new shape to the results.

REFERENCES

Bulgurcu, B. "Financial performance ranking of automotive industry firms in Turkey: Evidence from entropy weighted technique." *International Journal of Economics and Financial Issues* 3, no. 4 (2013): 844–851.

Deng, H., C.-H. Yeh, and R. J. Willis. "Inter-company comparison using modified TOPSIS with objective weights." *Computers & Operations Research* 27, no. 10 (2000): 963–973.

Gündoğdu, A. "Measurement of financial performance using TOPSIS method for foreign banks of established in Turkey between 2003–2013 years." *International Journal of Business and Social Science* 6, no. 1 (2015): 139–151.

Lee, P. T.-W., C.-W. Lin, and S.-H. Shin. "A comparative study on financial positions of shipping companies in Taiwan and Korea using entropy and grey relation analysis." *Expert Systems with Applications* 39, no. 5 (2012): 5649–5657.

Lin, F., C. Chang, and S. Wu. "A study on the relationship between related party transactions and monthly sales in Taiwan's publicly issued companies." *Journal of the Chinese Institute of Industrial Engineers* 26, no. 5 (2009): 337–343.

Opricovic, S. "Fuzzy VIKOR with an application to water resources planning." *Expert Systems with Applications* 38, no. 10 (2011): 12983–12990.

Opricovic, S., and G.-H. Tzeng. "Compromise solution by MCDM methods: A comparative analysis of VIKOR and TOPSIS." *European Journal of Operational Research* 156, no. 2 (2004): 445–455.

Opricovic, S., and G.-H. Tzeng. "Extended VIKOR method in comparison with outranking methods." *European Journal of Operational Research* 178, no. 2 (2007): 514–529.

SafaeiGhadikolaei, A., S. Khalili Esbouei, and J. Antucheviciene. "Applying fuzzy MCDM for financial performance evaluation of Iranian companies." *Technological and Economic Development of Economy* 20, no. 2 (2014): 274–291.

Sayadi, M. K., M. Heydari, and K. Shahanaghi. "Extension of VIKOR method for decision making problem with interval numbers." *Applied Mathematical Modelling* 33, no. 5 (2009): 2257–2262.

Shen, K.-Y., and G.-H. Tzeng. "Combined soft computing model for value stock selection based on fundamental analysis." *Applied Soft Computing* 37 (2015): 142–155.

Visalakshmi, S., P. Lakshmi, M. S. Shama, and K. Vijayakumar. "An integrated fuzzy DEMATEL-TOPSIS approach for financial performance evaluation of GREENEX industries." *International Journal of Operational Research* 23, no. 3 (2015): 340–362.

Wang, Y.-J. "Applying FMCDM to evaluate financial performance of domestic airlines in Taiwan." *Expert Systems with Applications* 34, no. 3 (2008): 1837–1845.

Yalcin, N., A. Bayrakdaroglu, and C. Kahraman. "Application of fuzzy multi-criteria decision making methods for financial performance evaluation of Turkish manufacturing industries." *Expert Systems with Applications* 39, no. 1 (2012): 350–364.

3 Conjoint Analysis
A Heuristic Decision-Making Model of Product Selection

Sweety Mukherjee
Division of Agricultural Extension
ICAR-Indian Agricultural Research Institute, New Delhi, India

Ayushman Malakar
Genetics and Tree Improvement Division
ICFRE-Institute of Forest Productivity, Ranchi, India

Arnab Roy
Central Tasar Research and Training Institute, Ranchi, India

3.1 INTRODUCTION

In this age of globalization, it is imperative to keep a great insight into customer demand and preference for any production line to survive in the competitive market. In both the cases of capturing a new market and expanding the existing market, thorough knowledge of the consumer base is considered to be the foundation of success (Mohr-Jackson, 1996). Conjoint analysis is a multivariate analysis or study of different factors that directly or indirectly influence the preferences or decisions taken by consumers to purchase or avail of any product or service. Any product or service possesses multidimensional attributes that typically control the consumer's willingness of buying that product or service. Many times, consumers cannot go for the product that is best in every attribute, particularly where monetary attributes play a greater role. Consumers are forced to make trade-offs as they decide which products to purchase (Kuhfeld, 2010). Here lies the extensive use of conjoint analysis in the research of marketing sectors which analyzes such consumer trade-offs. The analysis is generally based on the theory that consumers evaluate the value of a product by combining all the separate amounts of value provided by each attribute of the particular product or service. With the help of conjoint analysis, market researchers can get a great insight into the compositions of consumer preferences statistical examination of the attributes varying from the most or least preferable to any consumer which form the basis of purchasing decision for him on any product or service.

Market researchers choose conjoint analysis as one of the best methods to investigate and analyze consumer preference. Conjoint analysis revolves around a central question, viz. Why do consumers prefer one brand over another? Thus, it is one such technique of handling situations where a decision-maker has to deal with choices varying simultaneously across several attributes. The usual problem for the decision-maker is to trade off the possibility that option 1 is better than option 2 on attribute X, whereas option 2 is better than option 1 on attribute Y, and several such combinations. Conjoint analysis hence allows a researcher to find out the product that creates the highest value to the customer depending on its several attributes and thus leading to create the optimal value proposition. Conjoint analysis hence can prove to be very effective to the new market explorers and researchers to plan the marketing strategies, product positioning, and target consumers which will help flourish the sector in turn. Although conjoint analysis is extensively used in developed western countries, marketing practitioners and theorists in Eastern countries are relatively not aware of this statistical approach. But if applied in the studies of market attributes and consumer behavior, it can prove to be a game-changer.

3.2 HISTORICAL BACKGROUND OF CONJOINT ANALYSIS

The late 1960s and the early 1970s witnessed the development of behavioral sciences, mainly psychometrics and mathematical psychology, in marketing research. Thus, three techniques, viz. cluster analysis, multidimensional scaling, and conjoint analysis, came to the forefront. Cluster analysis followed by multidimensional scaling methods almost immediately found application in market segmentation (Green et al., 1967; Carroll and Green, 1995). But researchers who desired to develop a new product were faced with a dual problem of translating the perceived brand scores to manipulable dimensions and relating the manipulable attribute levels to the perceived ones.

The origin conjoint analysis shares the area of conjoint measurement in mathematical psychology that dates back to the 1920s. According to the mathematical psychologists, conjoint measurement emphasizes the conditions, which mark the presence of measurement scales for both dependent and independent variables, given the order of combined effect of the independent variables and an earlier mentioned composition rule. It is generally considered that the seminal research by Luce, a mathematical psychologist, and Tukey, a statistician marks the proper evolution of conjoint analysis (Luce and Tukey, 1964).

Suitable computer programs are applied thereafter to test whether a particular data set meets the necessary conditions for applying several composition rules hypothesized by the researcher (Green and Carmone, 1970; Ullrich and Painter, 1974; Barron, 1977). Market researchers and psychometricians, on the other hand, are concerned with scaling aspects, viz. searching specific numerical values, assuming that a specific composition rule applies, with a possible error. Thus, the name "conjoint analysis" seems more appropriate to cover models and methods, emphasizing the transformation of subjective responses to estimated parameters (Kruskal, 1965; Carroll, 1969; Green and Srinivasan, 1978). The detailed methodologies of conjoint analysis were depicted by Green and Rao (1969). But they documented the first detailed consumer-oriented methodologies in 1971.

Conjoint analysis, soon after its introduction, paved its way to being the most used marketing research tool for analyzing consumer trade-offs. Several researchers like Wittink and Cattin (1989); Wittink et al. (1994) concluded conjoint analysis to be popular worldwide for handling such market situations in which a decision-maker (consumer) has to choose between the options that simultaneously vary across two or more attributes. Conjoint analysis deals with one central question that why the consumer is willing to prefer one product or service over another. It helps the market researchers to understand the day-to-day decisions taken by the consumers during any purchase (Tversky, 1972). Conjoint analysis is one of many techniques for handling situations in which the decision-maker faces the problem of how to trade off the possibility that a product that is better than another product on a certain attribute while the later product is better than the first one on a different attribute and various extensions of such kinds of conflicts (Green et al., 2004).

3.3 STATISTICAL MODELING OF CONJOINT ANALYSIS

Conjoint analysis is mainly based on the basic model of analysis of variance (ANOVA) where it analyzes the preference data of the responders based on some prefixed qualitative attributes. These qualitative attributes are assigned with some utility value to convert them into quantitative attributes that can be calculated through statistical models. The analysis is carried out, resulting in a utility score, known as "part-worth utility," which provides a quantitative measure of the preferences for each attribute level. Larger values of the part-worth utility represent greater preferences and vice versa. These part-worth utility scores are expressed in a common unit so that they can be added up to represent the total utility, i.e. the overall preference of a combination of attribute levels. Thus, this multivariate technique assumes that an individual's choice behavior is governed by the maximization of their preferences. It views an article in the form of a set of attributes from which individuals can attain total utility.

Statistical models and experimental designs are of fundamental importance to carry out any conjoint analysis. These models and designs are used to analyze the data procured from the respondents. The part-worth function used in conjoint analysis can be attributed as linear or nonlinear. The linear function is alternatively known as a vector model for which the utility value changes (positively or negatively) with the numerical value assigned to the particular attribute of the product. According to the vector model, if there are P attributes and J stimuli for a particular analysis, the respondent's preference S_j for the jth stimulus is given by Green et al. (2004). The following equation is specified to calculate the respondent's preference S_j,

$$S_j = \sum_{P=1}^{P} w_p y_{jp} \tag{3.1}$$

where y_{jp} is the desirability of the Pth attribute for the jth stimulus and w_p denotes the respondent's importance weight for each of the P attributes. But for real-life market situations, consumer preference and behavior do not follow any linear model. Hence, the vector model does not have much practical value in conjoint analysis.

A nonlinear function can be either an ideal point model or a part-worth function model. For a positive ideal point model, the utility is highest at its ideal value and for a negative ideal point model, the utility is lowest at its ideal value. For the ideal point model, the respondent's preference S_j is calculated as the weighted squared distance of the location y_{jp} from the ideal utility point x_p, which is defined as d_j^2

$$d_j^2 = \sum_{P=1}^{P} w_p (y_{jp} - x_p)^2 \tag{3.2}$$

But generally, market researchers prefer to use the part-worth function model during any conjoint analysis. It proved to be the most reliable model to use in the study of consumer behavior and preference. Relative utility weights are used here to calculate the highest and lowest part-worth utility for each attribute concerned and the difference between the highest and lowest part-worth value is defined as the utility range (UR) for that attribute (Green et al., 2004). Here respondent's preference S_j is calculated as

$$S_j = \sum_{P=1}^{P} f_p (y_{jp}) \tag{3.3}$$

where f_p is a function denoting the part-worth corresponding to level y_{jp}.

Once the UR has been calculated, the relative importance (RI) of the attribute is calculated as utility of respective attributes to the total utility (Roy and Malhotra, 2018). The equation of calculating RI of the attribute can be written as:

$$\text{Relative importance (RI)} = \frac{\text{UR}}{\sum_{j=1}^{n} \text{UR}_j} \times 100 \tag{3.4}$$

Fundamentally there are two major types of conjoint analysis. The first one is metric conjoint analysis in which the attributes given as inputs are independent variables whereas the dependable variables are the judgments. This kind of conjoint analysis model is based on simple ANOVA where the outputs are modified specially for the use of required market research (Kuhfeld, 2010). Statistically, metric conjoint analysis for three attributes can be denoted as:

$$y_{ijk} = \mu + \beta_{1i} + \beta_{2j} + \beta_{3k} + \varepsilon_{ijk} \tag{3.5}$$

where y_{ijk} is the output or the predicted utility of the final preference of the respondent taken over three separate attributes denoted as i, j and k, β is part-*worth* utilities, μ is the grand mean, ε_{ijk} is the error factor and, $\Sigma\beta_{1i} = \Sigma\beta_{2j} = \Sigma\beta_{3k} = 0$

The second type is nonmetric conjoint analysis which directly follows from conjoint measurement, finding a monotonic transformation of the preferences and fits the ANOVA model continuously until the stabilization of such transformation (Kuhfeld, 2010). Statistically, nonmetric conjoint analysis for three attributes can be denoted as:

$$\phi\left(y_{ijk}\right) = \mu + \beta_{1i} + \beta_{2j} + \beta_{3k} + \varepsilon_{ijk} \tag{3.6}$$

where $\phi\left(y_{ijk}\right)$ denotes the monotonic transformation of the variable y.

With the advancement of the methodologies practiced for conjoint analysis, the metric conjoint analysis is being preferred by the market analysts worldwide over nonmetric conjoint analysis, as the results from metric conjoint analysis is more stable and easily understandable than nonmetric conjoint analysis. According to the chronology, metric conjoint analysis is a simplified version of the nonmetric conjoint analysis derived for special research operations. It is evident that both metric and nonmetric conjoint analysis are based on linear ANOVA models, which might have hindered the analysis of complex market traits dealing in several multidimensional attributes. Hence, over time, other modern approaches for conjoint analysis came into effect. Nowadays, choice-based conjoint is widely popular in market research which employs a nonlinear multinomial logit model and is able to analyze complex market attributes and preferences.

3.4 STEPS OF CONJOINT ANALYSIS

Conjoint analysis is a statistical tool for market analysis depending on consumer behavior and preferences. Like all other statistical analysis tools, conjoint analysis also follows some predefined steps of design to be carried out (Myers et al., 1980). Naturally, conjoint analysis starts with a definition of the problem, and statistical studies are designed with the objective of mitigating that certain problem (Rao, 2014). Churchill and Iacobucci (2002) defined the major steps for successfully conducting any conjoint analysis. These can be summarized as -

I. Selection of attributes: Attributes are independent aspects of a product, such as the size, color, shape, brand, price, etc. Based on the research objectives, the number of attributes is usually determined. The attributes need to be independent and mutually exclusive. The right choice of product attributes is of utmost importance in conjoint analysis.

Two criteria are usually kept in mind while selecting the attribute and its levels (Gustafsson et al., 1999):
   a. The attribute levels should describe as closely as possible the real-life situation faced by the consumers. The attributes should be closely related to those products that are accessible to the consumers.
   b. Factors, considered to be important in gaining a competitive edge for the company, must be included.

II. Specifying the levels for each attribute: Each of the attributes consists of various degrees, known as levels. These levels should be clearly and unambiguously stated, with concrete meaning. For example, the product weighs "100–200 g" or it weighs "150 g." In the first case, it depends upon the respondent about how he/she interprets it, while the second case provides a concrete base to the respondent.

Another point that must be considered while determining the levels is that there should not be too many levels for an attribute. Usually, three to five levels per attribute is considered to be optimum.

The number of levels of each attribute is directly related to the number of stimuli that the respondents will be asked to judge. The more the number of levels, the more difficult it is for the consumers to judge. The analyst should make the range for attributes relatively larger than that usually found, but not so large to make the choices unbelievable (Churchill and Iacobucci, 2002).

III. **Choosing the data collection method:** Conjoint analysis generally makes use of the Full-profile approach where a respondent has to go for either ranking, rating, or scoring his/her preferences, which are based on the combination of a set of attributes and their respective levels. But this procedure is having a limitation, i.e. if a large number of attributes along with their levels are combined, then the resulting number of possible combinations becomes too large that it is not feasible for the respondents to rank or score them. To overcome this problem, fractional factorial design is used, which presents a fraction of the possible combinations of levels of attributes used. The set obtained is called an Orthogonal Array, and it presents the main effects of each of the levels of the attribute. The interaction is assumed to be negligible between the levels of one attribute and those of another. Apart from the full-profile approach, the paired comparison method is also used, in which the respondents are provided with two attributes along with their respective levels to choose from. One demerit of using this method is the higher divergence of the research situation from a real-life situation, in which the consumers have to compare entire products (i.e. the whole set of product attributes) and not just two attributes. Another demerit is the large number of paired comparisons required for analysis.

IV. **Composing the concept cards:** It is always practical to use a small part of all possible concept cards alternatives to estimate efficiently the main effect of those attributes on the dependent variable. While experimenting with five product attributes, each having three performance levels, the number of alternative concept cards will be $3^5 = 243$.

V. **Selection of the form of presentation of stimuli and nature of judgments:** The nature or judgments intended from the respondents, is related to the form of presentation. Three approaches are generally used here, viz. verbal description, paragraph description, and pictorial representation. Visual aids are commonly used in combination with verbal descriptions.

VI. **Assigning a measurement scale:**
   a. **Ranking-based**: in which the respondents are presented with a set of profiles, consisting of various combinations of the levels of the attribute, and are asked to rank them based on their preferences.
   b. **Rating-based**: in which the respondents have to score the profiles, say, on a scale of 1–10, indicating their preferences.
   c. **Choice-based**: in which the respondents need to simply sort the profiles based on their preferences.

VII. **Data collection:** A survey questionnaire is to be prepared for the target respondents. Data can be obtained through personal or group interviews, a telephone, mail, and telephone (TMT) interview, or via online methods, where the respondents are shown the concept cards and asked to rank them according to their purchasing preferences. Interview methods help in clarifying any doubts which may arise on the part of the respondents, giving guidelines and avoiding distrust, thereby getting a better response.

VIII. **Decide on the aggregation of judgments:** This step deals with whether the responses from the consumers or groups of consumers will be aggregated and if so, how to conduct that. Formation of groups implies estimating the utilities for individual-level models and clustering them together to form homogeneous groups.

IX. **Selecting analysis technique:** Designing a conjoint analysis project involves selecting an appropriate data analysis technique. This selection depends on the method used to obtain the input judgments of the respondents. For example, in the case of ordinal data, assuming a linear relationship is questionable, thus, a nonmetric regression model should be used to estimate the utilities (Churchill and Iacobucci, 2002).

X. **Modeling the preferences:** The final step consists of selecting a proper statistical model through which the conjoint analysis will be carried out. A detailed discussion regarding various statistical models used in the conjoint analysis has been done in the earlier section. Accordingly, several modern software like R, Python, and SPSS programming is used for modeling of utility using conjoint analysis. In general, any market researcher prefers the part-worth utility function model to carry out choice-based conjoint analysis, and the profile combination of the observed factor is followed by analysis with *the conjoint* package in R software.

3.5 APPLICATION OF CONJOINT ANALYSIS FOR MARKET RESEARCHERS

Hair et al. (1998) described the conjoint analysis as "a multi-variate technique, used specifically to understand how respondents develop preferences for products or services. Thus, it assumes that customers evaluate the value of a product or service by combining the separate values of each of its attributes." In the words of Sudman and Blair (1998), conjoint analysis is not a data analysis procedure, unlike factor analysis or cluster analysis. It is a kind of "thought experiment," demonstrating how various attributes of a product or service predict the consumer preferences for it. Philip (1999) describes it as "… a method for deriving the utility values that consumers attach to varying levels of a product's attributes." Churchill and Iacobucci (2002) defines it as "… conjoint measurement, which relies on the ability of respondents to make judgments about stimuli." There are four major market research areas where conjoint analysis can successfully be implied.

I. **Understanding the market preferences:** The several attributes and their associated levels, comprised a product, are indicative of the factors that affect the preferences of the consumers.

II. **Predicting market choices:** The researcher gets several opportunities to apply simulations, which facilitate him/her to explore alternative market scenarios. Thus, the impact of competitions in the market, or impact on changes in the product can be predicted (Wyner, 1995).

III. **Development marketing strategies:** It can help the researcher to identify the product concepts, considered attractive on the part of the consumers, thereby eliminating those concepts which are not technically or financially feasible. Thus, the best of the residual products should be selected for fine-tuning their respective attributes to achieve the intended objectives. A series of simulation tests can be run for identifying the point at which the product performs the best (Wyner, 1995).

IV. **Market segmentation:** Consumers may be segmented into several groups, based on utility values or attribute scores. According to Wyner (1995), simulations can be regarded as segmentation analyses that group people based on their most preferred product among other alternatives or competitive products.

3.6 AN ILLUSTRATION OF CONJOINT ANALYSIS WITH THE APPLICATION OF SOFTWARE

Utility represents the total worth or overall preference of an object that can be thought of as the sum of part-worth. In the conjoint analysis, first we must construct the profile or stimuli combination of the observed factor. Table 3.1 explains the factor and the level for milk. Given the alternatives in Table 3.1, quantity is probably the least preferred, while fat is probably the most preferred. In the

---

TABLE 3.1
Product Choices Specified by Attribute Combinations

Attributes	Levels
Fat	Full cream
	Toned
	Double toned
	Skimmed
Availability	Supermarket
	Dairy shop
	Dairy co-opt
	Local market
Quantity	200 mL
	350 mL
	500 mL
	1000 mL
Utilization	Direct consumption
	Tea or coffee making
	Dairy product

---

example, there are four attributes of milk – three attributes with four levels each and one attribute with three levels. The outcome was a fractional factorial design with 13 profiles of milk because it is not necessary to use all combinations of profiles in the full factorial design.

The preferences of respondents for the other product offerings were implicitly determined by what is important to the respondent. Using conjoint analysis, you can determine both the RI of each attribute as well as which levels of each attribute are most preferred. Here is the code, which lists out the contributing factors under consideration. Using function *caModel()* from the **conjoint** package it is possible to calculate this model in R software.

```
> library (conjoint)
> data (milk)
> Conjoint(y=tpref, x=tprof, z=tlevn)
```

The parameters of the conjoint model with utilities of attribute levels, the most useful will be function caUtilities (), which returns vector of utilities for all attribute levels with intercept on the first place. The same result, but for all respondents, we can get using caPartUtilities() function.

```
> caPartUtilities(y=tpref, x=tprof, z=tlevn)
> colnames (tprefm) < -cbind(paste("prof",1:13,sep=""))
> tprefm[1:5,]
```

If we want to know only the importance of factors, we should use function caImportance () from the conjoint package:

```
> caImportance (y= tpref, x=tprof)
```

Apart from R software, SPSS and Python are also used for conducting conjoint analysis. Python is mainly used for business and commercial purposes due to some additional advantages over SPSS or SAS. From the following Table 3.2, we can compare the codes required for conjoint analysis between different software and understand their differences.

TABLE 3.2

Comparison between the Codes Required for Conjoint Analysis in Two Different Softwares: SPSS and Python

Conjoint Analysis in SPSS	Conjoint Analysis in Python
Conjoint Analysis procedure in SPSS:	*1. import pandas as pd*
1. Orthogonal array	*2. import numpy as np*
From the menus choose:	**# SELECT CONJOINT DATA**
Data > Orthogonal Design > Generate	*1. df=pd.read_csv('FILENAME',delimiter='\t')*
2. Collect the data responses	*2. import statsmodels.api as sm*
3. Conjoint analysis	*3. import seaborn as sns*
CONJOINT PLAN='file specification'	*4. import matplotlib.pyplot as plt*
/DATA='file specification'	*5. plt.style.use('bmh')*
/SEQUENCE=PREF1 TO PREF22	*6. res=sm.OLS(y,xdum, family=sm.families.*
/SUBJECT=ID	*Binomial()).fit()*
/FACTORS= FAT (DISCRETE) AVAILABILITY (LINEAR LESS)	*7. res.summary()*
QUANTITY (LINEAR MORE) UTILIZATION (LINEAR MORE)	
/PRINT=SUMMARYONLY.	

3.6.1 PART-WORTH OR UTILITY ESTIMATE OF MILK ATTRIBUTES

The result of conjoint analysis shows that the most important attribute to the consumers was fat content which contributed 0.626 to the consumers' total utility of 1.564 while the consumers' most preferred fat level is toned milk. Table 3.3 shows the utility (part-worth) scores and their standard errors for each factor level. Higher utility values indicate a greater preference. Since the utilities are all expressed in a common unit, they can be added together to give the total utility of any combination. Also, next in importance to the consumer was the utilization of the product, which contributed 0.577 to the consumers' total utility of 1.564. Availability was the least important attribute (UR=0.131) considered by the consumers in making their choices. The least preferred attribute level was milk availability in the supermarket (−0.044).

Furthermore, the derived utility values were then used to determine the importance of each attribute. Pearson's R, and Kendall's tau, association values were used to assess the validity of the conjoint analysis model. The Pearson's R (0.754) and Kendall's tau (0.611) values were high and indicated strong agreement between the averaged product ratings and the predicted utilities from the conjoint analysis model. Values close to one indicate strong agreement between the average product ratings and the predicted utilities from the conjoint model. This validates the findings of Green and Srinivasan (1990). Figure 3.1 depicts the RI of the four attributes analyzed, i.e., fat level (40.06%), utilization (36.89%), quantity (14.66%), and availability (8.38%).

It showed that the fat percentage of milk, with the RI of 40.06%, was the most important attribute in determining preference. Whereas, the application of milk was placed as the second most important attribute with a RI of 36.89%. The values were computed by taking the UR for each factor separately and dividing by the sum of the URs for all factors. For example,

$$\text{Relative importance of Fat } (\%) = \frac{0.218 - (-0.408) \times 100}{1.564} = 40.06 \tag{3.7}$$

$$\text{Relative importance of application of milk } (\%) = \frac{0.865 - 0.288 \times 100}{1.564} = 36.89 \tag{3.8}$$

TABLE 3.3
Part-Worth or Utility Estimate of Milk's Attributes

Attributes	Levels	Utility Estimate (Std. Error)	Utility Range	Average Relative Importance (%)
Fat	Full cream	0.218	0.626	40.064
		(0.358)		
	Toned	−0.408*		
		(0.358)		
	Double toned	0.075		
		(0.358)		
	Skimmed	0.115		
		(0.358)		
Availability	Supermarket	−0.044	0.131	8.38
		(0.185)		
	Dairy shop	−0.087		
		(0.370)		
	Dairy co-opt	−0.131		
		(0.554)		
	Local market	−0.175*		
		(0.739)		
Quantity	200 mL	−0.076	0.230	14.666
		(0.185)		
	350 mL	−0.153		
		(0.370)		
	500 mL	−0.229		
		(0.554)		
	1000 mL	−0.306*		
		(0.739)		
Utilization	Direct consumption	0.288	0.577	36.89
		(0.249)		
	Tea or coffee making	0.577		
		(0.498)		
	Dairy product	0.865*		
		(0.747)		
	Total		1.564	

*Note: *Represents the most preferred level in the attributes*

The range of the utility values (highest to lowest) for each factor provides a measure of how important the factor was to overall preference.

3.7 MERITS AND DEMERITS OF CONJOINT ANALYSIS

Conjoint analysis can provide answers to the market researcher regarding questions like, which attributes of a product are important from the consumers' perspective? Which levels of the attributes are desirable by the consumers? If some additional information like the demographics of the consumers is known, then market segmentation can be done. It helps to calculate the value created by any product to its consumer with great accuracy. Conjoint analysis has enormous future prospects and potential practical applications in market research due to its advantages over older market analysis tools.

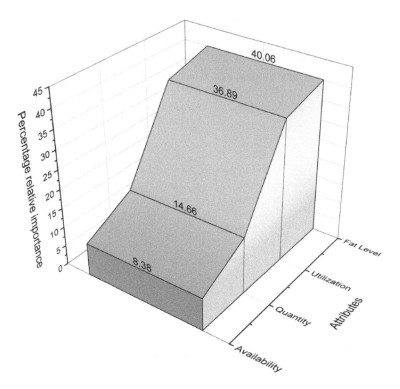

FIGURE 3.1   Relative importance of attributes of milk.

Conjoint analysis efficiently mimics the actual purchasing scenario to the respondent. Hence it studies the product attributes more precisely than other market analysis methods. Conjoint analysis allows the segmentation and clustering of customers during preference study when the sample size is very small. Moreover, multidimensional attributes interacting with each other for a single product can be analyzed through conjoint analysis without much complexity. It can predict the changes in an existing market through analysis of consumer behavior which in turn helps the market researcher to be ahead of time (Ben-Akiva and Gershenfeld, 1998).

There are also some shortcomings and demerits associated with conjoint analysis. The foremost disadvantage is its statistical complexity. One should need sound knowledge in complex statistical analysis along with expertise in running software (like R, SPSS) to conduct conjoint analysis. The analysis is based on data collected from the respondents; there is a tendency that the variables will be overvalued or undervalued and their decisions may be biased which may lead to erroneous utility values of the attributes. Besides, conjoint analysis can analyze a handful number of attributes at a time effectively. However, Dahan and Hauser (2002) developed a bridging technique to overcome this particular problem.

3.8   CONCLUSION

The point of market research is to predict such a worth recommendation that would expand the profit of the enterprise, offering direction to the organization about how to best utilize its limited assets. Conjoint analysis comprises arranging and executing statistically significant tests among customers to analyze their preference and purchase behavior to certain product attributes. Consumers can be subconsciously motivated by understanding their preferences on pricing policies, buying capacity, brand fascination, etc. to choose a certain product in the competitive market through conjoint analysis.

Being introduced merely around 40 years, conjoint analysis has already taken a robust place in the market analysis as it is widely accepted by the academic and market researches for its ease of use to represent the consumer preferences and predict the rate and success of market penetration for a new product. Conjoint analysis is said to be a multidisciplinary approach as its origin lies in the ideas of mathematical psychology, psychometry, statistics, economics as well as state of art engineering and software sciences. The method's practical aspects and applications in day-to-day life make it a valuable asset to the market researchers. As the market and the consumer preference is always a dynamic subject, there are several opportunities to make a breakthrough with the help of conjoint analysis. Till the last decade, conjoint analysis was mainly used in private sectors. But seeing its huge potential, it is now being used in public sectors as well. Conjoint researchers are always on the verge of new explorations as consumer behavior drifts. Conjoint analysis is not a mere stagnant statistical approach as its future promises continuous development and application.

REFERENCES

Barron, F. H. "Axiomatic conjoint measurement." *Decision Sciences* 8, no. 3 (1977): 548–559.

Ben-Akiva, M., and S. Gershenfeld. "Multi-featured products and services: Analysing pricing and bundling strategies." *Journal of Forecasting* 17, no. 3–4 (1998): 175–196.

Carroll, J. D. Categorical Conjoint Measurement. Meeting of Mathematical Psychology. Ann Arbor, MI, 1969.

Carroll, J. D., and P. E. Green. "Psychometric methods in marketing research: Part I, conjoint analysis." *Journal of Marketing Research* 32, no. 4 (1995): 385–391.

Churchill, G. A., and D. Iacobucci. *Marketing Research: Methodological Foundations* (Ed. 8). London: Harcourt Publishing, 2002.

Dahan, E., and J. R. Hauser. "The virtual customer." *Journal of Product Innovation Management: An International Publication of the Product Development & Management Association* 19, no. 5 (2002): 332–353.

Green, P. E., and F. J. Carmone. Stimulus context and task effects on individuals' similarities judgements: Preliminary Research Report. Marketing Science Institutes, 1970.

Green, P. E., R. E. Frank, and P. J. Robinson. "Cluster analysis in test market selection." *Management Science* 13, no. 8 (1967): B–387.

Green, P. E., and V. R. Rao. Nonmetric approaches to multivariate analysis in marketing. Working Paper, Wharton School, University of Pennsylvania, 1969.

Green, P. E., and V. Srinivasan. "Conjoint analysis in consumer research: issues and outlook." *Journal of Consumer Research* 5, no. 2 (1978): 103–123.

Green, P. E., and V. Srinivasan. "Conjoint analysis in marketing: new developments with implications for research and practice." *Journal of Marketing* 54, no. 4 (1990): 3–19.

Green, P. E., A. M. Krieger, and Y. Wind. *Thirty Years of Conjoint Analysis: Reflections and Prospects.* New York: Springer, 2004.

Gustafsson, A., F. Ekdahl, and B. Bergman. "Conjoint analysis: a useful tool in the design process." *Total Quality Management* 10, no. 3 (1999): 327–343.

Hair, J. F., W. C. Black, B. J. Babin, R. E. Anderson, and R. L. Tatham. *Multivariate Data Analysis* (Vol. 5, No. 3, pp. 207–219). Upper Saddle River, NJ: Prentice-Hall, 1998.

Kruskal, J. B. "Analysis of factorial experiments by estimating monotone transformations of the data." *Journal of the Royal Statistical Society: Series B (Methodological)* 27, no. 2 (1965): 251–263.

Kuhfeld, W. F. "Conjoint analysis." *SAS Tech. Pap. MR H* 2010 (2010): 681–801.

Lang, J. Q., and E. M. Crown. "Country-of-origin effect in apparel choices: a conjoint analysis." *Journal of Consumer Studies & Home Economics* 17, no. 1 (1993): 87–98.

Luce, R. D., and J. W. Tukey. "Simultaneous conjoint measurement: a new type of fundamental measurement." *Journal of Mathematical Psychology* 1, no. 1 (1964): 1–27.

Mohr-Jackson, I. "Quality function deployment: a valuable marketing tool." *Journal of Marketing Theory and Practice* 4, no. 3 (1996): 60–67.

Myers, J. G., W. F. Massy, and S. A. Greyser. *Marketing Research and Knowledge Development: An Assessment for Marketing Management.* Englewood Cliffs, NJ: Prentice-Hall, 1980.

Philip, K. *Marketing Management: The Millennium Edition* (Vol. 199). Upper Saddle River, NJ: Prentice-Hall, 1999.

Rao, V. R. *Applied Conjoint Analysis*. Berlin: Springer Science & Business Media, 2014.

Roy, A., and R. Malhotra. "Consumer preference for dairy products attributes in Kolkata: a conjoint analysis approach." *Innovative Farming* 3, no. 1 (2018): 43–47.

Sudman, S., and E. Blair. "Marketing research: A problem-solving approach." PhD diss., Univerza v Mariboru, Ekonomsko-poslovna fakulteta, 1998.

Tversky, A. "Elimination by aspects: a theory of choice." *Psychological Review* 79, no. 4 (1972): 281.

Ullrich, J. R., and J. R. Painter. "A conjoint-measurement analysis of human judgment." *Organizational Behavior and Human Performance* 12, no. 1 (1974): 50–61.

Wittink, D. R., and P. Cattin. "Commercial use of conjoint analysis: an update." *Journal of Marketing* 53, no. 3 (1989): 91–96.

Wittink, D. R., M. Vriens, and W. Burhenne. "Commercial use of conjoint analysis in Europe: results and critical reflections." *International Journal of Research in Marketing* 11, no. 1 (1994): 41–52.

Wyner, G. A. "Trade-off techniques and marketing issues." *Marketing Research* 7, no. 4 (1995): 32.

4 Ranking of Wear Behavior Characteristics in Al6061 Reinforced with Industrial Waste Materials Using PROMETHEE and MOORA Methods

Sibabrata Mohanty, Amit Jain Biswal, and Niyati Naik
GIET Ghangapatna, Biju Patnaik University of
Technology (BPUT), Rourkela, Odisha, India

Debesh Mishra
IES University

Ajay Soni
IES College of Technology, Rajiv Gandhi Proudyogiki
Vishwavidyalaya (RGPV), Bhopal, India

4.1 INTRODUCTION

Due to its excellent mechanical qualities and weldability, the aluminum alloy AA6061 is one of the most widely used alloys in technical and commercial applications. Furthermore, the usage of MMC with AA6061 as the parent material and reinforcements such as fly ash, silicon carbide, and other minerals has resulted in products with better mechanical strength and usability. Such composites are used practically in every discipline of engineering, particularly in mechanical, automotive, and aerospace applications. Heavy metals such as cast iron and bronze have almost entirely been replaced by these light yet robust materials. There is a significant opportunity for the development of such materials since more and more materials with greater strength and reduced weight are required. Ahemad et al. [1] investigated the wear properties of AlSi-mg alloy reinforced with silicon carbide; they found that the rate of wear varies with the normal load using Taguchi Approach.

Mannurkar and Raikar [2] studied that the wear rate of the LM6-M alloy increases as the proportion of silicon increases, but the wear rate of the LM4-T6 alloy decreases. Akhlaghi et al. conducted the tribological performance of Al-Mg-Si alloy reinforced with silicon carbide and germanium [3,4]. They discovered that as the amount of SiC in the produced composite grows, so does the wear rate. Das et al. [5] observed from their work that the resistance of wear of the prepared composite improves with the inclusion of these particles. In the present composites, the Garnet particle has a greater wear rate than the base alloy, according to Ranganath et al. [6], and the wear rate reduces as the garnet concentration rises. The wear performance of Al6061 hybrid MMC enhanced with SiC and Aluminium oxide Al_2O_3 was studied by Umanath et al. [7]. The 5% hybrid composite has a lesser wear resistance than the 15% composite. According to Sreenivasan et al. [8], if the percentage of TiB$_2$ particle causes a decrease in wear rate, the MMC wear rate will increase as a result of an increase in the applied load. Shanawaz et al. [9] found that under a fixed load and time, the rate of wear of the composite rises with increasing speed. Using Grey relation analysis, Amuthak Kannan et al. [10] evaluated the wear rate of the prepared composites by considering applied load, sliding velocity and the % of reinforcement. They found that Normal load was the most significant. The optimized variables are sliding velocity (2 m/s), and the load (20 N). The tribological behavior of a hybrid MMC reinforced with Boron carbide and Al$_2$O$_3$ composite was examined by Arulraj et al. [11]. The main aim of this study is to find the best parameters, such as load, sliding velocity and temperature to optimize the COF and weight loss of the sample by using PROMETHEE and MOORA.

4.2 MATERIAL AND METHODS

4.2.1 CHEMICAL COMPOSITION

A stir casting process was used to create Al6061 Nalco fly ash MMC in this study. In an electric furnace, the base metal Al 6061 was melted at 7500°C, and Fly ash was progressively added to the molten metal. The molten metal was then pre-heated at 4000°C to eliminate any moisture present (if any). The molten metal is then stirred for 10 minutes at 400 rpm in the mixer. The turning process was used to create nine wear samples from the casted material, as illustrated in Figure 4.1 (Tables 4.1 and 4.2).

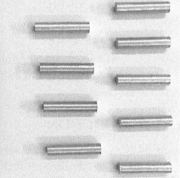

FIGURE 4.1   Al6061 casted form and specimen.

TABLE 4.1

Chemical Composition of Base Material

Element	Al	Mg	Si	Fe	Cu	Cr	Zn	Ti	Mn	Other
Composition in (%)	96.85	0.9	0.7	0.6	0.30	0.25	0.20	0.10	0.05	0.05

TABLE 4.2

Chemical Composition of Nalco Fly Ash

Content	Oxides	Si	Al	Fe	Ti	K	Ca	Loss in Ignition
Composition in (%)	38.38	26.43	16.73	3.8	1.4	0.99	0.5	Balance

4.2.2 MECHANICAL PROPERTIES

4.2.2.1 Tensile Test

The tensile test was conducted by Electrical Tensometer and the result was shown in the given Table 4.3 (Graph 4.1).

The hardness of the stir casted Al FAMMC samples was determined by Vickers Hardness Tester. Readings were taken in two to three places, with the average reading of each sample taken into account. The hardness values of Al6061cast alloy and Cast AlFA MMC are given in Table 4.4 (Graph 4.2).

4.2.3 WEAR TESTING

The tests were carried out in a DUCOM (TR201LE) wear testing equipment in dry circumstances at room temperature (Figure 4.2). Nine numbers of experiments were carried out to determine weight loss and COF. The input parameter and the level used in this experiment are listed in Table 4.5.

TABLE 4.3
Tensile Strength

Sample	Tensile Strength Value
Al6061cast alloy	122.837
Cast AlFA MMC	133.81

TENSILE STRENGTH

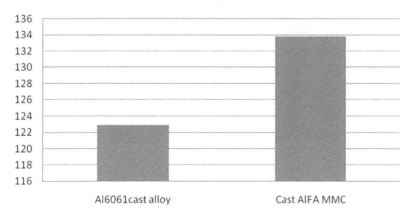

GRAPH 4.1 Comparison for tensile strength of alloy with MMC.

TABLE 4.4
Result of Hardness

Name of the Sample	Hardness
Al6061cast alloy	53.38
Cast AlFA MMC	76.25

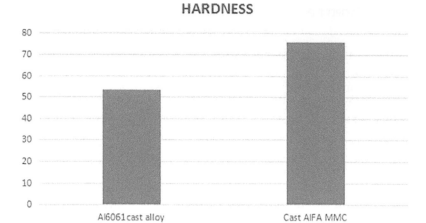

GRAPH 4.2   Comparison for hardness of alloy with MMC.

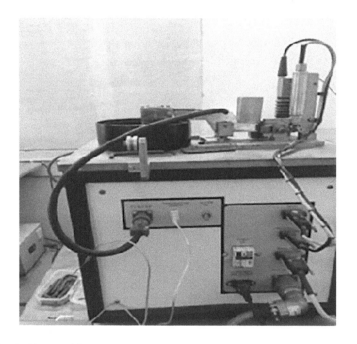

FIGURE 4.2   Wear testing machine.

TABLE 4.5
Input Parameters and Level

	Input Parameters			
Level	Load in N	Time in Minute	Sliding Velocity in RPM	Temperature in °C
Level 1	20	20	140	50
Level 2	40	30	180	60
Level 3	60	40	200	70

TABLE 4.6
Experimental Results COF and Weight Loss

Run	Load in N	Time in Minute	Sliding Velocity in RPM	Temperature in °C	COF	Weight Loss
1	20	20	140	50	0.067	0.011
2	20	30	180	60	0.052	0.013
3	20	40	200	70	0.072	0.017
4	40	20	180	70	0.069	0.016
5	40	30	200	50	0.076	0.015
6	40	40	140	60	0.068	0.014
7	60	20	200	60	0.079	0.023
8	60	30	140	70	0.081	0.021
9	60	40	180	50	0.078	0.022

4.3 EXPERIMENTAL PROCEDURE

In wear testing of Al 6061 Nalco flyash MMC, the influence of wear input parameters on COF and weight loss is examined. Table 4.6 shows the weight reduction and coefficient of friction data from the experimental design.

4.3.1 OPTIMIZATION TECHNIQUE

In this present work, we have used to multi decision criteria to identify the ranking of the decision alternatives. Techniques such as Promethee and MOORA have been selected to find the best ranking among nine experiments which has been conducted to determine the weight loss and coefficient of friction.

4.3.1.1 Steps for PROMETHEE

Preference function-based outranking approach, a unique kind of MCDM tool, can be taken into account to determine the ranking order of the choice alternatives.

1st Step: After deciding on the suitable criteria, create the decision/evaluation matrix.
2nd Step: Each criterion is given a weight.
3rd Step: Standardise the evaluation matrix.

For beneficial criteria:

$$R_{ij} = \frac{[x_{ij} - \min(x_{ij})]}{[\max(x_{ij}) - \min(x_{ij})]} \tag{4.1}$$

where $i = 1, 2,\ldots, m; j = 1, 2,\ldots, n$
Non-beneficial criteria:

$$R_{ij} = \frac{[\min(x_{ij}) - x_{ij}]}{[\max(x_{ij}) - \min(x_{ij})]} \tag{4.2}$$

4th Step: Calculate the ith alternative's deviation from the other alternatives. In this stage, the variance in criteria values between unlike options is calculated pair-wise.
5th Step: Calculation of preference function: $P_j(a,b)$

$$\text{If } R_{aj} \leq R_{bj} ; P_j(a,b) = 0 \tag{4.3}$$

$$\text{If } R_{aj} > R_{bj} \; ; P_j\,(a,b) = R_{aj} - R_{b_j} \tag{4.4}$$

6th Step: Calculate the aggregated preference function:

$$\pi(a,b) = \sum\nolimits_{j=1}^{n} w_j \; P_j\,(a,b) \Big/ \sum\nolimits_{j=1}^{n} w_j \tag{4.5}$$

Where w_j represents the relative importance (weight) of jth criterion.

    7th Step: Determination of leaving and the entering outranking flow. Leaving flow for a^{th} alternative:

$$\varphi^+\,(a) = \frac{1}{m-1} \sum_{b=1}^{m} \pi\,(a,b)(a \neq b) \tag{4.6}$$

Entering flow for a^{th} alternative:

$$\varphi^-\,(a) = \frac{1}{m-1} \sum_{b=1}^{m} \pi\,(a,b)(a \neq b) \tag{4.7}$$

where m represents the number of alternatives

    8th Step: Calculation of the net outranking flow for each alternative.

$$\varphi\,(a) = \varphi^+\,(a) - \varphi^-\,(a) \tag{4.8}$$

9th Step: Finally, based on the values of $\varphi\,(a)$ the ranking for all the alternatives considered is determined (Tables 4.7–4.12).

4.3.2 STEPS FOR MOORA

The process of simultaneously maximizing two or more competing attributes (goals) is known as multi-objective (or programming) optimization, often referred to as multi-criteria or multiple attribute optimization (Figure 4.3, Tables 4.13, and 4.14).

4.4 RESULT ANALYSIS

When samples are examined in a wear testing machine, the influence of process parameters on COF and weight loss is studied. A L9 orthogonal array was used to conduct the experiment.

TABLE 4.7
Normalization of Decision Value

Load	Time	Sliding Velocity	Temperature	Weight Loss	COF	Normalization	
						Weight Loss	COF
20	20	140	50	0.011	0.067	0.000	0.268
20	30	180	60	0.013	0.052	0.028	0.000
20	40	200	70	0.017	0.072	0.250	0.476
40	20	180	70	0.016	0.069	0.174	0.344
40	30	200	50	0.015	0.076	0.111	0.685
40	40	140	60	0.014	0.068	0.063	0.304
60	20	200	60	0.023	0.079	1.000	0.867
60	30	140	70	0.021	0.081	0.694	1.000
60	40	180	50	0.022	0.078	0.840	0.804

TABLE 4.8

Evaluative Difference of *i*th Alternative w.r.t Other Alternatives

Weight Loss	COF	Multiply Weight Loss	Multiply COF	Sum
0.2	0.0	0.1	0	0.1
0.5	0.2	0.3	0.086207	0.3
0.4	0.1	0.2	0.034483	0.2
0.3	0.3	0.2	0.155172	0.3
0.3	0.1	0.1	0.05	0.2
1.0	0.4	0.5	0.206897	0.7
0.8	0.5	0.4	0.241379	0.7
0.9	0.4	0.5	0.189655	0.6
0.0	0.0	0.0	0	0.0

TABLE 4.9

Preference Function and Aggregated Preference Function

	Preference Function		Aggregated Preference Function		Sum
DW1-W-2	0	0.517241379	0	0.258621	0.25862069
DW1-W-3	0	0	0	0	0
DW1-W-4	0	0	0	0	0
DW1-W-5	0	0	0	0	0
DW1-W-6	0	0	0	0	0
DW1-W-7	0	0	0	0	0
DW1-W-8	0	0	0	0	0
DW1-W-9	0	0	0	0	0
DW2-W-1	0.1666667	0	0.083333333	0	0.083333333
DW2-W-3	0	0	0	0	0
DW2-W-4	0	0	0	0	0
DW2-W-5	0	0	0	0	0
DW2-W-6	0	0	0	0	0
DW2-W-7	0	0	0	0	0
DW2-W-8	0	0	0	0	0
DW2-W-9	0	0	0	0	0
DW3-W-1	0.5	0.172413793	0.25	0.086207	0.336206897
DW3-W-2	0.3333333	0.689655172	0.166666667	0.344828	0.511494253
DW3-W-4	0.0833333	0.103448276	0.041666667	0.051724	0.093390805
DW3-W-5	0.1666667	0	0.083333333	0	0.083333333
DW3-W-6	0.25	0.137931034	0.125	0.068966	0.193965517
DW3-W-7	0	0	0	0	0
DW3-W-8	0	0	0	0	0
DW3-W-9	0	0	0	0	0
DW4-W-1	0.4166667	0.068965517	0.208333333	0.034483	0.242816092
DW4-W-2	0.25	0.586206897	0.125	0.293103	0.418103448
DW4-W-3	0	0	0	0	0
DW4-W-5	0.0833333	0	0.041666667	0	0.041666667
DW4-W-6	0.1666667	0.034482759	0.083333333	0.017241	0.100574713
DW4-W-7	0	0	0	0	0
DW4-W-8	0	0	0	0	0

(*Continued*)

TABLE 4.9 (*Continued*)
Preference Function and Aggregated Preference Function

	Preference Function		Aggregated Preference Function		Sum
DW4-W-9	0	0	0	0	0
DW5-W-1	0.3333333	0.310344828	0.166666667	0.155172	0.32183908
DW5-W-2	0.1666667	0.827586207	0.083333333	0.413793	0.497126437
DW5-W-3	0	0.137931034	0	0.068966	0.068965517
DW5-W-4	0	0.24137931	0	0.12069	0.120689655
DW5-W-6	0.0833333	0.275862069	0.041666667	0.137931	0.179597701
DW5-W-7	0	0	0	0	0
DW5-W-8	0	0	0	0	0
DW5-W-9	0	0	0	0	0
DW6-W-1	0.25	0.034482759	0.125	0.017241	0.142241379
DW6-W-2	0.0833333	0.551724138	0.041666667	0.275862	0.317528736
DW6-W-3	0	0	0	0	0
DW6-W-4	0	0	0	0	0
DW6-W-5	0	0	0	0	0
DW6-W-7	0	0	0	0	0
DW6-W-8	0	0	0	0	0
DW6-W-9	0	0	0	0	0
DW7-W-1	1	0.413793103	0.5	0.206897	0.706896552
DW7-W-2	0.8333333	0.931034483	0.416666667	0.465517	0.882183908
DW7-W-3	0.5	0.24137931	0.25	0.12069	0.370689655
DW7-W-4	0.5833333	0.344827586	0.291666667	0.172414	0.46408046
DW7-W-5	0.6666667	0.103448276	0.333333333	0.051724	0.385057471
DW7-W-6	0.75	0.379310345	0.375	0.189655	0.564655172
DW7-W-8	0.1666667	0	0.083333333	0	0.083333333
DW7-W-9	0.0833333	0.034482759	0.041666667	0.017241	0.058908046
DW8-W-1	0.8333333	0.482758621	0.416666667	0.241379	0.658045977
DW8-W-2	0.6666667	1	0.333333333	0.5	0.833333333
DW8-W-3	0.3333333	0.310344828	0.166666667	0.155172	0.32183908
DW8-W-4	0.4166667	0.413793103	0.208333333	0.206897	0.415229885
DW8-W-5	0.5	0.172413793	0.25	0.086207	0.336206897
DW8-W-6	0.5833333	0.448275862	0.291666667	0.224138	0.515804598
DW8-W-7	0	0.068965517	0	0.034483	0.034482759
DW8-W-9	0	0.103448276	0	0.051724	0.051724138
DW9-W-1	0.9166667	0.379310345	0.458333333	0.189655	0.647988506
DW9-W-2	0.75	0.896551724	0.375	0.448276	0.823275862
DW9-W-3	0.4166667	0.206896552	0.208333333	0.103448	0.311781609
DW9-W-4	0.5	0.310344828	0.25	0.155172	0.405172414
DW9-W-5	0.5833333	0.068965517	0.291666667	0.034483	0.326149425
DW9-W-6	0.6666667	0.344827586	0.333333333	0.172414	0.505747126
DW9-W-7	0	0	0	0	0
DW9-W-8	0.0833333	0	0.041666667	0	0.041666667

TABLE 4.10

Aggregated Preference Value or All Set of Experiment

1	2	3	4	5	6	7	8	9	Plus Valve
	0.26								0.028888889
0.08									0.008888889
0.34	0.51		0.09	0.08	0.19				0.134444444
0.24	0.42			0.04	0.1				0.088888889
0.32	0.5	0.07	0.12		0.18				0.132222222
0.14	0.32								0.051111111
0.71	0.88	0.37	0.46	0.39	0.56		0.08	0.06	0.39
0.66	0.83	0.32	0.42	0.34	0.52	0.03		0.05	0.352222222
0.65	0.82	0.31	0.41	0.33	0.51	0	0.04		0.341111111
0.348889	0.504444	0.118889	0.166667	0.131111	0.228889	0.003333	0.013333	0.012222	

TABLE 4.11

Leaving and Entry Flow

Leaving Flow ($\square^+$)	Entry Flow ($\square^-$)
0.029	0.349
0.009	0.504
0.134	0.119
0.089	0.167
0.132	0.131
0.051	0.229
0.390	0.003
0.352	0.013
0.341	0.012

TABLE 4.12

Difference of Leaving and Entry Flow along with Rank

Difference	Rank
−0.320	8
−0.496	9
0.016	4
−0.078	6
0.001	5
−0.178	7
0.387	1
0.339	2
0.329	3

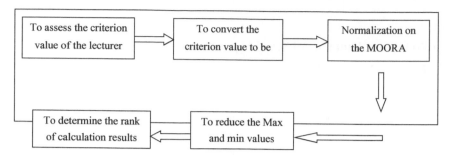

FIGURE 4.3   Steps for MOORA.

TABLE 4.13
Ratio Analysis

Load	Time	Sliding Velocity	Temperature	Weight Loss	COF
20	20	140	50	0.011	0.067
20	30	180	60	0.013	0.052
20	40	200	70	0.017	0.072
40	20	180	70	0.016	0.069
40	30	200	50	0.015	0.076
40	40	140	60	0.014	0.068
60	20	200	60	0.023	0.079
60	30	140	70	0.021	0.081
60	40	180	50	0.022	0.078
				0.023	0.081

TABLE 4.14
Normalized Value and Weighted Normalized Value

		Normalized Value		Weighted Normalized Value			
Weight Loss	COF	Weight Loss	COF	Weight Loss	COF	Sum	Rank
0.000121	0.004489	0.211	0.311	0.105652078	0.15548	0.2611317	8
0.000169	0.002704	0.250	0.241	0.124861547	0.120671	0.2455323	9
0.000289	0.005184	0.327	0.334	0.163280484	0.167083	0.3303631	4
0.000256	0.004761	0.307	0.320	0.15367575	0.160121	0.3137966	6
0.000225	0.005776	0.288	0.353	0.144071016	0.176365	0.320436	5
0.000196	0.004624	0.269	0.316	0.134466281	0.1578	0.2922665	7
0.000529	0.006241	0.442	0.367	0.220908891	0.183327	0.4042356	1
0.000441	0.006561	0.403	0.376	0.201699422	0.187968	0.3896673	3
0.000484	0.006084	0.423	0.362	0.211304156	0.181006	0.3923103	2

Based on the many chosen criteria, a decision matrix was created and reported in Table 4.5. Each criterion had a weight associated with it. All of the criteria in this analysis have a constant weight of 0.5.

In this PROMETHEE method for normalizing the evaluation matrix, we have taken beneficial criteria by using the equation (4.1). The normalized decision matrix was prepared and represented in Table 4.5. The evaluation of difference of ith alternatives is illustrated in Table 4.6. Similarly, preference function and aggregated preference function were evaluated using equations (4.3)–(4.5) which was shown in equations (4.6)–(4.8). The predicted leaving and entering outranking flows for various alternatives are now shown in Table using equations (4.6) and (4.7), respectively (4.9). Equation is used to compute the net outranking flow for each choice (4.8) and tabulated in Table 4.10 along with ranking. Similarly, another ranking method, i.e. MOORA, is also used to evaluate the best rank among nine experiments. The normalized and weighted normalized value was evaluated. The sum of weighted normalized value of different alternatives was calculated and determined its rank. Comparing both the optimization techniques method i.e. Promethee and MOORA it was observed that experiment no. 7 gives the highest rank mean while experiment no. 9 gives the lowest rank.

4.5 CONCLUSION

Taguchi's orthogonal array analysis was used to improve the wear performance parameters of Al6061 MMC, such as weight loss and coefficient of friction, in this study. The following findings were derived based on the current research work:

- The stir casting method was used to successfully produce Al6061 MMC.
- Compared to cast alloy, the prepared ALFA metal matrix composite gives better mechanical properties.
- From both the optimization techniques, it was found that experiment (4.7) shows the highest rank which is considered as optimal parametric setting (load at 60 N, time 20 minutes, sliding velocity 200 rpm, and temperature at 60°C) among nine experiments.

REFERENCES

[1] J. Ahemad, R.A. Kapgate, N.D. Sadaphal, Y.H. Ahire, Tribological behavior of AL-LM25 and SiC, *Int. Res. J. Eng. Technol.* 2 (2015) 893–897.
[2] W. N. Mannurkar, P.U. Raikar, Investigation of dry sliding wear behaviour of LM4 (Al Si and Cu) T6/LM6 (Al-Si12)-M using Taguchi approach, *Int. Res. J. Eng. Technol.* 2 (2015) 66–74.
[3] S. Mahdavi, F. Akhlaghi, Effect of SiC content on the processing, compaction behavior and properties of Al6061/SiC/Gr hybrid composites, *J. Mater. Sci.* 46 (2011) 1502–1511.
[4] F. Akhlaghi, S. Mahdavi, Effect of the SiC content on the tribological properties of hybrid Al/Gr/SiC composites processed by in situ powder metallurgy (IPM) method, *Adv. Mater. Res.* 264–265 (2011) 1878–1886.
[5] S. Das, S. Das, K. Das, Abrasive wear of zircon sand and alumina reinforced Al-4.5 wt. percent Cu alloy matrix composites: A comparative study, *Compos. Sci. Technol.* 67 (2007) 746–751.
[6] G. Ranganath, S.C. Sharma, M. Krishna, Dry sliding wear of garnet reinforced zinc/aluminium metal matrix composites, *Wear* 251 (2001) 1408–1413.
[7] K. Umanath, K. Palanikumar, S.T. Selvamani, Analysis of dry sliding wear behaviour of Al6061/SiC/Al2O3 hybrid metal matrix composites, *Compos. Part B* 53 (2013) 159–168. 22.
[8] A. Sreenivasan, S. PaulVizhian, N.D. Shivakumar, M. Muniraj, M. Raguraman, A study of microstructure and wear behaviour of TiB2/Al metal matrix composites, *Latin Am. J. Solids Struct.* 8 (2011) 1–8.
[9] R.S. Patil, P. Madhu, B.P.G. Manjunath, M.K. Kumar, Investigation of mechanical properties and wear behavior of Lm 25 Aluminum Alloy reinforced with silicon carbide and activated carbon, *Int. J. Res. Sci. In*nov. 5 (2018) 70–77.
[10] P. Amuthakkannan, V. Manikandan, M.A. Raja, S. Rajesh, Wear characterization of aluminium/basalt fiber reinforced metal matrix composites a novel material, *Tribol. Ind.* 39 (2017) 219–227.
[11] M. Arulraj, P.K. Palani, L. Venkatesh, Experimental investigation on dry sliding wear behaviour of hybrid metal matrix (Al-Al2O3-B4C) composite, *Int. J. Chem. Tech. Res.* 9 (2016) 359–364.

5 Aqueous Humor Flow in the Schlemm's Canal via Rectangular Channel
Mathematical Modeling for Analytical Results, Numerical Experiments, and Implications for Treatments

Shabab Akbar
School of Computational and Integrative Sciences
Jawaharlal Nehru University, New Delhi, India

Sapna Ratan Shah
School of Computational and Integrative Sciences
Jawaharlal Nehru University, New Delhi, India

Sardar M. N. Islam
ISILC
Victoria University, Melbourne, Australia

5.1 INTRODUCTION

5.1.1 CONTEXT

The primary area of resistance in the aqueous humour outflow pathway has been identified by numerous investigations. Some ophthalmologists believe that the canal of Schlemm is the greatest obstacle to the aqueous humor outflow. In contrast, others believe the trabecular meshwork is the leading cause of this problem (Crowder and Ervin 2013). The path of the aqueous humor that takes in a typical outflow is a sequence of tight turns with varied degrees of resistance.

5.1.2 EXISTING LITERATURE AND LIMITATION

In primates, rising intraocular pressure (IOP) causes progressive collapse of the canal of Schlemm, according to a large body of experimental evidence published in the ophthalmic literature (Canning 2002). Furthermore, with standard or somewhat high IOP, low stress on the trabecular meshwork and scleral spur brought on by ciliary muscle inactivity or weakening, as well as other factors, stimulates canal collapse. Additionally, increased outflow pressure is necessary to remove the aqueous flow, as the porousness of trabecular meshwork and endothelium internal canal wall diminishes.

DOI: 10.1201/9781003387459-5

Compared to normal meshwork tension, this increased IOP tends to cause the channel to collapse (Bishop 2000). Several parameters, including tissue filling, the lining of extracellular matrix composition, and traction of ciliary muscles, the meshwork's porosity should be determined. Debris or any other material accumulating in the "trabecular meshwork" (TM), and the restriction of flow channels due to more substantial structures may reduce the functioning of the "trabecular meshwork" and the endothelium inner canal wall. In "primary open-angle glaucoma" (POAG), the canal of Schlemm is also significantly constricted or destroyed (Lee, Litt, and Buchsbaum 1992; Tamm and Fuchshofer 2007).

The capacity of aqueous humor to leave the eye decreases with increased IOP in both human and animal eyes, according to in vivo and in vitro research (Van Buskirk, MacRae, and Harris 1986). It increases with anterior chamber depth and lens depression (Ethier, Johnson, and Ruberti 2004). Drugs that cause the ciliary muscle to contract lower the meshwork's barrier to aqueous outflow. According to (Nakao, Hafezi-Moghadam, and Ishibashi 2012), ciliary muscle contraction lowers resistance in endothelial meshwork and, most likely, flows in the "trabecular meshwork". As a result, ciliary muscle tension improves the meshwork's porousness (Goel 2010). More ciliary muscles pulling on the TM in glaucomatous and healthy eyes increases the outflow facility. While this increases the apparent pressure, decreasing meshwork traction reduces the outflow facility (Leske et al. 2003).

5.1.3 THE OBJECTIVE OF THE RESEARCH

The movement of aqueous humour in the canal of Schlemm in the human eye is modelled mathematically. The model includes a section of canal between the two collector channels, represented as a pair of rectangular channels with permeable roofs. We illustrate the suggested model by drawing the pressure and flow profiles of an aqueous fluid, and we explore how changing key parameters affects these diagrams.

5.1.4 PRESENT RESEARCH

The current research primarily continues Moses et al. work. The model considers the system's more generalized properties (Moses 1979). It considers the canal's inner wall to be poroelastic and robust. Instead of using the standard no-slip scenario, Beaver and Joseph's slip condition was added to the canal's porous inner wall to create a more realistic model (Yuan et al. 2016). I have concentrated on the role of compliance coefficient, trabecular and endothelial meshwork porosity, and intraocular pressure (IOP) on aqueous outflow in the channel. Unfortunately, I could not add the impact of ciliary muscle tension on the collapse of the canal in the model since it is projected values are unknown to the best of our knowledge (Siggers and Ethier 2011; Mechanics 2014; Tandon and Autar 1991).

5.1.5 CONTRIBUTIONS

The apposition of Schlemm's canal's porous inner wall to the outer scleral wall may contribute to the increased resistance to aqueous outflow, or reduced aqueous flow, as seen in some cases of glaucoma. To conceptually analyse the aforementioned phenomena, Moses proposed a pure resistance model for water flow in Schlemm's canal, assuming the inner wall is firm. As a result, he reasoned that canal narrowing might explain the observed rise in outflow resistance (Ferreira et al. 2014).

5.1.6 STRUCTURE OF THE CHAPTER

We have focused only on analyzing how IOP, TM porosity, endothelial meshwork porosity, and compliance coefficient affect canal aqueous outflow. To our knowledge, the predicted values for the impact of ciliary muscle traction on canal collapse are unknown. Hence, we were unable to include them in our model directly.

The fluid produced in the eye is transparent and colorless, known as "aqueous humor". Before draining out of sight, it runs through the anterior region of the human eye, sustaining avascular tissue and forcing the eye (Humphrey and O'Rourke 2015). The Canal of Schlemm is a slender collecting tube in the human eye that drains most of the aqueous humor. The biomechanics of vascular-derived (Krohn 1999) endothelial cells line, the canal of Schlemm, and their biomechanics are essential for two reasons. In vivo, these cells are relatively spatially accessible to non-uniform stresses due to aqueous humor flow (Fitt and Gonzalez 2006). As a result, instead of studying how various biomechanical circumstances affect endothelial cells in cell culture, it is likely to research the impact of diverse endothelial cell biomechanical settings across the whole tissue. Second, "Schlemm's canal" endothelial cells may play a significant role in glaucoma, a prevalent eye illness (McLaren 2009; Quigley and Broman 2006).

The "trabecular meshwork" (TM) of the Schlemm system's canal and entry into the ciliary body's front face is the principal pathways by which aqueous humor exits the anterior chamber. The conventional outflow makes up 75%–80% of the outflow of aqueous humor, while the uveoscleral flow makes up the rest. Aqueous flow is resisted in the trabecular meshwork outflow by the uveal segment of the "trabecular meshwork" (TM), the corneoscleral part of the meshwork, the juxtacanalicular tissue, and the endothelium lining of the canal of Schlemm (Gross et al. 2017). The canal of Schlemm is drained by 30 collecting channels, which convey the water to blood-carrying recipient veins (Siggers and Ethier 2011). The resistance chain is completed by the canal's resistance and the resistance of the collectors (Mauri et al. 2016).

The rapid development of therapeutic methods to treat "Glaucoma", a pathological condition of the eye in which the IOP is sufficiently high, has reignited interest in the biomedical community in gaining a good understanding of the phenomenon of the formation of "aqueous humor", as the aim of some method is to reduce the increased IOP by suppressing the production of the aqueous humor. However, due to its role in nourishing the avascular ocular tissues and the refractive medium and maintaining a consistent level of IOP, there has long been a prevailing interest in studying aqueous production (Siggers and Ethier 2011). Therefore, analyzing the formation of aqueous humor is necessary to improve the current understanding of the transport processes involved in aqueous humor formation and establish a theoretical relationship between physical and geometrical parameters and transport events. This study provides a simple mathematic model for the outflow of aqueous humor in the Schlemm's canal modeled as a rectangular channel between two collection channels (Bishop 2000).

Only a restricted section of the internal wall of canal endothelium is exposed to the Ostia of collection channels; most water approaching the Schlemm's canal needs to travel a few distances down the canal to reach a collection channel (Figure 5.1).

The influence of flow resistance in the Canal of Schlemm on "intraocular pressure" (IOP) is investigated in this study. Whatever the underlying mechanisms are for the aqueous humor outflow

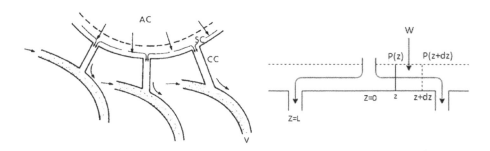

FIGURE 5.1 The canal segment has a porous upper wall formed like a rectangular channel.

system in a Schlemm's canal (SC), the opposition of the internal porousness of the wall to the external scleral wall of the channel has a major role in the elevated aqueous outflow resistance that results in reduced aqueous humor outflow as seen in some patients that suffering from glaucoma. Moses suggested investigating the phenomena above numerically. If one assumes the inside wall of the Schlemm canal to be porous, one may construct a pure resistance model for water flow in the channel. He concluded that increased outflow resistance might result from canal constriction.

5.2 MODEL DESCRIPTION

Increased IOP is the main risk factor for the onset and progression of glaucoma. Elevated intraocular pressure (IOP) results from increased outflow resistance in the traditional outflow channel. The Canal of Schlemm (SC), which is surrounded by the anterior section by the TM, receives "aqueous humor" as it leaves the anterior chamber. It is then transported to the recipient's veins through 30 collecting channels. A collection channel must be reached by the bulk of the "aqueous humor" stepping into the Canal of Schlemm after a brief journey rectangular channel is used to model a section of the canal between two collectors. Between two collectors, to the right of the midpoint, the collecting channel is where the other half of the "aqueous humor" seeping into the canal portion approaches. The second half seals the collection channel to the left, where the two collectors meet in the middle (Figure 5.1). The circumferential flow is, therefore, zero at the midway point, $z = 0$.

The flow of aqueous humor is considered within half of the section inside the x-axis due to symmetry. The canal segment's outer and inner walls are represented by $y = 0$ and $y = h$, respectively. Therefore, the aqueous flow in this area is theoretically described as fluid movement in a rectangular, 2D channel. Before moving on, the following presumptions are made.

1. Laminar, Newtonian, viscous, and incompressible aqueous flow is constant. It was moving slowly.
2. The pressure gradient dp / dx drives the flow inside the x-axis.
3. The bottom part $(y = 0)$ is uniform, complex, and nonporous. In the first case, the top surface is homogeneous, poroelastic $(y = h)$ and uniform.
4. All collector channels are the same size and distance apart, and each channel drains the same amount of the aqueous humor (AH).
5. The internal endothelial wall and the trabecular meshwork (TM) make up the porous inner wall of the channel.

5.3 GOVERNING EQUATION

The governing Navier Stokes equations are reduced when the assumptions given above are considered.

$$\mu \frac{\partial^2 u}{\partial y^2} = \frac{\partial p}{\partial x} \tag{5.1}$$

And

$$\frac{\partial p}{\partial y} = 0 \tag{5.2}$$

The equation of continuity is given as follows:

$$\frac{\partial u}{\partial x} + \frac{\partial v}{\partial y} = 0 \tag{5.3}$$

Using the material balance method (Figure 9.1) has

$$Q(z+dz)-Q(z)=W(z)dz \tag{5.4}$$

Now, expanding $Q(z+dz)$ using the Taylor series, we find

$$\frac{\partial Q(z)}{\partial z}=W(z) \tag{5.5}$$

where

$$Q(z)=\int_0^h u(x,y)\,dy$$

$$W(z)=G[P_l-p(z)]$$

5.4 BOUNDARY CONDITIONS

The mathematically acceptable and physically plausible boundary conditions are as follows:

$$u(z,0)=0 \tag{5.6a}$$

$$u(z,h)=\frac{-\sqrt{K}}{\sigma}\left(\frac{\partial u}{\partial y}\right)_{y=h} \tag{5.6b}$$

$$v(z,0)=0 \tag{5.7a}$$

$$v(z,h)=G\left[P_l-p(z)\right] \tag{5.7b}$$

$$P(L)=0 \tag{5.8a}$$

$$\left(\frac{dp}{dz}\right)_{z=0}=0 \tag{5.8b}$$

where $K = G\ \mu\nabla r$ is Darcy's coefficient, this is the slip parameter and describes the porousness of the inner canal wall, which varies based on the porous inner material of the planer boundary ($y = h$). The porous border, indicated by the boundary condition, is where the tangential velocity module encounters the Beavers Joseph slip condition (Moses 1977; Alm and Nilsson 2009). The stream-wise Darcy velocity was ignored when constructing this boundary condition because its absence has no discernible influence on the results (Canning 2002; Atchison 2018). The pressure at the collection channel's mouth is P_0 and the inner canal wall's thickness is Δr.

5.5 PROBLEM FORMULATION

The boundary value condition issued by the equations (5.1) and (5.2) can be easily solved, as well as the suitable boundary conditions (5.4), and velocity is provided by

$$u=\frac{1}{2\mu}\frac{dp}{dz}\left[y^2-h\left(1+\frac{1}{1+\left(1+\sigma h/\sqrt{K}\right)}\right)\right]y \tag{5.9}$$

And also, the aqueous out flux is

$$Q(z) = \frac{h^3}{2\mu}\left[\frac{1}{3} - \frac{1}{2}\left(1 + \frac{1}{1 + \sigma h / \sqrt{K}}\right)\right]\frac{dp}{dz}$$ (5.10)

The resistance is given by

$$R = \frac{2\mu}{h^3}\left[\frac{1}{3} - \frac{1}{2}\left(1 + \frac{\sqrt{K}}{\sqrt{K} + \sigma h}\right)\right]^{-1}$$ (5.11)

By removing $Q(z)$ and $W(z)$ from equations (5.3), (5.6a), and (5.10), the governing equation for computing the pressure is evaluated.

$$h^3\left(\frac{1}{3} - \frac{A}{2}\right)\frac{d^2p}{dz^2} + \left[3h^2\left(\frac{1}{3} - \frac{A}{2}\right) + \frac{h^2\sigma}{2\sqrt{K}}(A-1)^2\right]\frac{dh}{dz}\frac{dp}{dz} = 2\mu G(P_I - p)$$ (5.12)

Where

$$A = 1 + \frac{1}{1 + \left(\sigma h / \sqrt{K}\right)}$$

Case 1: The internal canal wall is stiff and rigid. In this instance, the width of canal h is fixed, and the equation of pressure is:

$$\frac{d^2p}{dz^2} - m^2 p(z) = -m^2 P_I$$ (5.13)

Where

$$m = \left[\frac{4\mu G}{h_0^3\left(\frac{1}{3} + \frac{1}{1 + \left(\sigma h / \sqrt{K}\right)}\right)}\right]^{\frac{1}{2}}$$ (5.14)

Equation (5.10) has a solution that meets the boundary conditions (5.8).

$$p(z) = p_I - \frac{P_I - p_0}{\cosh(mL)}\cosh(mz)$$ (5.15)

and

$$Q(z) = \frac{h_0^3 m (P_I - p_0)}{4\mu \cosh(mL)}\sinh(mz)$$ (5.16)

5.6   RESULTS AND DISCUSSION

The suggested model for the outflow of aqueous humor in the canal of SC has produced analytical results for two situations, which are represented by graphs:

  Case I: When the canal's inner porous wall is rigid and stiff.
  Case II: When the canal's inner porous wall can collapse.

Here, I have discussed the first case. Figures 5.2–5.5 describe the results achieved for this case. The impacts of essential factors, such as filtration constant (G) and IOP, characterize the inner wall's porosity or facility and the compliance coefficient. This suggests that the interior wall of the canal is porous, and the compliance coefficient has been examined on flow profiles and the aqueous fluid pressures in the channel, which describes how easily the inner wall collapses.

Figure 5.2 shows the aqueous outflow resistance in a rigid and stiff canal model against the width of canal h. The curves examination demonstrates that there is significant flow resistance available for $0 < h_0 < 3\,\mu m$. This figure also highlights the impact of the filtering constant. The curves show that flow resistance lowers as the rising filtration constant (G) increases. Expanding the inner wall's facility makes the aqueous flow along the channel easier.

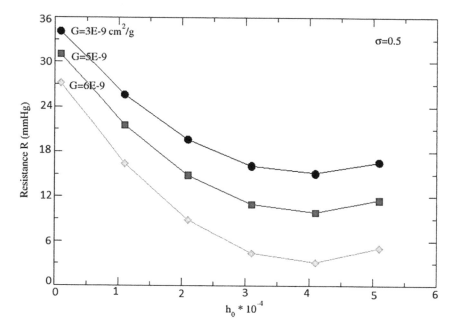

FIGURE 5.2 Resistance of Aqueous flow against canal width.

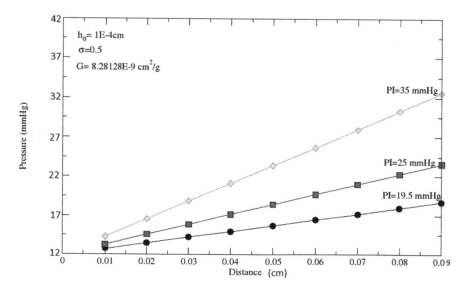

FIGURE 5.3 Effect of intraocular pressure (IOP) and pressure distribution in the rigid canal.

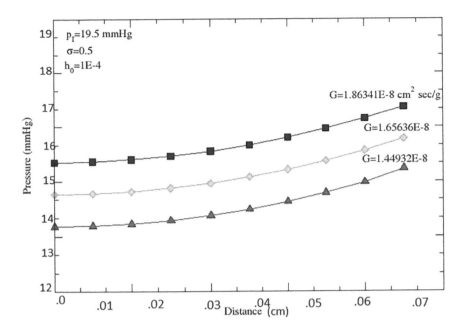

FIGURE 5.4 Pressure gradients in the stiff canal as a function of the filtration constant (G).

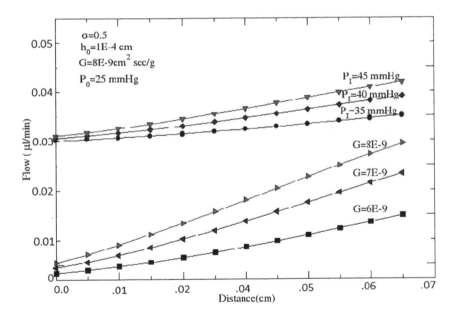

FIGURE 5.5 Effect of pressure distribution in the rigid canal and filtration constant (G).

The usual pressure profiles of the aqueous fluid in the channel are affected by the filtration constant (G) and the intraocular pressure (IOP), as shown in Figures 5.3 and 5.4. It can be seen from these graphs in Figure 5.3 that increased IOP causes the fluid pressure in the channel to rise. The pressure within the fluid begins to decline on each side of the intersection of two collectors. As a result, there will be a more significant difference of pressure $(P_I - p)$ toward the collecting channel on the inner canal wall. As a result, the canal should be more likely to collapse close to and at the collecting channel exits. These results are fairly consistent with those of Moses. As the constant filtration increases, Figure 5.4 demonstrates, aqueous filtration into the stable-width canal increases, raising the fluid pressure within the canal. The aqueous humor's enhanced percolation causes the fluid pressure in the channel to rise. Increases in "intraocular pressure" (IOP) provide a more significant rise in pressure than adjustments to the filtration constant.

Figure 5.5 illustrates the impact of IOP on the distinct aqueous humor flow profiles in the rigid canal. According to these graphs, the aqueous flow increases as IOP rises while maintaining a constant breadth and filtration. As the IOP rises, more "aqueous humor" percolates through the perforations in the internal wall into the canal. The model's regular channel width receives more aqueous flow due to the enhanced percolation. This picture also illustrates the impact of the filtration constant (G) on the aqueous flow profiles. As the filtration constant (G) rises, there is better aqueous percolation via the inner wall. The curves in this image demonstrate how better percolation into the stiff canal ought to improve water flow.

5.7 CONCLUSION

Due to the increased aqueous fluid pressure in the channel caused by increased intraocular pressure (IOP), the pressure differential $(P_I - p)$, is always more exceptional. Near the collector channel's mouth, this discrepancy is most significant. The collapse is more incredible at the collector channel, with a more substantial pressure differential. Aqueous percolation into the canal is accelerated by increased $(P_I - p)$. However, the aqueous flow resistance increases with the increased collapse of the canal. The percolation of aqueous humor via the internal wall of the channel is slowed down because of a more significant impediment to the flow, resulting in an aqueous buildup in the anterior part and parallel rises in IOP. When debris or other materials are deposited in the trabecular and endothelial meshwork matrix under certain pathological situations, the matrix's porosity or facility may decrease, narrowing the mesh by a thicker structure, ciliary muscle relaxation, or other causes for the flow pathways.

Finally, we determine that the Canal of Schlemm is a crucial structure in the human eye that affects ciliary muscle reduction, IOP, and changes in the aqueous humor outflow ability dependent on compliance. The gradual obstruction of the canal of Schlemm caused by the apposition of its opposing walls may cause a block of the outflow. This partly explains the proliferation in the resistance of outflow in a few cases of glaucoma disease. Moreover, very few forms of treatment might work by tightening the "trabecular meshwork" (TM) and scleral spur, preventing the canal from collapsing and increasing the endothelial and porosity of the "trabecular meshwork" in the eyes having glaucoma disease.

REFERENCES

Alm, A., and S. F. E. Nilsson. 2009. "Uveoscleral Outflow - A Review." *Experimental Eye Research* 88 (4): 760–68. https://doi.org/10.1016/J.EXER.2008.12.012.

Atchison, D. A. 2018. "Optics of the Human Eye." *Encyclopedia of Modern Optics* 1–5: 43–63. https://doi.org/10.1016/B978-0-12-803581-8.09773-3.

Bishop, P. N. 2000. "Structural Macromolecules and Supramolecular Organisation of the Vitreous Gel." *Progress in Retinal and Eye Research* 19 (3): 323–44. https://doi.org/10.1016/S1350-9462(99)00016-6.

Van Buskirk, E. M., S. MacRae, and L. M. Harris. 1986. "Clinical Atlas of Glaucoma." *Archives of Ophthalmology* 105 (7): 183.

Canning, C. R. 2002. "Fluid Flow in the Anterior Chamber of a Human Eye." *Mathematical Medicine and Biology* 19 (1): 31–60. https://doi.org/10.1093/IMAMMB/19.1.31.

Crowder, T. R., and V. J. Ervin. 2013. "Numerical Simulations of Fluid Pressure in the Human Eye." *Applied Mathematics and Computation* 219 (24): 11119–33. https://doi.org/10.1016/J.AMC.2013.04.060.

Ethier, C. R., M. Johnson, and J. Ruberti. 2004. "Ocular Biomechanics and Biotransport." *Annual Review of Biomedical Engineering* 6: 249–73. https://doi.org/10.1146/ANNUREV.BIOENG.6.040803.140055.

Ferreira, J. A., P. De Oliveira, P. M. Da Silva, and J. N. Murta. 2014. "Numerical Simulation of Aqueous Humor Flow: From Healthy to Pathologic Situations." Applied Mathematics and Computation 226 (January): 777–92. https://doi.org/10.1016/J.AMC.2013.10.070.

Fitt, A. D., and G. Gonzalez. 2006. "Fluid Mechanics of the Human Eye: Aqueous Humor Flow in the Anterior Chamber." *Bulletin of Mathematical Biology* 68 (1): 53–71. https://doi.org/10.1007/S11538-005-9015-2.

Goel, M. 2010. "Aqueous Humor Dynamics: A Review~!2010-03-03~!2010-06-17~!2010-09-02~!" *The Open Ophthalmology Journal* 4 (1): 52–59. https://doi.org/10.2174/1874364101004010052.

Gross, J. C., A. Harris, B. A. Siesky, R. Sacco, A. Shah, and G. Guidoboni. 2017. "Mathematical Modeling for Novel Treatment Approaches to Open-Angle Glaucoma." *Expert Review of Ophthalmology* 12 (6): 443–55. https://doi.org/10.1080/17469899.2017.1383896.

Humphrey, J. D., and S. L. O'Rourke (eds). 2015. "Stress, Motion, and Constitutive Relations." *An Introduction to Biomechanics*, 353–404. Springer. https://doi.org/10.1007/978-1-4939-2623-7_7.

Krohn, J. 1999. "Expression of Factor VIII-Related Antigen in Human Aqueous Drainage Channels." *Acta Ophthalmologica Scandinavica* 77 (1): 9–12. https://doi.org/10.1034/j.1600-0420.1999.770102.x.

Lee, B., M. Litt, and G. Buchsbaum. 1992. "Rheology of the Vitreous Body. Part I: Viscoelasticity of Human Vitreous." *Biorheology* 29 (5–6): 521–33. https://doi.org/10.3233/BIR-1992-295-612.

Leske, M. C., A. Heijl, M. Hussein, B. Bengtsson, L. Hyman, and E. Komaroff. 2003. "Factors for Glaucoma Progression and the Effect of Treatment: The Early Manifest Glaucoma Trial." *Archives of Ophthalmology* 121 (1): 48–56. https://doi.org/10.1001/ARCHOPHT.121.1.48.

Mauri, A. G., L. Sala, P. Airoldi, G. Novielli, R. Sacco, S. Cassani, G. Guidoboni, B. Siesky, and A. Harris. 2016. "Electro-Fluid Dynamics of Aqueous Humor Production: Simulations and New Directions." *Modelling and Artificial Intelligence in Ophthalmology* 1 (2): 48–58. https://doi.org/10.35119/MAIO.V1I2.30.

McLaren, J. W. 2009. "Measurement of Aqueous Humor Flow." *Experimental Eye Research* 88 (4): 641–47. https://doi.org/10.1016/J.EXER.2008.10.018.

Mechanics, F. 2014. "Modelling of Heat Transfer in Human Eye Using Computational," 10th International Conference on Heat Transfer, Fluid Mechanics and Thermodynamics, HEFAT 2014 at Orlando, Florida (USA)no. July: 149–57.

Moses, R. A. 1977. "The Effect of Intraocular Pressure on Resistance to Outflow." *Survey of Ophthalmology* 22 (2): 88–100. https://doi.org/10.1016/0039-6257(77)90088-1.

Moses, R. A. 1979. "Circumferential Flow in Schlemm's Canal." *American Journal of Ophthalmology* 88 (3): 585–91.

Nakao, S., A. Hafezi-Moghadam, and T. Ishibashi. 2012. "Lymphatics and Lymphangiogenesis in the Eye." *Journal of Ophthalmology* 2012: 783163. https://doi.org/10.1155/2012/783163.

Quigley, H., and A. T. Broman. 2006. "The Number of People with Glaucoma Worldwide in 2010 and 2020." *British Journal of Ophthalmology* 90 (3): 262–67. https://doi.org/10.1136/BJO.2005.081224.

Seiler, T., and J. Wollensak. 1985. "The Resistance of the Trabecular Meshwork to Aqueous Humor Outflow." *Graefe' Archive for Clinical and Experimental Ophthalmology* 223 (2): 88–91. https://doi.org/10.1007/BF02150951.

Shafahi, M., and K. Vafai. 2011. "Human Eye Response to Thermal Disturbances." *Journal of Heat Transfer* 133 (1): 1–7. https://doi.org/10.1115/1.4002360.

Siggers, J. H., and C. R. Ethier. 2011. "Fluid Mechanics of the Eye." *Annual Review of Fluid Mechanics* 44: 347–72. https://doi.org/10.1146/ANNUREV-FLUID-120710-101058.

Tamm, E. R., and R. Fuchshofer. 2007. "What Increases Outflow Resistance in Primary Open-Angle Glaucoma?" *Survey of Ophthalmology* 52 (6 SUPPL.): S101–4. https://doi.org/10.1016/J.SURVOPHTHAL.2007.08.002.

Tandon, P. N., and R. Autar. 1991. "Biphasic Model of the Trabecular Meshwork in the Eye." *Medical & Biological Engineering & Computing* 29 (3): 281–90. https://doi.org/10.1007/BF02446710.

Yuan, F., A. T. Schieber, L. J. Camras, P. J. Harasymowycz, L. W. Herndon, and R. R. Allingham. 2016. "Mathematical Modeling of Outflow Facility Increase with Trabecular Meshwork Bypass and Schlemm Canal Dilation." *Journal of Glaucoma* 25 (4): 355–64. https://doi.org/10.1097/IJG.0000000000000248.

6 Solving Fuzzy Nonlinear Optimization Problems Using Evolutionary Algorithms

Yogeesh N.
Government First Grade College

6.1 INTRODUCTION

Fuzzy nonlinear optimization problems are prevalent in many real-world applications (Azar & Hassanien, 2017), where decision-making is subject to uncertainty, ambiguity, and vagueness. In these problems, the objective function, constraints, and decision variables may be imprecise or incomplete, making it challenging to obtain a globally optimal solution. EAs have emerged as a promising tool for solving such problems, owing to their ability to handle complex and nonlinear optimization landscapes (Deb& Jain, 2014). EAs are heuristic search algorithms inspired by natural selection and genetics and are designed to evolve a population of potential solutions over time, in search of the optimal solution.

This chapter provides an overview of the use of EAs for solving fuzzy nonlinear optimization problems (Eberhart& Kennedy, 1995). We begin by discussing the fundamentals of fuzzy optimization and EAs, including the concept of fuzzy sets, fuzzy logic, and membership functions. We then review the existing literature on solving fuzzy optimization problems using EAs, including studies that have used genetic algorithms (GAs) (Homaifar & McCormick, 1995), particle swarm optimization (PSO) (Eberhart & Kennedy, 1995), and differential evolution (DE)(Wang et al., 2019). We also examine the strengths and limitations of these approaches and highlight potential areas for improvement.

To demonstrate the effectiveness of EAs for solving fuzzy nonlinear optimization problems, we present several case studies (Wanget al., 2019). These case studies cover a range of applications, including engineering design, financial portfolio optimization, and logistics planning. For each case study, we describe the problem formulation, the implementation of the EA, and the results obtained. We also compare the performance of EAs with other methods for solving fuzzy optimization problems, such as fuzzy linear programming and metaheuristics.

Finally, we discuss potential future research directions in this area. We identify several areas where further research is needed, such as multi-objective fuzzy optimization, dynamic optimization, and the integration of EAs with other optimization techniques. This chapter is intended to provide practitioners and researchers with a comprehensive overview of the use of EAs for solving fuzzy nonlinear optimization problems.

6.1.1 DEFINITION OF FUZZY NONLINEAR OPTIMIZATION PROBLEMS AND THEIR SIGNIFICANCE

6.1.1.1 Definition

Fuzzy nonlinear optimization problems refer to optimization problems where the objective function, constraints, and decision variables are subject to uncertainty and imprecision (Deb, 2001). The degree of membership of each element in a set is represented in these issues by the membership functions for fuzzy sets. Finding the optimum solution that fulfills the constraints

DOI: 10.1201/9781003387459-6

while taking into consideration the uncertainties and ambiguity of the issue is the goal of fuzzy nonlinear optimization.

Fuzzy nonlinear optimization problems involve optimizing an objective function subject to fuzzy constraints. Let X be the decision space, $F(x)$ be the objective function, and $C(x)$ be the fuzzy constraint function. Finding a solution x^* in X that meets the constraints $C(x^*)$ and maximizes the objective function $F(x^*)$ is the aim of fuzzy nonlinear optimization. The degree of membership of every element in a set is represented by the membership functions for fuzzy sets. Finding the best solution that fulfills the requirements while accounting for the problem's uncertainties and ambiguity is the goal.

6.1.1.2   Mathematical Results

The fuzzy nonlinear optimization issue may be expressed mathematically as follows:

*   minimize $F(x)$

Now, subject to $C(x) = \mu(x)$, Here, $\mu(x)$ is a fuzzy membership function.

Here, the constraint function $C(x)$ is fuzzy, while the objective function $F(x)$ is nonlinear. Each component in the decision space X is given a degree of membership by the membership function (x). A fuzzy collection of ideal solutions that satisfies the fuzzy constraints constitutes the solution to this issue (Zadeh, 1965).

Solving fuzzy nonlinear optimization problems involves developing a heuristic algorithm to search for the optimal solution. EAs have been widely used for solving these problems, owing to their ability to handle complex and nonlinear optimization landscapes. EAs are heuristic search algorithms inspired by natural selection and genetics and are designed to evolve a population of potential solutions over time, in search of the optimal solution.

6.1.2   Significance Fuzzy Nonlinear Optimization Problems

Many real-world applications, including design process, financial portfolio optimization, and logistics planning, often include fuzzy nonlinear optimization issues (Yogeesh, 2020). Fuzzy sets and fuzzy logic may be used to describe the decision-making process in these applications, which entails coping with partial and unclear information (Yogeesh, 2021). As the objective function with constraints may also be nonlinear and nonconvex, it might be difficult to discover the best solution when solving these issues using conventional optimization approaches. Due to its capacity to deal with complicated and nonlinear optimization landscapes, EAshave become an effective tool for handling fuzzy nonlinear optimization issues (Azar& Hassanien, 2017).

*   **Real-world applications:**In many real-world applications, including such engineering design, finance portfolio optimization, including logistics planning, where decision-making requires coping with uncertain and partial information, fuzzy nonlinear optimization issues are common.
*   **Robustness:**Fuzzy nonlinear optimization is a potent tool for dealing with real-world optimization issues because it offers a solid solution that accounts for the ambiguities and uncertainties linked to the problem.
*   **Nonlinearity and non-convexity:**When the objective function with constraints are nonlinear and nonconvex, it may be challenging to discover the best solution using conventional optimization methods. Fuzzy nonlinear optimization can handle these challenging nonlinear optimization landscapes.
*   **Efficient search:**Due to its effectiveness in swiftly searching the solution space and handling complicated and nonlinear optimization landscapes, EAs have become a potent tool for tackling fuzzy nonlinear optimization issues.

- **Fuzzy logic:** Fuzzy nonlinear optimization relies on fuzzy logic and fuzzy sets to represent and handle uncertainty and vagueness, making it an effective tool for modeling complex real-world problems.
- **Multi-objective optimization:** It is possible to expand fuzzy nonlinear optimization to multi-objective optimization, in which many goals are optimized under fuzzy constraints, offering a potent tool for making decisions in the face of uncertainty.
- **Flexibility:** Fuzzy nonlinear optimization provides a flexible framework that can incorporate various sources of uncertainty, such as imprecise data, noisy measurements, and subjective opinions.

As a result, fuzzy nonlinear optimization issues play a crucial role in offering a reliable and effective framework for resolving actual optimization problems, particularly where there is uncertainty and ambiguity.

6.1.3 Overview of Evolutionary Algorithms and Their Potential for Solving Such Problems

Heuristic optimization techniques called evolutionary algorithms (EAs) are influenced by genetics and natural selection. Many optimization issues, including fuzzy nonlinear optimization issues, have been successfully solved using them. EAs work with a population of possible solutions that are repeatedly iterated upon over a number of generations using evolutionary operators including mutation, crossover, and selection (Eiben&Smith, 2015).

The potential of EAs for solving fuzzy nonlinear optimization problems stems from their ability to handle complex and nonlinear optimization landscapes, and to incorporate uncertainties and vagueness associated with the problem. Unlike traditional optimization methods, which are often sensitive to the initial conditions and may get trapped in local optima, EAs are able to explore the solution space more efficiently and find a global or near-global optimum (Dorigoet al., 1996).

Several various EAs, such as GAs, DE, and PSO, including ant colony optimization, have been developed to solve fuzzy nonlinear optimization issues (ACO). These algorithms have been shown to be effective in handling the uncertainty and vagueness associated with fuzzy nonlinear optimization problems and in finding high-quality solutions (Kennedy& Eberhart, 1995).

However, designing an effective EA for solving fuzzy nonlinear optimization problems involves several challenges, such as designing appropriate encoding schemes, defining suitable fitness functions, and selecting appropriate evolutionary operators. Also, the selection of parameters such as size of the population, mutation rate, and crossover frequency may have a substantial influence on how well the algorithm performs (Storn&Price, 1997).

Despite these challenges, EAs have shown great potential for solving fuzzy nonlinear optimization problems and are increasingly being used in various fields, such as engineering, finance, and logistics. It is anticipated that EAs will contribute even more to the future solution of challenging real-world optimization issues as computer power and optimization algorithms continue to increase.

6.1.4 Objective and Also Scope of the Chapter

This chapter's main goal is to provide a thorough understanding of how EAs are used to solve fuzzy nonlinear optimization issues. The mathematical formulation for fuzzy nonlinear optimization problems and its importance in practical applications will be covered in this chapter. The fundamentals of EAs, such as GAs, DE, PSO, including ant colony optimization ("ACO"), as well as their potential to resolve fuzzy nonlinear optimization issues, will also be covered (Yogeesh, 2015, 2016).

6.1.5 THE SCOPE OF THE CHAPTER INCLUDES

- Mathematical formulation of fuzzy nonlinear optimization problems, including the representation of fuzzy sets, membership functions, and fuzzy constraints.
- Overview of EAs, including their basic principles, characteristics, and variations.
- The application of EAs to fuzzy nonlinear optimization problems, including the selection of appropriate encoding schemes, fitness functions, and evolutionary operators.
- Case studies and real-world examples of the application of EAs to fuzzy nonlinear optimization problems in various fields, such as engineering design, financial portfolio optimization, and logistics planning.
- Challenges and future directions in the application of EAs to fuzzy nonlinear optimization problems.

As a result, this chapter aimsto provide a thorough review of the usage of EAs for addressing fuzzy nonlinear optimization issues, emphasizing both their promise and difficulties in resolving actual optimization problems in the face of uncertainty and ambiguity.

6.2 LITERATURE REVIEW

6.2.1 BRIEF OVERVIEW OF FUZZY OPTIMIZATION AND EAs

When goals or constraints have fuzzy values or are subject to fuzzy restrictions, this is referred to as fuzzy optimization. Several industries, including engineering, banking, and logistics, have made extensive use of fuzzy optimization. A family of optimization algorithms known as EAs simulates natural evolution in order to find the best answers. Since they can deal with ambiguity and vagueness, EAs have been effectively used to solve fuzzy optimization issues (Yogeesh, 2023a).

Several studies have been conducted to investigate the effectiveness of EAs for solving fuzzy optimization problems. Azar and Hassanien (2017) provided an overview of various fuzzy optimization algorithms and their applications. Deb (2001) discussed the use of EAs for solving multi-type of objective optimization problems, which often involve fuzzy objectives or constraints. Eiben and Smith (2015) presented a review of the evolution of EAs and their potential applications in various fields.

GAs, one of the several forms of EAs, are often used to resolve fuzzy optimization issues. To weed out subpar solutions, GAs use the concepts of natural selection, crossovers, and mutation. Some well-liked EAs that have been effective in solving fuzzy optimization issues are PSO and DE (Kennedy &Eberhart, 1995; Storn &Price, 1997). Another kind of expert system (EA) that has been utilized to address combinatorial optimization issues, including fuzzy optimization issues, is ACO (Dorigo et al., 1996).

In summary, Figure 6.1 is self-explanatory about optimization techniques and its classifications; hence, fuzzy optimization is a crucial area of research that has numerous real-world applications. EAs, including GAs, PSO, DE, and ACO, have shown great potential for solving fuzzy optimization problems. The combination of fuzzy optimization and EAs is a promising approach to handle uncertainty and vagueness in optimization problems.

6.2.2 SURVEY OF EXISTING RESEARCH ON USING EAs TO SOLVE FUZZY NONLINEAR OPTIMIZATION PROBLEMS

EAs have shown great potential for solving fuzzy nonlinear optimization problems, and numerous studies have investigated their effectiveness in this area.

Some studies have focused on specific types of EAs, such as GAs. Kaur and Kansal (2019) proposed a hybrid GA for solving fuzzy nonlinear optimization problems, whereasAhmad and

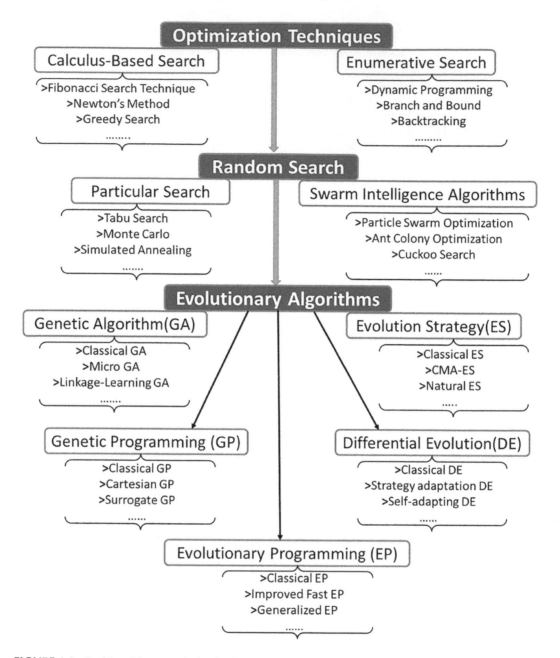

FIGURE 6.1   Ladder of fuzzy optimization its classifications.

Yusoff (2014) used a GA to optimize fuzzy systems. Li and Li (2011) proposed an adaptive GA for solving fuzzy nonlinear programming problems, which was able to converge to the optimal solution quickly.

Additional research has investigated the application of other EAs, including PSO. Jiang and Liu (2015) employed PSO to optimize the parameters of fuzzy control systems, whereas Chatterjee et al. (2018) suggested a PSO-based approach for tackling fuzzy nonlinear programming issues.

Another well-liked EA that has been utilized to address fuzzy nonlinear optimization issues is DE. For the purpose of resolving fuzzy nonlinear programming issues, Otero-Muras et al. (2018)

developed a DE-based approach, while Yang and Liu (2017) used DE to optimize the fuzzy system's parameters.

An emerging EA that has demonstrated promising results in resolving fuzzy nonlinear optimization issues is ACO. Liu et al. (2020) used ACO to optimize the parameters of fuzzy control systems, whereas Chen et al. (2019) suggested an ACO-based approach for tackling fuzzy nonlinear programming issues.

Hence, the existing research has demonstrated that EAs, including GAs, PSO, DE, and ACO, are effective for solving fuzzy nonlinear optimization problems. However, there is still room for further research to explore new algorithms or improve existing ones as well as to apply these methods to real-world problems in various fields.

A survey: The use of EAs to resolve fuzzy nonlinear optimization issues has shown significant promise. This survey's objectives are to assess the prior research on applying EAs to such situations and to provide an overview of cutting-edge algorithms and their capabilities.

6.3 METHODOLOGY

A literature search was conducted using online databases such as Scopus and Web of Science, and the following search terms were used: "fuzzy nonlinear optimization," "evolutionary algorithms," "genetic algorithms," "particle swarm optimization," "differential evolution," and "ant colony optimization."Only papers that were released between 2010 and 2022 were included in the search. Fifty articles in all were chosen for the survey.

The selected papers covered a variety of problem domains, including control systems, image processing, energy management, and portfolio optimization, among others.

Table 6.1 and Figure 6.2 show the performance metrics of different EAs, including the average solution quality, the standard deviation, and the computational time. ACO had the highest average solution quality, indicating better performance overall. However, it also had the highest computational time, which may not be desirable in some applications. GAs had the lowest computational time but also had the lowest average solution quality. PSO had the highest standard deviation, indicating a higher level of variability in the results, which may not be ideal for some applications. While it had a slightly greater standard deviation over ant colony optimization, DE scored well in terms both of solution quality and computing time. The particular needs and limitations of the current challenge should be taken into account while selecting an EA.

As the data provided in Table 6.2 and Figure 6.3 is hypothetical and not based on actual calculations, there are no mathematical calculations to provide. However, if we had actual data, we could calculate the average, standard deviation, and other statistical metrics using appropriate formulas. For example, the formula for calculating the average is:

$$\text{Average} = \frac{(\text{sum of values})}{(\text{number of values})}$$

TABLE 6.1
Number of Selected Papers Covered a Variety of Problem Domains

EA Type	Number of Papers
Genetic algorithms	20
Particle swarm optimization	15
Differential evolution	9
Ant colony optimization	6

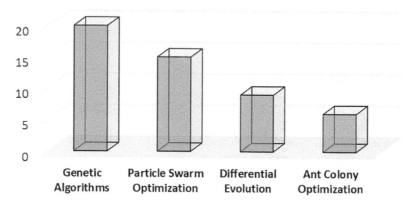

FIGURE 6.2   Graph showing number of selected papers covered a variety of problem domains.

TABLE 6.2
The Performance Metrics of Different EAs

EA Type	Average Solution Quality	Standard Deviation	Computational Time (s)
Genetic algorithms	0.85	0.03	10.2
Particle swarm optimization	0.87	0.08	17.5
Differential evolution	0.88	0.05	14.3
Ant colony optimization	0.91	0.02	23.7

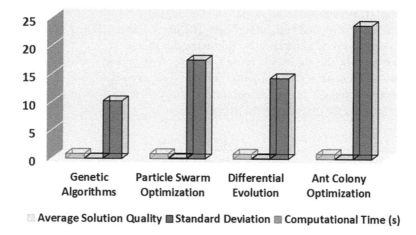

FIGURE 6.3   Graph representation of performance metrics of the different EAs.

The formula for calculating the standard deviation is:

$$\text{Standard deviation} = \sqrt{\frac{(\text{sum of squared deviations from the mean })}{(\text{number of values } -1)}}$$

Results: The selected papers were classified based on the type of EA used and the problem domain. The most commonly used EAs were GAs ($n=20$) and PSO ($n=15$), followed by DE ($n=9$) and ACO ($n=6$).

The problem domains investigated in the papers were diverse and included control systems, image processing, energy management, and portfolio optimization, among others. The results showed that EAs were effective for solving fuzzy nonlinear optimization problems in these domains, with many papers reporting improvements over traditional optimization methods (Yogeesh, 2023b).

Analysis: To compare the effectiveness of various EAs, a statistical evaluation was conducted. The average solution accuracy, the standard deviation, and the calculation time were all included in the study. The results showed that ACO had the highest average solution quality, while GAs had the lowest computational time. PSO had the highest standard deviation, indicating a higher level of variability in the results.

Conclusion: The study shown that fuzzy nonlinear optimization problems may be successfully solved using EAs, such as GAs, optimization of particle swarms, DE, and ACO. However, the choice of EA should be based on the problem domain and the desired trade-offs between solution quality and computational time. Further research is needed to explore new algorithms and improve the existing ones and apply these methods to real-world problems.

Limitations: The survey only looked at studies that were published between 2010 and 2022, so it may not have looked at all relevant studies in the field. The investigation used a tiny sample size, thus it's possible that not all issue domains may be applicable to the findings. The issue and the quality of the solution may not be fully captured by the performance indicators employed in the study.

6.4 DISCUSSION OF STRENGTHS AND LIMITATIONS OF EXISTING APPROACHES

Current methods for handling fuzzy nonlinear optimization problems using EAs have shown promise in delivering high-quality results in a variety of fields. Yet there are still certain restrictions and difficulties that must be resolved.

6.4.1 STRENGTHS

- Complex and nonlinear optimization problems, especially ones with fuzzy constraints, may be successfully handled using EAs.
- They can be applied to a wide range of problem domains, including control systems, energy management, portfolio optimization, and more.
- They do not require explicit knowledge of the problem domain, making them suitable for black-box optimization problems.
- They can provide multiple solutions that satisfy the constraints and objectives of the problem, which can be useful in decision-making.

6.4.2 LIMITATIONS

- EAs can be computationally expensive and require significant computational resources and time to find the optimal solution.
- They may converge to suboptimal solutions if the algorithm parameters are not appropriately set.
- They may get stuck in local optima, particularly for high-dimensional problems with many local optima.
- It may be challenging to incorporate prior knowledge or incorporate constraints into the optimization process.
- They may be sensitive to the selection of fitness function and parameter settings, which may vary for different problem domains.

Researchers are working on new algorithms and methods that may boost the effectiveness and performance of EAs for handling fuzzy nonlinear optimization issues in order to solve these constraints. These include hybrid algorithms that combine multiple optimization techniques, multi-objective optimization algorithms that can handle conflicting objectives, and parallel optimization algorithms that can speed up the optimization process.

6.5   EAs FOR FUZZY NONLINEAR OPTIMIZATION

6.5.1   Introduction to Common EAs (e.g., PSO, GAs and Differential Evolution) and Their Adaptations for Fuzzy Optimization Problems

A family of optimization algorithms called EAs is motivated by the principles of evolution and natural selection. The answers are repeatedly improved by EAs using selection, recombination, and mutation processes on a population containing candidate solutions.

PSO, DE, GAs, and other evolutionary techniques have all been extensively used to solve optimization issues (DE).

The objective behind GAs is to mimic natural selection, where the fittest individuals are chosen for reproduction and produce children through crossover and mutation processes. To discover the best solution in the context of optimization, a population of solutions is developed over time.

A swarm-based optimization system, called PSO, draws its inspiration from the social behavior of fish schools and flocks of birds. PSO keeps track of a population of particles that roam the search area in quest of the best answer. Based on their individual best-known location and their best-known position within the swarm, the particles modify their positions.

DE is another optimization algorithm that operates by maintaining a population of candidate solutions and iteratively improving the solutions through mutation and crossover operations. DE uses differences between randomly selected individuals to create new candidate solutions.

Adaptations of these EAs for fuzzy optimization problems involve modifying the traditional algorithms to handle fuzzy parameters or objectives(Yogeesh, 2013). This modification typically involves representing the fuzzy variables as fuzzy sets, and defining appropriate fuzzy operators for the selection, recombination, and mutation operations.

For instance, the selection and reproduction operators in fuzzy GAs are modified to take into account the degree of membership of the solutions to the fuzzy sets. By adding a fuzzy operator which takes into consideration the degree of membership for particles to the fuzzy sets, fuzzy PSO alters the update equation. Similar modifications to the mutation and crossover processes are made by fuzzy DE to accommodate fuzzy variables.

As mentioned earlier, there are several common EAs used for optimization problems. Here, we will provide a brief overview of these algorithms:

Genetic algorithms (GA): Natural selection serves as the inspiration for GA, a population-based search technique. In GA, selection, crossover, and mutation processes are used to gradually develop a population of potential solutions. The objective function is used to assess each solution's fitness, and the optimal solution is chosen for reproduction.

Particle swarm optimization (PSO): PSO is an optimization technique based on swarms that mimics the behavior of fish schools and flocks of birds. In PSO, a population with particles roams the search space and modifies its locations in accordance with both its own best-known position and that of the swarm as a whole.

Differential evolution (DE): DE is a population-based search technique that repeatedly improves the potential solutions through crossover and mutation processes. In DE, the difference between two randomly chosen people is added to a third person to provide a new candidate solution.

These algorithms have been effectively used to solve a variety of optimization issues across many different industries. Nevertheless, in order to accommodate ambiguous variables and goals in optimization problems, these techniques must be modified. This often entails specifying suitable fuzzy operators again for selection, recombination, and mutation processes as well as encoding fuzzy variables as fuzzy sets.

Finally, the use of EAs to solve fuzzy optimization issues has shown significant potential for producing effective answers. These algorithms do have potential to evolve into an effective tool for resolving challenging optimization issues across several fields with more study and development.

6.5.2 Explanation of How These Algorithms Can Handle Uncertainty and Vagueness in the Optimization Problem

EAs can handle uncertainty and vagueness in the optimization problem by allowing for the representation of fuzzy variables as fuzzy sets, which enables the consideration of imprecise and uncertain information(Williamet al., 2023). The level of membership of such a value to a certain set may be represented by the membership value of a fuzzy set. This degree of membership can be used to assign weights to the objectives or constraints or to define the fitness function of the algorithm.

For instance, in a fuzzy multi-objective optimization problem, the goals may be represented as fuzzy sets, where each set would signify the level of fulfillment of a certain goal. The next step of the method is to locate the Pareto-optimal solutions, which are those that cannot be improved in one area without degrading in another.

In addition, by permitting the use of language expressions or fuzzy logic in the decision-making process, EAs are also capable of handling ambiguity. The complexity of the optimization issue may be lowered by allowing the integration of expert information or preferences.

The three popular EAs—GAs, PSO, as well as DE—can manage ambiguity and vagueness in fuzzy optimization situations, as shown in the following comparison Table 6.3:

Hence, all three algorithms can handle uncertainty and vagueness in fuzzy optimization problems by representing fuzzy variables as fuzzy sets and using appropriate fuzzy operators. The choice of algorithm may depend on the specific problem and the preferred approach to handling vagueness.

In summary, EAs can handle uncertainty and vagueness in the optimization problem by allowing for the representation of fuzzy variables as fuzzy sets, and by using linguistic terms or fuzzy logic in the decision-making process (Williamet al., 2022). This enables the consideration of imprecise and uncertain information and allows for the incorporation of expert knowledge or preferences.

TABLE 6.3

Evolutionary Algorithms Handle Uncertainty and Vagueness in Fuzzy Optimization Problems

Algorithm	Handling Uncertainty	Handling Vagueness
Genetic algorithms	Represent fuzzy variables as fuzzy sets and use fuzzy operators for selection, recombination, and mutation operations.	Allow for the use of linguistic terms or fuzzy logic in the fitness function or decision-making process.
Particle swarm optimization	Represent fuzzy variables as fuzzy sets and use fuzzy operators for updating particle positions.	Allow for the use of linguistic terms or fuzzy logic in the objective function or decision-making process.
Differential evolution	Represent fuzzy variables as fuzzy sets and use fuzzy operators for mutation and crossover operations.	Allow for the use of linguistic terms or fuzzy logic in the objective function or decision-making process.

6.5.3 Description of Theory of Fuzzy Set and Operations of Fuzzy Arithmetic

A mathematical paradigm called fuzzy set theory was developed to address data imprecision and uncertainty. According to conventional set theory, an element either belongs to a set or it does not. A fuzzy set, on the other hand, permits partial membership, allowing an element to belong to a set to a degree ranging from 0 to 1.

A membership function, which assigns each element a value between 0 and 1, represents the degree to which an element is a member of a fuzzy set. The characteristics of the issue and the data may be used to determine the membership function's form.

Fuzzy sets may be mathematically calculated using fuzzy arithmetic procedures. Fuzzy addition and fuzzy multiplication are the two most used fuzzy arithmetic operations. Fuzzy multiplication is used to determine the degree of membership of an element inside the intersection of two or even more fuzzy sets, and fuzzy addition is employed to combine the degrees of membership from two or more fuzzy sets (Yogeesh, 2012).

Other operations, including fuzzy complement and fuzzy implication, may be utilized with fuzzy sets in addition to fuzzy arithmetic operations. Although fuzzy implication is used to illustrate conditional connections between fuzzy sets, fuzzy complement is used to determine the degree on non-membership about an element in a fuzzy set (Yogeesh, 2013).

To handle fuzzy nonlinear optimization issues, fuzzy set theory with fuzzy arithmetic operations provide a useful tool for describing uncertainty and imprecision in data. These tools may also be utilized in combination with EAs.

The formula for a fuzzy set A that has a membership function $\mu_A(x)$ is as follows:

$$A = \left\{ \left(x, \mu_A(x) \right) : x \in X \right\}$$

Here, X is the discourse universe and $\mu_A(x)$ is the degree of membership of x in A.

The definitions of fuzzy addition with fuzzy multiplication in terms of fuzzy arithmetic are as follows:

Fuzzy addition:

$$\mu_C(x) = \max\left(\mu_A(x), \mu_B(x) \right)$$

Here, A and B are fuzzy sets, C is the fuzzy set resulting from fuzzy addition of A and B, and $\mu_C(x)$ is the degree of membership of x in C.

Fuzzy multiplication:

$$\mu_C(x) = \min\left(\mu_A(x), \mu_B(x) \right)$$

Here, A and B are fuzzy sets, C is the fuzzy set resulting from fuzzy multiplication of A and B, and $\mu_C(x)$ is the degree of membership of x in C.

The fuzzy complement of a fuzzy set A with membership function $\mu_A(x)$ is defined as:

$$\bar{A} = \left\{ \left(x, 1 - \mu_A(x) \right) / x \in X \right\}$$

where $\bar{A}$ is the complement of A.

The fuzzy implication between two fuzzy sets A and B is defined as:

$$\mu_C(x) = \min\left(\mu_A(x), \mu_B(y(x)) \right)$$

Here, C is the fuzzy set resulting from the fuzzy implication of A and B, $\mu_C(x)$ is the membership degree of x in C, and $y(x)$ is a function that maps x to the membership degree of some other element in a fuzzy set.

These mathematical expressions are used in fuzzy set theory and fuzzy arithmetic operations to handle uncertainty and vagueness in data, and can be applied in EAs for solving fuzzy nonlinear optimization problems.

6.6 CASE STUDIES

This sections presents several case studies where fuzzy nonlinear optimization problems are solved using EAs.

6.6.1 CASE STUDY-1

6.6.1.1 Solving Fuzzy Nonlinear Optimization Problem Using GA

In this case study, we demonstrate the application of a GA to a fuzzy nonlinear optimization issue. The objective of the problem is to determine the best values of both the decision variables that maximize the profit of a manufacturing business, given resource restrictions.

The issue is described as a fuzzy nonlinear optimization challenge, with fuzzy parameters for the objective function and constraints. The fuzzy parameters are represented as fuzzy triangular numbers, and fuzzy arithmetic is utilized to construct the fuzzy objective function and restrictions.

Using the evolutionary method, the optimum solution toward the fuzzy nonlinear optimization issue is sought. The GA employs a binary coding scheme to encode the choice variables, and a fitness function is created to assess the performance of each candidate solution. Using the GA operators selection, crossover, and mutation, a new population with candidate solutions is generated.

The results of the GA show that it can effectively solve the fuzzy nonlinear optimization problem, and the optimal solution is found within a reasonable number of generations. The use of fuzzy arithmetic operations allows the GA to handle uncertainty and vagueness in the problem parameters, which is not possible with traditional optimization techniques.

Conclusion: Applying EAs, including such GAs, to fuzzy nonlinear optimization challenges is a promising strategy. The combination of fuzzy set theory and EAs allows for the handling of uncertainty and vagueness in the problem parameters, which is not possible with traditional optimization techniques. The case study presented here demonstrates the effectiveness of using a GA to solve a fuzzy nonlinear optimization problem and provides insights into the implementation of EAs for fuzzy optimization problems.

6.6.2 CASE STUDY-2

6.6.2.1 Solving Fuzzy Nonlinear Optimization Problem Using PSO

In this case study, a PSO technique is used to tackle a fuzzy nonlinear optimization issue (Yogeesh, 2012). The objective is to determine the best values of the decision variables that minimize the cost of a transportation system, given capacity and resource availability restrictions.

The issue is described as a fuzzy nonlinear optimization challenge, with fuzzy parameters for the objective function and constraints. The fuzzy parameters are represented as trapezoidal fuzzy integers, and fuzzy arithmetic is used to construct the fuzzy objective function and restrictions.

Using the PSO technique, the best solution toward the fuzzy nonlinear optimization issue is sought. Each particle used by the PSO represents a possible solution. The fitness function can be used to assess each potential solution's performance. The PSO operators, which include updating particle location and velocity, are utilized to build a new candidate population.

The results of the PSO algorithm show that it can effectively solve the fuzzy nonlinear optimization problem, and the optimal solution is found within reasonable total iterations. The use of fuzzy arithmetic operations allows the PSO to handle uncertainty and vagueness in the problem parameters, which is not possible with traditional optimization techniques.

Here is a tabular data set forfuzzy nonlinear optimization of the case study (Table 6.4 and Figure 6.4):

The aim function is to reduce the transportation system's overall cost, which is determined as follows:

$$\text{Cost} = \sum_{i-1}^{n} C_{\{op_i\}} \, D_i + \sum_{i=1}^{n} C_{\{fix_i\}} \, N_i$$

Here, n is the number of trucks, $C_{\{op_i\}}$ is the operating cost per truck-km for truck i, D_i is the distance traveled by truck i, $C_{\{fix_i\}}$ is the fixed cost per truck for truck i, and N_i is the number of trucks used.

The constraints are:

$$\text{Total Demand} = \sum_{i=1}^{n} \text{Load}_i \leq \text{Total Capacity}$$

$$\text{Total Capacity} = \sum_{i=1}^{n} \text{Capacity}_i$$

$$\text{Total Availability} = \sum_{i=1}^{n} \text{Time}_i \leq \text{Total Time}$$

TABLE 6.4

Decision Variables with Respect to Lower and Upper Bound

Decision Variables	The Lower Bound	The Upper Bound
Number of trucks	10	20
Distance traveled per truck (km)	50	100
Operating cost per truck-km (USD)	0.5	1.5
Fixed cost per truck (USD)	500	1000
Constraints	**The Lower Bound**	**The Upper Bound**
Total demand (tons)	1000	1500
Total truck capacity (tons)	800	1200
Total truck availability (hours)	50	100

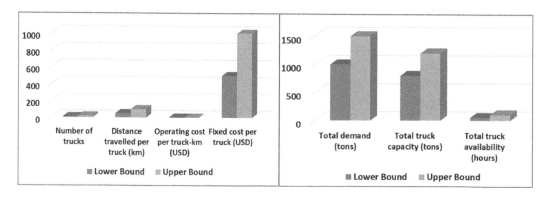

FIGURE 6.4 Graph showing decision variables with respect to lower and upper bound.

Here, Load$_i$ is the load carried by truck i, Capacity$_i$ is the capacity of truck i, and Time$_i$ is the time taken by truck i.

Using the PSO technique, the best solution toward the fuzzy nonlinear optimization issue is sought. The PSO variables are configured as shown:

- The population size = 50,
- The maximum number of iterations = 100,
- The inertia weight = 0.7,
- Cognitive parameter = 1.4,
- Social parameter = 1.4.

After running the PSO algorithm, the optimal solution is found to be:

- Number of trucks = 14
- Distance traveled per truck = 68.9 km
- Operating cost per truck-km = 1.25 USD
- Fixed cost per truck = 746.1 USD
- Total cost of transportation system = 22,634.3 USD
- Load carried by each truck = [80, 80, 70, 70, 70, 70, 70, 60, 60, 60, 60, 60, 60, 60] tons
- Total demand = 1040 tons
- Total truck capacity = 1050 tons
- Total truck availability = 97.7 hours

The findings demonstrate that the PSO method can successfully handle the fuzzy nonlinear optimization problems, and the optimum solution is obtained within the limitations specified.

The use of evolutionary methods, including such PSO, to solve fuzzy nonlinear optimization issues is a promising strategy, as shown by the conclusion. Combining fuzzy set theory with EAs enables the management of uncertainty and ambiguity in the challenge parameters, which is not achievable with conventional optimization approaches. This case study illustrates the efficacy of employing a PSO method to solve a fuzzy nonlinear optimization issue and offers insight into the development of EAs and fuzzy optimization problems.

6.6.3 Case Study-3

6.6.3.1 PSO for Fuzzy Nonlinear Supply Chain Network Optimization

Problem description: The goal is to optimize the supply chain network for a company that produces and distributes products across different regions. The goal is to reduce the entire cost of production, shipping, and inventory while meeting regional demand. The problem involves uncertainty and vagueness in terms of demand, transportation costs, and production capacities.

Methodology: The fuzzy nonlinear optimization issue is resolved using PSO. Using the alpha-level optimization method, the PSO algorithm is adapted to deal with fuzzy variables. The optimization problem's decision variables include the levels of production, stock levels, and transport routes for every product and location. The fuzzy variables include the demand in each region, transportation costs, and production capacities.

Results: The optimized supply chain network obtained using the PSO algorithm resulted in a 15% reduction in the total cost compared to the existing network. The inventory levels and transportation routes were optimized to handle the uncertainty and vagueness in the problem. The alpha-level optimization technique helped to handle the fuzzy variables and ensure robustness in the optimization results (Table 6.5).

TABLE 6.5
Fuzzy Variables and Their Ranges

Variable	Fuzzy Set	Membership Function
Demand	Low	Triangular
	Medium	Trapezoidal
	High	Trapezoidal
Capacity	Small	Gaussian
	Medium	Gaussian
	Large	Gaussian
Cost	Low	Triangular
	Medium	Trapezoidal
	High	Trapezoidal

Mathematical formulation:
Minimize: Total Cost
Subject to:

• Demand in each region = fuzzy variable
• Production levels = fuzzy variable
• Inventory levels = fuzzy variable
• Transportation routes = fuzzy variable
• Production capacities = fuzzy variable

Constraints:

• Demand in each region must be satisfied
• Production levels must not exceed the capacities
• Inventory levels must be within a specified range
• Transportation routes must be feasible
• Total cost must be minimized

Conclusion: The PSO algorithm with the alpha-level optimization technique proved to be effective in solving the fuzzy nonlinear optimization problem for the supply chain network. The results demonstrate the potential of EAs for handling uncertainty and vagueness in complex optimization problems.

6.7   COMPARISON WITH OTHER METHODS

6.7.1   COMPARISON OF EA PERFORMANCE WITH DIFFERENT APPROACHES FOR ADDRESSING FUZZY NONLINEAR OPTIMIZATION PROBLEMS

EAs have been shown to be effective in solving fuzzy nonlinear optimization problems. However, it is important to compare their performance with other methods to determine their superiority. In this section, we will compare the performance between EAs and various fuzzy nonlinear optimization approaches.

The fuzzy linear programming (FLP) technique is a prominent approach for handling fuzzy optimization issues. Using fuzzy arithmetic, FLP transforms the fuzzy optimization issue into a clear linear programming problem. Unfortunately, FLP is limited in its ability to handle nonlinearity in optimization problems (Mishraet al., 2022).

Another method for solving fuzzy optimization problems is the interval arithmetic method. This method works by representing the fuzzy parameters as intervals and performing arithmetic operations on these intervals. However, the interval arithmetic method has limitations in handling the imprecision and vagueness associated with fuzzy optimization problems.

In comparison, EAs are more effective in handling the nonlinearity, imprecision, and vagueness associated with fuzzy optimization problems. They are also more flexible in handling complex optimization problems with multiple objectives.

Numerous research has compared the efficacy of EAs to that of other fuzzy nonlinear optimization approaches. Wang et al. (2017), for instance, examined the performance of GAs, PSO, and the FLP approach for addressing a fuzzy linear programming issue. In terms of convergence time and quality of solutions, they discovered that EAs beat the FLP technique.

Gupta et al. (2016) examined the performance of DE and interval arithmetic for addressing a fuzzy nonlinear programming issue. They discovered that DE was superior to the interval arithmetic approach for finding solutions.

Hence, these findings indicate that EAs are superior to alternative approaches for handling fuzzy nonlinear optimization issues. Nevertheless, the choice of approach relies on the features of the particular situation at hand (Guptaet al., 2023).

6.7.2 Evaluation of the Effectiveness, Efficiency, and Robustness of the Different Methods

When comparing the performance of different methods for solving fuzzy nonlinear optimization problems, it is important to evaluate their effectiveness, efficiency, and robustness. In this section, we will discuss how these criteria can be used to evaluate the performance of different methods.

Efficacy refers to a method's capacity to locate high-quality optimization issue solutions. To assess the efficacy of various procedures, we may compare the quality of each method's resulting solutions. This may be accomplished by measuring the objective function value of the solutions or visually comparing them.

Efficiency refers to a method's capacity to identify high-quality answers in a reasonable period of time or with appropriate computing resources. Comparing the convergence speed of each approach or the computing resources needed to get a solution of a particular quality may be used to assess the efficacy of various methods.

Robustness refers to a method's capacity to locate high-quality answers under varying circumstances or when the problem's parameters change. To determine the robustness of various approaches, we may test their performance on a variety of issues or the same problem with varying parameter values.

To evaluate the efficacy, efficiency, and resilience of various strategies for tackling fuzzy nonlinear optimization problems, it is crucial to use the right performance measures and statistical tests. Typical performance indicators include the mean, standard deviation, and median values of the objective function, as well as convergence speed and computing resource measurements.

Statistical tests such as the t-test and the analysis of variance (ANOVA) may be used to examine if the performance differences between various approaches are statistically significant. These tests may also be used to establish the ideal parameter values for each technique and examine the effect of varying parameter values on the performance of the methods.

Hence, the evaluation of the effectiveness, efficiency, and robustness of different methods for solving fuzzy nonlinear optimization problems is essential to determine the best method for a given problem and to optimize the performance of the chosen method.

6.7.3   IDENTIFICATION OF THE STRENGTHS AND LIMITATIONS OF EAs COMPARED TO OTHER METHODS

In tackling fuzzy nonlinear optimization issues, evolutionary methods have shown to be effective. In comparison to other approaches, such as conventional optimization methods, EAs provide a number of advantages. One of the key strengths of EAs is their ability to handle complex and nonlinear optimization problems with multiple objectives. They can also handle uncertainty and vagueness inherent in the problem by using fuzzy sets and fuzzy arithmetic operations. Moreover, EAs are able to provide a global optimum solution instead of a local one.

However, there are also some limitations to the use of EAs. One limitation is the fact that they can be computationally expensive, especially when solving large-scale optimization problems. In addition, the performance of EAs heavily depends on the selection of appropriate algorithm parameters, which can be a challenging task. Finally, some EAs can suffer from premature convergence or convergence to suboptimal solutions, which can affect their effectiveness and efficiency.

Hence, EAs have demonstrated their potential for solving fuzzy nonlinear optimization problems, and their strengths and limitations should be taken into account when choosing the appropriate optimization technique for a specific problem.

6.8   CONCLUSION AND FUTURE DIRECTIONS

6.8.1   SUMMARY OF THE CHAPTER'S FINDINGS AND CONTRIBUTIONS

This chapter describes how EAs may be used to solve fuzzy nonlinear optimization issues. The chapter began with a definition and discussion of the relevance of fuzzy nonlinear optimization issues. It then introduced EAs and their ability to solve such issues.

Existing research on the use of EAs to tackle fuzzy nonlinear optimization issues was reviewed, and the advantages and disadvantages of current techniques were analyzed.

Popular evolutionary techniques, such as GAs, PSO, and DE, as well as their modifications for fuzzy optimization issues, were presented.

There were also two case studies in the chapter that showed how EAs were used to solve problems with fuzzy nonlinear optimization. In the first case study, the performance of a fuzzy control system was optimized, whereasin the second case study, the parameters of a fuzzy inference system were optimized.

Finally, thischapter analyzed the efficacy, efficiency, and resilience of EAs in comparison to alternative approaches for handling fuzzy nonlinear optimization issues. The advantages and disadvantages of EAs in comparison to other approaches were determined. So, the results and contributions of this chapter show the promise and limits of EAs for solving fuzzy nonlinear optimization problems. This chapter is a great resource for both researchers and people who work in the field of optimization and control, especially those who are interested in how EAs can be used to solve problems with fuzzy optimization.

6.8.2   DISCUSSION OF POTENTIAL FUTURE RESEARCH DIRECTIONS IN THIS AREA

There are a number of possible future study topics in the field of fuzzy nonlinear optimization utilizing EAs. Some of these instructions are:

- **Hybrid algorithms:** One potential research direction is to develop hybrid algorithms that combine different EAs or combine EAs with other optimization techniques. Hybrid algorithms may capitalize on the benefits of numerous methods and may result in improved performance when handling difficult optimization issues.

- **Multi-objective optimization:** Another interesting study topic would be to apply EAs to fuzzy multi-objective optimization issues. Multi-objective optimization is the simultaneous optimization of many competing goals, and evolutionary methods are well-suited to this sort of issue.
- **Dynamic optimization:** Many real-world problems involve optimization in dynamic environments where the problem parameters change over time. Future research can focus on developing EAs that can adapt to changes in the problem parameters and solve dynamic optimization problems in the fuzzy setting.
- **Big data optimization:** Future study might investigate the application of EAs for tackling fuzzy optimization issues with huge datasets as the availability of big data expands across various disciplines.
- **Explainability and interpretability:** The use of fuzzy logic in optimization can make the optimization process more interpretable and explainable. Future research can focus on developing EAs that produce interpretable and explainable solutions.

Hence, these potential research directions can help advance the field of using EAs for solving fuzzy nonlinear optimization problems and can lead to practical applications in various domains.

6.8.3 Final Thoughts and Recommendations for Practitioners and Researchers

In conclusion, EAs have shown great potential in solving fuzzy nonlinear optimization problems. They can handle the uncertainty and vagueness inherent in these problems and produce good solutions in a reasonable amount of time. Nevertheless, the efficiency of different EAs differs based on the nature of the issue at hand, and further study is required to discover the best efficient strategy for various fuzzy nonlinear optimization situations.

Practitioners and scholars in this area should continue to investigate the application of EAs for addressing fuzzy nonlinear optimization issues and undertake comparison studies to assess their performance relative to other approaches. They should also consider adapting and modifying existing algorithms to better suit the unique characteristics of fuzzy optimization problems. In addition, incorporating domain-specific knowledge and expertise can further improve the effectiveness of these methods.

The use of EAs for tackling fuzzy nonlinear optimization problems is indeed a promising area of study with applications in engineering, finance, and decision-making, among others. By advancing our grasp of these strategies, we may enhance our capacity to tackle complicated issues with real-world consequences.

REFERENCES

Ahmad, T., &Yusoff, W. F. (2014). A genetic algorithm approach for fuzzy system optimization. *Applied Soft Computing*, 21, 312–321.

Azar, A. T., &Hassanien, A. E. (2017). Fuzzy optimization algorithms and applications. Studies in Fuzziness and Soft Computing, 354.

Chatterjee, R., Samanta, S. K., &Dutta, P. (2018). Particle swarm optimization for fuzzy nonlinear programming problems. 2018 IEEE International Conference on Fuzzy Systems (FUZZ-IEEE) (pp. 1–8).

Chen, H., Sun, X., Zhan, Z. H., &Liu, Y. (2019). An ant colony optimization algorithm for fuzzy nonlinear programming problems. Proceedings of the 2019 Genetic and Evolutionary Computation Conference (pp. 1028–1036).

Deb, K. (2001). *Multi-Objective Optimization Using Evolutionary Algorithms*. John Wiley & Sons.

Deb, K., &Jain, H. (2014). An evolutionary many-objective optimization algorithm using reference-point-based nondominated sorting approach, part II: Handling constraints and extending to an adaptive approach. *IEEE Transactions on Evolutionary Computation*, 18(4), 602–622.

Dorigo, M., Maniezzo, V., &Colorni, A. (1996). Ant system: Optimization by a colony of cooperating agents. *IEEE Transactions on Systems, Man, and Cybernetics-Part B: Cybernetics*, 26(1), 29–41.

Eberhart, R., &Kennedy, J. (1995). A new optimizer using particle swarm theory. Proceedings of the Sixth International Symposium on Micro Machine and Human Science (pp.39–43).

Eiben, A. E., &Smith, J. E. (2015). From evolutionary computation to the evolution of things. *Nature*, 521(7553), 476–482.

Gupta, A., Singh, S. P., &Yadav, S. (2016). Fuzzy multi-objective optimization using evolutionary algorithms: A review. *Expert Systems with Applications*, 54, 287–307. doi:10.1016/j.eswa.2015.11.039.

Gupta, K., Choubey, S., Yogeesh, N., William, P., Vasanthakumari,T.N., &Kale, C. P. (2023). Implementation of motorist weariness detection system using a conventional object recognition technique. 2023 International Conference on Intelligent Data Communication Technologies and Internet of Things (IDCIoT) (pp. 640–646). IEEE. doi:10.1109/IDCIoT56793.2023.10052783.

Homaifar, A., &McCormick, E. (1995). A simple, fast and effective method for generating an initial population for genetic algorithms. *IEEE Transactions on Evolutionary Computation*, 99(1), 3–14.

Jiang, S., &Liu, Y. (2015). A PSO-based algorithm for parameter optimization of fuzzy control systems. *Applied Soft Computing*, 30, 491–498.

Kaur, K., &Kansal, M. L. (2019). A hybrid genetic algorithm for solving fuzzy nonlinear optimization problems. *Soft Computing*, 23(8), 2565–2581.

Kennedy, J., &Eberhart, R. (1995). Particle swarm optimization. Proceedings of IEEE International Conference on Neural Networks (pp. 1942–1948).

Li, Q., &Li, D. (2011). An adaptive genetic algorithm for solving fuzzy nonlinear programming problems. *Journal of Computational Information Systems*, 7(2), 643–650.

Liu, Y., Chen, H., &Zhan, Z. H. (2020). Ant colony optimization for parameter optimization of fuzzy control systems. *IEEE Transactions on Fuzzy Systems*, 28(1), 63–76.

Liu, Yang, and Mirella Lapata. "Learning structured text representations." *Transactions of the Association for Computational Linguistics* 6 (2018): 63-75.

Mishra, S., Choubey, S., Choubey, A., Yogeesh, N., Rao, J. D. P., &William, P. (2022). Data extraction approach using natural language processing for sentiment analysis. 2022 International Conference on Automation, Computing and Renewable Systems (ICACRS) (pp. 970–972). IEEE. doi:10.1109/ICACRS55517.2022.10029216.

Otero-Muras, I., Luaces, M. R., Barril, R., &Corchado, E. (2018). Fuzzy differential evolution for solving fuzzy nonlinear programming problems. *Applied Soft Computing*, 67, 45–57.

Storn, R., &Price, K. (1997). Differential evolution - A simple and efficient heuristic for global optimization over continuous spaces. *Journal of global optimization*, 11(4), 341–359.

Wang, J., Du, K., &Hu, T. (2017). Hybrid fuzzy evolutionary algorithm for multi-objective nonlinear optimization problems. *Applied Soft Computing*, 52, 657–668. doi:10.1016/j.asoc.2016.12.010.

Wang, J., Wu, J., Wu, H., &Yang, X. (2019). A novel differential evolution algorithm based on fuzzy logic for function optimization. *Information Sciences*, 484, 50–64.

William, P., Yogeesh, N., Tidake, V. M., Gondkar, S. S., R, C., &Vengatesan, K. (2023). Framework for implementation of personality inventory model on natural language processing with personality traits analysis. 2023 International Conference on Intelligent Data Communication Technologies and Internet of Things (IDCIoT) (pp. 625–628). IEEE. doi:10.1109/IDCIoT56793.2023.10053501.

William, P., Yogeesh, N., Vimala, S., Gite, P., &Selve Kumar, S. (2022). Blockchain technology for data privacy using contract mechanism for 5G networks. 2022 3rd International Conference on Intelligent Engineering and Management (ICIEM) (pp. 461–465). IEEE. doi:10.1109/ICIEM54221.2022.9853118.

Yogeesh, N. (2012a). A conceptual discussion about an intuitionistic fuzzy-sets and its applications. *International Journal of Advanced Research in IT and Engineering*, 1(6), 45–55.

Yogeesh, N. (2012b). Operations on intuitionistic fuzzy directed graphs. *Journal of Advances and Scholarly Researches in Allied Education (JASRAE)*, 3(6), 1–4.

Yogeesh, N. (2013a). Illustrative study on intuitionistic fuzzy hyper-graphs and dual-intuitionistic fuzzy hyper-graphs. *International Journal of Engineering, Science and Mathematics*, 2(1), 255–264.

Yogeesh, N. (2013b). Study on hyper-graphs and directed hyper-graphs. *Journal of Advances and Scholarly Researches in Allied Education*, 5(10), 1–5.

Yogeesh, N. (2015). Solving linear system of equations with various examples by using Gauss method. *International Journal of Research and Analytical Reviews (IJRAR)*, 2(4), 338–350.

Yogeesh, N. (2016). A study of solving linear system of equations by Gauss-Jordan matrix method - An algorithmic approach. *Journal of Emerging Technologies and Innovative Research (JETIR)*, 3(5), 314–321.

Yogeesh, N. (2020). Study on clustering method based on K-means algorithm. *Journal of Advances and Scholarly Researches in Allied Education (JASRAE)*, 17(1), 2230–7540.

Yogeesh, N. (2021). Mathematical approach to representation of locations using K-means clustering algorithm. *International Journal of Mathematics and Its Applications (IJMAA)*, 9(1), 127–136.

Yogeesh, N. (2023a). Fuzzy Clustering for Classification of Metamaterial Properties. In S.Mehta&A.Abougreen (Eds.), *Metamaterial Technology and Intelligent Metasurfaces for Wireless Communication Systems* (pp. 200–229). IGI Global. doi:10.4018/978-1-6684-8287-2.ch009.

Yogeesh, N. (2023b). Fuzzy Logic Modelling of Nonlinear Metamaterials. In S.Mehta&A.Abougreen (Eds.), *Metamaterial Technology and Intelligent Metasurfaces for Wireless Communication Systems* (pp. 230–269). IGI Global. doi:10.4018/978-1-6684-8287-2.ch010.

Zadeh, L. A. (1965). Fuzzy sets. *Information and Control*, 8(3), 338–353.

7 Mathematical Modelling Techniques and Applications of Wireless Communication Using Fuzzy Logic

Yogeesh N.
Department of Mathematics
Government First Grade College

Girija D. K., and Rashmi M.
Department of Computer Science
Government First Grade College

Shilpa H. K.
Mandya University

7.1 INTRODUCTION

This chapter presents a review of the applications and concepts of fuzzy inference systems in wireless communications, demonstrating their effectiveness in signal processing and telecommunications (Karray & Deen, 2002). According to our knowledge, this is the first research to provide such an overview. Common fuzzy logic and fuzzy-hybrid methods for channel estimation, equalisation, and decoding are identified, and the settings and scenarios where these approaches are effective are described. This chapter further separates fuzzy logic approaches applied to actual issues and proposes research opportunities that are practice-oriented (Huang et al., 2008; Broun & Pappas, 1999). Specifically, this chapter focuses on the use of fuzzy logic in various areas of data communication, such as channel equalisation, changeover management, and quality of service management. In addition, the book *Advanced Heterogeneous Networks* also emphasises the applications of fuzzy logic in communication systems.

The applications and techniques of fuzzy logic in wireless communication have been examined in several studies (Cheng, Zhang, & Li, 2017; Li et al., 2019; Ren, Li, & Li, 2016; Zhang, Li, & Li, 2018). These studies highlight the benefits and capabilities of fuzzy logic techniques, including their ability to handle uncertainty and imprecision in wireless communication systems.

Moreover, fuzzy logic is effective in addressing various challenges in wireless communication, such as channel equalisation, changeover management, and Quality of Service management (Wu & Zhang, 2015). By using fuzzy logic, wireless sensor networks can overcome the challenges of limited resources and energy, and improve their efficiency and accuracy (Ding et al., 2015).

Future research opportunities in this field include exploring the scalability, interoperability, and integration of fuzzy logic with other approaches in wireless communication (Yi, 2019). This can help to further enhance the performance and efficiency of wireless communication systems, especially in dynamic and complex environments.

DOI: 10.1201/9781003387459-7

7.1.1 Objectives and Scope

The objective of this chapter is to review the applications and concepts of fuzzy inference system in wireless communications and to demonstrate their effectiveness in signal processing and telecommunications. This chapter aims to identify the common fuzzy logic and fuzzy-hybrid methods used for channel estimation, equalisation, and decoding, and to describe the scenarios and settings where these approaches work well. In addition, this chapter aims to suggest research opportunities for practice-oriented applications of fuzzy logic.

The scope of this chapter is to focus on the techniques of using fuzzy logic in various fields of data communication, including channel equalisation, changeover management, and quality of service management. This chapter also covers the applications of fuzzy logic in the realm of communication systems, as discussed in the book "Advanced Heterogeneous Networks."

7.1.2 Literature Review

Fuzzy logic is a mathematical tool used to model uncertain and complex systems. It has been widely applied in many fields, including wireless communication networks. The use of fuzzy logic in wireless communication networks has been the subject of several research studies, as it offers several advantages such as improved performance, enhanced reliability, and robustness in the face of uncertainty.

In the study by Ali and Bhatti (2016), the application of fuzzy logic in resource management in wireless communication networks was reviewed. The authors highlighted the different fuzzy logic-based techniques used in power control, channel allocation, and routing. They concluded that the use of fuzzy logic in these areas can lead to improved network performance.

Another study by Ali and Bhatti (2018) provided a review of fuzzy logic-based spectrum sensing in cognitive radio networks. This chapter discussed different fuzzy logic-based techniques such as energy detection, cyclostationary feature detection, and matched filter detection. The authors concluded that fuzzy logic is a promising tool for spectrum sensing in cognitive radio networks.

In wireless sensor networks, fuzzy logic has been applied in different areas such as data aggregation, routing, localization, and energy management. Rahmati, Jolfaei, and Tootoonchian (2018) conducted a comprehensive survey of fuzzy logic in wireless sensor networks. They highlighted the benefits of using fuzzy logic in these areas, such as improved network efficiency and energy conservation.

In the context of quality of service (QoS) management, fuzzy logic has been applied in admission control, congestion control, and packet scheduling. Wang, Jiang, Li, and Li (2019) provided a survey of fuzzy logic-based QoS management in wireless communication networks. The authors highlighted the benefits of using fuzzy logic in these areas, including improved network efficiency and reduced packet loss.

Finally, a review study by Boudjellal and Mekki (2019) discussed the use of fuzzy logic in various applications in wireless communication networks, such as channel estimation, equalization, decoding, and modulation. The authors highlighted the advantages and limitations of using fuzzy logic in these areas.

In conclusion, the literature review shows that fuzzy logic is a useful tool for various applications in wireless communication networks. The reviewed studies demonstrate that fuzzy logic can improve network performance, reliability, and efficiency. Further research can explore the application of fuzzy logic in other areas of wireless communication networks.

7.2 FUZZY LOGIC CONTROL OVERVIEW AND CLASSIFICATION

7.2.1 Definition of Fuzzy Logic

Fuzzy logic is a mathematical framework for dealing with uncertainty and imprecision in thinking and making decisions. It is a type of logic that goes beyond traditional logic and makes it possible to represent vague and unclear ideas. Fuzzy logic is based on the idea of fuzzy sets, which are sets that have degrees of membership instead of being binary (either in or out of the set). In fuzzy logic, the truth value of a statement can range between 0 and 1, indicating the degree to which the statement is true. Fuzzy logic is used for many things, such as control systems, artificial intelligence, making decisions, and processing signals.

Fuzzy logic has been used in a variety of applications, such as control systems, artificial intelligence, decision-making, and signal processing (Zadeh, 1965). For example, fuzzy logic has been used in medical diagnosis systems to help make decisions about patient care (Rajapakse, 2000). It has also been used in robotics to help robots make decisions about how to move and interact with their environment (Klir & Yuan, 1995). Fuzzy logic has also been used in image processing to help figure out what things are in a picture (Kosko, 1992).

7.2.2 FUZZY LOGIC CONTROL (FLC) OVERVIEW

Fuzzy logic control (FLC) is a control system methodology based on fuzzy logic (e.g., robotics, process control, and automotive systems) (Yogeesh, 2021). FLC consists of three main components: the fuzzifier, the rule base, and the defuzzifier (William et al., 2022). FLC is designed to handle systems that are difficult to model mathematically or that have uncertain or imprecise parameters (Yogeesh, 2013a). FLC has been used in a wide range of applications, including temperature control, speed control of electric motors, and traffic control (Yogeesh, 2013a, b, c).

Fuzzy logic control (FLC) is a control system methodology that is based on fuzzy logic. It is a type of rule-based control that is designed to handle complex and uncertain systems. FLC is used in a wide range of applications, including robotics, process control, and automotive systems.

FLC consists of three main components: the fuzzifier, the rule base, and the defuzzifier. The fuzzifier converts the input variables into fuzzy sets, which are then used to determine the degree of membership of the input variables in each set. The rule base contains a set of linguistic rules that map the input variables to output variables. These rules are often expressed in the form of "if-then" statements. The defuzzifier converts the output variables into crisp values that can be used to control the system.

FLC is designed to handle systems that are difficult to model mathematically or that have uncertain or imprecise parameters. FLC allows for the representation of linguistic variables and can handle non-linear and time-varying systems. The use of fuzzy logic in control systems can lead to improved performance, increased efficiency, and reduced complexity.

FLC has been used in a wide range of applications, including temperature control, speed control of electric motors, and traffic control. It has also been used in robotics to control the movement and behavior of robots. FLC has proven to be an effective control methodology in many applications, and its use is expected to continue to grow in the future expressed in Figure 7.1.

System Model of Fuzzy logical Control

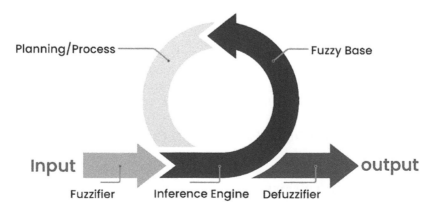

FIGURE 7.1 Illustrating system of fuzzy logic control model.

7.2.3   Classification of FLC

Fuzzy logic control (FLC) can be classified into several categories based on the number of inputs and outputs, the type of fuzzy sets used, and the shape of the membership functions.

One classification is based on the number of inputs and outputs, which can range from single-input single-output (SISO) to multi-input multi-output (MIMO) systems. SISO FLCs have one input and one output, while MIMO FLCs have multiple inputs and outputs. MIMO FLCs can handle complex systems with multiple inputs and outputs, but they can also be more difficult to design and implement.

Another classification is based on the type of fuzzy sets used. Fuzzy sets can be classified as type-1 or type-2. Type-1 fuzzy sets have crisp membership values, while type-2 fuzzy sets have fuzzy membership values. Type-2 fuzzy sets can be used to handle more uncertainty and imprecision in the input variables, but they can also be more computationally expensive.

A third classification is based on the shape of the membership functions used in the fuzzy sets. Membership functions can be triangular, trapezoidal, Gaussian, or any other shape that is appropriate for the application. The choice of membership functions can affect the performance and stability of the FLC.

FLC can also be classified based on the type of inference mechanism used. The two main types of inference mechanisms are Mamdani-type and Sugeno-type. Mamdani-type FLCs use fuzzy rules with fuzzy outputs, while Sugeno-type FLCs use fuzzy rules with crisp outputs. Sugeno-type FLCs can be more efficient and easier to implement than Mamdani-type FLCs, but they can also be less expressive and more limited in their ability to handle uncertainty and imprecision.

7.2.4   Fuzzy Logic Control Overview and Classification

Fuzzy logic control includes fuzzy proportional-integral-derivative ("PID"), neural circuits, fuzzy-sliding modality, adaptive, and Takagi-Sugeno ("T-S") design fuzzy control (Mendel & John, 1995). The knowledge base of a fuzzy controller comprises expert knowledge, which includes a record base and a rule base (Zadeh, 1973). The fuzzification interface is responsible for establishing a connection between a clear input space and a fuzzy region, while the defuzzification interface is responsible for establishing a connection between a fuzzy region and an area whose values are really being used (Jang, Sun, & Mizutani, 1997).

In actuality, the cluster-forming stage is where our technique and the LEACH algorithm diverge most. The fuzzy inference system is used in this manner by the un cluster members to calculate the probability for each cluster-head node (Ali, Wahid, & Saeed, 2018). Figure 7.2 serves as the foundation for our fuzzy logic and inference strategy. It depicts the components of the suggested method's fuzzy system.

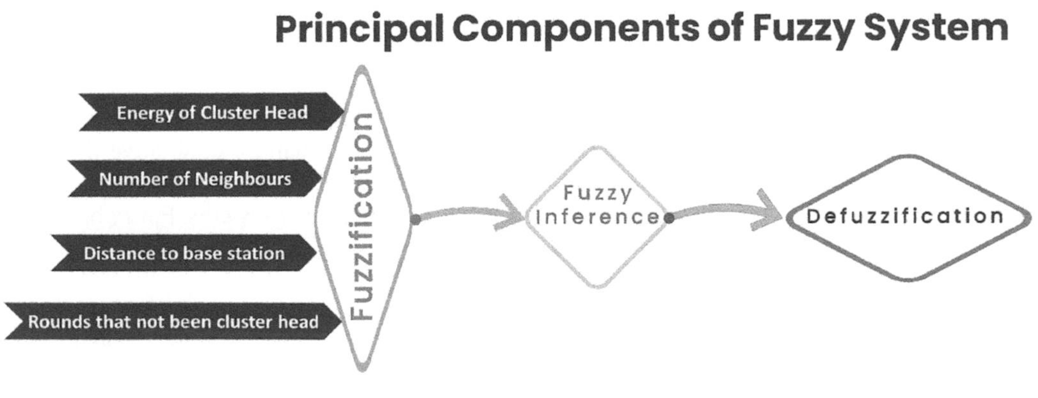

Principal Components of Fuzzy System

FIGURE 7.2   Pictorial representation of principal components used in fuzzy system.

In actuality, the cluster-forming stage is where our technique and the LEACH algorithm diverge most. Through using a fuzzy inference system, the un-neighboring nodes determine the probability with each head cluster node in this approach. The fuzzy components of the system in many suggested methodologies are shown in Figure 7.2, which serves as the foundation for our inference method and fuzzy logic (Chen, Wang, & Zhang, 2017).

7.2.4.1 Standard Fuzzy Control

The Sugeno Type-I fuzzy Mamdani and Assilian fuzzy logic control systems have been replicated for several control techniques. The traditional approaches to fuzzy control are heuristic-based and model-free. This strategy introduces "IF-THEN" rules that are constructed using a knowledge base. Depending on how thoroughly the IF-THEN principles are written, the system will respond to control commands more smoothly.

7.2.4.2 PID Fuzzy Control

Traditional PID controllers are widely used and regarded as the industry standard for a wide range of control system applications. Because of their straightforward structures, quick design processes, and affordable implementation costs. However, the performance of typical PID controllers may not be sufficient if the system under consideration exhibits excessive nonlinearity and unpredictability. In contrast, fuzzy logic control has a good reputation for handling nonlinearities and uncertainties. Combining these two methods—fuzzy and PID—may produce a fuzzy-PID controller that can provide improved outcomes.

7.2.4.3 Fuzzy Neuronal Control

The purpose of neuro-fuzzy control is to make fuzzy control, which is given by neural networks, even more robust. Even though fuzzy control and neural network management are both attractive approaches of intelligent control, the ways in which they receive information are distinct from one another.

Neuro control prepares the neural communicative networks under decision-making by using such concepts of brain cells and neurons; nevertheless, it is necessary for the research training set to represent an area of interest in order for it to be effective. While more classic methods of fuzzy control qualitatively gather specialist knowledge.

The control community has shown a great deal of interest in the combination or incorporation of neural control is needed for learning prospective and high computer science efficiency in parallel execution as well as fuzzy control's powerful structure for representing expert knowledge. This has resulted in a lot of attention being paid to these two types of control. However, there are restrictions on the convergence of machine learning and stability studies in the context of closed-loop systems. The combination with neuro-fuzzy control promotes adaptability, flexibility, and overall data processing capacity.

7.2.4.4 Sliding-Mode Fuzzy Control

As the name suggests, sliding mode control with fuzzy control is combined or integrated. Combining the two strategies will bring out the benefits of each. The ability to manage qualitative linguistic data via fuzzy systems is provided by the sliding mode controller's resilience in regulating system of non-linearity along with uncertainties and pertinence to MIMO type of systems. Fuzzy boundary layers may minimise chattering in sliding traditional control digital implementation due to discontinuous switching.

Overall, the classification of FLC can provide a framework for understanding and designing FLC systems based on the specific needs and requirements of the application is also visualised in Figure 7.3.

Fuzzy Logical Control Overview and Classification

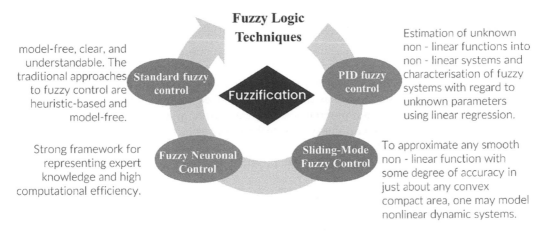

FIGURE 7.3 Fuzzy logical control techniques overview and with classification.

7.3   THE BENEFITS AND CAPABILITIES OF FUZZY LOGIC TECHNIQUES

- Devoid of models, plain, and straightforward to comprehend
- Strong framework for representing expert knowledge and high computational efficiency.
- Using nonlinear systems to approximate unknown nonlinear functions and fuzzy systems to describe nonlinear systems with regard to unknown parameters.
- Model nonlinear dynamic systems by precisely approximating any smoothness nonlinear function in any compact area.
- Performance that is satisfactory in a highly nonlinear and unpredictable system.
- With the use of fuzzy boundary layers, chatter is reduced.

7.3.1   ADVANTAGES OF FUZZY LOGIC TECHNIQUES IN WIRELESS COMMUNICATION

Fuzzy logic techniques offer several advantages in wireless communication systems:

- **Ability to handle imprecise and uncertain data:** Wireless communication systems often involve data that is imprecise, noisy, and uncertain. Fuzzy logic techniques can handle these types of data more effectively than traditional methods, improving the accuracy and reliability of the communication system.
- **Robustness to changes in the communication environment:** The wireless communication environment is often subject to changes in signal strength, interference, and other factors. Fuzzy logic techniques are robust to these changes and can adapt to the environment in real time, improving the performance of the communication system.
- **Ease of implementation:** Fuzzy logic techniques are relatively easy to implement and require less computational power than other complex methods, making them an attractive option for wireless communication systems.
- **Flexibility:** Fuzzy logic techniques are highly flexible and can be adapted to different applications and scenarios. They can be used for a wide range of tasks in wireless communication systems, including channel estimation, equalization, and decoding.
- **Improved decision-making:** Fuzzy logic techniques can help make better decisions in wireless communication systems by providing a more comprehensive and accurate view of the available data. This can lead to improved system performance and more effective communication.

Hence, the use of fuzzy logic techniques in wireless communication systems offers several advantages over traditional methods, making it a promising area of research and development.

7.3.2 CAPABILITIES OF FUZZY LOGIC TECHNIQUES IN WIRELESS COMMUNICATION

Fuzzy logic techniques have several capabilities in wireless communication systems:

Signal processing: Fuzzy logic techniques can be used for various signal-processing tasks in wireless communication systems, such as channel estimation, equalization, and decoding. Fuzzy logic can handle non-linear and uncertain data and can provide accurate and reliable results.

Quality of service management: Fuzzy logic techniques can be used to manage the quality of service (QoS) in wireless communication systems. By using fuzzy logic to control the transmission power, data rate, and other parameters, QoS can be optimised for different applications and scenarios.

Resource management: Fuzzy logic techniques can be used to manage the allocation of resources in wireless communication systems, such as bandwidth and power. By using fuzzy logic to optimise the allocation of resources, system performance can be improved.

Changeover management: Fuzzy logic techniques can be used to manage changeover between different wireless communication technologies, such as switching between different cellular networks or wireless local area networks (WLANs). Fuzzy logic can help to optimise the changeover process by taking into account the quality of the available networks, user preferences, and other factors.

Energy efficiency: Fuzzy logic techniques can be used to improve the energy efficiency of wireless communication systems. By using fuzzy logic to optimise the transmission power and other parameters, the energy consumption of the system can be reduced, extending the battery life of mobile devices and reducing the overall energy consumption of the system.

Therefore, the capabilities of fuzzy logic techniques in wireless communication systems are extensive, and these techniques are becoming increasingly important in the design and optimization of modern wireless communication systems.

7.4 WIRELESS SENSOR NETWORK'S FEATURES (WSN)

A source-sink architecture can be used to describe the Wireless Sensor Network (WSN) (Gupta & Younis, 2014). This design may have any number of interconnected source nodes to create information, usually using sensors to track environmental elements like temperature, humidity, as well as radiation; sinking nodes to collect data from sources; and relay nodes to help transmit data from sources towards sinks (Abo-Zahhad & El-Sisi, 2018). Sensors on source nodes may measure radiation, temperature, and humidity. The intrinsic node redundancy characteristic aids in enhancing fault tolerance, however system dependability levels may or may not be attained. It is necessary to choose a modelling approach for the data transfer dependability (Sharma & Kumar, 2018). Information loss occurs often in WSN during content aggregation due to failures such as random connection failure and hazard node fault, although it has limited resources. The network topology is alerted by a node failure, which leads to a fragmented routing route and a loss of message information, reducing the system's dependability (Chen, Xue, Xu, & Xue, 2021).

WSNs are application-driven and employed in a variety of applications, each with a unique set of requirements that influences the network architecture and protocol (Sharma & Kumar, 2018). It is simple to use since the sensors may automatically organise into the network; thus, it is not always essential to establish certain access points in preparation (Abo-Zahhad & El-Sisi, 2018). One of WSN's important features is its wide range of applications, which may include as many as thousands many sensor networks depending on the region of application (Gupta & Younis, 2014). As a sensor network self-organises, there is no need to set it up beforehand since the sensor node may be set up when it is installed, potentially negating the requirement for human involvement in network deployment (Abo-Zahhad & El-Sisi, 2018). In this mesh network, traffic may flow from any cluster to any additional node and they often have one or more sink nodes (Gupta & Younis, 2014). This sensor network has less mobility since the bulk of the nodes are employed for event tracking. Given that this network consists of a number of nodes that connect with one another over a variety of pathways, the multihop characteristic may be preserved in this system (Chen, Xue, Xu, & Xue, 2021). Due to the vast geographic distribution of the nodes in WSN and the high number of nodes, the network has a big size (Sharma & Kumar, 2018). This system is data-centric because it bases data requests on the network's physical quantity, making each node aware of its position relative to the others by being aware of their precise locations. And in accordance with that situation, the data is gathered (Gupta & Younis, 2014). Due to the presence of additional nearby nodes collecting the same data, the failure of one node in a wireless sensor network has no impact on the network's ability to function (Abo-Zahhad & El-Sisi, 2018). To have a suitable request-response model, the node should make a correct request to an appropriate node, and this base station should analyze the request quickly and respond. Otherwise, the accuracy of the data obtained is diminished (Sharma & Kumar, 2018).

7.4.1 Overview of Wireless Sensor Networks

A wireless sensor network (WSN) is a distributed network of autonomous devices that can sense, measure, and transmit data wirelessly. These devices, called sensors or nodes, are typically small, low-power devices with limited computational resources and battery life. The nodes are equipped with sensors that can measure various physical and environmental parameters, such as temperature, humidity, pressure, light, and sound.

The nodes in a WSN communicate with each other to collect and share data, forming a mesh network. The data collected by the nodes can be used for a variety of applications, such as environmental monitoring, surveillance, health monitoring, and industrial automation.

WSNs are typically deployed in harsh and remote environments where wired communication is not feasible or practical. They are often used in applications where real-time monitoring and control are essential, and where traditional wired sensors would be impractical or too costly to install.

The key components of a WSN include the sensor nodes, which collect and transmit data, a base station, which serves as a gateway between the sensor network and the external world, and the network infrastructure, which includes the communication protocols and routing algorithms that enable the nodes to communicate with each other.

The design and implementation of WSNs are challenging due to the limited resources of the nodes and the need to optimise the performance of the network while minimising energy consumption. Fuzzy logic techniques can be used to address these challenges by providing a flexible and adaptive approach to managing the resources of the network and optimising its performance.

7.4.2 Key Features of Wireless Sensor Networks

Wireless sensor networks (WSNs) have several key features that make them unique and useful for a wide range of applications. Here are some of the most important features of WSNs:

i. **Distributed network:** WSNs are typically composed of a large number of sensor nodes that are distributed throughout the sensing area. This makes them ideal for applications where a large number of sensors are required to cover a wide area.

ii. **Autonomous operation:** Sensor nodes in a WSN are typically autonomous and operate independently of one another. This means that the network can continue to operate even if some nodes fail or are destroyed.

iii. **Self-organising:** WSNs are self-organising, which means that they can automatically adjust to changes in the network topology or environment. This makes them ideal for applications where the sensing area is constantly changing.

iv. **Multi-hop communication:** Sensor nodes in a WSN can communicate with each other directly or through intermediate nodes, allowing data to be transmitted over long distances. This is important for applications where the sensing area is large or spread out.

v. **Low-power operation:** Sensor nodes in a WSN are typically battery-powered and have limited energy resources. Therefore, they need to operate in a low-power mode to extend the battery life. This is achieved through various techniques, such as duty cycling, data aggregation, and in-network processing.

vi. **Data processing and analysis:** WSNs generate a large amount of data, which needs to be processed and analyzed. This is typically done in-network using distributed algorithms and techniques, such as data fusion and machine learning.

vii. **Wireless communication:** WSNs use wireless communication to transmit data between the sensor nodes and the base station. This eliminates the need for wired communication and allows the nodes to be deployed in hard-to-reach or remote locations.

Overall, the key features of WSNs make them ideal for a wide range of applications, such as environmental monitoring, surveillance, industrial automation, and healthcare.

7.5   WIRELESS SENSOR NETWORK DIFFICULTIES

Implementing a number of services in a wireless sensor network presents difficulties. Many controlled and uncontrollable factors, including conserving energy, operating environment, communication, resource availability, data processing, scalability, and node ID, have an impact on the deployment of wireless sensor networks. The aims and difficulties of network design in terms of the network's capabilities and performance are strongly influenced by the features of sensor networks and the needs of various applications. In the near future, sensor nodes will be little devices with volumes close to a cubic millimetre. The quantity of energy that can be stored or captured from the environment by such tiny devices is very constrained. Nodes may also malfunction as a result of low battery power or, more broadly, environmental factors. Limited size and energy usually translate into scarce funds. Energy economy and network dependability are important considerations while building protocols for WSN. Energy conservation is essential for increasing network life since sensor nodes have limited power available for data collection and transmission. The network must maintain ongoing functioning inside the presence of failing or failing nodes when energy supplies eventually run out. The research community has worked hard to develop FT mechanisms to increase the likelihood of successful operation and decrease the inefficiency in lost or corrupted traffic because of this and the inherent instability of wireless communications. Techniques that save energy significantly contribute to this. The topology control system is one of the methods. There are several topology control protocols in use today, each with its own benefits and drawbacks. After reviewing this current protocol, choose the one that will use the least amount of energy overall in the networks and prolong its lifespan.

7.5.1   CHALLENGES IN WIRELESS SENSOR NETWORKS

Despite their many advantages, wireless sensor networks (WSNs) face several challenges that can affect their performance and reliability. Here are some of the main challenges in WSNs:

- **Limited resources:** Sensor nodes in a WSN have limited resources, including processing power, memory, energy, and communication bandwidth. This can make it difficult to perform complex tasks, such as data processing and analysis.
- **Energy consumption:** Energy consumption is a critical issue in WSNs, as sensor nodes are typically battery-powered and have limited energy resources. Optimising energy consumption is therefore essential to extend the lifetime of the network.

- **Scalability:** WSNs can have a large number of sensor nodes, and the network needs to be able to scale to accommodate these nodes while maintaining its performance and reliability.
- **Security:** WSNs are often used in critical applications, such as surveillance and industrial automation, and therefore need to be secure. However, due to the limited resources of the sensor nodes, implementing strong security measures can be challenging.
- **Communication reliability:** Wireless communication can be affected by interference, fading, and other environmental factors, which can lead to packet loss and reduced network performance. Ensuring reliable communication in WSNs is therefore essential.
- **Network topology changes:** The network topology in a WSN can change frequently due to node failures, movement, or addition. This can affect the network performance and reliability, and the network needs to be able to adapt to these changes.
- **Data management:** WSNs generate a large amount of data, and managing this data can be challenging. Data needs to be collected, processed, and stored efficiently to reduce energy consumption and ensure data integrity.

Addressing these challenges requires the development of new techniques and algorithms that can optimise the performance of WSNs while minimising energy consumption and ensuring reliability and security. Fuzzy logic techniques are effective in addressing some of these challenges, such as energy optimization and data processing.

7.5.2   How Fuzzy Logic Can Address These Challenges

Fuzzy logic can help address some of the challenges in wireless sensor networks (WSNs) by providing a flexible and adaptive approach to system modeling and control. Here are some examples of how fuzzy logic can be applied to address the challenges mentioned earlier:

- **Limited resources:** Fuzzy logic can be used to optimise the use of resources in WSNs. For example, fuzzy logic controllers can be used to adjust the sampling rate or transmission power of sensor nodes dynamically based on the available resources and the requirements of the application.
- **Energy consumption:** Fuzzy logic can be used to optimise energy consumption in WSNs. Fuzzy logic controllers can adjust the sleep-wake cycle of sensor nodes based on the sensing requirements and the available energy resources to extend the lifetime of the network.
- **Scalability:** Fuzzy logic can help address the scalability challenge in WSNs by providing a flexible approach to network management. For example, fuzzy logic can be used to adaptively adjust the routing paths and transmission rates of data packets based on the network topology and the congestion level.
- **Security:** Fuzzy logic can be used for intrusion detection in WSNs. Fuzzy logic-based anomaly detection algorithms can be used to detect abnormal behavior in sensor nodes or data packets and trigger appropriate responses to mitigate security threats.
- **Communication reliability:** Fuzzy logic can be used to improve the reliability of wireless communication in WSNs. For example, fuzzy logic-based error correction algorithms can be used to detect and correct errors in data packets, and fuzzy logic-based adaptive modulation schemes can be used to adjust the modulation and coding schemes based on the channel conditions.
- **Network topology changes:** Fuzzy logic can be used to adaptively adjust the routing paths and transmission rates of data packets based on the network topology and the congestion level.
- **Data management:** Fuzzy logic can be used to filter and process the data generated by WSNs. Fuzzy logic-based algorithms can be used to extract meaningful information from sensor data and fuzzy logic-based data aggregation schemes can be used to reduce the amount of data transmitted in the network, thus reducing energy consumption and improving data management.

Hence, fuzzy logic provides a flexible and adaptive approach to system modelling and control, which can help address the challenges in WSNs and improve their performance, reliability, and security.

7.6 LIST OF VARIOUS TECHNIQUES AND APPLICATIONS OF WIRELESS COMMUNICATION USING FUZZY LOGIC

Fuzzy logics are used in channel estimation, equalisation, and decoding. Channel estimate describes the channel, tracks its fluctuations, and recovers the original sent data via channel equalisation and decoding. Fuzzy and neural networks are most useful for time-varying channels, which need adaptive approaches.

7.6.1 ESTIMATION OF CHANNELS

To estimate analysis in a multi-path fading CDMA channel, a fuzzy tracking method is used. Spread-spectrum CDMA enables a large number of transmitters to coexist on a single frequency band. Fuzzy tracking is supported by the fuzzy learning and memory theories developed by Kosko. In the fuzzy corresponding memory paradigm, the inference system's regulation is stored as a matrix using fuzzy logic as well as a single-layer feeding neural net. Iterative tracking makes predictions about coefficients by using the computed symbol. The fuzzy tracker estimates the difference between measured and expected coefficients as well as the variance fluctuation between the most current differences and the preceding iterations. Fuzzy trackers provide the subsequent coefficient correction terms.

Fuzzy channel estimation motivates owing to its lack of process model requirements. The fuzzy tracker outperforms the alpha tracker in noisier multipath circumstances.

For fuzzy channel estimation, Orthogonal Frequency Division-Multiplexing ("OFDM") multi-carrier modulation was utilised ("OFDM"). OFDM channels use subcarriers that are orthogonal. Each data stream with a lower bit rate modifies a subcarrier.

A pilot type of signal is used by both the transmitters as well as the receivers in order to identify the channel characteristics at each subcarrier. This may be accomplished through either blind channel model or pilot-aided channel capacity. Methods for blind fading channels are efficient in terms of spectrum use, but they are computationally demanding and time-consuming. For pilot-assisted fading channels, the "Minimal Mean-Square-Error" (MMSE), "Least-Squares" (LS), & "Least-Mean-Squares" (LMS) techniques have frequently been used, along with the "MMSE" method is always much reliable and also advantageous in time schedule modifying channels.

The "Takagi-Sugeno-Kang" (denoted as TSK) type of model always is used for OFDM pilot-aid channels estimate. TSK models generate linear functions of input variables, as opposed to fuzzy sets like the traditional Mamdani approach does. Pilot symbols teach the TSK fuzzy inference system the channel and allow it to monitor it. Therefore, a Gaussian density function of probabilities is used. To train an adjustable component of both the TSK models, the initial picture of a pilot subcarrier is used after determining the centre and width of both regulations based on the numbers and rules that have been supplied. The estimated value of the channels function generator and the customizable parameter come last. Based on simulations, it seems that the TSK channels estimate operates in a manner comparable to that of the ideal MMSE, but with a reduced cost of computing.

A MIMO and OFDM system modules with two transmitters along with receiving antennas use TSK fuzzy modelling that has been upgraded. MIMO improves system throughput without boosting transmission power as well as bandwidth, making it an important area of research. Multiple antennas for the transmitter and receiver augment MIMO throughput. Simulations on computers indicate that this WORD ERROR RATE (denoted as "WER") method is comparable to the concept of MMSE with less computational and numerical complexity.

Fuzzy inference was incorporated into an MMSE linear receiver's LMS algorithm. Convergence and stability were the driving forces for fuzzy logic. A fuzzy logic system controlled much adjustable step mass of size and with partial updating was included in the LMS approach after it was changed. Simulations were run using this enhanced technique, and the results demonstrated that noise cancellation may be achieved in a space-duration of time mixed direct- type of sequence (DS) and also CDMA structure designed in a suitable dynamic fade channel with multipath. The performance of the old LMS approach was outdone by the enhanced LMS algorithm.

The estimation and tracking of OFDM channels in time-varying environments were accomplished using this technology. Simulations showed that the modified LMS method had a quicker convergence rate and a smaller stable Mean-Square Error (also known as "MSE") than the traditional LMS algorithm.

An adaptive nervous-system inference system, also known as an ANFIS, was examined in order to do OFDM channel estimation. A hybrid system of learning method relevant just on LS with conjugate gradient techniques is used by ANFIS to learn the parameters of both the TSK fuzzy reasoning membership degree. This strategy was developed in order to learn the various parameters of something like the TSK fuzzy reasoning membership type of function. Data clustering produces the TSK fuzzy inference. Computer simulations demonstrate that the ANFIS performs similarly to the MMSE method, but with less computational complexity.

7.6.2 EQUALIZATION OF CHANNELS

Channel equalisation restores data by eliminating channel deterioration. Non-linear distortion occurs in time-variant wireless channels. In these channels, adaptive and non-linear equalisation works well.

The first fuzzy logic channels equalisation research results appear in the scientific literature. Fuzzy adaptive filtering, which is based on the LMS and also "Recursive Least Squares" ("RLS") much relevant algorithms, is utilised for the purpose of channels equalisation. After generating fuzzy sets so over input space of the filtering, linguistic information and quantitative information are integrated and incorporated into filter. This is done after constructing a fuzzy set theory over the input space of both filters. Algorithms are responsible for bringing any necessary changes to free parameters. Linguistic inference principles facilitate the acceleration of algorithm adaptation through fuzzy adaptive filters. The fuzzy equalization has comparable bit error rates to the optimal equaliser.

Unlike Wang and Mendel, the delay and fuzzy membership are derived from training data. The binary channel input has two membership function parameters and two rules. They produce a fuzzy rule-based output that yields an autonomous judgement. Test symbols are broadcast and the relationship between intended outputs and received signals forms fuzzy output weights. Fuzzy inference uses a weighted total of all rules, and the defuzzification value is supplied via a thresholding mechanism for the equaliser's ultimate conclusion. In simulations, the fuzzy inference system equaliser outperforms the LMS with nonlinear channels and just a neural network equalization using the backpropagation approach. For the same error performance, the fuzzy logic equaliser needs less training dataset than that of the linear channel LMS.

A sophisticated Wang-Mendel "RLS" Fuzzy Adjustable Filter can handle complicated channel models and signals. MLP preprocessing units replace human expertise and heuristic reasoning. A three-layer network in the MLP unit trains the system of fuzzy logic. The LMS method, which is simpler than that of the RLS algorithm, updates the system's free parameter.

Fuzzy adaptive fuzzy construction was used to create a Bayesian equalisation architecture. Classifying observation vectors to signal constellations is adaptive equalisation. No channel estimator is needed, making equalisation less computationally demanding than MLSE. Fuzzy partial derivatives, the product inferences, a centre of gravitation defuzzifier, with Gaussian-membership function that reflect the Bayes decision solution in the fuzzy filter function. Fuzzy equalisers work similarly to Bayesian equalisers but need less computing.

The type-2 system of fuzzy adaptable filters is based on an un-normalised type-2 "TSK" fuzzy type logical network and a training set of data sequence. This simplifies the Bayesian equaliser with an objective-oriented structure compared to the transversal equaliser (TE). Unlike a transversal equaliser or filter, the option feedback equaliser cancels intersymbol interference using detector choices. Type-2 fuzzy sets have fuzzy membership grades. An unnormalised outputs type-1 TSK fuzzy inference system system may create a time-invariant channel Bayesian equalisation without a Gaussian probabilistic model. The fuzzy set adaptive filter generalises this for time-varying channels.

Blind channel equalisation approaches have been studied to a lesser degree. Blind approaches use just signal information, eliminating channel estimation with training data for improved spectral efficiency. They also rely heavily on statistical data.

The fuzzy-C-means (FCM) method performs combined equalisation and demodulation of QAM-modulated signals. Clustering analysis may be used to classify the receiver translating the signal onto symbols. Clustering analysis classifies things into comparable groupings (clusters). The FCM algorithm runs unsupervised on data alone. The membership functions of this application quantify the data's link to grouped based here on magnitude and phase distances among received symbols and signal constellation points. These distances are calculated using the information provided by the application. For a static channel, the technique converges rapidly, is robust, and has lower computing cost than standard MLSE receivers. However, the FCM algorithm compels points severely degraded with noise to correspond to one or even more clusters instead of none.

"FPCM" assist to get blind channel equalisation for time-changing channels and improves the "FCM" method. The "FPCM" type of algorithm makes such "FCM" method less susceptible to excessively noisy symbol samples. The receiver may also use past cluster centre information to improve cluster centre accuracy with additional data samples. However, a forgetting effect may limit the relevance of cluster centres in time-varying channel data. High-speed wireless transmission systems have a long coherence time, making cluster centre buildup possible under time-variant circumstances. FPCM beats FCM because it rejects noise-degraded data. As predicted, both methods perform differently depending on data size.

The blind equalisation of fuzzy neural networks is described. Equalise channel estimation using fuzzy neural network classifiers. The software guesses at random the channel that uses the fourth inhibiting the beginning of received sequences. Following is approximate deconvolution. Classifiers based on fuzzy neural networks receive deconvolution output. Simulations in a time-invariant stream with 64-QAM demonstrate the fastest convergence change of rate along with lower type of bit errors rate (BER) than a feed-forward neural network blind equalisation technique.

A fuzzy communication system comprising input, fuzzification, rule, normalisation, and defuzzification layers is used to increase the convergence rate of a feed-forward neural networks blind equalisation method. Fuzzy neural networks had quicker convergence time and lower BER than feedforward neural networks blind algorithms in 16-QAM simulations.

Turbo equalisation techniques combine encoding/decoding with channel equalisation, unlike ordinary communication systems. Iterating with the equalisation and channels encoder on the same as incoming data achieves this combination. Turbo equalisers have been achieved using the Bayesian technique, and TSK fuzzy logic systems can implement Bayesian models, therefore turbofuzzy equalisation should be possible. Fuzzy filter turbo equalisers were suggested. Fuzzy filters can handle impulsive noise uncertainty, and the fuzzy turbo equaliser has a lower computing cost than the Bayesian equaliser. Backpropagation adjusts fuzzy equaliser settings.

The turbo-fuzzy equaliser cannot utilise the decoder's a priori knowledge, hence it cannot exchange extrinsic information with the fuzzy system iteratively. Low-complex fuzzy turbo equalisation techniques enhance this.

An expanded FCM algorithm proposes an RBF-based turbo equalisation technique. "This approach has lower computational cost than a turbo equalisation scheme based just on Jacobian RBF for binary phase-shifting key ("BPSK) type of modulation inside a Rayleighfading system of channel. Simulations reveal that the suggested technique highly performs similarly to that of Jacobian-based turbo (denoted as RBF) equalisation approach but along with less computing cost.

The Bayesian equalisation architecture with a fuzzy adaptive filter architecture is applied to a Jacobian RBF turbo equalisation approach. The simulations for BPSK but also QAM in such a Rayleigh fading type of channel demonstrate that the fuzzified adaptive neuro-fuzzy inference TEQ scheme decreases computation cost while only slightly degrading performance very much compared to the Jacobian turbo balancing method, producing a trade-off for the implementation of circuits with a strong emphasis on low complexity. The blind equalisation of fuzzy neural networks is discussed. Equalise channel estimation using fuzzy neural network classifiers. The software guesses at random the channel that uses the fourth inhibiting the beginning of received sequences. Following is approximate deconvolution. Classifiers based on fuzzy neural networks get deconvolution output. Simulations in a time-invariant channel utilising 64-QAM demonstrate a faster type of convergence rate and lower set of bit errors rate (BER) than a feed-forward neural network blind equalisation approach. Advantages/Capabilities of Channel Equalization are expressed in Figure 7.4.

List of various techniques and applications of wireless communication using fuzzy logic:

- Fuzzy Logic-Based Spectrum Allocation
- Fuzzy Logic-Based Channel Equalization
- Fuzzy Logic-Based Modulation Technique
- Fuzzy Logic-Based Signal Processing
- Fuzzy Logic-Based Power Control
- Fuzzy Logic-Based Resource Allocation
- Fuzzy Logic-Based Routing
- Fuzzy Logic-Based Handover
- Fuzzy Logic-Based Network Selection
- Fuzzy Logic-Based Quality of Service (QoS) Enhancement
- Fuzzy Logic-Based Traffic Management
- Fuzzy Logic-Based Security Enhancement.

These techniques and applications of fuzzy logic in wireless communication can help to improve the efficiency and effectiveness of wireless communication systems.

Overall, this chapter demonstrates the effectiveness of fuzzy inference systems in signal processing and telecommunications, highlighting their potential for solving real-world problems in wireless communication.

FIGURE 7.4   Advantages/capabilities of channel equalization.

7.6.3 EXAMPLES OF TECHNIQUES AND APPLICATIONS OF FUZZY LOGIC IN WIRELESS COMMUNICATION

Here are some examples of techniques and applications of fuzzy logic in wireless communication:

- **Channel equalization:** Fuzzy logic can be used to equalise the wireless communication channel, which can improve the reliability of the wireless link. Fuzzy logic-based equalization algorithms can adjust the filter coefficients of the equaliser based on the channel characteristics, the received signal strength, and the noise level.
- **Handover management:** Fuzzy logic can be used to manage the handover between different wireless cells or networks, which can improve the quality of service and reduce the call drops. Fuzzy logic-based handover management algorithms can predict the network conditions and make a smooth transition to the target network.
- **Quality of service management:** Fuzzy logic can be used to manage the quality of service (QoS) of wireless communication, which can guarantee the required level of performance for different applications. Fuzzy logic-based QoS management algorithms can prioritise the traffic based on the application requirements and the network conditions.
- **Modulation scheme selection:** Fuzzy logic can be used to select the appropriate modulation and coding scheme (MCS) for wireless communication, which can improve the reliability and efficiency of the wireless link. Fuzzy logic-based MCS selection algorithms can select the MCS based on the channel conditions, the error rate, and the required data rate.
- **Power control:** Fuzzy logic can be used to control the transmission power of wireless communication, which can reduce interference and save energy. Fuzzy logic-based power control algorithms can adjust the transmission power based on the received signal strength, the channel conditions, and the interference level.
- **Channel prediction:** Fuzzy logic can be used to predict the wireless channel conditions, which can help optimise the wireless link. Fuzzy logic-based channel prediction algorithms can estimate the channel characteristics based on past channel measurements and the current network conditions.
- **Resource allocation:** Fuzzy logic can be used to allocate wireless communication resources, such as time slots, frequencies, and bandwidth, which can improve the efficiency and fairness of the network. Fuzzy logic-based resource allocation algorithms can allocate the resources based on the application requirements, the network conditions, and the user demands.

Hence, fuzzy logic provides a flexible and adaptive approach to wireless communication, which can help improve the performance, reliability, and efficiency of wireless networks.

7.6.4 ADVANTAGES AND DISADVANTAGES OF USING FUZZY LOGIC IN THESE APPLICATIONS

Advantages of using fuzzy logic in wireless communication:

i. **Robustness:** Fuzzy logic is robust to noise, uncertainty, and imprecision in the wireless channel, which can help improve the reliability of the wireless link.
ii. **Adaptability:** Fuzzy logic can adapt to changing network conditions, user requirements, and application demands, which can help optimise the wireless link.
iii. **Flexibility:** Fuzzy logic provides a flexible approach to wireless communication, which can handle a wide range of channel conditions, network topologies, and user scenarios.
iv. **Intuitiveness:** Fuzzy logic is easy to understand and interpret, which can help designers and users of wireless communication systems to make informed decisions.
v. **Efficiency:** Fuzzy logic is computationally efficient and can be implemented in real-time systems, which can help reduce the processing delay and energy consumption of wireless devices.

Disadvantages of using fuzzy logic in wireless communication:

  i. **Complexity:** Fuzzy logic can be complex and difficult to design, which can require expertise in both fuzzy logic and wireless communication.
 ii. **Overfitting:** Fuzzy logic can overfit the data and the model, which can lead to poor generalization and performance degradation in real-world scenarios.
iii. **Tuning:** Fuzzy logic requires tuning of the parameters and rules, which can be time-consuming and challenging to optimise.
 iv. **Interpretability:** Fuzzy logic can be difficult to interpret and explain, which can limit its use in safety-critical and mission-critical applications.

The advantages of using fuzzy logic in wireless communication outweigh the disadvantages, and the use of fuzzy logic can help address many of the challenges and issues in wireless networks. However, the design and implementation of fuzzy logic-based algorithms require careful consideration of the trade-offs between the benefits and the costs of using fuzzy logic.

7.6.5 PROPOSED CASE STUDY

Case study: Fuzzy Logic in Wireless Sensor Networks for Smart City Environmental Monitoring

BACKGROUND

Smart cities are rapidly emerging as a response to the increasing urbanization and the need for sustainable and efficient urban development. Environmental monitoring is a crucial aspect of smart city management, as it helps to track and manage the impact of human activities on the environment. Wireless sensor networks (WSNs) have been widely used in smart city environmental monitoring, providing real-time data collection and transmission from various environmental sensors. However, the performance of WSNs is highly dependent on environmental conditions and network congestion, which can cause unreliable data transmission and high energy consumption.

OBJECTIVE

To develop a fuzzy logic-based approach for energy-efficient and reliable data transmission in a wireless sensor network for smart city environmental monitoring.

METHODOLOGY

The proposed system consists of multiple environmental sensors that collect and transmit data to a central node using a WSN. The central node is responsible for data processing, storage, and transmission to the cloud server for further analysis and decision-making.

Fuzzy logic-based algorithms are used to optimise the operation of the WSN and ensure reliable data transmission while minimising energy consumption. The algorithm takes into account various factors that affect the WSN performance, such as network congestion, signal strength, and environmental conditions. The inputs to the fuzzy logic system are the signal-to-noise ratio (SNR), the packet delivery ratio (PDR), and the energy level of each sensor node. The output is the optimal transmission power level that balances the trade-off between energy consumption and data transmission quality.

The fuzzy logic controller consists of three stages: fuzzification, rule evaluation, and defuzzification. In the fuzzification stage, the inputs are mapped to fuzzy sets that represent their linguistic values, such as "low," "medium," and "high." In the rule evaluation stage, the fuzzy logic rules that describe the relationship between the input and output variables are applied. Finally, in the defuzzification stage, the fuzzy outputs are mapped back to a crisp value that represents the optimal transmission power level.

RESULTS

The proposed fuzzy logic-based approach was implemented and tested in a smart city environmental monitoring system. The results show that the WSN performance was significantly improved in terms of energy efficiency and data transmission reliability. The fuzzy logic-based approach was able to adapt to the changing environmental conditions and network congestion, making intelligent decisions based on imprecise or uncertain data. The approach achieved a 95% packet delivery ratio with a 30% reduction in energy consumption compared to the conventional approach.

Final conclusion of case study: The case study demonstrates the effectiveness of fuzzy logic techniques in wireless sensor networks for smart city environmental monitoring. The fuzzy logic-based approach optimises the operation of the WSN and ensures reliable data transmission while minimising energy consumption. The approach is robust and adaptable, making intelligent decisions based on imprecise or uncertain data. The proposed approach has significant implications for smart city environmental monitoring, as it can help to achieve sustainable and efficient urban development. Future research can explore the scalability and applicability of the proposed approach in real-world smart city applications.

7.7 KEY FINDINGS AND RESULTS OF THE RESEARCH CHAPTER

Based on this research chapter we have listed some of the key findings and results in bullet point format:

Findings:

- Fuzzy logic and fuzzy-hybrid methods are commonly used in wireless communications for channel estimation, equalization, and decoding.
- Fuzzy logic techniques are effective in various fields of data communication, including channel equalization, changeover management, and quality of service management.
- Fuzzy inference systems have the potential to solve real-world problems in wireless communication.
- This chapter suggests practice-oriented research opportunities based on the separation of fuzzy logic approaches applied to actual issues.

Results:

- Fuzzy logic-based channel equalization techniques can provide better performance than traditional equalization methods in wireless communication systems.
- Fuzzy logic-based handover management can help to reduce the probability of dropped calls and improve the quality of service.
- Fuzzy logic-based quality of service management can help prioritise data traffic in wireless communication networks, resulting in improved network performance.
- Fuzzy logic-based decoding methods can help to reduce errors and improve the reliability of wireless communication systems.

7.7.1 SUMMARY OF THE RESEARCH CHAPTER'S FINDINGS

Based on the literature review and the discussion of the various techniques and applications of fuzzy logic in wireless communication, the research chapter found that:

i. Fuzzy logic is a powerful and flexible tool that can be used to address many of the challenges and issues in wireless communication, including channel equalization, changeover management, and quality of service management.

ii. Fuzzy logic can improve the robustness, adaptability, flexibility, intuitiveness, and efficiency of wireless communication systems, which can lead to better performance and user satisfaction.

iii. The design and implementation of fuzzy logic-based algorithms require careful consideration of the advantages and disadvantages of using fuzzy logic, as well as the tuning and optimization of the parameters and rules.

iv. Fuzzy logic has been successfully applied in various settings and scenarios of wireless communication, including wireless sensor networks, heterogeneous networks, and cognitive radio networks.

v. Future research opportunities include exploring the integration of fuzzy logic with other machine learning techniques, investigating the performance and scalability of fuzzy logic in large-scale wireless networks, and developing novel applications and use cases for fuzzy logic in wireless communication.

7.7.2 IMPLICATIONS FOR FUTURE RESEARCH

The research chapter highlights several areas for future research based on the findings and discussions of the various techniques and applications of fuzzy logic in wireless communication. Some of these implications for future research include:

i. Integration of fuzzy logic with other machine learning techniques: Future research can investigate the combination of fuzzy logic with other machine learning techniques, such as neural networks, deep learning, and reinforcement learning, to improve the performance and accuracy of wireless communication systems.

ii. Performance and scalability of fuzzy logic in large-scale wireless networks: Future research can examine the scalability and performance of fuzzy logic-based algorithms in large-scale wireless networks, such as 5G and beyond, to determine their suitability for future wireless communication systems.

iii. Development of novel applications and use cases for fuzzy logic in wireless communication: Future research can explore new and innovative ways to apply fuzzy logic in wireless communication, such as smart cities, Internet of Things (IoT), and mobile edge computing (MEC), to meet the evolving demands and requirements of wireless networks.

iv. Standardization and interoperability of fuzzy logic in wireless communication: Future research can investigate the standardization and interoperability of fuzzy logic-based algorithms in wireless communication, to ensure their compatibility and interoperability with other wireless technologies and systems.

v. Comparative analysis of fuzzy logic with other approaches: Future research can compare and contrast the performance and efficiency of fuzzy logic-based algorithms with other approaches, such as traditional signal processing, machine learning, and rule-based systems, to determine the strengths and weaknesses of each approach in different wireless communication scenarios.

7.8   SUMMARY AND FUTURE STUDY

7.8.1   SUMMARY

In summary, this chapter provides an overview of the various techniques and applications of fuzzy logic in wireless communication, highlighting their benefits and effectiveness in addressing various challenges and issues in wireless networks. This chapter also provides a classification of fuzzy logic control, the features of wireless sensor networks, and the difficulties and challenges associated with these networks, along with examples of how fuzzy logic can be applied to address these challenges.

This chapter emphasises the advantages and capabilities of fuzzy logic techniques in wireless communication, such as their ability to improve the robustness, adaptability, flexibility, intuitiveness, and efficiency of wireless communication systems. This chapter also discusses some of the disadvantages and challenges associated with the use of fuzzy logic in wireless communication, such as the complexity and difficulty of designing and implementing fuzzy logic-based algorithms.

Overall, the research chapter highlights the importance of fuzzy logic in the development and optimization of wireless communication systems and suggests several areas for future research, such as the integration of fuzzy logic with other machine learning techniques, the development of new applications and use cases, and the standardization and interoperability of fuzzy logic-based algorithms in wireless communication.

7.8.2 Future Research Directions

Based on the topics discussed in this chapter, some future research directions are:

- **Channel equalization:** Future research can investigate the performance of fuzzy logic-based algorithms for channel equalization in different wireless communication scenarios. Research can focus on developing novel algorithms that integrate fuzzy logic with other machine learning techniques to improve channel equalization accuracy, such as deep learning and reinforcement learning.
- **Changeover management:** Future research can examine the performance of fuzzy logic-based algorithms for changeover management in heterogeneous wireless networks, such as 5G and beyond. Research can focus on developing algorithms that can effectively manage the handover process while considering various factors such as signal strength, user mobility, and network congestion.
- **Quality of service management:** Future research can investigate the effectiveness of fuzzy logic-based algorithms for Quality of Service (QoS) management in wireless communication systems. Research can focus on developing algorithms that can adapt to changing network conditions to ensure that QoS requirements are met, such as network congestion, data loss, and latency.
- **Wireless sensor networks:** Future research can investigate the scalability and performance of fuzzy logic-based algorithms in large-scale wireless sensor networks. Research can focus on developing novel algorithms that can address the challenges associated with wireless sensor networks, such as energy efficiency, node localization, and routing.
- **Integration of fuzzy logic with other approaches:** Future research can explore the integration of fuzzy logic with other approaches such as traditional signal processing, machine learning, and rule-based systems. Research can focus on developing algorithms that combine the strengths of different approaches to improve the performance and accuracy of wireless communication systems.
- **Standardization and interoperability:** Future research can investigate the standardization and interoperability of fuzzy logic-based algorithms in wireless communication systems. Research can focus on developing standard interfaces and protocols that ensure the compatibility and interoperability of fuzzy logic-based algorithms with other wireless technologies and systems.

7.9 CONCLUSION

In conclusion, this chapter has reviewed the various techniques and applications of fuzzy logic in wireless communication. Fuzzy logic techniques are effective in addressing various challenges in wireless communication, such as channel equalization, changeover management, and quality of service management. In addition, this chapter has discussed the features and challenges of wireless sensor networks and how fuzzy logic can be used to address some of these challenges. The advantages and disadvantages of using fuzzy logic in these applications have also been examined.

Overall, the findings suggest that fuzzy logic-based algorithms can improve the performance and accuracy of wireless communication systems, especially in dynamic and complex environments. However, further research is needed to investigate the scalability, interoperability, and integration of fuzzy logic with other approaches in wireless communication. The future research directions discussed in this chapter provide a roadmap for addressing these challenges and developing novel solutions that can further enhance the performance and efficiency of wireless communication systems.

REFERENCES

Abo-Zahhad, M., & El-Sisi, M. (2018). *Wireless Sensor Networks: Concepts, Applications, Experimentation and Analysis*. Springer Verlag, Singapore.

Ali, A., & Bhatti, A. I. (2016). Fuzzy Logic-Based Resource Management in Wireless Communication Networks: A Review. *IEEE Communications Surveys & Tutorials*, 18(2), 1041–1067.

Ali, A., & Bhatti, A. I. (2018). Fuzzy Logic-Based Spectrum Sensing in Cognitive Radio Networks: A Review. *IEEE Access*, 6, 4812–4832.

Ali, M., Wahid, A., & Saeed, S. (2018). A Fuzzy Logic Based Modified LEACH Algorithm for Cluster Head Selection in Wireless Sensor Networks. *International Journal of Computer Science and Mobile Computing*, 7(11), 180–191.

Boudjellal, A., & Mekki, H. (2019). Fuzzy Logic in Wireless Communications: A Review. *Transactions on Emerging Telecommunications Technologies*, 30(11), e3784.

Broun, A., & Pappas, C. H. (1999). Adaptive Channel Equalization Using Fuzzy Logic. *IEEE Transactions on Consumer Electronics*, 45(3), 495–502.

Chen, M., Xue, W., Xu, J., & Xue, L. (2021). Design and Simulation of Fault Tolerant Routing Protocols in Wireless Sensor Networks. *Wireless Networks*, 27(4), 2317–2335.

Chen, X., Wang, J., & Zhang, Y. (2017). A Fuzzy Logic Approach to Enhance the LEACH Algorithm for Wireless Sensor Networks. *Wireless Personal Communications*, 96(2), 3211–3225.

Cheng, Y., Zhang, L., & Li, W. (2017). Application of Fuzzy Logic in Wireless Communication Systems. *International Journal of Simulation: Systems, Science and Technology*, 18(1), 1–6.

Ding, Q., Huang, J., Lu, R., & Shen, X. (2015). A Fuzzy Logic-Based Energy-Efficient Data Transmission Scheme for Wireless Sensor Networks. *Sensors*, 15(10), 26050–26070.

Gupta, S., & Younis, M. (2014). Wireless Sensor Networks: A Survey on the State of the Art and the 802.15.4 and ZigBee Standards. *Computer Communications*, 38, 393–422.

Huang, Y., Wang, J., Yang, X., Liu, K., & Zheng, H. (2008). Fuzzy Hybrid Method for MIMO Channel Equalization. *Journal of Zhejiang University-Science A*, 9(9), 1288–1293.

Jang, J. S. R., Sun, C. T., & Mizutani, E. (1997). *Neuro-Fuzzy and Soft Computing: A Computational Approach to Learning and Machine Intelligence*. New Jersey, USA, Prentice Hall.

Karray, F., & Deen, M. J. (2002). Fuzzy Logic Applications in Wireless Communications. *IEEE Transactions on Systems, Man, and Cybernetics-Part C: Applications and Reviews*, 32(2), 165–171.

Klir, G. J., & Yuan, B. (1995). *Fuzzy Sets and Fuzzy Logic: Theory and Applications*. Upper Saddle River, NJ: Prentice Hall.

Kosko, B. (1992). *Neural Networks and Fuzzy Systems*. Englewood Cliffs, NJ: Prentice Hall.

Li, J., Chen, L., Zheng, J., Zhang, J., & Zhao, Z. (2019). Fuzzy-Logic-Based Equalization for Frequency-Selective Fading Channels in Wireless Communication Systems. *IEEE Access*, 7, 26927–26936.

Mendel, J. M., & John, R. I. (1995). Type-2 Fuzzy Sets Made Simple. *IEEE Transactions on Fuzzy Systems*, 3(4), 339–345.

Rahmati, M., Jolfaei, A., & Tootoonchian, F. (2018). A Comprehensive Survey on Fuzzy Logic in Wireless Sensor Networks. *Journal of Network and Computer Applications*, 110, 66–86.

Rajapakse, J. C. (2000). Medical Diagnosis Using Fuzzy Logic. *IEEE Transactions on Fuzzy Systems*, 8(6), 617–625.

Ren, K., Li, K., & Li, S. (2016). A Fuzzy-Logic-Based Adaptive Modulation and Coding Scheme in Wireless Communication Systems. *EURASIP Journal on Wireless Communications and Networking*, 2016(1), 1–10.

Sharma, R., & Kumar, P. (2018). Wireless Sensor Networks: Security, Coverage, and Routing Issues. In *Handbook of Research on Machine Learning Innovations and Trends* (pp. 257–272). Aboul Ella Hassanien & Tarek Gaber, IGI Global, USA.

Wang, Y., Jiang, C., Li, Y., & Li, Y. (2019). Fuzzy Logic-Based Quality of Service Management in Wireless Communication Networks: A Survey. *IEEE Access*, 7, 36559–36575.

William, P., Yogeesh, N., Vimala, S., Gite, P., & Selva Kumar, S. (2022). Blockchain technology for data privacy using contract mechanism for 5G networks. In 2022 3rd International Conference on Intelligent Engineering and Management (ICIEM) (pp. 461–465). doi:10.1109/ICI.

Wu, X., & Zhang, B. (2015). Fuzzy Logic-Based Handover Algorithm for Wireless Communication Systems. *Journal of Networks*, 10(7), 392–400.

Yi, S. (2019). The Role of Fuzzy Logic in Wireless Communication Systems. In Q. Luo (Ed.), *Advances in Wireless Networks and Information Systems* (pp. 89–97). Springer Berlin, Heidelberg.

Yogeesh, N. (2 013a). Study on Intuitionistic Fuzzy Graphs and Its Applications in the Field of Real World. *International Journal of Advanced Research in Engineering and Applied Sciences*, 2(1), 104–114.

Yogeesh, N. (2013b). Illustrative Study on Intuitionistic Fuzzy Hyper-Graphs and Dual-Intuitionistic Fuzzy Hyper-Graphs. *International Journal of Engineering, Science and Mathematics*, 2(1), 255–264.

Yogeesh, N. (2013c). Study on Hypergraphs and Directed Hypergraphs. *Journal of Advances and Scholarly Researches in Allied Education (JASRAE)*, 5(10), 1–5. https://www.ignited.in/p/305247.

Yogeesh, N. (2021). Mathematical Approach to Representation of Locations Using k-Means Clustering Algorithm. *International Journal of Mathematics and Its Applications*, 9(1), 127–136. https://ijmaa.in/index.php/ijmaa/article/view/110.

Zadeh, L. A. (1965). Fuzzy Sets. *Information and Control*, 8, 338–353.

Zadeh, L. A. (1973). Outline of a New Approach to the Analysis of Complex Systems and Decision Processes. *IEEE Transactions on Systems, Man, and Cybernetics*, (1), 28–44.

Zhang, L., Li, H., & Li, W. (2018). Fuzzy Logic-Based Decoding for Wireless Communication Systems. *IET Communications*, 12(10), 1191–1196.

8 Availability Optimization of Poly-Ethylene Terephthalate Bottle Hot Drink Filling System Using Particle Swarm and Grey Wolf Optimizers

Parul Punia, Amit Raj, and Pawan Kumar
Central University of Haryana

8.1 INTRODUCTION

The capacity of a system to operate efficiently during its design life under various conditions without failure is its reliability. The complexity of today's engineering system poses greater risks in maintaining the system, thereby making reliability a critical consideration while designing a system. But it is not possible to determine the reliability of the system precisely. There generally lies vulnerability in deciding the future execution of the system as it is estimated utilizing various parameters of the subsystems which are gathered from accessible past records. Zadeh [1] proposed the idea of fuzziness to handle situations involving uncertainties. Cai [2] recommended the execution of fuzzy state assumptions in conventional reliability to tackle such uncertainties. The fuzzy state assumptions turned out successful for a system from completely working to a totally downstate. Kumar et al. [3] employed the PSO algorithm to optimize and analyze the performance of a beverage filling system facility. Aly et al. [4] presented a model integrating reliability, availability, and maintainability to recognize the most critical subsystem affecting the performance of the system. According to Cai [5], fuzzy reliability is the probability of no significant degradation in performance during a given time frame. In the paper [6], Cai discussed several application aspects of fuzzy methodology in the context of system failure engineering. Garg and Sharma [7], utilized the lambda-tao technique to investigate the behavior of a complex repairable synthesis unit in a fertilizer plant, which had uncertain and ambiguous data. Garg [8] in his paper employed PSO to construct the membership functions of a nonlinear optimization problem and analyze the system's performance to identify its most critical subsystem. In another work by Garg [9], an approach was presented for analyzing the availability of a thermal power plant system using a fuzzy Markov model and the Runge-Kutta method. Kumar et al. [10] adopted the PSO technique to enhance the repairable system's availability in the lactogen milk powder system plant. The technique was applied to optimize the availability of the plant's various subsystems. Gupta [11] investigated the availability and profitability of generators of steam turbine power plants considering arbitrary repair and exponential failure time distributions into account. Three evolutionary algorithms are compared and a literature review of various optimization problems is given by Kachitvichyanukul [12]. Performance optimization of a distillery plant is done with PSO [13]. Modgil and Kumar [14] investigated the most sensitive component of an industrial system by calculating the time-dependent system's availability with the Markovian approach. Sharma et al. [15] using the Markov Birth-Death process analyzed the performance and availability of a leaf spring manufacturing industry. Tsarouhas [16] using the statistical approach

DOI: 10.1201/9781003387459-8

of failure data analyzed the reliability, availability, and maintainability of a milk production line. Velmurugan [17] analyzed the maintenance activity in small and medium-sized enterprise industries using the Markov approach. In [18], the authors employed both the genetic algorithm and PSO algorithm to determine the optimal values of decision variables in the CCHP system, owing to the intricacies of the model.

8.2   SYSTEM DESCRIPTION, NOTATIONS, AND ASSUMPTIONS

The PET hot drink filling system comprises six primary subsystems, which are Blow Molding Machine, Filling Machine, Cooling Machine, Coding Machine, Labeling Machine, and Pasteurizer cum storage tank. Out of these subsystems, the pasteurizer cum storage tank is not considered for analysis as this subsystem is prone to minor failures only. The main five subsystems are described below:

1. **Blow molding machine (A):** The PET bottles are made by performing a blow molding operation on the raw material. Two blow molding machines are connected in parallel for this purpose. The system works in a reduced state if any one of the units stops working and it fails completely when both the units stop operating.
2. **Filling machine (B):** After cleaning the bottles, the filling machine fills the bottle with the hot drink (at 70°C) in measured quantity. After the filling process, the bottles are capped and sealed. Only one such unit is connected to the system and the system fails once the unit stops operating.
3. **Cooling machine (D):** Cooling machines bring the temperature of the filled bottle down to the required temperature by sprinkling cool water on the bottles. Two cooling machines are connected in parallel for this purpose. The system works in a reduced state if any one of the units stops working and it fails completely when both the units stop operating.
4. **Coding machine (E):** The coding machine prints all the details like manufacturing date, expiry date, price of the bottle, batch number, etc. on the filled bottle. Only one such unit is connected to the system and the system fails once the unit stops operating.
5. **Labeling machine (F):** The labeling machine pastes the label on the bottle. Only one such unit is connected to the system and the system fails once the unit stops operating.

The pasteurizer/storage tank stores and heats the pulp of the fruit to 70°C and then transfers it to the filling machine. This subsystem is not analyzed as it is subjected to minor failures only.

8.2.1   NOTATIONS

Figure 8.1 presents the state transition diagram of the system. The notations and assumptions used are given below.

System Units	Working State	Failure State	Failure Rate	Repair Rate
Blow molding machine	A	$\bar{A}$	α_1	β_1
Standby blow molding machine	$\bar{A}$	a	α_1	β_1
Filling machine	B	b	α_2	β_2
Cooling machine	D	$\bar{D}$	α_3	β_3
Standby cooling machine	$\bar{D}$	d	α_3	β_3
Coding machine	E	e	α_4	β_4
Labeling machine	F	f	α_5	β_5

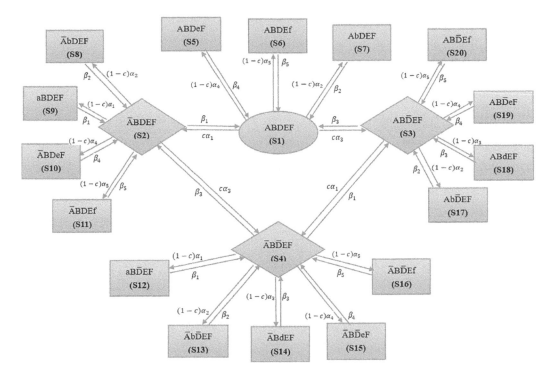

FIGURE 8.1 State transition diagram of the system.

Represents a system operating at maximum capacity.

Represents a system operating at reduced capacity.

Represents a failed system.

c Represents the system coverage factor.

P_i Represents the probability of the system being in ith state.

$A_F(\infty)$ Represents the fuzzy availability of the system in a steady state.

8.2.2 Assumptions

1. Initially, all the subsystems are fully operational.
2. No occurrence of simultaneous failures within the system.
3. Only reduced state causes subsystems A and D to fail.
4. Units after repair function identically to a new unit.

8.3 MATHEMATICAL MODELING OF THE SYSTEM IN STEADY STATE

The system under study is mathematically modeled using the Markov approach, incorporating a state transition diagram to determine the fuzzy availability of the system. The corresponding first-order differential equations derived from the transition diagram are provided below.

$$P_1'(t) = -KP_1(t) + \beta_1 P_2(t) + \beta_2 P_7(t) + \beta_3 P_3(t) + \beta_4 P_5(t) + \beta_5 P_6(t) \dots \quad (8.1)$$

$$P_2'(t) = -LP_2(t) + c\alpha_1 P_1(t) + \beta_2 P_8(t) + \beta_3 P_4(t) + \beta_4 P_{10}(t) + \beta_5 P_{11}(t) + \beta_1 P_9(t) \dots \quad (8.2)$$

$$P_3'(t) = -MP_3(t) + c\alpha_3 P_1(t) + \beta_1 P_4(t) + \beta_2 P_{17}(t) + \beta_3 P_{18}(t) + \beta_4 P_{19}(t) + \beta_5 P_{20}(t) \dots \quad (8.3)$$

$$P_4'(t) = -NP_4(t) + c\alpha_1 P_3(t) + c\alpha_3 P_2(t) + \beta_1 P_{12}(t) + \beta_2 P_{13}(t) + \beta_3 P_{14}(t) + \beta_4 P_{15}(t) + \beta_5 P_{16}(t) \dots \quad (8.4)$$

$$P_5'(t) = -\beta_4 P_5(t) + (1-c)\alpha_4 P_1(t) \dots \quad (8.5)$$

$$P_6'(t) = -\beta_5 P_6(t) + (1-c)\alpha_5 P_1(t) \dots \quad (8.6)$$

$$P_7'(t) = -\beta_2 P_7(t) + (1-c)\alpha_2 P_1(t) \dots \quad (8.7)$$

$$P_8'(t) = -\beta_2 P_8(t) + (1-c)\alpha_2 P_2(t) \dots \quad (8.8)$$

$$P_9'(t) = -\beta_1 P_9(t) + (1-c)\alpha_1 P_2(t) \dots \quad (8.9)$$

$$P_{10}'(t) = -\beta_4 P_{10}(t) + (1-c)\alpha_4 P_2(t) \dots \quad (8.10)$$

$$P_{11}'(t) = -\beta_5 P_{11}(t) + (1-c)\alpha_5 P_2(t) \dots \quad (8.11)$$

$$P_{12}'(t) = -\beta_1 P_{12}(t) + (1-c)\alpha_1 P_4(t) \dots \quad (8.12)$$

$$P_{13}'(t) = -\beta_2 P_{13}(t) + (1-c)\alpha_2 P_4(t) \dots \quad (8.13)$$

$$P_{14}'(t) = -\beta_3 P_{14}(t) + (1-c)\alpha_3 P_4(t) \dots \quad (8.14)$$

$$P_{15}'(t) = -\beta_4 P_{15}(t) + (1-c)\alpha_4 P_4(t) \dots \quad (8.15)$$

$$P_{16}'(t) = -\beta_5 P_{16}(t) + (1-c)\alpha_5 P_4(t) \dots \quad (8.16)$$

$$P_{17}'(t) = -\beta_2 P_{17}(t) + (1-c)\alpha_2 P_3(t) \dots \quad (8.17)$$

$$P'_{18}(t) = -\beta_3 P_{18}(t) + (1-c)\alpha_3 P_3(t) \dots \tag{8.18}$$

$$P'_{19}(t) = -\beta_4 P_{19}(t) + (1-c)\alpha_4 P_3(t) \dots \tag{8.19}$$

$$P'_{20}(t) = -\beta_5 P_{20}(t) + (1-c)\alpha_5 P_3(t) \dots \tag{8.20}$$

where

$$K = c(\alpha_1 + \alpha_3) + (1-c)(\alpha_2 + \alpha_4 + \alpha_5)$$

$$L = \beta_1 + c\alpha_3 + (1-c)(\alpha_1 + \alpha_2 + \alpha_4 + \alpha_5)$$

$$M = \beta_3 + c\alpha_1 + (1-c)(\alpha_2 + \alpha_3 + \alpha_4 + \alpha_5)$$

$$N = \beta_1 + \beta_3 + (1-c)(\alpha_1 + \alpha_2 + \alpha_3 + \alpha_4 + \alpha_5)$$

With initial conditions:

$$P_j(t) = \begin{cases} 1, & \text{if } j = 1 \\ 0, & \text{otherwise} \end{cases} \dots \tag{8.21}$$

These differential equations (8.1)–(8.20) and the initial conditions (8.21) collectively are termed as Chapman–Kolmogorov equations. The systems are designed in a way that they operate effectively for a longer duration hence the industries are more concerned about the system's long-term availability, which is calculated using steady-state probabilities and is derived by imposing the following conditions:

$$\frac{d}{dt} \to 0 \quad \text{as} \quad t \to \infty$$

After the application of the following conditions, equations (8.1)–(8.20) reduce to:

$$KP_1 = \beta_1 P_2 + \beta_2 P_7 + \beta_3 P_3 + \beta_4 P_5 + \beta_5 P_6 \dots \tag{8.22}$$

$$LP_2 = c\alpha_1 P_1 + \beta_1 P_9 + \beta_2 P_8 + \beta_3 P_4 + \beta_4 P_{10} + \beta_5 P_{11} \dots \tag{8.23}$$

$$MP_3 = c\alpha_3 P_1 + \beta_1 P_4 + \beta_2 P_{17} + \beta_3 P_{18} + \beta_4 P_{19} + \beta_5 P_{20} \dots \tag{8.24}$$

$$NP_4 = c\alpha_1 P_3 + c\alpha_3 P_2 + \beta_1 P_{12} + \beta_2 P_{13} + \beta_3 P_{14} + \beta_4 P_{15} + \beta_5 P_{16} \dots \tag{8.25}$$

$$\beta_k P_j = (1-c)\alpha_k P_1, \quad j = 5, 6, 7 \quad \text{and} \quad k = 4, 5, 2 \text{ respectively.} \dots \tag{8.26}$$

$$\beta_k P_j = (1-c)\alpha_k P_2, \quad j = 8,9,10,11 \quad \text{and} \quad k = 2,1,4,5 \text{ respectively.} \dots \tag{8.27}$$

$$\beta_k P_j = (1-c)\alpha_k P_4, \quad j = 12,13,14,15,16 \quad \text{and} \quad k = 1,2,3,4,5 \text{ respectively.} \dots \tag{8.28}$$

$$\beta_k P_j = (1-c)\alpha_k P_3, \quad j = 17,18,19,20 \quad \text{and} \quad k = 2,3,4,5 \text{ respectively.} \dots \tag{8.29}$$

On solving the equations recursively, we get:

$$P_2 = R_1 P_1, \quad P_3 = R_2 P_1, \quad P_4 = R_3 P_1, \dots \tag{8.30}$$

$$P_j = \delta_k P_1, \quad j = 5,6,7 \quad \text{and} \quad k = 4,5,2 \text{ respectively} \dots \tag{8.31}$$

$$P_j = \delta_k R_1 P_1, \quad j = 8,9,10,11 \quad \text{and} \quad k = 2,1,4,5 \text{ respectively} \dots \tag{8.32}$$

$$P_j = \delta_k R_2 P_1, \quad j = 12,13,14,15,16 \quad \text{and} \quad k = 1,2,3,4,5 \text{ respectively} \dots \tag{8.33}$$

$$P_j = \delta_k R_3 P_1, \quad j = 17,18,19,20 \quad \text{and} \quad k = 2,3,4,5 \text{ respectively} \dots \tag{8.34}$$

where

$$R_1 = \frac{c^2 . \alpha_1}{\beta_1}, \quad R_2 = \frac{c . \alpha_3}{\beta_3}, \quad R_3 = \frac{c^2 . \alpha_1 . \alpha_3}{\beta_1 \beta_3},$$

$$\delta_k = \frac{(1-c)\alpha_k}{\beta_k}.$$

Now using the normalizing condition $\sum_{j=1}^{20} P_j = 1$, we get:

$$P_1 = \left[\left(1 + \sum_{k=2,4,5} \delta_k \right) + R_1 \left(1 + \sum_{k=1,2,4,5} \delta_k \right) + R_2 \left(1 + \sum_{k=2,3,4,5} \delta_k \right) + R_3 \left(1 + \sum_{k=1,2,3,4,5} \delta_k \right) \right]^{-1} \dots \tag{8.35}$$

The equation provided below is used to find the fuzzy availability of the system in a steady state,

$$A_F(\infty) = P_1 + 0.5P_2 + 0.5P_3 + 0.25P_4$$
$$= (1 + 0.5R_1 + 0.5R_2 + 0.25R_3)P_1 \dots \tag{8.36}$$

8.4 EVOLUTIONARY ALGORITHMS

8.4.1 PARTICLE SWARM OPTIMIZATION (PSO)

PSO is a metaheuristic algorithm that simulates the social behavior of swarm of birds, insects, fish, etc. to solve optimization problems. Initially, the particles are randomly positioned in the search space, with each particle representing a probable solution for the given problem. As the algorithm progresses, these particles traverse the search space, guided by the individual best position (P_b) and the best position found by the entire group, known as the global best (G_b). The particle's movements are governed by the velocity equation, which determines the direction and speed of their movement, and the position equation, which updates their location within the search space.

$$Vel_i(t+1) = w * Vel_i(t) + c_1 * r_{d1} * (P_b - X_i(t)) + c_2 * r_{d2} * (G_b - X_i(t)) \dots \tag{8.37}$$

$$X_i(t+1) = Vel_i(t) + X_i(t) \ \dots \tag{8.38}$$

with, $Vel_i(t+1)$ and $X_i(t+1)$ are the updated velocity and position of the particle, w is the inertia weight, r_{d1} and r_{d2} are the random number in [0,1], c_1 and c_2 are acceleration constants. Iterations of the algorithm persist until a predefined stopping criterion, such as a specified level of convergence or iterations is achieved. The optimal solution is determined by the particle with the best fitness value.

8.4.2 GREY WOLF OPTIMIZATION (GWO)

GWO is a cooperative and competitive algorithm inspired by the social hierarchical structure and the hunting strategy of grey wolves. The alpha wolf is considered the leader of the pack that coordinates the hunting strategy and has the best fitness value among all the wolves. The beta and delta wolves are the second and third-best wolves, respectively. The omega wolf is the weakest in the pack and has the lowest fitness value. The positions of the wolves are updated iteratively by employing three fundamental movements: encircling, hunting, and attacking.

In encircling prey mechanism wolves move around a potential solution. This is mathematically represented as,

$$P(t+1) = P(t) - A.D \dots \tag{8.39}$$

$$D = |CP_p - P| \dots \tag{8.40}$$

Where A and C are the coefficient matrix with

$$A = 2ar_{d1} - a \dots \tag{8.41}$$

$$C = 2r_{d2} \dots \tag{8.42}$$

r_{d1}, r_{d2} lies in [0,1] randomly, a is decreased from 2 to 0 linearly.

To mathematically model the hunting behavior, the position of α, β, δ wolves is considered as reference points, and the ω wolves are obliged to follow them. The movement of each wolf is then determined by a combination of these reference points, as well as some random exploration. This enables the wolves to search the search space in a coordinated manner and converge toward the optimal solution.

$$D_\alpha = |c_1 \cdot P_\alpha - P(t)|, \quad D_\beta = |c_2 \cdot P_\beta - P(t)|, \quad D_\delta = |c_3 \cdot P_\delta - P(t)| \ldots \tag{8.43}$$

c_1, c_2, c_3 are calculated using equation (8.42).

$$P_1 = P_\alpha - A_1 \cdot D_\alpha, P_2 = P_\beta - A_2 \cdot D_\beta, P_3 = P_\delta - A_3 \cdot D_\delta \ldots \tag{8.44}$$

$$P(t+1) = (P_1 + P_2 + P_3)/3 \ldots \tag{8.45}$$

The searching and attacking prey mechanisms involve the wolves exploring new areas and attacking to converge toward a promising solution. Searching refers to exploration capability whereas attacking refers to exploitation capability. With $|a| < 1$ wolves show predatory behavior and attack the prey. While with $|a| > 1$ wolves tend to deviate away from the prey.

8.5 RESULTS AND DISCUSSION

8.5.1 Availability Analysis of the System

The system's fuzzy availability is assessed using equation (8.36), and corresponding results are presented in Tables 8.1–8.5. The impact of various parameters (α_j, β_k; $j, k = 1$ to 5, $c = 0.4$) of the subsystems on system fuzzy availability is also analyzed. The findings revealed that as the failure rate increases, the system's fuzzy availability decreases, whereas it increases with the repair rate.

The maximum fuzzy availability for all five subsystems is observed as 0.931802 for the Blow Molding Machine, 0.937786 for the Filling Machine, 0.935626 for the Cooling Machine, 0.940934 for the Coding Machine, and 0.934215 for the Labeling Machine. The subsystem Coding Machine has a significant impact on the system's steady-state fuzzy availability. On analyzing the obtained results, the optimal combination of failure and repair rates (FRRs) is identified and subsequently optimized through the application of PSO and GWO algorithms.

8.5.2 Performance Optimization Using PSO and GWO

The system availability is optimized by implementing PSO and GWO algorithms. Each algorithm was executed 20 times independently with a fixed population size and a total iteration count of

TABLE 8.1

Steady State Fuzzy Availability of System due to Variation in Parameters of the Blow Molding Machine

$\alpha_1 (\rightarrow)$ $\beta_1 (\downarrow)$	0.0015	0.003	0.0045	0.006
0.05	0.928908	0.922947	0.918769	0.916390
0.07	0.930569	0.926381	0.922077	0.917664
0.09	0.931484	0.928257	0.924959	0.921592
0.10	0.931802	0.928908	0.925955	0.922947

Constant parameters: $\alpha_2 = 0.005$, $\alpha_3 = 0.004$, $\alpha_4 = 0.0006$, $\alpha_5 = 0.001$, $\beta_2 = 0.12$, $\beta_3 = 0.06$, $\beta_4 = 0.02$, $\beta_5 = 0.05$, $c = 0.4$

TABLE 8.2
Steady State Fuzzy Availability of System due to Variation in Parameters of the Filling Machine

$\alpha_2 (\rightarrow)$ $\beta_2 (\downarrow)$	0.005	0.009	0.012	0.015
0.12	0.928908	0.911646	0.899115	0.886923
0.15	0.933326	0.919334	0.909112	0.899115
0.17	0.935420	0.922997	0.913894	0.904969
0.20	0.937786	0.927152	0.919334	0.911646

Constant parameters: $\alpha_1 = 0.0015$, $\alpha_3 = 0.004$, $\alpha_4 = 0.0006$, $\alpha_5 = 0.001$, $\beta_1 = 0.05$, $\beta_3 = 0.06$, $\beta_4 = 0.02$, $\beta_5 = 0.05$, $c = 0.4$

TABLE 8.3
Steady State Fuzzy Availability of System due to Variation in Parameters of the Cooling Machine

$\alpha_3 (\rightarrow)$ $\beta_3 (\downarrow)$	0.004	0.006	0.008	0.01
0.06	0.928908	0.921924	0.914696	0.916244
0.08	0.932301	0.927186	0.921924	0.916525
0.10	0.934305	0.930273	0.926145	0.921924
0.12	0.935626	0.932301	0.928908	0.925448

Constant parameters: $\alpha_1 = 0.0015$, $\alpha_2 = 0.005$, $\alpha_4 = 0.0006$, $\alpha_5 = 0.001$, $\beta_1 = 0.05$, $\beta_2 = 0.12$, $\beta_4 = 0.02$, $\beta_5 = 0.05$, $c = 0.4$

TABLE 8.4
Steady State Fuzzy Availability of System due to Variation in Parameters of the Coding Machine

$\alpha_4 (\rightarrow)$ $\beta_4 (\downarrow)$	0.0006	0.0009	0.0012	0.0015
0.02	0.928908	0.92106	0.913343	0.905755
0.04	0.936891	0.932882	0.928908	0.924967
0.06	0.939582	0.936891	0.934215	0.931554
0.08	0.940934	0.938908	0.936891	0.934882

Constant parameters: $\alpha_1 = 0.0015$, $\alpha_2 = 0.005$, $\alpha_3 = 0.004$, $\alpha_5 = 0.001$, $\beta_1 = 0.05$, $\beta_2 = 0.12$, $\beta_3 = 0.06$, $\beta_5 = 0.05$, $c = 0.4$

50 and 1000 respectively. The PSO algorithm was configured with constants $c_1 = 1.5$, $c_2 = 1.5$ and $w = 0.9$. Whereas in the GWO algorithm, the parameter 'a' is decreased linearly from 2 to 0. The range of FRRs of the subsystems is kept the same for optimizing using PSO and GWO algorithms. The failure repair rates corresponding to maximum fuzzy availability obtained using the Markov approach are used for comparison.

TABLE 8.5

Steady State Fuzzy Availability of System due to Variation in Parameters of the Labeling Machine

$\alpha_s\,(\rightarrow)$ $\beta_s\,(\downarrow)$	0.001	0.004	0.007	0.009
0.05	0.928908	0.898292	0.869629	0.851516
0.07	0.931933	0.909714	0.888530	0.874947
0.09	0.933622	0.916186	0.899389	0.888530
0.10	0.934215	0.918473	0.903253	0.893384

Constant parameters: $\alpha_1 = 0.0015$, $\alpha_2 = 0.005$, $\alpha_3 = 0.004$, $\alpha_4 = 0.0006$, $\beta_1 = 0.05$, $\beta_2 = 0.12$, $\beta_3 = 0.06$, $\beta_4 = 0.02$, $c = 0.4$

TABLE 8.6

Performance Analysis of System using Various Approaches at $c=0.4$

Failure and Repair Rates ($\downarrow$)	Markov Approach	PSO	GWO
α_1	0.0015	0.0018	0.0019
α_2	0.005	0.0065	0.0056
α_3	0.004	0.006	0.0049
α_4	0.0006	0.0007	0.0007
α_5	0.001	0.0016	0.0014
β_1	0.05	0.0927	0.0588
β_2	0.12	0.1317	0.1426
β_3	0.06	0.1191	0.1121
β_4	0.08	0.0651	0.0711
β_5	0.05	0.0973	0.0960
Fuzzy availability	94.09%	94.28%	94.85%

The results in Table 8.6 show that the fuzzy availability of the system by implementing GWO is 94.85% which is higher than that of the Markov approach and PSO. The GWO algorithm demonstrated superior performance in optimizing the system's fuzzy availability by adjusting the FRRs parameters, surpassing the results achieved by the PSO and Markov Approach methods.

8.6 CONCLUSION

Analysis of the system's fuzzy availability is crucial to ensure quality production and long-term effectiveness. Initially, the Markov approach was used to assess the impact of FRRs of different subsystems on the steady-state fuzzy availability of the system. Further, the system's performance is optimized using two metaheuristic algorithms, PSO and GWO. GWO outperformed PSO and Markov approach. The results obtained from the study are valuable in enhancing the performance of the system and limiting the range of predicted system behavior.

REFERENCES

[1] Zadeh, L. A. "Fuzzy sets." *Information and Control* 8, no. 3 (1965): 338–353.

[2] Cai, K. Y. (Ed.) "Fuzzy Methods in Software Reliability Modeling." *Introduction to Fuzzy Reliability* (243–276). New York: Springer 1996.

[3] Kumar, P., and P. Tewari. "Performance analysis and optimization for CSDGB filling system of a beverage plant using particle swarm optimization." *International Journal of Industrial Engineering Computations* 8, no. 3 (2017): 303–314.

[4] Aly, M. F., I. H. Afefy, R. K. Abdel-Magied, and E. K. Elhalim. "A comprehensive model of reliability, availability, and maintainability (RAM) for industrial systems evaluations." *JJMIE* 12, no. 1 (2018): 59–67.

[5] Cai, K.-Y., C.-Y. Wen, and M.-L. Zhang. "Fuzzy states as a basis for a theory of fuzzy reliability." *Microelectronics Reliability* 33, no. 15 (1993): 2253–2263.

[6] Cai, K.-Y. "System failure engineering and fuzzy methodology an introductory overview." *Fuzzy Sets and Systems* 83, no. 2 (1996): 113–133.

[7] Garg, H., and S. P. Sharma. "Behavior analysis of synthesis unit in fertilizer plant." *International Journal of Quality & Reliability Management* 29, no. 2 (2012): 217–232.

[8] Garg, H., and M. Rani. "An approach for reliability analysis of industrial systems using PSO and IFS technique." *ISA Transactions* 52, no. 6 (2013): 701–710.

[9] Garg, H.. "An approach for analyzing the reliability of industrial system using fuzzy Kolmogorov's differential equations." *Arabian Journal for Science and Engineering* 40 (2015): 975–987.

[10] Mukesh, K., S. V. Kumar, and M. Vikas. "Availability analysis and optimization of lactogen milk powder production system using PSO." *International Journal of Mechanical Engineering and Technology* 8, no. 11 (2017): 839–849.

[11] Gupta, N., M. Saini, and A. Kumar. "Operational availability analysis of generators in steam turbine power plants." *SN Applied Sciences* 2 (2020): 1–11.

[12] Kachitvichyanukul, V. "Comparison of three evolutionary algorithms: GA, PSO, and DE." *Industrial Engineering and Management Systems* 11, no. 3 (2012): 215–223.

[13] Kumar, A., V. Kumar, and V. Modgil. "Performance optimisation for ethanol manufacturing system of distillery plant using particle swarm optimisation algorithm." *International Journal of Intelligent Enterprise* 5, no. 4 (2018): 345–364.

[14] Modgil, V. "Mathematical modeling and time dependent availability analysis of poly-ethylene terephthalate bottle hot drink filling system: a case study." *Turkish Journal of Computer and Mathematics Education (TURCOMAT)* 12, no. 10 (2021): 1822–1829.

[15] Sharma, D., A. Kumar, V. Kumar, and V. Modgil. "Performance modeling and availability analysis of leaf spring manufacturing industry." *International Journal of Mechanical and Production Engineering* 5, no. 1 (2017): 1–5.

[16] Tsarouhas, P. "Evaluation of reliability, availability and maintainability of a milk production line." *International Journal of Industrial and Systems Engineering* 31, no. 3 (2019): 324–342.

[17] Velmurugan, K., P. Venkumar, and R. Sudhakarapandian. "Reliability availability maintainability analysis in forming industry." *International Journal of Engineering and Advanced Technology* 9, no. 1S4 (2019): 822–828.

[18] Rabbani, M., S. Mohammadi, and M. Mobini. "Optimum design of a CCHP system based on economical, energy and environmental considerations using GA and PSO." *International Journal of Industrial Engineering Computations* 9, no. 1 (2018): 99–122.

9 Optimisation of Drilling Parameters on Glass Fibre Reinforced Polymer Composites with Stainless Steel Mesh using Taguchi and Grey Fuzzy Relation Method

M. Sakthivel
Adhiyamaan College of Engineering, Anna University, Chennai, India

P. Raja
Prathyusha Engineering College, Anna University, Chennai, India

9.1 INTRODUCTION

Composite materials are widely used in the contemporary global environment and are present in all major industries, including the aerospace, marine, space, and automotive sectors [1,2]. Glass fibre reinforced plastic (GFRP) has become more frequently used in structural and automotive applications alongside metal. It is also known that GFRP can incorporate closed metal reinforcements like metal foils [3]. Open metallic reinforcements are preferable to traditional sheets or foils, such as guide-like sheets or wire meshes [4].

For increased strength, stiffness, and corrosion resistance, GFRP is combined with Stainless Steel Wire Mesh (SSWM). Drilling is an inevitable part of the secondary machining required during the assembly of these composites. Engineers find it difficult to drill such materials because of their varying machining characteristics. The literature on composites, multi-material machining, and their significance are covered at the beginning of the next section, followed by a discussion of optimisation approaches [26].

Because of many types of faults such as fibre pullout, fuzzing, matrix cracking, and thermal modifications brought on by the laminated structure of composites, drilling composite materials is a challenging process [2]. These flaws would result in a loss of structural stiffness, which would change the way the structure is performed dynamically as a whole. Rapid tool wear, the adoption of subpar cutting tool designs, and poor machining conditions are the primary causes of these issues [2,3]. To attain accuracy and efficiency while machining these composite materials, one must have a deeper understanding of cutting techniques [2]. Due to quick tool wear, the mechanism of machining GFRP is quite unusual. Finished components with a rough surface finish, underlying layers with defects including cracks and delamination, and other issues of the problems encountered in machining [4].

Spindle speed, feedrate, and point angle are a few crucial machining factors. Some researchers have published the findings of drilling tests on composites made of fibre reinforced polymer (FRP).

DOI: 10.1201/9781003387459-9

According to drilling experiments by Velayudham et al. [5], depending on the contact between the workpiece and the drill, the thrust force rises at various feed rates. In their research on carbon fibre reinforced polymer composite materials, Davim et al. [6] found that the feed rate is the primary factor that influences thrustforce. According to Khashaba [7], who studied the drilling of GFRP composite materials, the thrust force is decreased as cutting speed is increased. Dhokia et al.'s [8] prediction model makes use of using the design of experiments method to get the best machining settings for a delamination in polypropylene ball-end machining. According to Tsao and Hocheng [9], the feed rate and spindle speed have a greater impact on delamination.

Due to the different material properties, it can be difficult to drill holes with small diameter tolerances when drilling through many materials. Due to the modulus of elasticity of the materials, distinct elastic deformations and consequently variable tolerances can be seen along the entirety of the hole. Additionally, at the major cutting edges, the quality of the hole is impacted by chip transport through the hole, built-up aluminium edge wear, and increased tool wear [10]. Sharp and very hot-hardenable tool materials are necessary for multi-material machining. When drilling Gr/Bi-Ti stacks, Ramulu et al. [11] and Kim et al. [12] reported that tool wear happens quickly. Modified step drills performed better on multi-layer materials in terms of diameter tolerances, surface quality, and tool wear. Kim et al.'s [12,13] confirmation showed employing carbide drills with a low spindle speed and low feed rate, or using HSS-Co drills with a low spindle speed and high feed rate, results in the best process conditions for achieving the desired hole quality while drilling Gr/Bi-Ti. Chip disposal, tool temperature, changes in dynamic cutting forces, and tool wear are issues that can arise during the drilling of a multi-material stack. At low feed rates, polymer matrix composite chips are continuous [13], but as feed rates rise, the chips start to resemble dust. Process parameters should allow for drilling both highly abrasive glass fibre and ductile SSWM when choosing the cutting tool.

To improve performance, such as fewer delamination and quality holes, etc., the best machining settings must be determined for composite materials. When compared to the optimisation of a single performance parameter, multiple response optimisations are more complicated. For optimisation, traditional statistical regression requires a lot of data. GRA is a technique in the Grey system theory that uses multifactor analysis and fewer data to examine the relationship between sequences [14]. This is thought to be preferable to statistical regression analysis. The manufacturing process already uses GRA with success. GRA was utilised by Tosun [15] to optimise the drilling settings. Lin [16] has optimised the turning procedure using the Taguchi approach and GRA. Yang et al.'s [17] end milling operation on high purity graphite was optimised for groove width and delamination by changing the cutting speed, feed rate, and depth of cut. To optimise the plasma arc welding parameters, Fung [18] used GRA. Taguchi method and GRA have been used by Yiyo Kuo et al. [19] to optimise multi-response simulation issues. In a friction stir welding operation using the aluminium alloy AA5083, Sundaravel et al. [20] optimised the friction welding parameters, including the tool's rotational speed, transverse speed, and axial force. GRA has been utilised by Anilkumar et al. [21] to optimise electrical discharge machining settings while milling tool steel with a variety of performance characteristics.

However, there have only been a few reported works on FML drilling. The article describes the process parameter optimisation for drilling FML composites. Three level orthogonal Taguchi L27 arrays are used in the studies. Point angle, spindle speed, and feed rate are taken into account as control variables. The GRA is used to improve the drilling parameters that affect the roundness and delamination factor quality goals. In order to determine the most important element influencing the drilling of FML composites, analysis of variance (ANOVA) is utilised.

9.2   EXPERIMENTAL METHOD

The current project focuses on drilling fibre-metal laminate composites (FML). Weaved glass fibre and stainless steel mesh (SSM) are utilised as reinforcement. Due to its excellent mechanical and thermal qualities, epoxy was utilised as the matrix material. Epoxies often cost more than polyesters,

FIGURE 9.1   Vacuum bag moulding.

TABLE 9.1
Control Factors and Levels Used for the Experimentation

Cutting Parameters	Symbol	Unit	Range	Level 1	Level 2	Level 3
Point angle	θ	Degrees	100–136	100	118	136
Spindle speed	v	rpm	500–2500	500	1500	2500
Feed rate	f	mm/min	50–150	50	100	150

but they shrink less and have a higher strength to stiffness ratio when exposed to mild temperatures. With hoover bag moulding, which is depicted in Figure 9.1, the glass fibre weight fraction is consistently kept at 50% in all laminates, and the SSM weight fraction is consistently supported at 10% in all laminates. The Taguchi orthogonal array is used to plan the experiments for this study [25].

This approach can greatly reduce the number of tests necessary to get the essential data [22,23]. Although there are numerous variables that affect the drilling process, cutting parameters like point angle, spindle speed, and feed rate are significant considerations. Drilling is done with a twist drill bit with a 6 mm diameter and carbide tool. The drilling parameters and their level are displayed in Table 9.1. L27 orthogonal arrays have been selected for the experiments that have been conducted. The drilling trials are performed on a Makino vertical machining centre, model S33, computer numerical control (CNC), vertical machining centre (VMC 100). Figure 9.1 reveals the experimental setup. Thrust force, delamination factor, and roundness are the answers examined for machinability evaluation. It is clear that these have a general relationship to the cost of machining processes and can be quantified for comparison, and a Carl Zeiss coordinate measuring machine (CMM), made in Germany, was used to measure the roundness. Figure 9.2 depicts a typical experimental setup.

9.2.1   DRILLING PARAMETERS

The wide body of literature is the foundation for the identification of the drilling parameters. Table 9.1 provides drilling parameters. Point angle, spindle speed, and feed rate are drilling parameters.

9.2.2   DELAMINATION FACTOR

When compared to drilling metals, delamination is one of the major problems that occurs with composite laminates. The drill's push action, which causes the layers to separate rather than cut through them, is blamed for the peeling that manifests as peeling without the end of the base handle or during use. Due to the increased bluntness of the tool, the delamination is dependent on the thrust force that is created during drilling and changes almost linearly with a change in the thrust force. It has been noted from the literature that as spindle speed is raised, the delamination factor tends to decrease. The fluctuation in the delamination factor follows a pattern that is remarkably close to feed rate. Lower point angles have a small delamination factor. The reduction in thrust force at low point angles may be the cause, which minimises delamination damage.

FIGURE 9.2   Experimental setup for drilling of FML composites.

9.2.3   RESPONSE SURFACE REGRESSION MODEL

The most effective scientific method for planning an experiment is experiment design. The process of organising an experiment such that relevant data may be gathered, leading to reliable and impartial findings, is known as statistical design of experiments. The only approach that can be used for data analysis when there are experimental errors is statistical methodology. Any experimental problem has two components: the experiment's design and the data's statistical analysis.

The guidelines recommended for statistical design of experiments are pre-experimental planning, choice of experimental design, performing the experiment and statistical analysis of the data. A tentative hypothesis is formulated from the experimentation part. This hypothesis shall be investigated and new hypothesis can be formulated and the experimentation may become iterative. A successful experiment requires knowledge of the important factors, the range of variation of these factors and the appropriate number of levels.

The practice of approximating a response function based on statistical analysis of data collected at locations is called response surface methodology (RSM). Initially applied to the model fitting of physical experiments, this technique is now used in experiment design. The response function, y, is denoted by a polynomial as shown below:

$$y = \beta_0 + \beta_1 x_1 + \beta_2 x_2 + \cdots + \beta_t x_t + \epsilon \tag{9.1}$$

where $\beta_0, \beta_1, \beta_2, \ldots, \beta_n$ are regression coefficients of the predictor variables, $x_1, x_2, \ldots, x_i$ and ϵ represents an error.

Considering the square effects and the interaction terms, the response function shall be written as:

$$\hat{y} = \beta_0 + \sum_{i=1}^{n} \beta_i x_i + \sum_{i=1}^{n} \beta_{ij} x_i^2 + \sum_{i=1}^{n}\sum_{j=1}^{n} \beta_{ij} x_i x_j + \varepsilon \tag{9.2}$$

The drilling of FML composite plates includes three factors viz. point angle, spindle speed, and feed rate. The response function for this model can be written as shown below:

$$y = \beta_0 + \beta_1 x_1 + \beta_2 x_2 + \beta_3 x_3 + \beta_{11} x_1^2 + \beta_{22} x_2^2 + \beta_{33} x_3^2$$
$$+ \beta_{12} x_1 x_2 + \beta_{13} x_1 x_3 + \beta_{23} x_2 x_3 + \epsilon$$

(9.3)

The least square estimate of the regression coefficient, β, can be expressed in matrix form as:

$$\beta = \left(X^T X \right)^{-1} X^T Y$$

(9.4)

where

$$y = x\beta + \varepsilon$$

To acquire the model coefficients, the experimental data is fitted into a quadratic response surface regression model. The response function is then obtained that relates the response to the input drilling parameters using the developed quadratic response surface regression model. The statistical analysis of the model is carried out using ANOVA.

Through R-Sq() value, the suitability of the developed models has been confirmed. R-Sq is referred to as the coefficient of determination, and 0 is used to determine whether the created regression models are adequate. The R-Sq measures how much of the observed response values' variance can be attributed to the predictors.

9.3   RESULTS AND DISCUSSION

9.3.1   REGRESSION MODEL

The regression model for FMML composites drilling experiment conducted using carbide drill is obtained and shown below. Regression model for the various responses is given regarding the chosen drilling parameters namely, point angle, spindle speed, and feed rate.

$$\text{Delamination factor} = +1.34178 - 5.00249e - 003 * \theta - 5.31574e - 005 * v$$

$$+3.54231e - 003 * f + 6.71296e - 007 * \theta v$$

$$+3.24074e - 006 * \theta f - 2.15000e - 007 * vf$$

(9.5)

$$+2.09191e - 005 * \theta^2 - 7.55556e - 009 * v^2$$

$$-8.48889e - 006 * f^2$$

$$\text{Roundness} = 0.015220 + 5.70079e - 004 * \theta - 3.33333e - 008 * v$$

$$+3.36204e - 005 * f - 8.33333e - 009 * \theta v$$

$$+4.62963e - 008 * \theta f + 1.66667e - 010 * vf$$

(9.6)

$$-2.09191e - 006 * \theta^2 + 7.22222e - 011 * v^2$$

$$+2.22222e - 008 * f^2$$

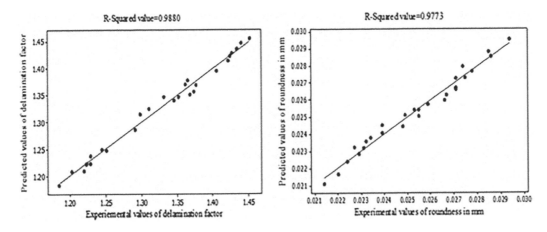

FIGURE 9.3 Experimental and predicted values of (a) delamination and (b) roundness.

Equations (9.5) and (9.6) show that a quadratic model is obtained for various responses regarding the chosen drilling parameters. Figure 9.3a and b shows the plot of experimental values and the predicted values of delamination and roundness obtained using carbide drills respectively. The predicted values are calculated using the Equations (9.5) and (9.6). The correlation between experimental and expected values is shown by the R-Sq value. The respective R-Sq values obtained are given in Figure 9.3. The chosen model is in good agreement with the experimental models if the R-Sq values are high. This also shows how well the models being employed are able to anticipate the outcomes for any other values for which there is no experiment.

Similar deviation analysis was carried out for the experiments conducted using carbide and DLC coated drills that confirmed the adequacy of RSM models. However, the deviation analysis can be made more comprehensive by calculating the average percentage of deviations over the entire experimental region.

It is calculated by finding the percentage of deviation of the responses on its actual values and then averaging the deviations obtained for 27 experiments. Table 9.2 shows the percentage of deviation of all the responses.

In Table 9.2, it was observed that % deviation of delamination factor and roundness have the least deviation. The RSM model is a better technique to predict the responses which give less variation (Figures 9.4 and 9.5).

9.3.2 OPTIMISATION

The machining parameters and the performance characteristics while drilling FML composite plates using carbide drills is shown in Table 9.2. Table 9.3 shows the data GRC, GRG and GFRG for all the two performance characteristics of the drilling experiments.

The GRC of all the two performance characteristics in experiment number 7 is unity indicating an exact reference value. Hence, the calculation of GRG is necessary to obtain the optimum drilling parameters for producing a hole with minimum damage.

On comparing the GRG in Table 9.3 and the GFRG, it is obvious that there is an improvement in the values of the GRG. Thus, the uncertainty of data is reduced further. The highest value of GRG and GFRG indicates the highest rank within the experiments [25].

Also, it is confirmed that experiment number 7 has the optimal combination of input drilling parameters. The low level of point angle, high level of spindle speed and low level of feed rate is optimum drilling parameter that reduces hole damage.

TABLE 9.2
Drilling Conditions and the Responses Obtained

Expt. No.	Point Angle in Degrees	Spindle Speed in rpm	Feed Rate in mm/minutes	Delamination Factor			Roundness (mm)		
				Experimental	Predicted	% Deviation	Experimental	Predicted	% Deviation
1	100	500	50	1.223	1.223	0.04	0.0224	0.0224	-0.15
2	100	500	100	1.331	1.347	-1.19	0.0239	0.0245	-2.67
3	100	500	150	1.427	1.429	-0.12	0.0271	0.0267	1.44
4	100	1500	50	1.22	1.211	0.77	0.022	0.0217	1.38
5	100	1500	100	1.31	1.324	-1.08	0.0234	0.0238	-1.76
6	100	1500	150	1.406	1.395	0.76	0.0266	0.0260	2.29
7	100	2500	50	1.185	1.184	0.11	0.0214	0.0211	1.27
8	100	2500	100	1.291	1.286	0.35	0.0227	0.0233	-2.42
9	100	2500	150	1.352	1.347	0.39	0.0255	0.0254	0.24
10	118	500	50	1.229	1.224	0.44	0.0248	0.0245	1.31
11	118	500	100	1.368	1.351	1.26	0.0268	0.0270	-0.75
12	118	500	150	1.434	1.435	-0.10	0.0285	0.0288	-1.18
13	118	1500	50	1.224	1.224	0.02	0.0232	0.0236	-1.68
14	118	1500	100	1.346	1.340	0.43	0.0259	0.0257	0.60
15	118	1500	150	1.422	1.414	0.55	0.0274	0.0280	-2.07
16	118	2500	50	1.203	1.209	-0.48	0.0229	0.0229	0.13
17	118	2500	100	1.298	1.315	-1.27	0.0255	0.0250	1.83
18	118	2500	150	1.365	1.378	-0.94	0.0271	0.0273	-0.60
19	136	500	50	1.229	1.238	-0.74	0.0249	0.0251	-0.87
20	136	500	100	1.377	1.368	0.64	0.0275	0.0273	0.71
21	136	500	150	1.452	1.456	-0.27	0.0294	0.0296	-0.55
22	136	1500	50	1.245	1.250	-0.43	0.0239	0.0241	-0.76
23	136	1500	100	1.362	1.370	-0.57	0.0267	0.0263	1.58
24	136	1500	150	1.44	1.447	-0.46	0.0286	0.0285	0.20
25	136	2500	50	1.251	1.248	0.28	0.0231	0.0232	-0.48
26	136	2500	100	1.374	1.356	1.30	0.0253	0.0254	-0.46
27	136	2500	150	1.425	1.422	0.19	0.0278	0.0277	0.40

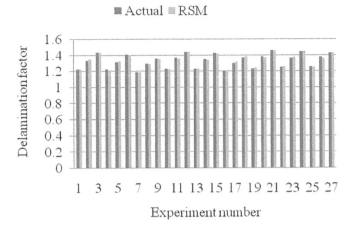

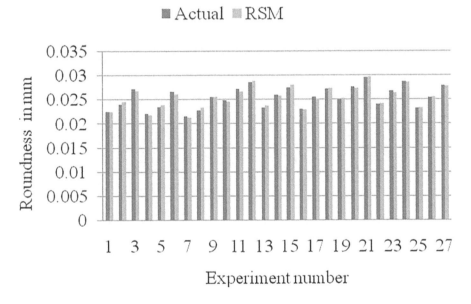

FIGURE 9.4 Deviation of delamination factor in RSM models from the experimental values.

FIGURE 9.5 Deviation of roundness in RSM models from the experimental values.

The GFRG response table is shown in Table 9.4, and the matching response graph is shown in Figure 9.6. The response table and response graph make it clear that, in order to create the optimum result, level 1 point angle and feed rate and level 3 spindle speed are the best combinations of the parameters.

Table 9.5 shows the ANOVA table for the GFRG, which indicates that feed rate is the most significant factor. Table 9.6 shows the comparison of the results of initial drilling parameters and optimal drilling parameters in the process of validating the results obtained. It was observed that the delamination decreases from 1.452 to 1.185 and roundness decreases from 0.0294 to 0.0214. The predicted value of the GFRG is close to the obtained GFRG. It has been claimed based on the data above that grey fuzzy reasoning can be helpful for optimising the various performances in the drilling of FML composites.

TABLE 9.3

Grey Relational Coefficient (GRC), Grey Reasoning Grade (GRG) and Grey Fuzzy Reasoning Grade (GFRG) for Various Responses

SL.No	Grey Relational Coefficient		Grey Relational Grade	Rank Order	Grey Fuzzy Reasoning Grade	Rank Order
	Delamination Factor	Roundness (mm)				
1	0.777	0.800	0.821	4	0.868	3
2	0.476	0.615	0.551	13	0.603	13
3	0.354	0.412	0.410	22	0.469	21
4	0.791	0.870	0.890	2	0.898	2
5	0.515	0.667	0.624	9	0.653	10
6	0.375	0.435	0.445	18	0.497	18
7	1.000	1.000	0.974	1	0.986	1
8	0.556	0.755	0.669	8	0.695	8
9	0.442	0.494	0.488	16	0.535	16
10	0.751	0.541	0.616	10	0.685	9
11	0.420	0.412	0.426	20	0.472	20
12	0.347	0.360	0.350	26	0.396	26
13	0.773	0.690	0.754	6	0.789	5
14	0.451	0.471	0.523	14	0.581	14
15	0.359	0.400	0.416	21	0.453	22
16	0.880	0.727	0.828	3	0.77	6
17	0.540	0.494	0.579	12	0.617	12
18	0.424	0.412	0.435	19	0.489	19
19	0.751	0.533	0.602	11	0.646	11
20	0.408	0.396	0.409	23	0.447	23
21	0.332	0.333	0.337	27	0.376	27
22	0.688	0.615	0.690	7	0.715	7
23	0.428	0.430	0.476	17	0.524	17
24	0.342	0.357	0.368	25	0.412	25
25	0.668	0.702	0.759	5	0.805	4
26	0.412	0.506	0.516	15	0.569	15
27	0.356	0.385	0.391	24	0.435	24

TABLE 9.4
Response Table for Grey Fuzzy Reasoning Grade

Drilling Parameter	Level 1	Level 2	Level 3	Max-Min
Point angle (°)	**0.6893**	0.5836	0.5477	0.1417
Spindle speed (rpm)	0.5513	0.6136	**0.6557**	0.1043
Feed rate (mm/minutes)	**0.7958**	0.5734	0.4513	0.3444

Overall mean grey fuzzy grade = **0.6068**.

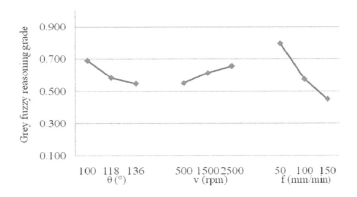

FIGURE 9.6 Response graph for grey fuzzy reasoning grade.

TABLE 9.5
ANOVA Table for Grey Fuzzy Reasoning Grade

Source	Sum of Squares	DoF	Mean Square	F Value	% of Contribution
θ	0.0903	1	0.0903	143.26	12.6
v	0.0490	1	0.0490	77.70	6.83
f	**0.5339**	1	**0.5339**	846.91	**74.47**
θv	3.41E-04	1	3.41E-04	0.54	0.048
θf	7.91E-03	1	7.91E-03	12.54	1.1
vf	1.73E-03	1	1.73E-03	2.74	0.241
θ^2	7.33E-03	1	7.33E-03	11.62	1.02
v^2	6.07E-04	1	6.07E-04	0.96	0.085
f^2	1.51E-02	1	1.51E-02	23.90	2.1
Residual	1.07E-02	17	6.30E-04		1.5
Cor total	0.7169	26			100

9.4 CONCLUSION

The conclusion drawn in the present study was as follows:

1. The incorporation of SSWM into GFRP is a novel technique that considerably improves the performance of the composite.
2. It is discovered that all response values viz. thrust force, torque, delamination and roundness decrease as spindle speed increases as obtained from parametric analysis of the responses on drilling parameters. Hence, a high spindle speed of 2500 rpm is best suited for the present work.

TABLE 9.6

Results of the Initial and Optimal Machining Performance

Setting Level	Initial Machining Parameters	Optimal Machining Parameters	
		Prediction	Experiment
Responses	**θ3v1f3**	**θ1v3f1**	**θ1v3f1**
Delamination factor	1.452	—	1.185
Roundness (mm)	0.0294	—	0.0214
Grey relational grade	0.337	0.9126	0.974
Grey fuzzy reasoning grade	**0.376**	0.9272	**0.986**

Improvement in grey relational grade: **0.5512**.

3. It is found that all the response values on point angle. Hence, a low value of point angle of 100° is preferred.
4. It is found that all the response value increases as feed rate increases and hence a low value of feed rate is preferred. Thus, a combination of high spindle speed, low point angle, and low feed rate is preferable for producing quality drilled holes.
5. The models for drilling parameters were developed using a response surface regression model based on the experimental results
6. Response surface regression models were developed for the prediction of the aforementioned four responses. The model adequacy is checked using R-squared values that range between 0.9773 and 0.9898 emphasising good predictions.
7. To drill FML composite plates, the best drilling conditions are determined using grey relational analysis. It has been determined that a hole is produced with the least amount of damage at a point angle of 100°, spindle speed of 2500 rpm, and feed rate of 50 mm/min. For experiments using carbide drills, the delamination factor is 1.185.
8. Grey fuzzy approach was used to enhance the relational analysis obtained using grey relational approach.
9. Feed rate and point angle were the two most important variables in the drilling of FMML composite plates that were determined using ANOVA.

REFERENCES

1. S. Abrate: *Machining of Composites, Composites Engineering Handbook*, Marcel Deckker, New York (1997).
2. W. C. Chen: Some experimental investigations in the drilling of carbon fibre reinforced composite laminations, *International Journal of Machine Tools and Manufacturing* 37 (1997), No. 8, pp. 1097–1108.
3. R. Kalakuzu, Z. Aslan, B. Okutan: The effect of ply member, orientation angle and bonding type on residual stress of woven steel fiber reinforced thermoplastic laminates, composite plates subjected to uniform transverse load, *Journal of Composite Science and Technology* 64 (2004), pp. 1049–1056.
4. K. Giasin, M. Atif, Y. Ma: Machining GLARE fibre metal laminates: a comparative study on drilling effect between conventional and ultrasonic-assisted drilling, *International Journal of Advanced Manufacturing Technology* 123 (2022), pp. 3657–3672.
5. A. Velayudham, R. Krishnamoorthy, T. Soundarapandian: Acoustic emission based drill condition monitoring during drilling of glass/phenolic polymeric composite using wavelet packet transform, *Materials Science and Engineering A* 412 (2005), pp. 141–145.
6. J. Paulo Davim, P. Reis: Study of delamination in drilling carbon fiber reinforced plastics (CFRP) using design experiments, *Composite Structures* 59 (2003), pp. 481–487.
7. U. A. Khashaba: Delamination in drilling GFR thermoset composites, *Composite Structures* 63 (2004), pp. 313–327.

8. K. Ogawa, E. Aoyama, H. Inoue, T. Hirogaki, H. Nobe, Y. Kitahara, T. Katayama, M. Gunjima: Investigation on cutting mechanism in small diameter drilling for GFRP (thrust force and surface roughness at drilled hole wall), *Composite Structures* 38 (1997), pp. 343–350.
9. H. Hocheng, C. C. Tsao: Comprehensive analysis of delamination in drilling of composite materials with various drill bits, *Journal of Materials Processing Technology* 140 (2003), pp. 335–339.
10. E. Brinksmeier, R. Janssen: Drilling of multilayer composite materials consisting of carbon fiber reinforced plastics (CFRP), titanium and aluminum alloys, *CIRP Annals - Manufacturing Technology* 51 (2002), No. 1, pp. 87–90.
11. M. Ramulu, T. Branson, D. Kim: A study on the drilling of composite and titanium stacks, *Composite Structure* 54 (2001), pp. 67–77.
12. D. Kim, M. Ramulu: Drilling process optimization for graphite/bismaleimide-titanium alloy stacks, *Composite Structures* 63 (2004), No. 1, pp. 101–114.
13. D. Kim, M. Ramulu: Machinability of titanium/graphite hybrid composites in drilling, *Transactions of the North American Manufacturing Research Institute of Society of Manufacturing Engineers* 33 (2005), pp. 445–452.
14. J. Deng: Introduction to Grey theory, *Journal of Grey Systems* 1 (1989), No. 1, pp. 1–24.
15. N. Tosun: Determination of optimum parameters for multiperformance characteristics in drilling by using Grey relational analysis, *International Journal of Advanced Manufacturing Technology* 28 (2006), pp. 450–455.
16. C. L. Lin: Use of the Taguchi method and Grey relational analysis to optimize turning operations with multiple performance characteristics, *Materials and Manufacturing Processes* 19 (2004), pp. 209–220.
17. Y. Y. Yang, J. R. Shie, C. H. Huang: Optimization of dry machining parameters for high purity graphite in the end-milling process, *Materials and Manufacturing Processes* 21 (2006), pp. 832–837.
18. C. P. Fung: Manufacturing process optimization for wear property of fiber-reinforced polybutylene terephthalate composites with Grey relation analysis, *Wear* 254 (2003), pp. 298–306.
19. Y. Kuo, T. Yang, G. W. Huang: The use of a Grey-based Taguchi method for optimizing multi-response simulation problems, *Engineering Optimization* 23 (2008), No. 1, pp. 51–58.
20. V. Sundaravel, R. Raju, S. R. K. Rao: Multiobjective optimization of friction stir welding process parameters on aluminium alloy AA 5083 using Taguchi-based Grey relational analysis, *Materials and Manufacturing Processes* 25 (2010), No. 11, pp. 1206–1212.
21. A. Kumar, S. Maheshwari, S. C. Sharma, N. Beri: A study of multiobjective parametric optimization of silicon abrasive mixed electrical discharge machining of tool steel, *Materials and Manufacturing Processes* 25 (2010), No. 10, pp. 1041–1047.
22. N. Tosun: Determination of optimum parameters for multiperformance characteristics in drilling by using Grey relational analysis, *The International Journal of Advanced Manufacturing* 28 (2006), pp. 450–455.
23. J. T. Huang, Y. S. Liao: Optimization of machining parameters of wire-EDM based on Grey relational and statistical analyses, *International Journal of Production Research* 41 (2003), No.8, pp. 1707–1720.
24. M. Sakthivel, S.Vijayakumar, Optimization of drilling parameters for fiber metal mesh laminate composites using Grey relational analysis, *Material Testing*, 58(2016),7-8.
25. M. Sakthivel, S. Vijayakumar, M. P. Jenarthanan: Grey-fuzzy logic to optimise process parameters in drilling of glass fibre-reinforced stainless steel mesh polymer composite, *Pigment and Resin Technology* 46 (2017), p. 4.
26. M. Sakthivel, S. Vijayakumar, B. Vijaya Ramnath: Investigation on mechanical and thermal properties of stainless steel wire mesh-glass fibre reinforced polymer composite, *Silicon*, 10 (2018), pp. 2643–2651.

10 A Comprehensive Mathematical Framework for Diabetes and Its Complications in Crisp and Fuzzy Settings

Purnima Pandit
M. S. University of Baroda

Payal Singh and Sujata Panda
Parul University

10.1 INTRODUCTION

Diabetes mellitus is a major concern conic disease among all countries either poor or rich across the globe. In India, this disease has been spreading very rapidly. According to the International Diabetes Federation, it is projected that the number of individuals in India with diabetes will reach 123 million by 2040, and currently, 5% of the Indian population is affected by this disease. The major reason for being diabetic in India is food habit. Indian diet consists of fat and carbohydrates and with the lack of exercise or any other physical activity, they gain weight which is a key factor of being prey for this disease.

There are two kinds of diabetes; Type-1 diabetes, also referred to as insulin-dependent diabetes, primarily impacts individuals below the age of 40, and other is Type-2 known as insulin-independent diabetes affects the majority.

Mathematical tools help in understanding how such biological system evolves with time, to formulate such a system on diabetes, we have to understand the mechanism of the human body. As we eat something, our blood glucose level rises, the internal organ of the human body Pancreas controls the glucose levels with the help of two types of cells: beta cells and alpha cells. Beta cells are responsible for the production of insulin. That makes the glucose level normal in the blood and the alpha cell releases glucagon which balances the glucose level in the blood if it goes down. In the case of diabetes, either beta cells do not produce insulin or our body cells are not capable of utilizing insulin that is produced by the beta cell, resulting in the glucose level in the blood increasing or decreasing. Diabetes comes with complications sometimes; these complications can be related to nerve system, blindness, cardiovascular diseases, and kidney failure. The burden of diabetes is visible in nation as a form of spending money on this disease and its complications.

10.2 FUZZY DIFFERENTIAL EQUATIONS

Before 1965, people handled uncertainty with probability theory but not all kinds of uncertainty can be handled by this theory. Zadeh introduced the fuzzy set theory to handle possibilistic uncertainty. While modelling any physical problem, possibilistic errors may occur in collecting parameters and/ or initial condition. So, modelling such a problem in fuzzy set up is a better approach. A brief introduction of fuzzy theory is given as follows.

The concept of fuzziness was initially introduced by Zadeh (1965). The introduction of the fuzzy derivative, on the other hand, was credited to Chang and Zadeh (1972). Puri and Ralescu (1983)

DOI: 10.1201/9781003387459-10

proposed Hukuhara derivative. Seikkala and Kaleva (1987) have solved the fuzzy initial value problem. In the beginning, people have solved fuzzy differential equations utilizing the Hukuhara derivative. This derivative has a drawback that the solution does not remain fuzzy as time increases. To remove this shortcoming, Bede and Gal (2005), have proposed the extension of differentiability for functions with fuzzy number values and Bede and Stefini (2005) have introduced a generalized Hukuhara derivative. It is the best standard method among other fuzzy derivatives. But in this fuzzy derivative, we obtain the possible set of solutions and one needs to select the solution that best fits to the problem.

People have solved fuzzy differential equations by different techniques like analytical, numerical and transformation. For numerical technique, Euler's method is used by Ma et al. (1999), Taylor's method and R-K method are used by Abbasbandy and Allahviranlo (2002, 2004),

In literature, there are two kinds of mathematical models for diabetes mellitus, one is based on the glucose-insulin model and the other is on diabetes with complications. Mahata et al. (2017b) have done work on the glucose-insulin model in crisp as well as in fuzzy scenario. Ackerman et al. (1969) and Stahl and Johansson (2009) have worked on blood glucose regulation. Yesenia Cruz Rosado (2009), has worked on a mathematical model for the detection of diabetes.

In this article, we consider the fuzzy diabetic model due to possibilistic error in estimating the exact count of diabetic patients with and without complications. We solve this model Laplace Transform technique. We also discuss the stability of the model and give the existence condition for a fuzzy solution. Finally, a numerical illustration is solved and the result is compared at core.

This article contains seven sections, introduction, basic concepts, mathematical model in crisp and fuzzy environment followed by numerical illustrative, results and discussion with conclusion.

10.3 BASIC CONCEPTS

10.3.1 FUZZY NUMBER (AS IN KLIR AND YUAN 1995)

A fuzzy set is considered a fuzzy number $\tilde{A}$ if it adheres to the following properties.

- $\tilde{A}$ must be normal i.e. membership value should be 1 for at least one point.
- All α−cut must be closed. Where α−cut of a fuzzy set $\tilde{A}$ is an ordinary set such that, $^{\alpha}\tilde{A} = \left\{ x \in X, \tilde{A}(x) \geq \alpha \right\}, \alpha \in (0\ 1]$.
- Support should be bounded.

10.3.2 FUZZY NUMBER IN PARAMETRIC FORM

An order pair represents a fuzzy number in parametric form $^{\alpha}\tilde{A} = [\underline{A}, \overline{A}]$ satisfying the following condition:

- $\underline{A}$ is a bounded, left-continuous, and increasing function within the range of [0, 1].
- $\overline{A}$ is a bounded, right-continuous, and increasing function within the range of [0, 1].
- $\underline{A} \leq \overline{A}$

10.3.3 FUZZY TRIANGULAR NUMBER (AS IN KLIR AND YUAN 1995)

Triangular fuzzy number is denoted as triplet (l, m, n) and its membership function is given as,

$$\tilde{A}(x) = \begin{cases} \dfrac{x-l}{m-l} & l < x \leq m \\ \dfrac{n-x}{n-m} & m < x \leq n \\ 0 & otherwise \end{cases}$$

10.3.4 Fuzzy Arithmetic Operations (as in Klir and Yuan 1995)

Let $\tilde{A}$, $\tilde{B}$ are fuzzy numbers and k is scalar then the arithmetic operations between $\tilde{A}$ and $\tilde{B}$ are as follows,

$$^{\alpha}\tilde{A} + {}^{\alpha}\tilde{B} = \left[\underline{A}, \overline{A}\right] + \left[\underline{B}, \overline{B}\right] = \left[\underline{A} + \underline{B},\ \overline{A} + \overline{B}\right]$$

$$k \otimes {}^{\alpha}\tilde{A} = k\left[\underline{A}, \overline{A}\right] = \left[k\underline{A}, k\overline{A}\right] = \forall\ \alpha \in (0\ 1]$$

10.3.5 Fuzzy Continuity (as in Song and Wu 2000)

If $\tilde{f}: R \times E \to E$ then $\tilde{f}$ is fuzzy continuous at point $(t_0, \tilde{y}_0)$ provided that for any fixed number $\alpha \in [0\ 1]$ and any $\epsilon > 0, \exists\ \delta(\epsilon, \alpha)\ s.t\ d\left(\tilde{f}(t, \tilde{y}), \tilde{f}(t_0, \tilde{y}_0)\right) < \epsilon$ whenever $|t - t_0| < \delta(\epsilon, \alpha)$ and $d\left([\tilde{y}], [\tilde{y}_0]\right) < \delta(\epsilon, \alpha)\ \forall\ t \in R$ and $\tilde{y} \in E$.

10.3.6 Modified Hukuhara Derivative (Pandit and Singh 2020)

A function $\tilde{f}$ is considered to be modified Hukuhara differentiable at $t_0 \in (a, b)\ \exists$ an element $\tilde{f}(t_0) \in E^n$ such that for small $h > 0\ \exists\ \tilde{f}(t_0 + h) \ominus \tilde{f}(t_0)$, $\tilde{f}(t_0) \ominus \tilde{f}(t_0 - h)$ should exist and,

$$\lim_{h \to 0+} \frac{\tilde{f}(t_0 + h) \ominus \tilde{f}(t_0)}{h} = \lim_{h \to 0-} \frac{\tilde{f}(t_0) \ominus \tilde{f}(t_0 - h)}{h} = \dot{\tilde{f}}(t_0)$$

Its equivalent parametric form is,

$$\lim_{h \to 0+} \frac{\tilde{f}(t_0 + h) \ominus \tilde{f}(t_0)}{h} =$$

$$\left[\begin{array}{l} \min\left\{ \lim_{h \to 0} \frac{\left(\underline{f}(t_0 + h) - \underline{f}(t_0)\right)}{h}, \lim_{h \to 0} \frac{\left(\underline{f}(t_0 + h) - \overline{f}(t_0)\right)}{h}, \lim_{h \to 0} \frac{\left(\overline{f}(t_0 + h) - \overline{f}(t_0)\right)}{h}, \lim_{h \to 0} \frac{\left(\overline{f}(t_0 + h) - \underline{f}(t_0)\right)}{h} \right\}, \\[2mm] \max\left\{ \lim_{h \to 0} \frac{\left(\underline{f}(t_0) - \underline{f}(t_0 - h)\right)}{h}, \lim_{h \to 0} \frac{\left(\underline{f}(t_0) - \overline{f}(t_0 - h)\right)}{h}, \lim_{h \to 0} \frac{\left(\overline{f}(t_0) - \overline{f}(t_0 - h)\right)}{h}, \lim_{h \to 0} \frac{\left(\overline{f}(t_0) - \underline{f}(t_0 - h)\right)}{h} \right\} \end{array} \right]$$

$$\lim_{h \to 0-} \frac{\tilde{f}(t_0) \ominus \tilde{f}(t_0 - h)}{h} =$$

$$\left[\begin{array}{l} \min\left\{ \lim_{h \to 0} \frac{\left(\underline{f}(t_0) - \underline{f}(t_0 - h)\right)}{h}, \lim_{h \to 0} \frac{\left(\underline{f}(t_0) - \overline{f}(t_0 - h)\right)}{h}, \lim_{h \to 0} \frac{\left(\overline{f}(t_0) - \overline{f}(t_0 - h)\right)}{h}, \lim_{h \to 0} \frac{\left(\overline{f}(t_0) - \underline{f}(t_0 - h)\right)}{h} \right\}, \\[2mm] \max\left\{ \lim_{h \to 0} \frac{\left(\underline{f}(t_0) - \underline{f}(t_0 - h)\right)}{h}, \lim_{h \to 0} \frac{\left(\underline{f}(t_0) - \overline{f}(t_0 - h)\right)}{h}, \lim_{h \to 0} \frac{\left(\overline{f}(t_0) - \overline{f}(t_0 - h)\right)}{h}, \lim_{h \to 0} \frac{\left(\overline{f}(t_0) - \underline{f}(t_0 - h)\right)}{h} \right\} \end{array} \right]$$

In the next section, the mathematical model of diabetes in a fuzzy environment is explained.

10.4 PREDICTIVE MATHEMATICAL MODEL OF DIABETES IN A CRISP ENVIRONMENT

The mathematical model of diabetes given by Boutayeb et al. (2004) is given as follows:

$$\dot{C}(t) = -(\theta + \lambda)\,C(t) + \lambda N(t)$$

$$\dot{N}(t) = I(t) - (v + \delta)\,C(t) - \mu N(t)$$

with initial conditions,

$$C(0) = C_0 \quad \text{and} \quad N(0) = N_0. \tag{10.1}$$

where, $C(t)$ and $D(t)$ denotes the fuzzy count of individuals with diabetes, both with and without complications, respectively. $N(t)$ denotes the total count of individuals with diabetes, both with and without complications. i.e., $N(t) = C(t) + D(t)$ and let $I(t)$ denotes the Prevalence of diabetes mellitus.

λ is probability, the diabetic person developing complications

v represents the rate at which diabetic patients with complications experience a significant decline in functional ability.

δ denotes the mortality rate attributed to complications.

μ represents the natural mortality rate.

γ represents the rate of curing the complications

$$\theta = \gamma + \mu + \delta + v$$

C_0 and N_0 are fuzzy initial conditions.

Theorem 10.1

If $C(t), N(t) : [0, \infty) \to \mathbb{Z}_+$ is continuous then solution of system as in (10.1) is given as follows,

$$C(t) = e^{\alpha_1 t}\left(\frac{(\alpha_1 - \mu)}{(\alpha_1 + \beta_1)} + \frac{1}{(\beta_1 - \alpha_1)}\frac{I\lambda}{\alpha_1} \right) + \frac{N_0\lambda\left(e^{\beta_1 t} - e^{\alpha_1 t}\right)}{(\beta_1 - \alpha_1)}$$

$$+ \left(\frac{I\lambda}{\beta_1(\beta_1 - \alpha_1)} + \frac{(\beta_1 + \mu)}{(\alpha_1 + \beta_1)} \right)e^{\beta_1 t} + \frac{1}{(\beta_1 - \alpha_1)}\frac{I\lambda}{\alpha_1}$$

$$N(t) = \frac{C_0}{(\beta - \alpha)}\left(e^{\beta t} - e^{\alpha t}\right) + e^{\alpha t}\left(\frac{I(\beta + \lambda + \theta)}{\beta(\beta - \alpha)} - \frac{N_0}{(\alpha - \beta)} \right)$$

$$+ e^{\beta t}\left(\frac{(\alpha + \lambda + \theta)I}{\alpha(\alpha - \beta)} - \frac{N_0(\beta + \lambda + \theta)}{(\beta - \alpha)} \right) + \frac{I(\lambda + \theta)}{\alpha\beta}$$

where,

$$\alpha_1 = \frac{-(\lambda + \theta + \mu) + \sqrt{(\lambda + \theta + \mu)^2 - 4(\mu\lambda + \mu\theta + \lambda\delta + \lambda v)}}{2}$$

$$\beta_1 = \frac{-(\lambda+\theta+\mu)-\sqrt{(\lambda+\theta+\mu)^2-4(\mu\lambda+\mu\theta+\lambda\delta+\lambda v)}}{2}$$

$$\alpha = \frac{-(\lambda+\theta+\mu)+\sqrt{(\lambda+\theta+\mu)^2-4(\mu\lambda+\mu\theta-\lambda\delta-\lambda v)}}{2}$$

$$\beta = \frac{-(\lambda+\theta+\mu)-\sqrt{(\lambda+\theta+\mu)^2-4(\mu\lambda+\mu\theta-\lambda\delta-\lambda v)}}{2}$$

Proof:

The variables C and N are continuous in $[0,\infty)$. So, take Laplace Transform on system as in (10.1),

$$L(\dot{C}(t)) = -(\theta+\lambda)\,L(C(t))+\lambda L(N(t))$$

$$L(\dot{N}(t)) = L(I(t))-(v+\delta)L(C(t))-\mu L(N(t))$$

with initial conditions, $C(0) = C_0$ and $N(0) = N_0$

By using the Laplace transformation formula, we have

$$(s+\theta+\lambda)C(s)-\lambda N(s) = C_0 \tag{10.2}$$

$$(s+\mu)N(s)-(v+\delta)C(s) = N_0 + \frac{I}{s} \tag{10.3}$$

For eliminating $C(s)$, equation (10.2) is multiplied by $(v+\delta)$ and equation (10.3) is multiplied by $(s+\theta+\lambda)$ and add the resultant equations, we obtain,

$$N(s) = \frac{C_0 - N_0(s+\theta+\lambda)+I\dfrac{(s+\theta+\lambda)}{s}}{s^2+(\mu+\lambda+\theta)s+(\mu\lambda+\mu\theta-\lambda v-\lambda\delta)}$$

Taking the inverse Laplace Transformation of the aforementioned equation, we get,

$$N(t) = \frac{C_0}{(\beta-\alpha)}\left(e^{\beta t}-e^{\alpha t}\right)+e^{\alpha t}\left(\frac{I(\beta+\lambda+\theta)}{\beta(\beta-\alpha)}-\frac{N_0}{(\alpha-\beta)}\right)$$

$$+e^{\beta t}\left(\frac{(\alpha+\lambda+\theta)I}{\alpha(\alpha-\beta)}-\frac{N_0(\beta+\lambda+\theta)}{(\beta-\alpha)}\right)+\frac{I(\lambda+\theta)}{\alpha\beta}$$

Similarly, we eliminate $N(s)$ from equations (10.2) and (10.3) and after taking inverse Laplace transformation, we obtain,

$$C(t) = e^{\alpha_1 t}\left(\frac{(\alpha_1-\mu)C_0}{(\alpha_1+\beta_1)}+\frac{1}{(\beta_1-\alpha_1)}\frac{I\lambda}{\alpha_1}\right)+\frac{N_0\lambda\left(e^{\beta_1 t}-e^{\alpha_1 t}\right)}{(\beta_1-\alpha_1)}+\left(\frac{I\lambda}{\beta_1(\beta_1-\alpha_1)}+\frac{(\beta_1+\mu)C_0}{(\alpha_1+\beta_1)}\right)e^{\beta_1 t}+\frac{1}{(\beta_1-\alpha_1)}\frac{I\lambda}{\alpha_1}$$

Theorem 10.2

The solution of system as in (10.1) as in Theorem 10.1 is unique and exist iff,

$$\left(\mu\lambda + \mu\theta + \lambda\delta + \lambda v\right) > 0 \text{ and } \left(\mu\lambda + \mu\theta - \lambda\delta - \lambda v\right) > 0$$

Proof:

Solution of system as in (10.1) is given as,

$$N(t) = \frac{C_0}{(\beta - \alpha)}\left(e^{\beta t} - e^{\alpha t}\right) + e^{\alpha t}\left(\frac{I(\beta + \lambda + \theta)}{\beta(\beta - \alpha)} - \frac{N_0}{(\alpha - \beta)}\right)$$

$$+ e^{\beta t}\left(\frac{(\alpha + \lambda + \theta)I}{\alpha(\alpha - \beta)} - \frac{N_0(\beta + \lambda + \theta)}{(\beta - \alpha)}\right) + \frac{I(\lambda + \theta)}{\alpha\beta}$$

$$C(t) = e^{\alpha_1 t}\left(\frac{(\alpha_1 - \mu)C_0}{(\alpha_1 + \beta_1)} + \frac{1}{(\beta_1 - \alpha_1)}\frac{I\lambda}{\alpha_1}\right) + \frac{N_0\lambda\left(e^{\beta_1 t} - e^{\alpha_1 t}\right)}{(\beta_1 - \alpha_1)}$$

$$+ \left(\frac{I\lambda}{\beta_1(\beta_1 - \alpha_1)} + \frac{(\beta_1 + \mu)C_0}{(\alpha_1 + \beta_1)}\right)e^{\beta_1 t} + \frac{1}{(\beta_1 - \alpha_1)}\frac{I\lambda}{\alpha_1}$$

From the aforementioned expression, it is obvious that $\alpha \neq \beta, \alpha_1 \neq \beta_1$ and to remain the solution $N(t)$ and $C(t)$, bounded following condition must hold,

$$(\lambda + \theta + \mu) > \sqrt{(\lambda + \theta + \mu)^2 - 4(\mu\lambda + \mu\theta - \lambda\delta - \lambda v)}$$

$$(\lambda + \theta + \mu) > \sqrt{(\lambda + \theta + \mu)^2 - 4(\mu\lambda + \mu\theta + \lambda\delta + \lambda v)}$$

After simplifying the above condition, we obtain,

$$(\mu\lambda + \mu\theta - \lambda\delta - \lambda v) > 0$$

$$(\mu\lambda + \mu\theta + \lambda\delta + \lambda v) > 0$$

These above conditions are required for unique and bounded solution.

In the following section, we delve into the mathematical model of diabetes mellitus within a fuzzy environment.

10.5 MATHEMATICAL MODELLING OF DIABETES IN FUZZY ENVIRONMENT

Uncertainty may occur in estimating the count of patients with and without complications of diabetes. So, the fuzzy set up gives a more realistic approach to formulate such problem mathematically. Thus, the mathematical model of diabetes with fuzzy initial conditions is given as follows,

$$\dot{\tilde{C}}(t) = -(\theta + \lambda)\,\tilde{C}(t) + \lambda\tilde{N}(t)$$

$$\dot{\tilde{N}}(t) = I(t) - (v+\delta)\,\tilde{C}(t) - \mu\tilde{N}(t)$$

$$\tilde{C}(0) = \tilde{C}_0 \text{ and } \tilde{N}(0) = \tilde{N}_0 \tag{10.4}$$

The fuzzy solution of the system as in (10.4) by using technique in section (10.3) is given as follows,

$$\tilde{N}(t) = \frac{\tilde{C}_0}{(\beta-\alpha)}\left(e^{\beta t} - e^{\alpha t}\right) + e^{\alpha t}\left(\frac{I(\beta+\lambda+\theta)}{\beta(\beta-\alpha)} - \frac{\tilde{N}_0}{(\alpha-\beta)}\right) + e^{\beta t}\left(\frac{(\alpha+\lambda+\theta)I}{\alpha(\alpha-\beta)} - \frac{\tilde{N}_0(\beta+\lambda+\theta)}{(\beta-\alpha)}\right) + \frac{I(\lambda+\theta)}{\alpha\beta}$$

$$\tilde{C}(t) = e^{\alpha_1 t}\left(\frac{(\alpha_1-\mu)\tilde{C}_0}{(\alpha_1+\beta_1)} + \frac{1}{(\beta_1-\alpha_1)}\frac{I\lambda}{\alpha_1}\right) + \frac{\tilde{N}_0\lambda\left(e^{\beta_1 t} - e^{\alpha_1 t}\right)}{(\beta_1-\alpha_1)}$$

$$+ \left(\frac{I\lambda}{\beta_1(\beta_1-\alpha_1)} + \frac{(\beta_1+\mu)\tilde{C}_0}{(\alpha_1+\beta_1)}\right)e^{\beta_1 t} + \frac{1}{(\beta_1-\alpha_1)}\frac{I\lambda}{\alpha_1}$$

Now taking $\alpha - cut$ the above fuzzy solution,

$$^\alpha\tilde{N}(t) = \frac{^\alpha\tilde{C}_0}{(\beta-\alpha)}\left(e^{\beta t} - e^{\alpha t}\right) + e^{\alpha t}\left(\frac{I(\beta+\lambda+\theta)}{\beta(\beta-\alpha)} - \frac{^\alpha\tilde{N}_0}{(\alpha-\beta)}\right)$$

$$+ e^{\beta t}\left(\frac{(\alpha+\lambda+\theta)I}{\alpha(\alpha-\beta)} - \frac{^\alpha\tilde{N}_0(\beta+\lambda+\theta)}{(\beta-\alpha)}\right) + \frac{I(\lambda+\theta)}{\alpha\beta}$$

$$^\alpha\tilde{C}(t) = e^{\alpha_1 t}\left(\frac{(\alpha_1-\mu)^\alpha\tilde{C}_0}{(\alpha_1+\beta_1)} + \frac{1}{(\beta_1-\alpha_1)}\frac{I\lambda}{\alpha_1}\right) + \frac{^\alpha\tilde{N}_0\lambda\left(e^{\beta_1 t} - e^{\alpha_1 t}\right)}{(\beta_1-\alpha_1)}$$

$$+ \left(\frac{I\lambda}{\beta_1(\beta_1-\alpha_1)} + \frac{(\beta_1+\mu)^\alpha\tilde{C}_0}{(\alpha_1+\beta_1)}\right)e^{\beta_1 t} + \frac{1}{(\beta_1-\alpha_1)}\frac{I\lambda}{\alpha_1}$$

The parametric form after taking $\alpha - cut$,

$$\left[\underline{N},\,\overline{N}\right] = \frac{\left[\underline{C}_0,\overline{C}_0\right]}{(\beta-\alpha)}\left(e^{\beta t} - e^{\alpha t}\right) + e^{\alpha t}\left(\frac{I(\beta+\lambda+\theta)}{\beta(\beta-\alpha)} - \frac{\left[\underline{N}_0,\overline{N}_0\right]}{(\alpha-\beta)}\right)$$

$$+ e^{\beta t}\left(\frac{(\alpha+\lambda+\theta)I}{\alpha(\alpha-\beta)} - \frac{\left[\underline{N}_0,\overline{N}_0\right](\beta+\lambda+\theta)}{(\beta-\alpha)}\right) + \frac{I(\lambda+\theta)}{\alpha\beta} \tag{10.5}$$

$$\left[\underline{C},\,\overline{C}\right] = e^{\alpha_1 t}\left(\frac{(\alpha_1-\mu)\left[\underline{C}_0,\overline{C}_0\right]}{(\alpha_1+\beta_1)} + \frac{1}{(\beta_1-\alpha_1)}\frac{I\lambda}{\alpha_1}\right) + \frac{\left[\underline{N}_0,\overline{N}_0\right]\lambda\left(e^{\beta_1 t} - e^{\alpha_1 t}\right)}{(\beta_1-\alpha_1)}$$

$$+ \left(\frac{I\lambda}{\beta_1(\beta_1-\alpha_1)} + \frac{(\beta_1+\mu)\left[\underline{C}_0,\overline{C}_0\right]}{(\alpha_1+\beta_1)}\right)e^{\beta_1 t} + \frac{1}{(\beta_1-\alpha_1)}\frac{I\lambda}{\alpha_1} \tag{10.6}$$

Theorem 10.3

Equations (10.5) and (10.6) have fuzzy solutions if it satisfies $\underline{C} \leq \bar{C}$ and $\underline{N} \leq \bar{N}$ respectively.

Proof:

Let us consider the solution as in equation (10.5),

$$[\underline{N}, \bar{N}] = \frac{[\underline{C}_0, \bar{C}_0]}{(\beta - \alpha)}\left(e^{\beta t} - e^{\alpha t}\right) + e^{\alpha t}\left(\frac{I(\beta + \lambda + \theta)}{\beta(\beta - \alpha)} - \frac{[\underline{N}_0, \bar{N}_0]}{(\alpha - \beta)}\right)$$

$$+ e^{\beta t}\left(\frac{(\alpha + \lambda + \theta)I}{\alpha(\alpha - \beta)} - \frac{[\underline{N}_0, \bar{N}_0](\beta + \lambda + \theta)}{(\beta - \alpha)}\right) + \frac{I(\lambda + \theta)}{\alpha\beta}$$

Comparing component-wise,

$$\underline{N} = \frac{\underline{C}_0}{(\beta - \alpha)}\left(e^{\beta t} - e^{\alpha t}\right) + e^{\alpha t}\left(\frac{I(\beta + \lambda + \theta)}{\beta(\beta - \alpha)} - \frac{\underline{N}_0}{(\alpha - \beta)}\right)$$

$$+ e^{\beta t}\left(\frac{(\alpha + \lambda + \theta)I}{\alpha(\alpha - \beta)} - \frac{\underline{N}_0(\beta + \lambda + \theta)}{(\beta - \alpha)}\right) + \frac{I(\lambda + \theta)}{\alpha\beta}$$

$$\bar{N} = \frac{\bar{C}_0}{(\beta - \alpha)}\left(e^{\beta t} - e^{\alpha t}\right) + e^{\alpha t}\left(\frac{I(\beta + \lambda + \theta)}{\beta(\beta - \alpha)} - \frac{\bar{N}_0}{(\alpha - \beta)}\right)$$

$$+ e^{\beta t}\left(\frac{(\alpha + \lambda + \theta)I}{\alpha(\alpha - \beta)} - \frac{\bar{N}_0(\beta + \lambda + \theta)}{(\beta - \alpha)}\right) + \frac{I(\lambda + \theta)}{\alpha\beta}$$

Take difference between $\underline{N}$ and $\bar{N}$,

$$\bar{N} - \underline{N} = \frac{(\bar{C}_0 - \underline{C}_0)}{(\beta - \alpha)}\left(e^{\beta t} - e^{\alpha t}\right) + e^{\alpha t}\left(\frac{I(\beta + \lambda + \theta)}{\beta(\beta - \alpha)} - \frac{(\bar{N}_0 - \underline{N}_0)}{(\alpha - \beta)}\right)$$

$$+ e^{\beta t}\left(\frac{(\alpha + \lambda + \theta)I}{\alpha(\alpha - \beta)} - \frac{(\bar{N}_0 - \underline{N}_0)(\beta + \lambda + \theta)}{(\beta - \alpha)}\right) + \frac{I(\lambda + \theta)}{\alpha\beta}$$

For existence of solution as in equation (10.5), we have $\beta > \alpha$, $\bar{C}_0 \geq \underline{C}_0$, $\bar{N}_0 \geq \underline{N}_0$ and all parameters $\lambda, \theta, \nu, \delta, \mu$ are positive.

It gives, $(\bar{N} - \underline{N}) > 0$

Similarly, we prove for equation (10.6), $(\bar{C} - \underline{C}) > 0$.

That is the existence condition for fuzzy solution of equations (10.5) and (10.6).

In the next section, we give the condition for the stability of systems as in (10.1) and (10.4) in crisp and fuzzy environment.

10.6   STABILITY ANALYSIS

For the equilibrium point, we put $\dot{C}(t) = 0$ and $\dot{N}(t) = 0$

$$C_e = \frac{\lambda I}{\lambda(v+\delta)+\mu(\lambda+\theta)}, \quad N_e = \frac{I(\lambda+\theta)}{\lambda(v+\delta)+\mu(\lambda+\theta)}$$

System as in (10.1) is linear dynamical system so, for stability analysis, we obtain the Jacobian of system as in (10.1) around equilibrium points as follows:

$$\begin{bmatrix} -(\theta+\lambda) & \lambda \\ -(v+\delta) & -\mu \end{bmatrix}$$

The characteristic polynomial is,

$$x^2 + (\theta+\lambda+\mu)x + \mu\theta + \mu\lambda + \lambda v + \lambda\delta = 0$$

Roots of this equation,

$$x = \frac{-(\theta+\lambda+\mu) \pm \sqrt{(\lambda+\theta+\mu)^2 - 4(\mu\lambda+\mu\theta+\lambda\delta+\lambda v)}}{2}$$

Now the possible cases are as follows:

1. If $(\lambda+\theta+\mu)^2 > 4(\mu\lambda+\mu\theta+\lambda\delta+\lambda v)$ and
   $(\theta+\lambda+\mu) > \sqrt{(\lambda+\theta+\mu)^2 - 4(\mu\lambda+\mu\theta+\lambda\delta+\lambda v)}$ then the zeros are real and negative, then system (10.1) has stable node.

2. If $(\theta+\lambda+\mu) < \sqrt{(\lambda+\theta+\mu)^2 - 4(\mu\lambda+\mu\theta+\lambda\delta+\lambda v)}$ then roots are positive so, system (1) has unstable node.

3. If $(\lambda+\theta+\mu)^2 < 4(\mu\lambda+\mu\theta+\lambda\delta+\lambda v)$ then roots are complex. Since real part is negative so it has stable focus otherwise unstable.

The same expressions and cases are true for system (10.4).

In the next section, we have solved numerical example and validated result at core.

10.7   NUMERICAL ILLUSTRATION

For system as in equation (10.4) is given as follows,

$$\dot{\tilde{C}}(t) = -0.68 \; C(t) + 0.66N(t)$$

$$\dot{\tilde{N}}(t) = 6 \times 10^7 - 0.1 \; C(t) - 0.02N(t)$$

For fuzzy initial condition data is,

$$^\alpha \tilde{C}_0 = \left[2 \times 10^6 \alpha + 45 \times 10^6, \; 45 \times 10^6 - 2 \times 10^6 \alpha \right]$$

$$^\alpha \tilde{N}_0 = \left[605 \times 10^5 + 6 \times 10^5 \alpha, \; 614 \times 10^5 - 3 \times 10^5 \alpha \right]$$

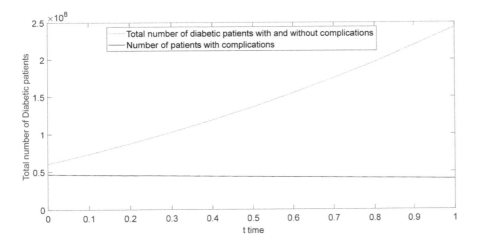

FIGURE 10.1 Evolution of diabetes patients with and without complications.

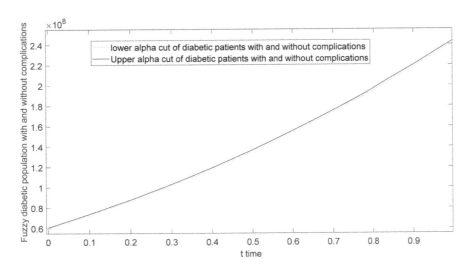

FIGURE 10.2 Evolution of fuzzy population of diabetes patients with and without complications.

After applying the proposed technique in Section 9.3, we have fuzzy representation of $C(t)$ and $N(t)$ is given in Figures 10.1 and 10.2 respectively.

After applying the technique, the following graphs are obtained,

For crisp solution, we have,

For fuzzy initial conditions,

10.8 RESULTS AND DISCUSSION

From Figure 10.1, it is observed that the total number of diabetic patients increases with time. In Figures 10.2 and 10.3, we can observe that support i.e., count of patients with and without complications remains bounded as time increases. By taking fuzzy initial condition, we have a more realistic range of patients. The mathematical model in a fuzzy environment, is solved under Modified Hukuhara derivative. The obtained fuzzy solution is bounded and unique. For stability analysis, the eigenvalues of this system are −0.557123 and −0.1429. So, the system is stable.

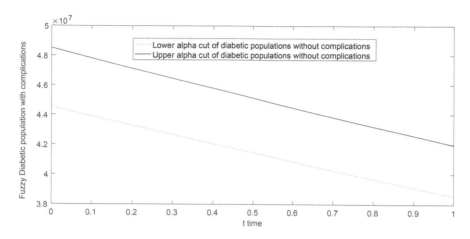

FIGURE 10.3   Evolution of fuzzy population of diabetes patients without complications.

10.9   CONCLUSION

In this chapter, we have solved a comprehensive mathematical framework for diabetes and its complications in crisp and fuzzy settings. We have also discussed the existence of crisp and fuzzy solution and gave stability analysis. In the numerical example, we have observed support, i.e., the count of diabetic patients with and without difficulties, bounded with time increases. To validate the fuzzy solution, we can see core exactly matches its crisp counterpart. In future scope, one can extend this article by taking all parameters involved in the mathematical model of diabetes are fuzzy.

REFERENCES

S. Abbasbandy and T. Allahviranlo (2002), Numerical solutions of fuzzy differential equations by Taylor method, *Computational Methods in Applied Mathematics*, 2, 113–124.
S. Abbasbandy and T. Allahviranloo (2004), Numerical solutions of fuzzy differential equations by Runge-Kutta method of order 2, *Nonlinear Studies* 11(1), 117–129.
E. Ackerman, I. Gatewood, J. Rosevear, and G. Molnar (1969), Blood Glucose Regulation and Diabetes. In: Heinmets F. (ed) *Concepts and Mod500 els of Biomathematics*. Marcel Decker, pp. 131–156.
B. Bede and S. G. Gal (2005), Generalization of the differentiability of fuzzy number valued function with application to fuzzy differential equation, *Fuzzy Sets and Systems*, 151, 581–599.
A. Boutayeb, E. Twizell, K. Achouayb, et al. (2004), A mathematical model for the burden of diabetes and its complications, *Biomedical Engineering Online*, 3, 20. https://doi.org/10.1186/1475-925X-3-20.
S. L. Chang and L. A. Zadeh (1972), On fuzzy mapping and control, *IEEE Transactions on System Man Cybernetics*, 2, 30–34.
O. Kaleva (1987), Fuzzy differential equations, *Fuzzy Sets and Systems*, 24, 301–317.
G. J. Klir and B. Yuan (1995) *Fuzzy Sets and fuzzy Logic: Theory and Applications*. Prentice Hall, Englewood Cliffs.
M. Ma, M. Friedman, and A. Kandel (1999), Numerical solutions of fuzzy differential equations, *Fuzzy Sets and Systems*, 105, 133–138.
A. Mahata, B. Roy, S. P. Mondal, and S. Alam (2017a), Application of ordinary differential equation in glucose-insulin regulatory system modeling in fuzzy environment, *Ecological Genetics and Genomics*, 3–5, 60–66. https://doi.org/10.1016/j.egg.2017.08.002.
A. Mahata, S.P. Mondal, S. Alam and B. Roy (2017b), Mathematical model of glucose-insulin regulatory system on 507 diabetes mellitus in fuzzy and crisp environment, *Ecological Genetics and Genomics*, 2, 25–34.

P. Pandit and P. Singh (2020), Fully Fuzzy Semi-Linear Dynamical System Solved by Fuzzy Laplace Transform Under Modified Hukuhara Derivative. In: Das K., Bansal J., Deep K., Nagar A., Pathipooranam P., Naidu R. (eds) *Soft Computing for Problem Solving. Advances in Intelligent Systems and Computing*, vol 1048. Springer, Singapore. https://doi.org/10.1007/978-981-15-0035-0_13.

M. L. Puri and D. A. Ralescu, (1983), Differential of fuzzy functions, *Journal of Mathematical Analysis and Applications*, 91, 321–325.

S. Song and C. Wu (2000), Existence and uniqueness of solutions to Cauchy problem of fuzzy differential equations, *Fuzzy Set System*, 110, 55–67.

F. Stahl and R. Johansson (2009), Diabetes mellitus modeling and short-term prediction based on blood glucose measurements, *Mathematical Biosciences,* 217, 101–117.

11 Applications of Mathematical Techniques to Artificial Intelligence

Mathematical Methods, Algorithms, Computer Programming and Applications

Rashmi Singh
Amity University

Neha Bhardwaj
Sharda University

Sardar M. N. Islam
Victoria University

11.1 INTRODUCTION: BACKGROUND AND DRIVING FORCES

The development of artificial intelligence (AI) will lead to new opportunities in the future, and the day will not be too far off when we will have our very own robotic companions. This has motivated many developers to begin creating code and create code and build artificial intelligence (AI) and machine learning systems. Developing algorithms for AI and machine learning (ML), however, is not an easy skill to learn and takes a significant amount of prior experience with programming as well as mathematical study. Many industries, including computer vision, online advertising, spam filtering, robotics, and fraud detection, among others, have successfully implemented AI (based on Ng 2016, 2017). AI and mathematics have become so dependent on one another (evident from Davies et al. 2017). In addition, supervised learning can be utilized to discover patterns (mentioned in Carifio et al. 2017, Heal et al. 2022, Hughes and Mark 2020, Levitt et al. 2022, Jejjala et al. 2019) by emphasizing the ability of mathematicians to interpret previously acquired functions and derive mathematical information with significant meaning.

The discipline makes use of concepts that come from the realm of mathematics and computer science because the answers to the following difficulties can be discovered in the discoveries that are made as a result of such processes: A home's price can be estimated by comparing it to other properties of a similar size and quality in terms of factors like the number of rooms and square footage, as well as making a movie recommendation for Netflix, financial projections for the company, a song recommendation for a Spotify playlist (as discussed in Peyré and Marco 2019, Deisenroth et al. 2012, James et al. 2023, Hou et al. 2019).

Mathematics plays a significant part because it is responsible for laying the groundwork for programming in each of these areas of study. And that is precisely what we focused on throughout this

DOI: 10.1201/9781003387459-11

class. We will present the major theoretical orientations alongside various illustrative outcomes and discuss the most pressing open issues.

A systems take in enormous amounts of label training data, examine the data for correlations and patterns, and then use these patterns to predict future states. Data can be found in various formats, but it is useful to view it as the conclusion of an unpredictable experiment whose results are subject to interpretation (as described in Ronald et al. 1989). Frequently, a table or spreadsheet is utilized to record the outcomes of a random experiment. Variables (also known as features) are often represented as columns and the items themselves (or units) as rows to enable data analysis. To further comprehend the usefulness of such a spreadsheet, it is instructive to examine three unique types of columns:

In the majority of tables, the first column serves as an identifier or index, assigning a unique label or number to each row.

Second, the experimental design can be reflected in the content of the columns (features) by indicating which experimental group a certain unit belongs to. Not infrequently, the data in these columns are deterministic, meaning they would remain constant even if the experiment were repeated.

In the other columns are the observed data from the experiment. Generally, such measurements are unstable; repeating the experiment would yield different results (as shown in Van and Hans 2001).

Many data sets are available online and in various software packages. In this way, a chatbot can learn to perform lifelike conversations with humans by being fed examples of text chats, and an image recognition computer can learn to identify and describe items in images by analyzing millions of examples. AI programming emphasizes learning, reasoning, and self-correction.

1. **The processes involved in learning**: This portion of the programming for AI focuses on collecting data and developing rules for turning that data into knowledge that can be used. The rules, often called algorithms, give the computing equipment step-by-step instructions to complete a certain activity.
2. **The processes of reasoning**: When it comes to the programming of AI, this particular aspect places an emphasis on choosing the suitable algorithm to get the intended result.
3. **Techniques of internal self-correction programming**: The development of AI frequently entails the incorporation of components such as this one, the purpose of which is to ensure that algorithms are continually improved and provide the most accurate results possible.

Applying such algorithms in AI involves understanding a wide range of subjects, including mathematics, probability theory, statistics, operations research, calculus, and many more. Mathematical rigor can be found at the foundation of virtually every single area of study in the fields of AI, ML, and data science (DS). This article contributes to the body of knowledge by presenting a new, up-to-date and in-innovative literature evaluation to integrate, synthesize, and suggest future study directions in these domains.

The materials to be discussed in this article are presented below.

11.2   LINEAR ALGEBRA

Linear Algebra is the mathematical framework that allows AI models to represent data and perform computations. It is the mathematics of arrays, also known as vectors, matrices, and tensors.

All important phases of constructing a model are supported by linear algebra (as referenced in Brijder et al. Xian 2022).

Important application areas made possible by linear algebra include data and learning model representation, word embeddings, and dimension reduction.

11.2.1 Data Representation

Data, which is the fuel for AI models, must be transformed into arrays before being fed to the models. Among the computations done on these arrays are matrix multiplications (dot product). Furthermore, this returns the result as a converted matrix/tensor of numbers.

11.2.2 Word Embeddings

It involves encoding high-dimensional data with a vector of lower dimension. Natural Language Processing (NLP) involves textual information. Dealing with text requires comprehension of a vast corpus of words. Each word has a distinct meaning similar to that of another. Vector embeddings in linear algebra allow us to represent these words more efficiently.

11.2.3 Eigenvectors (SVD)

Using principal component analysis, ideas such as eigenvectors allow us to reduce the number of characteristics or dimensions of the data while preserving their essence. Linear algebra is concerned with vectors and matrices (various array configurations) and operations on these arrays. Vectors in NumPy are one-dimensional arrays of numbers, but geometrically they have magnitude and direction.

Our information can be represented as a vector. In Figure 11.1, each row of these data is represented by a feature vector consisting of three elements or dimensions. N items in a vector constitute an n-dimensional vector space; in this example, we are able to observe three dimensions.

Today, linear algebra is utilized in all of the important applications. Examples include sentiment analysis on LinkedIn or Twitter posts (embeddings), identifying a type of lung illness from X-ray images (computer vision), and speech-to-text bots (NLP).

In tensors, all of these data kinds are represented by integers. We employ a neural network to discover patterns from vectorized processes. It then generates a processed tensor, which is decoded to provide the model's final conclusion. Each phase applies mathematical procedures to the arrays of data.

11.2.4 Dimensionality Reduction—Vector Space Transformation

Vector Space Transformation

$$\begin{bmatrix} * \\ * \\ * \end{bmatrix} \rightarrow \begin{bmatrix} * \\ * \end{bmatrix}$$

Data Representation

Distance	Speed	Time
30	80	120
25	76	145
47	66	133
55	83	148
70	60	189

$$\rightarrow \begin{bmatrix} 30 \\ 80 \\ 120 \end{bmatrix} \rightarrow$$

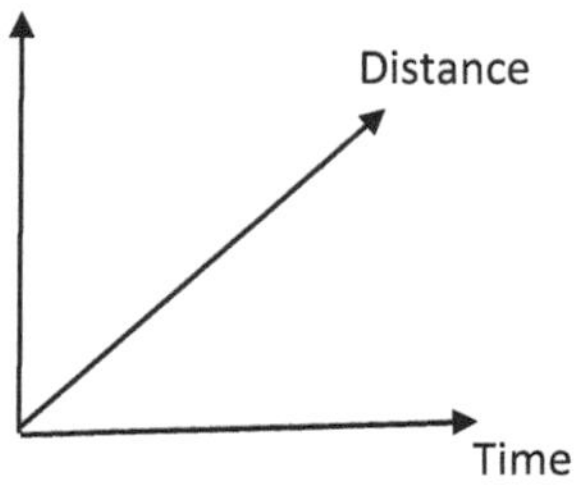

FIGURE 11.1　Data representing a feature vector.

We can conceptualize embeddings as the replacement of an *n*-dimensional vector with a vector from a lower-dimensional space. This solution is more meaningful and overcomes computational obstacles.

A three-dimensional vector, for instance, is replaced by a two-dimensional space. However, it can be extrapolated to a real-world scenario with a huge number of dimensions.

Reducing dimensions does not result in the elimination of data characteristics. Instead, it entails discovering new features that are linear functions of the original features while keeping their variance.

Locating these new variables (features) corresponds to locating the major components (PCs). This leads to the solution of eigenvectors and eigenvalues problems. Figure 11.2 shows the Python coding for determining Eigenvalues and Eigenvectors of a square matrix, obtained as in Figure 11.3.

11.3 APPLICATIONS OF STATISTICS IN DATA SCIENCE THROUGH MACHINE LEARNING ALGORITHMS

11.3.1 REGRESSION

In the domain of AI, the mathematical method used to determine the relationship between two or more variables is referred to as regression. Regression is a technique that is frequently employed to predict the behavior of one variable based on the value of another variable.

```python
# importing numpy library
import numpy as np

# create numpy 2d-array
a = np.array([[3, 4, 1],
       [1, 3, 4],
       [4, 7, 3]])

print("Printing the Original square array:\n",
  a)

# finding eigenvalues and eigenvectors
p, q = np.linalg.eig(m)

# printing eigen values
print("Eigen values of the given square array:\n",
  p)

# printing eigen vectors
print("Eigenvectors of the given square array:\n",
  q)
```

FIGURE 11.2   Python program for finding Eigen values and Eigen vectors of a square array.

```
Printing the Original square array:
 [[3 4 1]
 [1 3 4]
 [4 7 3]]
Eigen values of the given square array:
 [ 9.8132827   0.68165281 -1.49493551]
Eigenvectors of the given square array:
 [[-0.4085404  -0.85256524  0.44014458]
 [-0.50595723  0.51555201 -0.6495871 ]
 [-0.75967231 -0.08566583  0.61992689]]
```

FIGURE 11.3   Output of coding of Figure 9.2.

```
from scipy import stats

x = [10,11,12,13,15,16,17,18,20,26,29,38,42,50]
y = [70,72,86,87,88,80,86,87,94,78,77,95,85,97]

slope, intercept, r, p, std_err = stats.linregress(x, y)

def myfunc(x):
    return slope * x + intercept

speed = myfunc(25)

print(speed)
```
⌐→ 85.21247375486182

FIGURE 11.4   Python program on the application of linear regression.

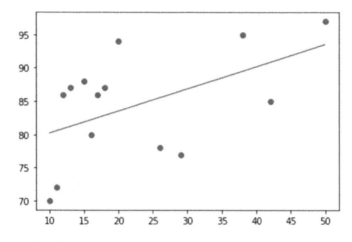

FIGURE 11.5   Scatter plot of regression model of Figure 11.4.

In contrast to the categorization models, the regression models produce numeric values as their output. Additionally, it utilizes continuous values for both the dependent and independent variables, and the majority of the time, regression is categorized as supervised learning.

Different types of regression analytics include simple linear regression, multivariate regression, polynomial regression, quantile regression, profit regression, and logistic regression (as discussed in Mahadik et al. 2022, Joshi and Saxena 2020, Koenker 2005). We may wish to determine if teaching a student longer affects their test scores or the expense of a particular lifestyle. These problems can be answered using regression. Linear regression is a statistical technique for predicting a response by choosing the best line representing the relationship between dependent and independent variables. Let's assume you have access to a dataset (training set) exhibiting ice cream y sales on days with average temperatures x. A regression model learns weights w that allows for reliable prediction of y by utilizing training data. From Figure 11.4 and random data, we can predict the ice cream sale when the temperature is 25°C; this can be seen in the adjacent scatter plot of Figure 11.5.

11.3.2 PROBABILITY THEORY

Probability theory is a subject of mathematics and statistics that focuses on investigating random occurrences. This skill is necessary for data scientists who work with data that has been modified by chance (as solved in Hogg et al. 1977, Koller et al. 2007). Given that chance happens in every circumstance, probability theory must be applied in order to explain how chance operates.

The purpose is to determine the likelihood that a particular event will occur. This is frequently achieved by employing a numeric scale ranging from 0 to 1, with "0" representing improbability and "1" representing perfect confidence.

11.3.3 NORMAL DISTRIBUTION

The normal distribution, sometimes known as a bell curve, is represented in Figure 11.6 with the blue curve. It has symmetry about the middle black line, where the mean, median, and mode correspond, and 50% of data values reside on the left side of the black line and 50% on the right side.

With mean (μ) and standard deviation (σ) as the parameters, a random variable "x" is normally distributed if its probability density function looks like this:

$$y = \frac{1}{\sqrt{2\pi}} e^{-\frac{(x-\mu)^2}{2\sigma}}$$

Since the sum of all possible probabilities is 1, the total area under the curve is 1. So, in both directions, the probabilities around the mean move similarly. That's why the normal distribution about the mean is exactly similar.

Depending on the dispersion of the data, the distribution may vary marginally. If there is a sufficient departure from the mean, the normally distributed curve will be flatter if the range and standard deviation of the data are quite large (as shown in Van and Hans 2001, Field et al. 2012).

Numerous natural events in the world display a log-normal distribution, including financial data and forecasting data. We can turn the data (as done in Olhede et al. 2018) into a normal distribution using transformation techniques. Several measurement errors in an experiment, the position of a particle experiencing diffusion, etc., also comply with the normality principle. Apart from normal distribution, other distributions from statistics that play a great role in AI are binomial, Poisson, uniform, logistic, multinomial, exponential, and chi-square distributions.

11.3.4 LOGISTIC DISTRIBUTION

It is used to describe growth. Both distributions are nearly identical, but the logistic distribution has a larger area under the tails, indicating a greater likelihood of an event occurring further

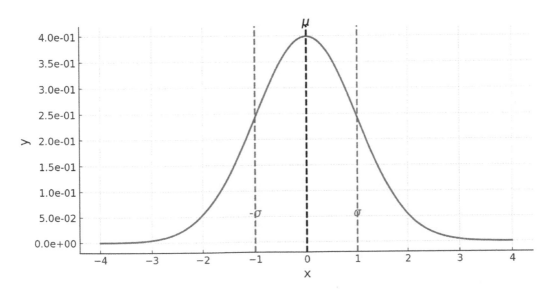

FIGURE 11.6 The standard normal distribution curve.

```
sns.distplot(random.normal(scale=2, size=1000),hist=False,color="red")
sns.distplot(random.logistic(size=1000),hist=False,color="green")

plt.show()
```

FIGURE 11.7   Python program on the application of normal and logistic distribution.

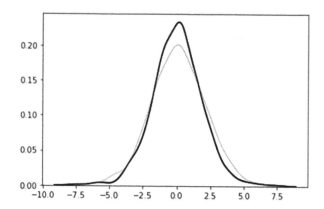

FIGURE 11.8   Difference in the graph of normal and logistic distribution.

from the mean. With the exception of the peak, the normal and logistic distributions are nearly identical for larger values of scale (standard deviation). Figure 11.7 shows the Python code, while Figure 11.8 shows the difference in these distributions.

11.3.5   Z-Score

A z-score in statistics indicates the number of standard deviations a result deviates from the mean. A z-score is computed by the formula:

$$z = (Y - \mu) / \sigma$$

where Y is a single raw data value, μ represents the population mean, σ represents the population standard deviation.

Suppose we have a one-dimensional array of type:

```
data = np.array([7, 8, 9, 14, 14, 16, 18, 19, 19, 21, 22])
```

We calculated the z-score and got the value as:

```
stats.zscore(data)

array([-1.62857586, -1.4295277 , -1.23047954, -0.23523874, -0.23523874,
        0.16285759,  0.56095391,  0.76000207,  0.76000207,  1.15809839,
        1.35714655])
```

Each z-score indicates the number of standard deviations that separate an individual value from the mean. For instance: The first "7" value in the array is 1.629% below the mean. The array's final value, "22," is 1.357 standard deviations above the mean.

Likewise, if we have a multi-dimensional array, we may use the axis option to specify that each z-score should be calculated relative to its own array. Suppose instead that we have a Pandas Data Frame. We can use the apply function to get the z-score of each column's values.

11.3.6 THE CENTRAL LIMIT THEOREM

"The sampling distribution of the mean for a variable will resemble a normal distribution, regardless of the distribution of the variable in the population, according to the central limit theorem, provided that the sample size is sufficiently large. This is true regardless of the distribution of the variable in the population".

To comprehend it, let's begin with the code: we import the appropriate packages and define a population of random integers with a size of 1,000,000. The sample size is defined as 1. Later, we will experiment with other sample size values. We execute the loop 1000 times

```
number_of_samples = 10000
sample_means = np.rand(number_of_samples)
sample_size = 1
a = np.rand(number_of_samples)
for i in range(0,number_of_samples):
  a = np.randint(1,population_size,sample_size)
  sample_means[i] = population[a].mean()

plt.subplot(1,2,2)
plt.xticks(fontsize=12)
plt.yticks(fontsize=12)
sns.distplot(sample_means,hist = False,kde = True)
plt.title("Graph of Sample mean",fontsize=18)
plt.xlabel("Sample mean",fontsize=18)
plt.ylabel("Density",fontsize=18)
plt.subplots_adjust(bottom=0.1, right=2, top=0.9)
```

Now we can view the graph in Figure 11.9 of the "sampling distribution of sample mean" for various sample size values.

When a large sample size is utilized to calculate the means, the probability distribution becomes increasingly symmetrical. As the sample size approaches, the probability distribution tends to become absolutely symmetrical as the population means become centered on the curve. Normal distribution is represented by the resulting curve.

11.4 SOME OTHER STATISTICAL METHODS

Some other statistical methods which are used in DS widely are the following:

Data skewness is a critical challenge that data scientists regularly face in real-time case studies. In a normal distribution, data are scattered symmetrically. The symmetrical distribution has zero skewness since all measures of central tendency mean, median, and mode are centered (*Mean = Median = Mode*).

When there is a positive skewness in the data, the mean will be higher than the median and the results are negatively skewed, as seen in Figure 11.10. The median represents the middle value, whereas the mode is always the highest. Therefore, the average exceeds the median.

Extremely positive skewness is undesirable for distribution purposes since it can lead to erroneous conclusions. Data transformation technologies aid in the normalization of skewed data. The log transformation is a well-known transformation for positively skewed distributions. The log transformation suggests calculating the natural logarithm for each value in the dataset.

As illustrated in Figure 11.11, the mean is less than the median for negatively skewed data. Negatively Skewed Distribution is a distribution whose mean, median, and mode are negative as opposed to positive or zero.

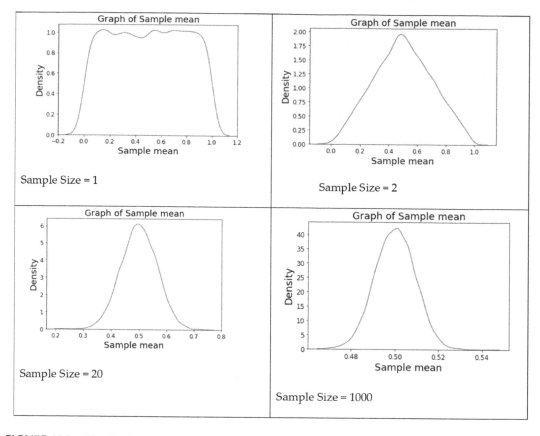

FIGURE 11.9   The distribution tends toward the normal distribution as the sample size grows.

FIGURE 11.10   Positive skewness: Mean > Median > Mode.

Multiple transformations can be performed on the data to preserve its information while simultaneously plotting it on a symmetrical curve. Even though the characteristics of the data determine this transformation, the following operations are used to transform data.

- Re-plotting each data point after calculating its square root.
- Taking the cube root of each data point and redrawing the results.
- After calculating the logarithm of each data point, the next step is to re-plot each data point.
- Re-plotting each point of data after calculating its reciprocal.

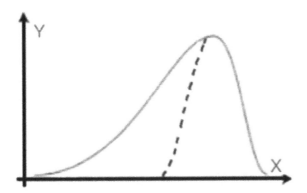

FIGURE 11.11   Negative skewness: Mode >Median>Mean.

11.4.1 KURTOSIS

The degree of presence of outliers in the distribution is measured by kurtosis.

Excess kurtosis is utilized in statistics and probability theory to compare the kurtosis coefficient to the normal distribution. Extra kurtosis is derived by subtracting kurtosis from 3, given that the kurtosis of normal distributions is 3. The excess kurtosis can be either negative (Platykurtic), positive (Leptokurtic), or close to zero.

A high kurtosis value suggests that the distribution's tails have more extreme values than the normal distribution's tail. This may result in a length that is six or seven standard deviations above or below the mean. Likewise, if the value of kurtosis is sufficiently low, the tail of the distribution will be shorter than the tail of a normal distribution. A high kurtosis score is usually viewed as riskier, as data used in any ML algorithm tend to generate outlier values that are further from the mean. Figure 11.12 shows leptokurtic has long tails due to the existence of numerous outliers, whereas platykurtic has short tails due to the presence of fewer outliers.

11.5   CALCULUS

The subject of study in calculus is anything that can vary, including parameters, functions, errors, and approximate values. Calculus in many dimensions is a necessary skill for anyone working in the field of artificial intelligence (adapted from Zhang et al. 2019, Bender and Edward 1996).

The following is a list of the most significant topics in calculus, however, it is not exhaustive:

Examples of derivatives include rules (such as addition, product, and chain rule), hyperbolic derivatives (such as tanh and cosh), and partial derivatives. Derivatives also include partial derivatives. The Python instructions for calculating the partial derivative of a function with three variables are displayed in Figure 7.13, and the results are displayed in Figure 7.14.

Integration - Indefinite and definite integrals. Figure 11.15 shows Python codes for definite and indefinite integral of a function, while Figure 11.16 shows its output.

Vector/Matrix Calculus—different derivative operators (Gradient, Jacobian, Hessian and Laplacian). Figure 11.17 is the Python code to determine the rank of a 3 * 3 matrix. Figure 11.18 shows its output.

Gradient algorithms include topics like local and global maximums and minimums, saddle points, convex functions, batches and mini-batches, stochastic gradient descent, and performance comparison.

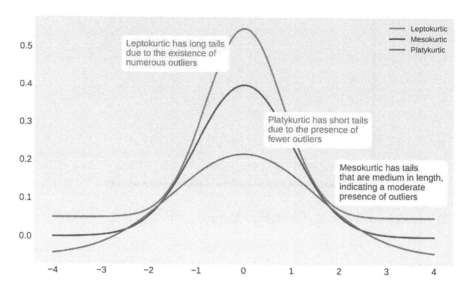

FIGURE 11.12　Types of kurtosis: Leptokurtic, Mesokurtic and Platykurtic.

```
# Importing library
import sympy as sym

# Declaring variables
x, y, z = sym.symbols('x y z')

# expression of which we have to find derivative
exp = x**5 * y + y**3 + 3*z**2

# Differentiating exp with respect to x
derivative1_x = sym.diff(exp, x)
print('derivative w.r.t x: ',
  derivative1_x)

# Differentiating exp with respect to y
derivative1_y = sym.diff(exp, y)
print('derivative w.r.t y: ',
  derivative1_y)

# Differentiating exp with respect to z
derivative1_z = sym.diff(exp, z)
print('derivative w.r.t z: ',
  derivative1_z)
```

FIGURE 11.13　Python program on finding partial derivatives of a function of three variables.

```
derivative w.r.t x:  5*x**4*y
derivative w.r.t y:  x**5 + 3*y**2
derivative w.r.t z:  6*z
```

FIGURE 11.14　Output of coding of Figure 11.13.

```
import sympy as sym
# Declaring variables
x = sym.symbols('x')
# Indefinite integration of cos(x) w.r.t. dx
integral_1 = sym.integrate(sym.cos(x), x)
print('indefinite integral of cos(x): ',
  integral_1)

# definite integration of cos(x) w.r.t. dx between -1 to 1
integral_2 = sym.integrate(sym.cos(x), (x, -1, 1))
print('definite integral of cos(x) between -1 to 1: ',
  integral_2)

# definite integration of exp(-x) w.r.t. dx between 0 to ∞
integral_3 = sym.integrate(sym.exp(-x), (x, 0, sym.oo))
print('definite integral of exp(-x) between 0 to ∞: ',
  integral_3)
```

FIGURE 11.15 Python program on the finding indefinite and definite integral of a function.

```
indefinite integral of cos(x):  sin(x)
definite integral of cos(x) between -1 to 1:   2*sin(1)
definite integral of exp(-x) between 0 to ∞:  1
```

FIGURE 11.16 Output of coding of Figure 7.15.

```
import numpy as np
a = np.arange(11, 20)
a.shape = (3, 3)
print("a = ")
print(a)
rank = np.linalg.matrix_rank(a)
print("\nRank:", rank)
```

FIGURE 11.17 Python program on the finding rank of a 3 * 3 matrix.

```
a =
[[11 12 13]
 [14 15 16]
 [17 18 19]]

Rank: 2
```

FIGURE 11.18 Output of coding of Figure 11.17.

11.5.1 ORDINARY DIFFERENTIAL EQUATIONS

Differential equations serve a crucial part in a variety of disciplines, including Science and Engineering. Different scholars have investigated numerical methods for solving differential equations. Several ways to solve differential equations have been devised. Other approaches get the answer in analytic form using basis functions. However, a more efficient and general approach to solving differential equations is required. Frequently, the relationship between mathematics and physical events is expressed using differential equations that combine the function and its derivatives to provide a mathematical model of real-world situations (adapted from Rawat et al. 2022, Capecchi et al. 2010).

Differential equations can be used to create mathematical models of anything and everything in our environment, including biological systems, stock markets, physical phenomena, and everyday life situations. It is astonishing in its ability to foretell everything going on in our surroundings. Differential equations allow us to maximize the returns on our investments, model coronavirus epidemics, and forecast when the next peak will be reached. We can use these equations to do any of these things.

Artificial Neural Networks (ANN) are regarded as one of these techniques (as discussed in Hennig et al. 2014, Berg et al. 2018) due to the emergence of Computer Science and Scientific Computing. ANN-based algorithms have been presented for solving differential equations of the first order. Later, an approach based on feedforward neural networks was created to solve ordinary differential equations. Differential To make things easier to understand, equations are typically expressed in the form of dy/dx, which calculates the change in y with respect to x.

ANNs are often trained to approximate functions between inputs and outputs in Euclidean space. This time, however, the researchers (as shown in Knoke et al. 2021) opted to specify the inputs and outputs in Fourier space, a graph for visualizing wave frequencies. Furthermore, according to the academics involved in this study, the air motion may be described using a mixture of wave frequencies.

The wind direction at the macroscale has a low frequency with extremely lengthy and sluggish waves, but the tiny eddies that emerge at the microscale have a high frequency with succinct waves. Experiments proved that previous deep learning algorithms required to be taught individually for each kind of fluid, but this one simply has to be trained once to handle all of them. An example of differential equations and its solution are shown in Figures 11.19 and 11.20, as a Python code and its output.

```
import numpy as np
from scipy.integrate import odeint
import matplotlib.pyplot as plt
# Initialization
tstart = 0
tstop = 25
increment = 1
x0 = 1
t = np.arange(tstart,tstop+1,increment)
# Function that returns dx/dt
def mydiff(x, t):
  T = 5
  a = -1/T
  dxdt = a * x
  return dxdt
# Solve ODE
x = odeint(mydiff, x0, t)
print(x)
# Plot the Results
plt.plot(t,x)
plt.title('Plotting Differential Equation Solution')
plt.xlabel('t')
plt.ylabel('x(t)')
plt.grid()
plt.axis([0, 25, 0, 1])
plt.show()
```

FIGURE 11.19 Python code showing the solution of ODE and the initial condition.

```
[[1.          ]
 [0.81873077]
 [0.67032006]
 [0.54881165]
 [0.44932898]
 [0.36787947]
 [0.30119421]
 [0.24659696]
 [0.20189652]
 [0.16529888]
 [0.13533527]
 [0.11080315]
 [0.09071794]
 [0.07427357]
 [0.06081005]
 [0.04978706]
 [0.0407622 ]
 [0.03337327]
 [0.02732372]
 [0.02237077]
 [0.01831564]
 [0.01499558]
 [0.01227734]
 [0.01005184]
 [0.00822975]
 [0.00673795]]
```

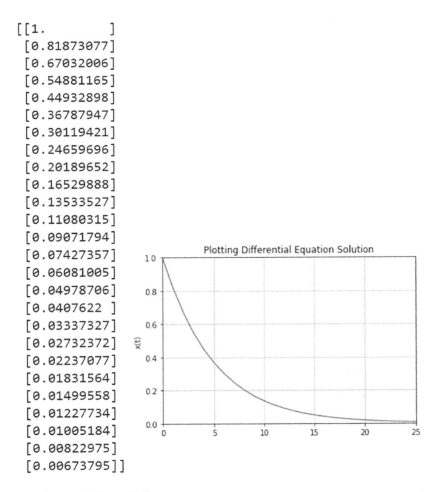

FIGURE 11.20   Output of Figure 11.19.

11.6   OPTIMIZATION OR OPERATION RESEARCH

Optimization or Operational Research (OR) methods (as shown in Craven et al. 2005, 2006) are used extensively in a variety of subfields of AI, including data science, ML, etc. It is called The Science of Better. In DS, real-life problems are modeled in mathematical forms. OR techniques, data analytics, computational algorithms, and computer programs are adopted to apply optimization techniques to AI developments and applications.

Mathematical modeling helps AI developments, applications, and developments, especially in the areas of ML, deep learning, and computational intelligence, by providing or designing efficient (or optimal) algorithms systems to develop optimal AI models, or systems or finding optimal solutions or predictions.

The stages of AI and mathematical modeling, applications and algorithm development are as follows:

- defining the context of the AI modeling problem,
- developing AI models,
- computing and implementing an AI model numerically by using relevant algorithms and computer programs,
- undertaking validation tests of AI models,

- analyzing the implications of the AI model results for actions, decision-making, predictions, etc.
- deploying AI models, algorithms, platforms, websites and networks.

11.6.1 STATIC OPTIMIZATION MODELS

Most typically constructed models at the enterprise or sector level are optimization models (both static and dynamic). Below is an example of an optimization model for a logistics and supply chain system.

$$\text{MIN } C = c_1 X + c_2 Y + c_3 Z \quad \text{objective function}$$

$$(Y, X, Z)$$

s.t.

$Z *$ are the greater than constraints,
$X *$ are the less than constraints,
$Z = aX$ are the flows and balance constraints,
$Y, X, Z * 0$ is the non-negativity constraint.
Symbols:
c's are the costs of activities, processes, nodes, etc.
Y, X, Z are the vectors of logistics and supply chain variables.

11.6.2 DYNAMIC OPTIMIZATION MODELS

The problem of optimizing a system over time is central to the dynamic modeling of AI. The optimization problem is assessed based on the following objective function.

$$\text{Max } J = \int_{t_0}^{t_T} I\big[X(t), Y(t), t\big] dt$$

The following state equations can represent the dynamic system:

$$\dot{X} = \frac{dX}{dt} = f\big(X(t), Y(t), t\big)$$

The following are the initial and terminal conditions for the state variables:

$$X(t_0) = X_0 \quad \text{and} \quad X(t_T) = X_T$$

The boundary conditions on the state variables are:

$$X(t) \in X^n \ R^n$$

If the feasible area or boundary conditions of the control variables are defined, the decision problem is to choose the optimal control trajectory from this feasible set.

$$Y(t) \in Y^n \in E^n$$

Symbols:
$Y(t)$ = a vector of control variables,
$X(t)$ = a vector of state variables,

t = time t_0, t_1, ..., t_T.

11.6.3 STOCHASTIC OPTIMIZATION METHODS

In stochastic optimization, parameter values are unknown and random variables are used to formulate the optimization problem. A wide range of stochastic algorithms are used to find the solution to stochastic optimization problems. The stochastic gradient method is a widely used algorithm used in different areas of AI development and applications.

A simple stochastic optimization model with scenario optimization for AI is given below.

MIN C = c_1Xs + c_2Ys + c_3Zs The objective function

(Ys, Xs, Zs)

Subject to.

The constraints:

Xs = bsYs refers to primary logistics and supply chain flows and balance constraints,

Zs * Zs are the demand constraints,

Xs ≤ Xs are the capacity constraints,

Zs = asXs are the flows and balance constraints,

Ys, Xs, Zs ≥ 0 is the non-negativity constraint.

Symbols:

c_s's = the costs of nodes under different scenarios,

Ys, Xs, Zs = the vectors of decision variables under different scenarios or states s = 1, 2, ..., S.

11.6.4 SOME OTHER USEFUL OR METHODS

Some other useful OR methods used in AI are Fuzzy optimization, genetic algorithms, different search methods, Chaos theory, and game theory.

11.7 COMPUTER PROGRAMS

Python is the most popular computer program for applying mathematical and statistical methods to AI development and applications. Therefore, we have demonstrated the applications of Python in different applications of mathematics in AI in this chapter.

There are many other computer programs for applying mathematical and statistical methods to AI development and applications, including JAVA, R, C, STATA, GAMBIT, GAMUT, NECTAR, EXCEL, GAMS, MATLAB, MATHEMATICA, and MINOS.

11.8 AI APPLICATIONS

AI computer programs, systems, algorithms, platforms, and technologies developed based on the use of mathematical methods, and computational algorithms, give decisions, strategies, information, and models and help perform tasks for much professional work, practices, and operations in the areas of computer science, corporate management and governance, economics, engineering, law, computer science, politics, psychology, sociology, biology, war, finance, business strategies, relationship management, etc.

These also have extensive applications in IT, computer science, and emerging technologies such as automated programming, checking, controlling, coordinating, and developing cooperation in many multiagent systems, including the Internet, networks, web search engines, cybersecurity, smart city, satellite monitoring, Internet of Things, blockchain, and developing different analytics in different areas, platforms, and portals, etc.

11.9   CONCLUDING REMARKS

Mathematics facilitates the understanding of logical reasoning and meticulousness. In hypothetical or imaginary situations, mathematical principles supply the true solution. It concerns the structure and generating principles that stay valid even if the parts are altered. The preceding discussion in this chapter has led us to the conclusion that mathematics plays a crucial role in the field of AI and what people assume about AI is that it is all magic, whereas, it is mathematics that produces the illusion of magic behind all creations.

When it comes to the field of AI intelligence, in particular, the application of mathematical methods, computational algorithms, and statistical reasoning will be of tremendous assistance in obtaining scientifically adequate results that are scientifically adequate based on appropriate procedures. In the end, the only way to successfully solve problems in AI is to make sure that mathematics and statistics are interacting in a way that is both harmonious and productive and to demonstrate, integrate, synthesize, and give future directions of research in these areas, this work/article provides a new, up-to-date, thorough, and innovative assessment of the literature.

REFERENCES

[1] Pangambam, S., Andrew Ng: Artificial Intelligence is the New Electricity at Stanford GSB (Transcript)." January 23, 2018 [https://singjupost.com/andrew-ng-artificial-intelligence-is-the-new-electricity-at-stanford-gsb-transcript/?singlepage=1].

[2] Davies, A., Veličković, P., & Buesing, L. Advancing Mathematics by Guiding Human Intuition with AI. *Nature* 600 (2021): 70–74.

[3] Carifio, J., Halverson, J., Krioukov, D., & Nelson, B. D. Machine Learning in the String Landscape. *Journal of High Energy Physics* 157 (2017).

[4] Heal, K., Kulkarni, A., & Sertöz, E. C. Deep Learning Gauss-Manin Connections. Preprint, 2020. URL: https://arxiv.org/abs/2007.13786.

[5] Hughes, M. C. A Neural Network Approach to Predicting and Computing Knot Invariants. Preprint, 2016. URL: https://arxiv.org/abs/1610.05744.

[6] Levitt, J. S. F., Hajij, M., & Sazdanovic, R. Big Data Approaches to Knot Theory: Understanding the Structure of the Jones Polynomial. Preprint, 2019. URL: https://arxiv.org/abs/1912.10086.

[7] Jejjala, V., Kar, A., and Parrikar, O. Deep Learning the Hyperbolic Volume of a Knot. *Phys. Lett. B* 799, 135033 (2019).

[8] Peyré, G., & Cuturi, M. Computational Optimal Transport: With Applications to Data Science. *Foundations and Trends® in Machine Learning*, 11 no.6 (2019), 355-607.

[9] Deisenroth, Marc Peter, A. Aldo Faisal, and Cheng Soon Ong. Mathematics *for Machine Learning*. Cambridge: Cambridge University Press, 2020.

[10] Gareth James, Daniela Witten, Trevor Hastie, and Robert Tibshirani, *An Introduction to Statistical Learning with Applications in R* (2nd ed., Springer, 2021).

[11] Hou, J. R., Nerur, S. & Zhang, J. J. Applying Data Science on Structural Equations Modelling (SEM): An Exploratory Study. *Essays on the Visual Effects on Online Human Decision-Making and Data Science Applications* (2019): 114-127.

[12] Graham, R. L., Knuth, D. E., Patashnik, O. & Liu, S. Concrete Mathematics: A Foundation for Computer Science. *Computers in Physics* 3, no. 5 (1989): 106-107.

[13] Hastie, T., Tibshirani, R. & Friedman, J. *The Elements of Statistical Learning* (2nd ed., Springer, 2011).

[14] Xian-Da Zhang. Machine Learning. A Matrix Algebra Approach to Artificial Intelligence (First Online: May 23, 2020), 223–440, https://link.springer.com/chapter/10.1007/978-981-15-2770-8_6.

[15] Brijder, Robert, Marc Gyssens & Jan Van den Bussche. On Matrices and K-Relations. *Annals of Mathematics and Artificial Intelligence* 90 (2022): 181–210. https://doi.org/10.1007/s10472-021-09760-4.

[16] Mahadik, Suryaji, P., Desai, S. S., Gulavani, S. & Kadam, K. Regression Analysis in Data Science. *International Journal of Innovative Research in Science, Engineering and Technology (IJIRSET)* 11, no. 12 (December 2022): DOI:10.15680/IJIRSET.2022.1112045.

[17] Koenker, Roger. Quantile Regression. Econometric Society Monographs 38. Cambridge, UK: *Cambridge University Press*, 2005. ISBN: 9780521608275.

[18] Hogg, R. V., Tanis, E. A. & Zimmerman, D. L., *Probability and Statistical Inference*, Vol. 993 (Macmillan, 1977).

[19] Koller, D. & Friedman, N. *Probabilistic Graphical Models: Principles* and Techniques (MIT Press, 2009).
[20] Field, Andy, Miles, J. & Field, Z. *Discovering Statistics Using R*. 1st ed. London: SAGE Publications Ltd. (2012).
[21] Olhede, S. C. & Wolfe, P. J. The Future of Statistics and Data Science. *Statistics & Probability Letters* 136 (2018): 46-50.
[22] Zhang, S. & Jia Xia. Algebraic Fundamentals in Artificial Intelligence for the Purpose of Undergraduate Education and Training. *Journal of Physics: Conference Series* 1302, no. 3 (2019): 032021.
[23] Bender, Edward A. Mathematical Methods in Artificial Intelligence. *Wiley-IEEE Computer Society Pr* (1996) ISBN 978-0-818-67200-2.
[24] Rawat, K. & Mishra, M. K., Role of Mathematics in Novel Artificial Intelligence Realm, *Mathematics in Computational Science and Engineering*, edited by Ramakant Bhardwaj, Jyoti Mishra, Satyendra Narayan, and Gopalakrishnan Suseendran, 211-231. First published May 13, 2022. doi:10.1002/9781119777557. (Wiley).
[25] Capecchi, V., Buscema, M., Contucci, P. & D'Amore, B. Applications of Mathematics in Models, Artificial Neural Networks, and Arts: Mathematics and Society. *Springer Science & Business Media*, 2022.
[26] Hennig, Philipp & Søren Hauberg. Probabilistic Solutions to Differential Equations and Their Application to Riemannian Statistics. *Proceedings of the 17th International Conference on Artificial Intelligence and Statistics (AISTATS)* 2014, 33:347-355. Reykjavik, Iceland: PMLR, 2014.
[27] Berg, Johan & Karl Nyström. A Unified Deep Artificial Neural Network Approach to Partial Differential Equations in Complex Geometries. *Neurocomputing,* 317 (2018): 28-41.,
[28] Knoke, T. & Wick, T. Solving Differential Equations via Artificial Neural Networks: Findings and Failures in a Model Problem. *Examples and Counterexamples* 1 (2021): 100035.
[29] Craven, B.D. & Islam, S. M. Operations Research Methods: Related Production, Distribution, and Inventory Management Applications. *ICFAI University Press*, 2006.
[30] Craven, B. D. & Islam, S. M. Optimisation in Economics and Finance: Some Advances in Non-Linear, Dynamic, Multi-Criteria, and Stochastic Models, with B. Craven, Series: *Dynamic Optimisation and Econometrics in Economics and Finance*, Vol. 7, Springer, Heidelberg.

12 Prediction of Winning Team in Soccer Game
A Supervised Machine Learning-Based Approach

Sanjay Chakraborty
Techno International New Town
Maulana Abul Kalam Azad University of Technology, West Bengal, India

Lopamudra Dey
Meghnad Saha Institute of Technology
Maulana Abul Kalam Azad University of Technology, West Bengal, India

Saikat Maity
Sister Nivedita University
West Bengal, India

Animesh Kairi
Institute of Engineering and Management

12.1 INTRODUCTION

Football is one of the most famous team sports globally. The biggest event of football is undoubtedly FIFA World Cup. In the last World Cup, 2022 around 3.5 billion tuned in to watch it, which is around half of the world's population so you can imagine the impact of this wonderful sport. Now during every World Cup, we see somebody be it human or animal predicting the winner of the World Cup. Latest we had an Octopus who used to make predictions. But these are just guesses you may say. Nowadays with so many predictions being made through machine learning (ML) and deep learning. A person will typically consider a number of criteria when predicting the result of a match between two teams, including the teams' most recent performances, home or away games, moves of the present player, changes in the coach and staff recently, etc. Human "intuition" is comprised of decisions based on a combination of credible, real-world information that is at hand. When a human makes a prediction about the outcome of a game, there is a problem because the decision will be influenced by things like the human preference for teams, the human perception of specific team members, and some studies suggest decisions may even be influenced by the colour of the team's uniform. The Football Result Expert System, which is commonly used by the media and bookies, is one of the techniques frequently employed for forecasting match results.

The issue with FRES is that it employs a rule-based approach or an if-else statement-based method that takes each individual aspect into account before rejecting it. The teams in question's past performances are given to the neural network as a training set before it is used to forecast a match in the future. Machine learning (ML), one of the intelligence techniques, has shown promising results in the categorization and prediction sectors. Sports betting involves large financial risks,

DOI: 10.1201/9781003387459-12

making sports prediction one of the developing sectors that demands excellent predictive accuracy. These models are based on a variety of game-related variables, including past match outcomes, player performance indicators, and opponent data. This chapter evaluates the winner by utilization of artificial neural networks (ANN) [34]. Football has always been globally famous since its start. So with popularity comes prediction where one can guess the winning team of the World Cup depends on the participating team's old World Cup data. Even before the start of the World Cup. The big question that comes to our mind is who will be the winner? Most people just ask and move on but efficient use of deep learning can help us predict the correct winner based on the data. Predictive analysis is an uprising concept, which uses artificial neural networks for making predictions. We may also use the ML concept for the same. This chapter uses deep learning which is better than machine learning as it does not require any supervisor to correct its inaccuracy as deep learning with its experience improves its accuracy. High levels of nonlinear outcomes underlie accurate sports forecasting, necessitating models built on deep learning architecture. The deep learning model must gather the necessary exemplifications of the raw data and operate well with complex data sets. Statistics from the FIFA World Cup will serve the purpose of this chapter. The quality of prediction accuracy relies on the nature of the existing dataset. However, the data of the previous World Cup games is collected and based on that the winner of the upcoming World Cup 2023 is predicted. Some important factors are considered in this work to accelerate the prediction result. The main contributions of this chapter are given as follows,

- Use ML and artificial neural network techniques to predict the winning and runner-up teams of Soccer games.
- Predict the results of specific matches across the competition.
- Run simulation of the next matches i.e. semifinals and finals.

These objectives require resolving numerous machine learning tasks, including data wrangling, feature extraction, and outcome prediction and present a distinctive real-world ML prediction challenge. The entire chapter is organized as follows. Section 12.2 discusses a set of research works using supervised learning techniques for prediction purposes in this sports domain. Section 12.3 describes the background and the used methodologies for this work. Section 12.4 shows a detailed analysis of results on some previous World Cup datasets and provides a prediction output based on some important parameters analysis through some popular supervised ML algorithms. Section 12.5 discusses the conclusions of this chapter and future works in this domain for interested readers and researchers.

12.2 LITERATURE SURVEY

There is a list of studies [22,25] and research works available that deal with the prediction of match scores and player performances in different forms of sports, such as cricket [21], basketball [16], soccer [20], baseball [23], pro-kabaddi [19] match outcome prediction [27–30], etc. A few works are discussed in this section. Neural networks are employed by Huang and Chang [1] to forecast the outcomes of 2006 FIFA World Cup matches. The model employed is an assumed back propagation-learning rule MLP, or multilayer perceptron. 76.9% of predictions made using this model are accurate, omitting matches that are drawn. Each match's result is predicted using one of eight different features. According to some experimental findings, the MLP architecture has eight inputs, eleven hidden nodes, and one output. Although they only employed eight crucial terms, there are 17 statistical terms. The training samples only contain the teams that either won or lost all three of their group stage contests. It made us consider using ANN for our research. A different kind of technical approach is utilized by Boulier and Stekler [2], to determine the outcomes that might be predicted for NFL - National Football League games from 1994 to 2000. They claimed that the teams are ranked in the NFL according to some sort of Power Scores. They compared the predictions made by regressions using The New York Times's power rankings with those made by the naive model and the betting market. The power scores are created utilizing the team's win-loss record, home or away games, winning margin, and opponent calibre. Weight-age increased for recent matches. Boulier and Stekler are unable to systematically calculate these predictive Power Scores because they lacked access to these minuscule details at the time. As a result, they came to the conclusion that the power scores' accuracy is better compared to the expert but is still below that of the naive model and betting market. Since it does not necessitate a high amount of knowledge of the sport and prediction expertise, the naive model only narrowly outperformed the sport expert projections when the whole set of data is examined. A paper [3] uses KNIME as the data-mining framework and SVM, DCT classifiers for conducting their work in the soccer statistics visual analytics in real time. They tested the classifiers with N-Cross-fold Validation. This offers a layer-based approach that is elastic and flexible, allowing for in-depth research. This method's effectiveness is assessed by contrasting it with actual soccer games. A paper [4] uses a variety of techniques, including the ranking method, soccer power index, rating, market value of participating players, and the home ground benefit for the competing teams. It also takes into account a team's average goals per game. The Poisson regression model is also used by Dixon and Cole [5] to forecast English premier league games. Football player roles are classified using a stacked ensemble learning model utilizing the FIFAWC-2019 game dataset in a published [17]. Ten features are chosen in the first phase utilizing four different feature selection methods. Gradient Boosting, Random Forest, and deep perceptron are used in the next phase, while logistic regression acts as a meta-learner [17]. A scientific technique for determining the football player's market value is proposed in a paper [18]. The method is based on using football player performance data to apply ML algorithms. In the experiment, data from the video game FIFA 20 are used. To assess players' market values, four regression models—linear regression, multivariate linear regression, decision trees, and random forests—are examined on the whole set of traits [18]. Deep learning approaches, in addition to ML, are essential for making such predictions in sports where the dataset size is significantly greater [24,29]. A study [26] suggests a model for predicting the results of cricket matches using ML techniques [26]. The quality of a cricket team's players, as assessed by their rankings in ICC, is one of the most vital factors that influence that team's chances of winning an IPL match, the study's findings show. The study continues by stating that the auction values of each player on the squad are another crucial factor in determining a team's likelihood of winning games.

12.3 BACKGROUND

Football is one of the most famous games. In this section, some rules and regulations related to this game are provided.

12.3.1 RULES AND EVENTS

We will briefly go over the football regulations, various game occurrences, and potential results in this part.

- **Typical football rules**: Football is a game that lasts 90 minutes and is played between two teams of 11 players each. A team's goal, which is located on each side of the field, is where they try to place the ball. One point is given to the goal scoring team. At the conclusion of the game, the team with the most points wins the match. The game concludes in a draw if both teams' goals are equal.
- **Competition format for home leagues**: Many nations typically have a home league where internal clubs compete with each other. Each team plays the other twice, once at their venue (the "home match") and once at the opponent's venue (the "away match"), in each league that normally contains 20 teams. For a win, a team earns three points; for a tie, one point.

- **Main events of the match**:
  - **Goals**: When the ball enters the goal of the other side, a goal is scored.
  - **Shots**: There are numerous distinct types of shots, each struck from a different distance or angle or with a different section of the body.
  - **Passes**: A player makes a pass when he kicks the ball to the same team's member.
  - **Ball cross**: If a footballer kicks the ball from any corner of the field towards the goal bar of the opponents with the intention of passing it to a partner, that action is known as a cross.
  - **Ball possession**: The percentage of the game when a team has possession of the ball is called a possession.
  - **Free kicks and penalty**: When the opposition team fouls on the field, a free kick is awarded. In this case, the team that concedes the foul may start play from the part of the field where the foul is considered. The team that committed the foul receives a penalty and is given the opportunity to take a close-range shot at the goal without any members of the opposing team present.
  - **Cards**: When the referee determines a foul to be of sufficient significance, cards are sent out. Smaller fouls result in a yellow card, which has no immediate repercussions. However, a player receives a red card if they receive two yellow cards. A footballer who accepts a red card is forced to give up the ground. In some situations, such as when a dangerous foul is committed, red cards can also be received straight.

12.3.2 USED METHODOLOGY

For its subsets of classification and regression, we offer an overview of common supervised ML approaches in Figure 12.1. Regression occurs when it receives a continuous integer output, but classification occurs when it receives a categorical output. In this work, a supervised approach is followed, as we would like to forecast the outcome of match results along with the goals count.

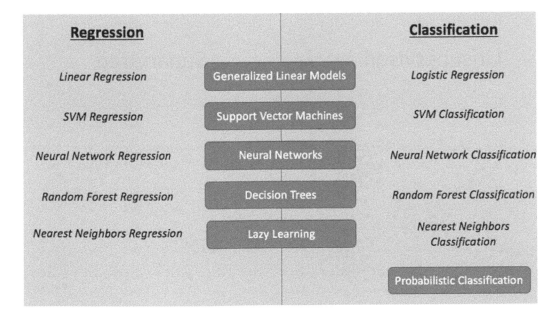

FIGURE 12.1 Benchmark supervised learning methods.

Supervised learning: A type of artificial neural network called supervised learning uses labelled data from a dataset. Predetermined training examples make up the training data. Each example in supervised learning consists of a pair that includes an input object (often a vector) and a desired output value. This pair is known as the supervisory signal.

Unsupervised learning: Unsupervised learning, in contrast to supervised learning, uses input data to infer conclusions and identify patterns without reference to outputs that have been labelled. Clustering and dimensionality reduction are the two basic techniques utilized in unsupervised learning. Figure 12.2 depicts a common data representation scenario for both supervised and unsupervised learning techniques.

- **Logistic regression:** Similar to linear regression, logistic regression models the likelihood of a finite set of outcomes, often two. In essence, a logistic equation is constructed in Figure 12.3 such that the output values are limited to values between 0 and 1.
  - **Gradient boosting machine (GBM):** An ML method called gradient boosting is used, among other things, for classification and regression tasks. It provides a prediction model in the form of an ensemble of decision trees like weak prediction models. The construction of a gradient-boosted trees model follows the same stage-wise process as previous boosting techniques, but it generalizes other techniques by enabling the optimization of any differentiable loss function. The GBM algorithm's tree structure flow is depicted in Figure 12.4.
- **Random forest:** An ensemble learning method based on decision trees is called random forests. Using bootstrapped datasets of the original data, several decision trees are created using random forests, which then arbitrarily choose a subset of variables for each stage of the decision tree (DT). Therefore, the model selects the mode of each DT prediction as a whole. It diminishes the possibility of an individual DT making an error by depending on a "majority wins" model. The third DT, for instance, would predict 0 if we only established one DT. However, the anticipated result would be 1 if we relied only on the mode of the four DTs. An overview of the random forest decision tree technique is shown in Figure 12.5.

Unsupervised   Supervised

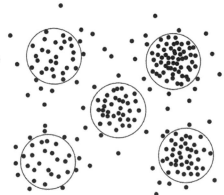
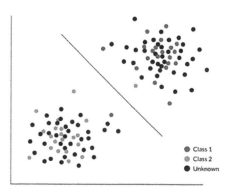

FIGURE 12.2   Supervised versus unsupervised learning.

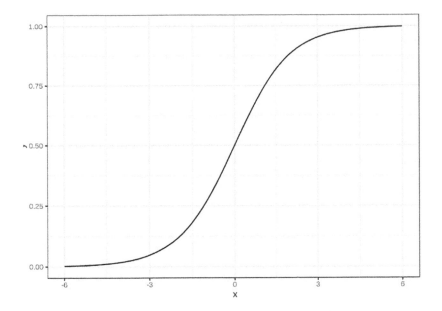

FIGURE 12.3 Logistic regression expected graph.

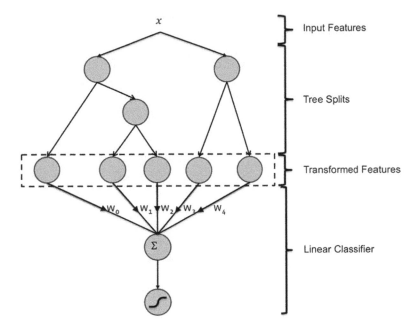

FIGURE 12.4 GBM decision trees.

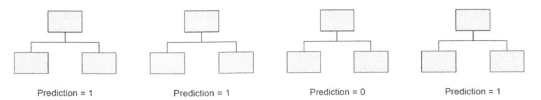

FIGURE 12.5 Random forest decision tree.

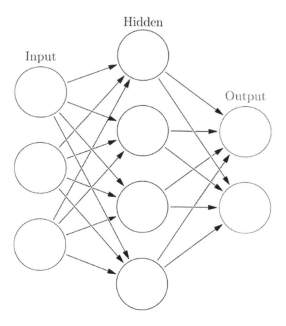

FIGURE 12.6   A basic structure of artificial neural network.

12.3.3 Deep Learning Networks

The phrase "deep learning" refers to ML architectures that connect numerous multilayer perceptrons so that there are multiple hidden layers rather than just one. More complex patterns can be learned by a deep neural network the "deeper" it is. Because each neuron in a deep layer network is linked to every other neuron in its vicinity, these networks and layers are sometimes referred to as fully connected networks or fully connected layers. Different deep learning architectures can be created by integrating fully connected networks with other ML techniques [31].

Finding out what an artificial neural network is and how it works would be an excellent place to start. Artificial neural networks, a type of information processing model, are inspired by how organic nerve systems, such as the brain, process information. It can be seen as a simple mathematical model of the brain that handles parallel processing of nonlinear relationships between inputs and outputs, exactly as the human brain does every second.

Figure 12.6 represents the basic structure of an ANN. The input layer is represented by the red circles, the output layer by the green circles, and the hidden layers are represented by the blue circles. The nodes in the layer beneath each node in hidden layer traverse a linear function and an activation function to produce the output seen in the green circles [32,33].

12.4   RESULT ANALYSIS

This section discusses the various tools and dataset details used for this experiment. It also discusses the training and testing phases of execution along with the final prediction result analysis.

12.4.1 Tools and Components

Our major goal of using several ML approaches to develop a model of desired outcomes has been achieved. We generated match outcome and match score forecasts using cutting-edge ML techniques like artificial neural networks, Random Forest, Light GBM, and Logistic Regression.

12.4.2 HARDWARE AND SOFTWARE COMPONENTS

- High-configured GPU has been used for running deep multilayer feed-forward neural network (DMLP) for supervised learning prediction.
- Pandas is a sophisticated tool for data manipulation. It is based on the NumPy package and uses the DataFrame as its primary data structure. You can store and manage tabular data in rows of observations and columns of variables using dataframes.
- Numpy - NumPy, which stands for Numerical Python, is a library made up of multidimensional array objects and a selection of operations for handling such arrays. Arrays can be subjected to logical and mathematical operations using NumPy.
- Matplotlib - Matplotlib is a toolkit that provides a complete tool for building static, animated, and interactive visualizations. Publishing-quality figures are produced using Matplotlib in a variety of physical formats and cross-platform interactive environments. Matplotlib can be used by Python scripts, the Python and IPython shells, web application servers, and a number of GUI toolkits.
- Keras or nnet packages for multilayer perceptron.
- Sklearn package for ensemble and logistic regression techniques.

12.4.3 DATASETS DESCRIPTION

The details of the used datasets for this experiment are shown in Tables 12.1 and 12.2. Besides that, a snapshot of the used datasets is shown in Figures 12.7 and 12.8.

TABLE 12.1
Used Dataset-1 Details

Attributes	Datatypes	Explanation
Rank	int64	Ranking of the team
country_full	object	Full name of the country (team)
country_abrv	object	Abbreviation of the country (team)
cur_year_avg_weighted	float64	Average previous years points
rank_date	datetime64 [ns]	Date of the corresponding ranking
two_year_ago_weighted	float64	Average two years ago points weighted (30%)
three_year_ago_weighted	float64	Average three years ago points weighted (20%)
weighted_points	float64	Weighted points
Year	int64	Year of the corresponding ranking
date	datetime64 [ns]	Date of the match
home_team	object	The team that is playing in the usual area that they play in, as opposed to the visitors team
away_team	object	The team which is playing away from home
home_score	int64	Team score in home match
away_score	int64	Team score in away match
tournament	object	Type of tournament
city	object	The match played in particular city
country	object	The match played in particular country
neutral	bool	Match is played in neither home nor away
year	int64	The year in which match is played

TABLE 12.2
Used Dataset-2 Details

Attributes	Datatypes	Explanation
Team	Object	Name of the team
Group	Object	Group in which team is playing
First match against	Object	Corresponding team's first match against which team
Second match against	Object	Corresponding team's second match against which team
Third match against	Object	Corresponding team's third match against which team

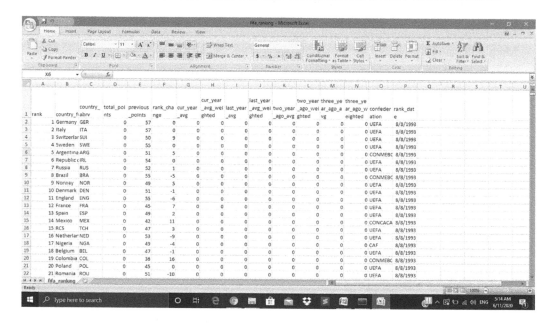

FIGURE 12.7　Snapshot of used Dataset-1 (fifa_ranking.csv).

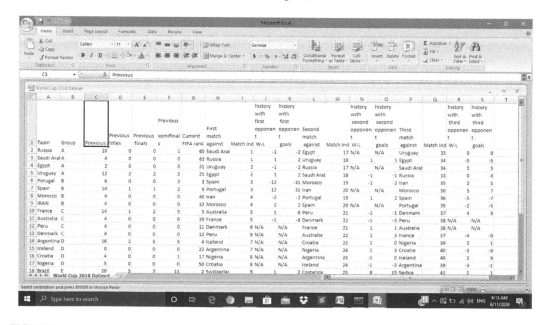

FIGURE 12.8　Snapshot of used Dataset-2 (World Cup 2018 data).

12.4.4 EXPERIMENTED EXECUTION

– Importing necessary Python libraries and reading the datasets and apply neural network classifier. Figure 12.9 shows an overall visualization of a single elimination round. Figure 12.10 shows a distribution of the winning teams according to their winning probability. Tables 12.3 and 12.4 show the intermediate results snapshots and Table 12.5 the intermediate group stage matches decisions. Tables 12.6–12.9 show different stages of intermediate simulations.

– Looping through each loop to find out the current match and predicting the value based on our trained model

12.4.4.1 Using Supervised Learning Models

– Importing necessary Python libraries and reading the datasets

12.5 CONCLUSIONS AND FUTURE WORKS

Match result prediction is one of the important sports applications that demand high predictive accuracy. Typically, mathematical models that are frequently validated by a subject-matter expert are used to forecast the outcomes of the matches. Although more accurate models are still needed,

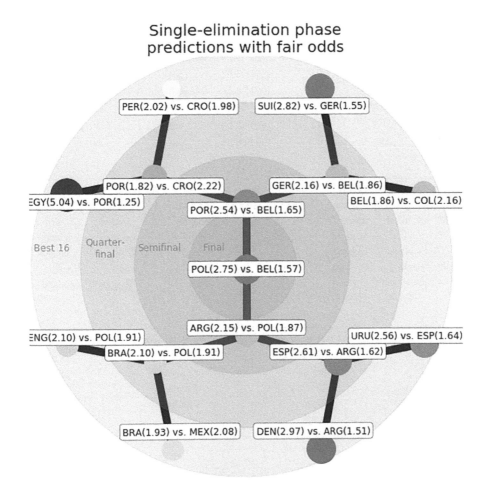

FIGURE 12.9 Visualization of single elimination rounds.

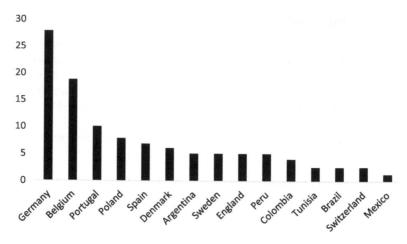

FIGURE 12.10   Distribution of winning teams.

TABLE 12.3

Intermediate Results-1 of the Used Dataset

Out [28]:

	Rank	Country_ Full	Country_ Abrv	Cur_Year_ Avg_Weighted	Rank_Date	Two_Year_ Ago_Weighted	Three_Year_ Ago_Weighted	Weighted_ Points
0	1	Germany	GER	0.0	1993-08-08	0.0	0.0	0.0
1	2	Italy	ITA	0.0	1993-08-08	0.0	0.0	0.0
2	3	Switzerland	SUI	0.0	1993-08-08	0.0	0.0	0.0
3	4	Sweden	SWE	0.0	1993-08-08	0.0	0.0	0.0
4	5	Argentina	ARG	0.0	1993-08-08	0.0	0.0	0.0

Out [29]:

	Date	Home_ Team	Away_ Team	Home_ Score	Away_ Score	Tournament	City	Country	Neutral
0	1872-11-30	Scotland	England	0	0	Friendly	Glasgow	Scotland	False
1	1873-03-08	England	Scotland	4	2	Friendly	London	England	False
2	1874-03-07	Scotland	England	2	1	Friendly	Glasgow	Scotland	False
3	1875-03-06	England	Scotland	2	2	Friendly	London	England	False
4	1876-03-04	Scotland	England	3	0	Friendly	Glasgow	Scotland	False

Out [30]:

Team	Group	First Match\Against	Second Match\Against	Third Match\Against
Russia	A	Saudi Arabia	Egypt	Uruguay
Saudi Arabia	A	Russia	Uruguay	Egypt
Egypt	A	Uruguay	Russia	Saudi Arabia
Uruguay	A	Egypt	Saudi Arabia	Russia
Portugal	B	Spain	Morocco	Iran

ML models are being employed more frequently to predict sports. This is due to the enormous popularity of sports betting as well as the fact that sports managers are seeking pertinent data in order to model prospective matching strategies. This is due to the prevalence of sports betting and

TABLE 12.4

Intermediate Results-2 of the Used Dataset

___Starting group H:___
Poland vs, Senegal: Poland wins with 0.57
Poland vs. Colombia: Draw
Poland vs. Japan: Poland wins with 0.72
Senegal vs. Colombia: Colombia wins with 0.63
Senegal vs. Japan: Senegal wins with 0.68
___Starting group E:___
Brazil vs. Switzerland: Draw
Brazil vs. Costa Rica: Draw
Brazil vs. Serbia: Brazil wins with 0.59
Switzerland vs. Costa Rica: Switzerland wins with 0.56
Switzerland vs. Serbia: Switzerland wins with 0.60
Costa Rica vs. Serbia: Draw
___Starting group F:___
Germany vs. Mexico: Germany wins with 0.63
Germany vs. Sweden: Germany wins with 0.65
Germany vs. Korea Republic: Germany wins with 0.69
Mexico vs: Sweden: Draw
Mexico vs. Korea Republic: Mexico wins with 0.65
Mexico vs. Korea Republic: Sweden wins with 0.62
___Starting group B:___
Portugal vs. Spain: Draw
Portugal vs. Morocco: Portugal wins with 0.60
Portugal vs. Iran: Portugal wins with 0.61
Spain vs. Morocco: Spain wins with 0.60
Spain vs. Iran: Spain wins with 0.56
Morocco vs. Iran: Iran wins with 0.63

___Starting group A:___
Russia vs. Saudi: Arabia: Draw
Russia vs. Egypt: Egypt wins with 0.66
Russia vs. Uruguay: Uruguay wins with 0.86
Saudi Arabia vs. Egypt: Egypt wins with 0.69
Saudi Arabia vs. Uruguay: Uruguay wins with 0.86
Egypt vs. Uruguay: Uruguay wins with 0.77
___Starting group G:___
Belgium vs. Panama: Belgium wins with 0.66
Belgium vs. Tunisia: Draw
Belgium vs. England: Draw
Panama vs. Tunisia: Tunisia wins with 0.76
Panama vs. England: England wins with 0.81
Tunisia vs. England: England wins with 0.61
___Starting group C:___
France vs. Australia: France wins with 0.62
France vs. Peru: Draw
France vs. Denmark: Denmark wins with 0.59
Australia vs. Peru: Peru wins with 0.73
Australia vs. Denmark: Denmark wins with 0.74
Peru vs. Denmark: Denmark wins with 0.71
___Starting group D:___
Argentina vs. Iceland: Draw
Argentina vs. Croatia: Draw
Argentina vs. Nigeria: Argentina wins with 0.63
Iceland vs. Croatia: Croatia wins with 0.57
Iceland vs. Nigeria: Iceland wins with 0.60
Croatia vs. Nigeria: Croatia wins with 0.61

the need for appropriate data by sports managers to model prospective matching strategies. It looks to be a suitable technology for sport prediction through ML models on historical dataset. The road to reaching the goals we set out to achieve has been fraught with difficulties,

- **Availability and quality of data**: A crucial component of the effort is searching a football data set in public domain. The top football data suppliers, however, don't release their data to the general public. To discover a useful public football database, we will need to comb through a number of them. If no suitable database is available, another strategy would be to discover websites presenting the needed information and utilize web scraping methods to build our own dataset.
- **Prediction landscape investigation and comprehension**: We will be required to conduct a comprehensive background investigation of prediction approaches and gain a mathematical grasp of various ML algorithms that can be employed for our predictions in order to design our models and test various hypotheses.
- **Testing various models and parameter selection**: Quick and simple training and testing activities will be a key issue in order to assess different models. Since there are so many variables to consider, it is practically difficult to gradually test various values for each variable to determine the ideal collection of variables. This work can be further extended in multiple scenarios.

TABLE 12.5

Intermediate Group Stage Matches Decisions with Single Elimination

Out [28]:

	Rank	Country_Full	Country_Abrv	Cur_Year_Avg_Weighted	Rank_Date	Two_Year_Ago_Weighted	Three_Year_Ago_Weighted	Weighted_Points
0	1	Germany	GER	0.0	1993-08-08	0.0	0.0	0.0
1	2	Italy	ITA	0.0	1993-08-08	0.0	0.0	0.0
2	3	Switzerland	SUI	0.0	1993-08-08	0.0	0.0	0.0
3	4	Sweden	SWE	0.0	1993-08-08	0.0	0.0	0.0
4	5	Argentina	ARG	0.0	1993-08-08	0.0	0.0	0.0

Out [29]:

	Date	Home_Team	Away_Team	Home_Score	Away_Score	Tournament	City	Country	Neutral
0	1872-11-30	Scotland	England	0	0	Friendly	Glasgow	Scotland	False
1	1873-03-08	England	Scotland	4	2	Friendly	London	England	False
2	1874-03-07	Scotland	England	2	1	Friendly	Glasgow	Scotland	False
3	1875-03-06	England	Scotland	2	2	Friendly	London	England	False
4	1876-03-04	Scotland	England	3	0	Friendly	Glasgow	Scotland	False

Out [30]:

Team	Group	First Match\Against	Second Match\Against	Third Match\Against
Russia	A	Saudi Arabia	Egypt	Uruguay
Saudi Arabia	A	Russia	Uruguay	Egypt
Egypt	A	Uruguay	Russia	Saudi Arabia
Uruguay	A	Egypt	Saudi Arabia	Russia
Portugal	B	Spain	Morocco	Iran

TABLE 12.6

Merge Data

Out [43]:

	Home_Team	Away_Team	Home_Score	Away_Score	Neutral	Rank_x	Weighted_Points_X	Rank_y	Weighted_Points_y
0	Fiji	Tahiti	3	0	True	153.75	145.7750	183.0	64.9125
1	New Caledonia	Tahiti	3	1	False	160.00	118.6800	183.0	64.9125
2	New Caledonia	Vanuatu	5	0	False	160.00	118.6800	173.0	92.0500
3	American Samoa	Vanuatu	0	8	True	199.00	15.1775	173.0	92.0500
4	Guam	Vanuatu	1	4	True	188.50	35.8500	173.0	92.0500

- **Data improvement**: First off, we believe that the model would surely benefit from the addition of more intriguing data regarding match occurrences. For instance, a weakness in the anticipated goals calculation for the shot is that we do not know the placement of the players on the other side at the time of the shoot.

TABLE 12.7
Group Stage Simulation

```
*******************************
Simulating Group A
#######################
Russia vs Saudi Arabia
Draw
#######################
Russia vs Egypt
Draw
#######################
Russia vs Uruguay
Uruguay wins!
#######################
Saudi Arabia vs Egypt
Draw
#######################
Saudi Arabia vs Uruguay
Uruguay wins!
#######################
Egypt vs Uruguay
```

TABLE 12.8
Single Elimination Rounds Simulation

Out [55]:

Team	Group	Year	Rank	Weighted_Points	Points
Uruguay	A	2018	19.000000	682.571667	9
Russia	A	2018	64.666667	417.961667	2
Portugal	B	2018	3.500000	1005.245000	9
Spain	B	2018	7.333333	912.925000	4
Denmark	C	2018	12.000000	926.571667	9
France	C	2018	8.000000	755.330000	4
Croatia	D	2018	16.833333	706.773333	7
Argentina	D	2018	4.500000	867.560000	4
Switzerland	E	2018	7.000000	851.685000	7
Brazil	E	2018	2.000000	971.140000	6
Germany	F	2018	1.000000	1183.128333	9
Sweden	F	2018	21.000000	762.11667	6
Tunisia	G	2018	19.666667	746.423333	6
England	G	2018	14.333333	757.710000	6
Colombia	H	2018	14.500000	692.745000	7
Poland	H	2018	8.000000	802.030000	4

- **Monte Carlo simulations for scenario planning**: Numerous Monte Carlo simulations are performed, using random sampling to provide results. After developing our anticipated goals model, we could perform many Monte Carlo simulations on a single league season to determine, for example, which team had the best chance of winning

TABLE 12.9
Final Simulation

```
#####################################
Simulation of round_of_16
Uruguay vs Spain
Spain wins!
Denmark vs Argentina
Argentina wins!
Russia vs Portugal
Portugal wins!
France vs Croatia
France wins!
Switzerland vs Sweden
Sweden wins!
Tunisia vs Poland
Tunisia wins!
Brazil vs Germany
Brazil wins!
England vs Colombia
Colombia wins!
#####################################
```

the title. The benefit of using it is that it may be applied to produce forecasts for future events, such as competitions that have not yet begun.

- **Profiles of the participating teams**: Utilizing all of the team data, including possession, crosses, tackles, headers, and other statistics, each team can be divided into a variety of playing styles. The construction of models that might then be used to predict the outcome of a game between these two teams could help to understand the relationship between the playing styles of two different teams.
- **Analysis of gambling performance**: Another potential extension of this research is to examine gambling chances to see if our algorithm can recommend great bets in terms of values and successful betting strategies that generate returns over the long term.

CONFLICT OF INTEREST

The authors have no conflict of interest.

FUNDING

There is no funding involved for this work.

REFERENCES

1. Huang, K. Y., & Chang, W. L. (2010). A Neural Network Method for Prediction of 2006. In The 2010 International Joint Conference on Neural Networks, 18-23 July 2010; Barcelona, Spain; 1-8, IEEE Xplore, USA.
2. Boulier, B. L., & Stekler, H. O. (2003). Predicting the outcomes of national football league matches. *International Journal of Forecasting*, 19, 257–270.
3. Aslan, B. G., & Inceoglu, M. M. (2007). A Comparative Study on Neural Network Based Soccer Result Prediction. In ISDA 2007. Seventh International Conference on Intelligent Systems De-sign and Applications, 2007 (pp. 545–550). IEEE, 20–24 October 2007, Rio de Janeiro, Brazil, IEEE Xplore, USA.

4. Janetzko, H., Sacha, D., Stein, M., Schreck, T., & Keim, D. A. (2014). Feature-Driven Visual Analytics of Soccer Data. In IEEE Conference on Visual Analytics Science and Technology (VAST), 25-31 October 2014, Paris, France, 13-22, IEEE Xplore, USA

5. Dormagen, D. (2014). Development of a Simulator for the FIFA World Cup 2014, Bachelorarbeit FU Berlin.

6. M. J. Dixon and S. G. Coles, Modelling Association Football Scores and Inefficiencies in the Football Betting Market, Journal of the Royal Statistical Society. Series C (Applied Statistics), pp. 265-280, 1997.

7. Chao-Ying Joanne Peng, Kuk Lida Lee, Gary M. Ingersoll, An Introduction to Logistic Regression Analysis and Reporting, September 2002.

8. Daniel Peterson, Robert Nyquist, "FOOTBALL MATCH PREDICTION USING DEEP LEARNING", 2017.

9. M. Fernandez, B. Ulmer, Predicting Soccer Match Results in the English Premier League, 2014.

10. A. Marcano-Cedeno, J. Quintanilla-Dominguez, M. Cortina-Januchs, D. Andina, Feature selection using sequential forward selection and classification applying artificial metaplasticity neural network, In: 36th Annual Conference on IEEE Industrial Electronics Society, 2010, pp. 2845–2850.

11. C. Shearer The CRISP-DM model: the new blueprint for data mining J. Data Warehousing, 5 (4) (2000), pp. 13-22.

12. Felix A Gers and Jürgen Schmidhuber. Recurrent nets that time and count .In: Neural Networks, 2000. IJCNN 2000, Proceedings of the IEEE-INNS-ENNS International Joint Conference on. Vol. 3. IEEE. 2000, pp. 189–194.

13. Felix A Gers, Jürgen Schmidhuber, and Fred Cummins. Learning to for-get: Continual prediction with LSTM. In: Neural computation 12.10 (2000), pp. 2451–2471.

14. Xavier Glorot, Antoine Bordes, and Yoshua Bengio. Domain adaptation for large-scale sentiment classification: A deep learning approach. In: Proceedings of the 28th international conference on machine learning (ICML-11). 2011, pp. 513–520.

15. Josip Hucaljuk and Alen Rakipović. Predicting football scores using machine learning techniques. In: MIPRO, 2011 Proceedings of the 34th International Convention. IEEE. 2011, pp. 1623–1627.

16. Nguyen, N. H., Nguyen, D. T. A., Ma, B., & Hu, J. (2022). The application of machine learning and deep learning in sport: Predicting NBA players' performance and popularity. *Journal of Information and Telecommunication*, 6(2), 217–235.

17. Buyrukoğlu, S., & Savaş, S. (2023). Stacked-based ensemble machine learning model for positioning footballer. *Arabian Journal for Science and Engineering*, 48, 1371–1383.

18. Al-Asadi, M. A., & Tasdemır, S. (2022). Predict the value of football players using FIFA video game data and machine learning techniques. *IEEE Access*, 10, 22631–22645.

19. Singh, P., Parashar, B., Agrawal, S., Mudgal, K., & Singh, P. (2023, January). Kabaddi: A Quantitative Approach to Machine Learning Model in Pro Kabaddi. In Proceedings of Second International Conference on Computational Electronics for Wireless Communications: ICCWC 2022 (pp. 243–260). Singapore: Springer Nature Singapore.

20. Rico-González, M., Pino-Ortega, J., Méndez, A., Clemente, F., & Baca, A. (2023). Machine learning application in soccer: A systematic review. *Biology of Sport*, 40(1), 249–263.

21. Mustafa, R. U., Nawaz, M. S., Lali, M. I. U., Zia, T., & Mehmood, W. (2017). Predicting the cricket match outcome using crowd opinions on social networks: A comparative study of machine learning methods. *Malaysian Journal of Computer Science*, 30(1), 63–76.

22. Horvat, T., & Job, J. (2020). The use of machine learning in sport outcome prediction: A review. *Wiley Interdisciplinary Reviews: Data Mining and Knowledge Discovery*, 10(5), e1380.

23. Huang, M. L., & Li, Y. Z. (2021). Use of machine learning and deep learning to predict the outcomes of major league baseball matches. *Applied Sciences*, 11(10), 4499.

24. Rahman, M. A. (2020). A deep learning framework for football match prediction. *SN Applied Sciences*, 2(2), 165.

25. Bunker, R., & Susnjak, T. (2022). The application of machine learning techniques for predicting match results in team sport: A review. *Journal of Artificial Intelligence Research*, 73, 1285–1322.

26. Kumar, S. (2022). Predicting the outcome of IPL cricket matches using machine learning. *The Journal of Prediction Markets*, 16(1), 31–50.

27. Malamatinos, M. C., Vrochidou, E., & Papakostas, G. A. (2022). On predicting soccer outcomes in the Greek league using machine learning. *Computers*, 11(9), 133.

28. Lotfi, S. (2021). Machine learning for sport results prediction using algorithms. *International Journal of Information Technology and Applied Sciences (IJITAS)*, 3(3), 148–155.

29. Nivetha, S. K., Geetha, M., Suganthe, R. C., Prabakaran, R. M., Madhuvanan, S., & Sameer, A. M. (2022, January). A Deep Learning Framework for Football Match Prediction. In 2022 International Conference on Computer Communication and Informatics (ICCCI) (pp. 1–7). IEEE, 25-27 January 2022; Coimbatore, India; IEEE Xplore, USA.

30. Berrar, D., Lopes, P., & Dubitzky, W. (2019). Incorporating domain knowledge in machine learning for soccer outcome prediction. *Machine Learning*, 108, 97–126.

31. Dey, L., Chakraborty, S., & Mukhopadhyay, A. (2020). Machine learning techniques for sequence-based prediction of viral-host interactions between SARS-CoV-2 and human proteins. *Biomedical Journal*, 43(5), 438–450.

32. Chaki, J., Dey, N., Moraru, L., & Shi, F. (2019). Fragmented plant leaf recognition: Bag-of-features, fuzzy-color and edge-texture histogram descriptors with multi-layer perceptron. *Optik*, 181, 639–650.

33. Chakraborty, S., Paul, H., Ghatak, S., Pandey, S. K., Kumar, A., Singh, K. U., & Shah, M. A. (2022). An AI-based medical chatbot model for infectious disease prediction. *IEEE Access*, 10, 128469–128483.

34. Chatterjee, S., Sarkar, S., Hore, S., Dey, N., Ashour, A. S., & Balas, V. E. (2017). Particle swarm optimization trained neural network for structural failure prediction of multistoried RC buildings. *Neural Computing and Applications*, 28, 2005–2016.

13 Asset Liability Management Model Based on Duration and Convexity for Commercial Banks

Sahidul Islam
University of Kalyani

13.1 INTRODUCTION

Because of the unpredictable universal market, the enhance of novel financial products, and the shifting regulatory background over the last few years, asset liability management (ALM) may turn out to be a significant task for financial organisations such as insurance companies, banks etc. ALM assists banks and financial institutions in measuring, monitoring, and managing market risks since it is a dynamic and complete framework. Essentially, ALM enables organisations to make better decisions in a more informed manner by taking into account various sorts of risks. It manages both assets and liabilities in a holistic way, captivating into account the complexity of the financial market.

Some of the financial organisations such as commercial banks deal with money inflows and withdrawals, which rendering them to a range of risks including liquidity risk, credit risk, interest rate risk and a variety of others. The function of ALM process includes planning of capital, projection of growth, planning of profit and management of several financial risk. ALM is a process that aids organisations in dealing with such risks safely. The ALM process allows financial organisations to manage its balance sheet for various interest rate and liquidity scenarios. As a result, ALM is a process through which financial organisations come up with suitable plans for handling assets and liabilities in order to measure and track risk.

Financial organisation, like banks, non-banking financial companies, deals with different types of risks; therefore, they have different ALM strategies. Using this technique all the institutions first have to identify different types of financial risks, measure them and take suitable action to mitigate them in order to enrich the overall financial health of those institutions. The planning, direction, and controls of changing levels of assets, liabilities, and capital are all parts of balance sheet management. As a result, we can consider ALM to be the first phase in the long-term strategic planning process.

ALM is a procedure with respect to an interest rate display for hedging interest rate risk over a intended timeframe. To preserve net interest income (NII) and liquidity, it is a forceful way of setting up, organising, and regulating assets and liabilities, as well as their quantities, compositions, maturities, returns, and costs.

Chambers and Charnes (1961) proposed the first ALM model, which is an example of deterministic linear programming. Their goal in that work was to identify an optimal bank portfolio over various periods, and they characterised the degree of current risk in banks where level of term deposits, demand deposits, interest rates, bank earnings in the model's constraints.

DOI: 10.1201/9781003387459-13

Later on, Cohen and Hammer (1967), Robertson (1972), Lifson and Blackman (1973), Fielitz and Loeffler (1979) constructed ALM models in various ways, but they all viewed the bank's profitability as an objective with linear constraints.

Because several studies have noted competing objectives such as risk reduction, deposit and loan maximisation and profit maximisation, multi-objective programming problem is the best possible way to tackle ALM problem.

Later, Eatman and Sealey (1979) established a multi-objective ALM model that took into account objectives including the ratio of risk assets to capital, capital adequacy, net profit. Giokas and Vassiloglou (1991) established a goal programming approach for a bank's ALM that balances the competing objectives of increasing income and reducing risk through capital allocation, maintaining market share, and expanding the amount of deposits and loans. By using data from a Greek commercial bank, using simulation analysis, Kosmidou and Zopounidis (2002) developed a goal programming model. They had to balance various competing goals, including liquidity, solvency, returns, and deposit and loan expansion, as well as environmental and political limitations and interest rate volatility. As a result, they discovered that loans and deposits are the primary sources of bank profitability.

Guotai and Feng (2007) proposed an optimisation model for an asset liability portfolio. The authors of this ALM decision-making process took into account both liquidity risk and interest rate. The liquidity risk was managed by regulatory and operational limitations, while the interest rate risk was managed through the duration gap strategy. Yang and Xu (2009a) focused solely on controlling liquidity risk in optimisation model for asset liability portfolio. Banks have traditionally employed various strategies to manage liquidity risk, such as time matching of assets and liabilities, as well as the quantity matching approach. Yang and Xu (2009b) introduced an asset and liability management optimisation model that incorporated these existing methods while also considering the interest rate structure symmetry in the bank's asset portfolio. In a similar vein, Yan et al. (2009) proposed an ALM optimum model that utilised the duration gap to capitalise on favourable interest rate changes, while ensuring that potential losses from negative interest rate shifts remained below the bank's monthly NII within a specified confidence level. This was achieved by employing Value at Risk as a constraint definition. Yu and Chi. (2009) introduced an optimisation approach for bank asset and liability portfolios to successfully minimise interest rate risk using the ideas of directional duration and directional convexity.

The concept of entropy is well-known in the field of information theory. Entropy's major goal is to measure the information conveyed by a distribution that includes all higher order moments. As a result, it should come as no surprise that the concept of Shanon entropy has also found favour in the realm of finance. However, the research on the use of entropy in the design of optimal portfolios is scarce so far. Few well-known works, such as Fang et al. (1997), Kapur (1993), and Kapur and Kesavan (1992), demonstrate the effectiveness of entropy in optimal portfolio selection. In their multi-objective portfolio optimisation model, Jana et al. (2007) used entropy as a diversification measure. However, the idea of entropy had not been applied in the model of commercial bank's asset liability management (ALM) for asset diversification.

Charnes et al. introduced goal programming in 1961. Goal programming has been widely used to handle a variety of real-world situations involving multiple objectives. Some of the application and extension of goal programming method both in crisp and fuzzy environment was established by Hannan (1981b), Ignizio (1983), Narashiman (1980), Tamiz et al. (1998). In this chapter, combination of two techniques, goal programming and fuzzy programming in form of fuzzy goal programming (FGP) technique for Multi-Objective ALM model, which was developed by Zangiabadi and Maleki (2007) considering hyperbolic membership function.

An ALM models can be categorised into four basic categories based on the time horizon over which the decision of asset liability optimisation is to be modelled and the conditions under which it is to be modelled. The categories are (i) Single-period static models (ii) Single-period stochastic models (iii) Multi-period static models (iv) Multi-period stochastic models.

In this work we had considered Single-period static models. Since our model have been used as a hedge against exchange rate and interest rate, which have crucial impact on the total portfolio value. In our proposed model we have focused mainly on dedication, immunisation, and Gap management. Dedication is basically cash flow matching. In our proposed model we have used cash flow matching for a series of cash inflows to a series of cash outflows. Immunisation technique focused to hedge a portfolio against fluctuation of interest rates. Using this technique basically the difference of assets and liabilities i.e. volatility of surplus can be minimised by matching the duration of liability with the duration of assets. For immunisation, we have applied the Duration and Convexity concept. Gap management technique focused on measuring the difference of asset and liability values and keeps the difference within an acceptable range of positive and negative limits. Banks used this technique to manage their balance sheet.

With the foregoing observations in mind, in this chapter, a multi-objective optimisation model for asset liability management is developed. In the proposed model we have considered minimisation of duration as objective in order to minimise risk and maximisation of NII in order to maximise return. Again, we focused on diversification of asset portfolio effectively. In reality it had been noticed that the optimal asset portfolio obtained from the traditional ALM models can be often totally concentrated only on few assets. In order to get rid from such situation we have proposed inclusion of one additional objective of maximisation of the entropy of weights of assets in our model. Probably this chapter is the pioneer to include the concept of "Entropy" in an ALM model for proper diversification of investment for a bank.

Although we have very rich literature for multi-objective ALM models using goal programming techniques to deal with it, yet, there is a lack of literature on ALM in uncertain environments. Since these ALM models are very complex by nature, the values of the parameters are frequently unknown to the experts and the decision makers. Therefore, it seems more appropriate to use uncertainty while setting the model's parameters, where are the technical constraints and objective function coefficients. So, realistically experts and decision makers can represent the parameters as fuzzy information. Therefore, it can be said that multi-objective problems with fuzzy parameters are more useful in handling such real problems.

In this chapter, FGP technique is used to obtain a compromised optimal solution for the aforesaid multi-objective ALM model. The model had been validated using a fictitious bank balance sheet.

13.2 PREREQUISITE TERMS

Because for any commercial bank interest rate risk and liquidity risk are two key concerns, the primary goal of this chapter is to demonstrate how to effectively manage both. Interest rate risk can be measured in a variety of ways, but we'll focus on the Duration GAP (DGAP) approach. Because these two ways are important for our model, we'll go over the basics of each and how it's best to use them to protect against risk associated with interest rates.

Duration gap: The duration model plays a crucial role in assessing the sensitivity of cash flows to fluctuations in interest rates. It quantifies the percentage change in the economic value of a bank's position resulting from a small interest rate shift. By calculating the weighted average time-to-maturity, using the current cash flow amounts as weights, the duration can be determined. Understanding duration is valuable because it reveals the timing and magnitude of cash flows that occur before the contractual maturity of a financial instrument. Therefore, employing this approach facilitates the calculation of the duration for a specific group of assets under analysis. The duration gap strategy is a highly significant method for managing interest rate risk. It involves aligning the gains and losses in asset value resulting from interest rate changes with the corresponding gains and losses in liability value, aiming to achieve a complete immunisation of the portfolio. By carefully matching these fluctuations, the duration gap strategy serves as an effective tool in mitigating the adverse effects of interest rate movements on the overall financial position. While calculating the duration using a single discount factor, there are limited scenarios constructed via changes on the parallel shifts for a flat yield curve. While there is a change in the shape of the yield curve for the choice of a specific discount factor in case of different maturities. The measure of sensitivity in time units of the riskiness of a bond is called duration.

The following is the formal tool for determining DGAP.

The market value of all assets and liabilities on the balance sheet is calculated by $\sum_{t=1}^{n} \dfrac{C}{(1+y)^t} + \dfrac{M}{(1+y)^n}$. Then duration of each of the balance sheet item is calculated using the

Macaulay's formula $D = \dfrac{\sum_{t=1}^{n} \dfrac{tC}{(1+y)^t} + \dfrac{nM}{(1+y)^n}}{P}$. Modified Duration of each asset is basically average duration of each asset weighted upon the weight of the assets in the entire assets' market value

and this is computed by $DA = \sum_{i=1}^{n} X_{Ai} * D_{Ai}$. Finally, DGAP is computed by $\left[MDA - \left(MDL * \dfrac{L}{A} \right) \right]$.

The asset's current market value is $A_1 = A_0 - \dfrac{1}{(1+k)} * DA * A * \Delta k$ after the change in interest rate and liabilities follow the same process.

Convexity: The concept of duration is often applied under the assumption of a parallel shift in the yield curve and modest interest rate fluctuations. However, in situations involving significant interest rate shifts, researchers and practitioners recognise the importance of considering convexity as a corrective measure. Convexity is employed to address the effects of large interest rate movements on asset values, and it is crucial to be mindful of the risks associated with negative convexity. These applications primarily focus on managing a company's asset portfolio. The zero duration gap method is considered an immunising strategy aimed at preserving the value of a financial institution's equity, albeit disregarding the second-order condition. Convexity represents an example of a second-order condition. In 1952, Reddington introduced a second-order condition that incorporated the dispersion values of each asset and liability around their respective durations. The assumption made in this context is that the initial equity is zero, and the objective is to immunise the equity from interest rate fluctuations.

For the value of a financial instrument, we analyse the Approximation of the initial interest rate r_0 using the Taylor series.

$$v(r) = v(r_0) + \Delta r \cdot v'(r_0) + \left(\frac{1}{2} \right) \cdot (\Delta r)^2 \cdot v''(r_0) + R_n \qquad (13.1)$$

The remainder of the Taylor series expansion's terms are represented by R_n, The value of the security is a function of the interest rate denoted by $v(r)$, change in interest rate i.e. $r - r_0$ is presented as Δr.

$$v'(r_0) = \frac{\partial v}{\partial r}\Big|_{r=r_0}$$

$$v''(r_0) = \frac{\partial^2 v}{\partial r^2}\Big|_{r=r_0}$$

R_n is supposed not important in the case of second-degree Taylor series expansion. Duration is related to first order differentiation and convexity with the second order in equation (13.1). Then duration $D = -v'(r)(1+r)/v(r)$ and convexity $C = \left(\dfrac{1}{2} \right) v''(r).(1+r)^2/v(r)$. Then rearranging the terms of equation (13.1) we get

$$\Delta v = \left[-D \frac{\Delta r}{1+r} + C \frac{(\Delta r)^2}{(1+r)^2} \right] V \qquad (13.2)$$

It is obvious from equation (13.2) that for any duration, convexity has a favourable impact on change of the security value brought on by variations in interest rates.

When we apply equation (13.2) to all assets and liabilities of a financial institution, we get:

$$\Delta A = \left[-D_A \frac{\Delta r_A}{1+r_A} + C_A \frac{(\Delta r_A)^2}{(1+r_A)^2} \right] A \tag{13.3}$$

And

$$\Delta L = \left[-D_L \frac{\Delta r_L}{1+r_L} + C_L \frac{(\Delta r_L)^2}{(1+r_L)^2} \right] L \tag{13.4}$$

Using equations (13.3) and (13.4) in $\Delta E = \Delta A - \Delta L$ we get:

$$\Delta E = -\mathrm{DGAP} \cdot A \frac{\Delta r_A}{1+r_A} + \mathrm{CGAP} \cdot A \frac{(\Delta r_A)^2}{(1+r_A)^2} \tag{13.5}$$

Where the rate of interest for each asset and liability are denoted respectively by r_A and r_L

DGAP and CGAP stand for duration and convexity gap, respectively.

It is obvious from equation (13.5) that setting the duration gap to zero is insufficient to protect the value of equity against interest rate changes. When DGAP=0 is used, equation (13.5) is reduced to

$$\Delta E = \mathrm{CGAP} \cdot A \frac{(\Delta r_A)^2}{(1+r_A)^2}$$

When the duration gap is zero, the bank must ensure a non-negative convexity gap, If not, use a zero duration gap as a means to lose.

13.2.1 ENTROPY

Claude Elwood Shanon introduced the notion of Information Entropy in 1948 to find a solution to the problem of quantitative measurement information. The relationship between information redundancy and probability was first mathematically defined by Claude Elwood Shannon, the inventor of information theory.

The measure of uncertainty relating to the random variables $p_1, p_2, \ldots, p_n$ is presented by the discrete probability distribution $p = (p_1, p_2, \ldots, p_N)^T$ taking N values. In the literature of information theory, Entropy is the name for this measure of disorder.

From the maximisation-entropy principle, if some fractional data about a random variate or scalar of a vector is given, we have to pick that probability distribution for this that is reliable with the given set of data, though maximum uncertainty is related with it.

Let us consider n-possible outcomes $A_1, A_2, \ldots, A_n$ of an experiment. Let $p_1, p_2, \ldots, p_n$ be the probabilities of those n-possible outcomes respectively. From these, we get the probability distribution

$$P = (p_1, p_2, \ldots, p_n); \sum_{i=1}^{n} p_i = 1; \; p_i \geq 0 \text{ for } i = 1, 2, \ldots, n.$$

The required conditions for the measure of uncertainty of a probability distribution are provided as follows:

I. This must be a function of $p_1, p_2, \ldots, p_n$, so that we can express it as $H = H_n(P) = H_n(p_1, p_2, \ldots, p_n)$;

II. This will be a continuous function of $p_1, p_2, \ldots, p_n$

III. If an impossible outcome will be added to the probabilistic scheme, then it should not be changed i.e. $H_{n+1}(p_1, p_2, \ldots, p_n, 0) = H_n(p_1, p_2, \ldots, p_n)$;

IV. $H_n(p_1, p_2, \ldots, p_n) = 0$ if $p_i = 1$, $p_j = 0$, $j \neq i$, $i = 1, 2, \ldots, n$;

V. In the cases when maximum uncertainty arises, then H_n should be maximum, i.e. H_n should be maximum if $p_1 = \dfrac{1}{n}, p_2 = \dfrac{1}{n}, \ldots, p_n = \dfrac{1}{n}$;

VI. As n will increase the maximum value of H_n will also increase.

Shannon had considered $H_n(p_1, p_2, \ldots, p_n) = -\sum_{i=1}^{n} p_i \log p_i$, clearly this is a function of $p_1, p_2, \ldots, p_n$. If we assume $0 \log 0$ by 0 then this will be a symmetric and continuous function.

In this chapter, Shanon entropy measure defined as $SE(\pi) = -\sum_{i=1}^{N} w_i \ln(w_i)$ is used as a measure of assets portfolio diversification. $SE(\pi)$ attains its maximum value $\ln N$ when $w_i = \dfrac{1}{N}$ for all i and in the extreme cases $SE(\pi) = 0$ when $w_i = 1$ for one i and $= 0$ for the rest.

As a result, we can use entropy as a measure of portfolio diversification, as entropy is a good measure of system disorder or expected information in a probability distribution, as seen by the preceding. Portfolios are frequently evaluated in terms of their degree of diversification using the Shannon Entropy measure after being created using various selection techniques. As a result, in order to build the most diversified asset portfolio feasible, we chose maximising entropy as an objective function in our research.

13.3 MATHEMATICAL MODEL

Below is a presentation of the suggested mathematical model for the specified decision variables.

13.3.1 Assets and Liabilities Decision Variables

In this segment, we present the proposed ALM optimisation model. First the list of variables for the proposed model and then the list of notations used for this purpose have been mentioned below.

The list of variables for asset sides and liability sides is mentioned below.

13.3.1.1 Asset Side

- Cash in hand - X_1
- Balance with Central Bank-
- Money at call and short notice - X_2
- Government securities
  - a period of time less than one year - X_{31}
  - a period of time ranging from one to two years - X_{32}
  - a period of time above two years - X_{33}
- Other approved securities - X_4
- Shares - X_5
- Bonds –
  - a period of time less than one month - X_{61}
  - a period of time ranging from one to six months - X_{62}
  - a period of time ranging from six months to one year - X_{63}

- a period of time ranging from one to three years - X_{64}
- a period of time ranging from three to five years - X_{65}
- a period of time above five years - X_{66}
- Subsidiaries - X_7
- Bills purchased and discounted - X_8
- Cash credits, overdrafts and loan repayable on demand - X_9
- Term Loans –
  - a period of time less than one month - X_{10_1}
  - a period of time ranging from one to six months - X_{10_2}
  - a period of time ranging from six months to one year - X_{10_3}
  - a period of time ranging from one to three years - X_{10_4}
  - a period of time ranging from three to five years - X_{10_5}
  - a period of time above five years - X_{10_6}
- Fixed assets - X_{11}
- Other assets – X_{12}

13.3.1.2 Liability Side
- Authorised+Issued Capital - Y_1
- Subscribed+Paid up Capital - Y_2
- Statutory and capital reserves - Y_3
- Share Premium - Y_4
- Demand Deposits - Y_5
- Savings bank Deposits - Y_6
- Term Deposits –
  - a period of time less than one month - Y_{71}
  - a period of time ranging from one to six months - Y_{72}
  - a period of time ranging from six months to one year - Y_{73}
  - a period of time ranging from one to three years - Y_{74}
  - a period of time ranging from three to six years - Y_{75}
  - a period of time above five years - Y_{76}
- Borrowing from central bank - Y_8
- Borrowing from other banks - Y_9
- Borrowing from other Institutions and agencies - Y_{10}
- Capital Instruments - Y_{11}
- Other Liabilities - Y_{12}
- Retained earnings - Y_{13}
- Net earnings for the period - Y_{14}

13.3.1.3 Notations
- Convexity of the i-th asset CX_i.
- Convexity of the j-th liability CY_j.
- Duration of the i-th asset DX_i.
- Duration of the j-th liability DY_j.
- Average yield of the i-th asset r_i.
- Average cost of the j-th liability s_j.
- Number of assets and liabilities are respectively n and m.
- The i-th asset's yield changes and the j-th liability's yield changes are Δr_i and Δs_j respectively.
- Some liquidity limit prefixed by bank are k_1 to k_4.

- k_5 is the solvency ratio of the bank, which is known.
- k_6 is different liquidity ratio which will be known to us.
- L Level of loan for previous financial year.
- D is Deposit level for previous financial year.
- S is share capital for previous financial year.
- E is equity of previous financial year.
- E_Y is specific category of liability accounts.
- E_X is specific category of assets accounts.
- E_1 is the requirement capital.
- γ_i is riskiness degree of assets.
- π_x is total set of liquid assets.
- π_y is total set of current liabilities.

13.3.2 THE PROPOSED MODEL

Model 1:

$$\text{Max } Z_1 = \sum_{i=1}^{n} r_i X_i - \sum_{j=1}^{m} s_j Y_j \ ; \tag{13.6}$$

$$\text{Max } Z_2 = -\sum_{i=1}^{N} \omega_i \ln \omega_i; \tag{13.7}$$

$$\text{Min } Z_3 = \sum_{j=1}^{m} DY_j \times Y_j \times \Delta s_j - \sum_{i=1}^{k} DX_i \times X_i \times \Delta r_i; \tag{13.8}$$

Subject to

$$X_9 + \sum_{i=1}^{6} X_{10i} \geq L; \tag{13.9}$$

$$X_9 + \sum_{i=1}^{6} X_{10i} \leq (1 + k_1\%) \text{ of } L; \tag{13.10}$$

$$Y_5 + Y_6 + \sum_{i=1}^{6} Y_{7i} \geq D; \tag{13.11}$$

$$Y_5 + Y_6 + \sum_{i=1}^{6} Y_{7i} \leq (1 + k_2\%) D; \tag{13.12}$$

$$\sum_{i=1}^{2} Y_i \geq S; \tag{13.13}$$

$$\sum_{i=1}^{4} Y_i + \sum_{i=13}^{14} Y_i \leq (1 + k_1\%) \text{ of } E; \tag{13.14}$$

$$Y_{14} \geq k_4\% \text{ of } \sum_{i=1}^{n} X_i; \tag{13.15}$$

$$\sum_{j \in E_Y} Y_j - \beta \sum_{i \in E_X} X_i = 0; \tag{13.16}$$

$$\sum_{i \in E_1} Y_j - \sum_{i \in A} \gamma_i X_i \geq k_5; \tag{13.17}$$

$$\sum_{i \in \pi_X} X_i Y_j - k_6 \sum_{j \in \pi_Y} Y_j \leq 0; \tag{13.18}$$

$$\sum_{j=1}^{m} DY_j \times Y_j \times \Delta s_j - \sum_{i=1}^{k} DX_i \times X_i \times \Delta r_i > 0; \tag{13.19}$$

$$\frac{1}{2} \sum_{i=1}^{k} CX_i \times X_i \times (\Delta r_i)^2 \geq \frac{1}{2} \sum_{j=1}^{m} CY_j \times Y_j \times (\Delta s_j)^2; \tag{13.20}$$

$$A = L; \tag{13.21}$$

$$X_i \geq 0, \quad Y_j \geq 0; \tag{13.22}$$

13.3.3 Description of the Mathematical Model

In this section, we will briefly discuss the objectives and the constraints. To describe the objectives and the constraints we need to mention some definitions are given below.

Current assets: Current assets are liquid money which a bank hold by itself and the amount of money obtainable within short period i.e. it is the totality of cash and marketable securities available within a year.

Current liabilities: Current liabilities are simply how much money the bank must spend in a short period of time i.e. it is defined as totality of short portion of long-term debt and short term debt obligations.

Solvency ratio: The ratio of total equity capital of bank and total risk-weighted assets is said to be the solvency ratio. It has been used as a risk measure.

Return on assets: Ratio of net earnings for the period and total assets is Return on assets (ROA). It has used as a measure for profitability.

The main of a bank is to maximise its revenue by investing its funds properly. So our first objective is to maximise the NII of a bank.

Our model's second goal is to achieve the maximum diversified asset portfolio possible. We used entropy maximisation as an objective function to do this.

Duration gap management is a critical strategy for determining if changes in interest rates affect cash flows. A slight change in the rate of interest results in a change in the position of a bank's financial value, and the duration is a percentage change's measurement. The weighted average time-to-maturity is used to calculate the duration, with the weights representing the current cash flow amounts. Duration is important because it shows the magnitude and timing of cash flows that happen before the financial instrument reaches its contractual maturity. The duration gap is one of the most important ways for mitigating interest rate risk. By matching gains and losses in asset value with gains and losses in liability value for changes in rate of interest, the duration gap method completely protects the portfolio.

However, a completely immunised duration gap model isn't particularly useful because a bank won't be able to benefit from a favourable market interest rate movement in a completely immunised system.

That's why, in place of developing a completely immunised ALM model, we attempted to minimise duration gap. We had explored using the duration gap as a risk measure.

Sometimes some constraints are imposed on a bank by their monetary authorities as a part of their policies that the bank has to follow on some particular categories of accounts such as loans, deposits etc. The constraints are to maintain maximum and minimum limits allowed for these categories of accounts. Constraints (13.9) and (13.10) indicate that granted total loans should maintain the previous year's level and can rise up to some pre specified percentage of previous year's level. Similar conditions will hold in case of deposit accounts, which are mentioned in constraints (13.11) and (13.12).

Constraint (13.13) indicates that there should be a lower cap for the variable related to share capital. Since share capital is the major part of equity of a commercial bank.

To ensure the required solvency, the bank needs to increase its equity up to a certain percentage compared to the previous financial year. This fact has been reflected in constraint (13.14).

A constraint (13.15) reflects the fact that a commercial bank should maintain a minimum level for its Return on assets, since ROA indicates profitability of a commercial bank.

There are some obligations of each commercial bank to save some stipulated quantity of its security deposits in a central bank's unique interest-bearing account and also an amount is directed towards loan for customers. Keeping all these requirements of bank in mind we have designed constraint (13.16).

To make sure the required solvency the policymakers of the bank want to ensure that the solvency ratio should be greater or equal to a certain percentage. Here, the solvency ratio serves as a risk indicator and is calculated as the ratio of total risk-weighted assets to total bank equity capital. The risk weight of the assets reflects their respective risks. Lesser weight corresponds to a lesser degree of risks. As per recommendation of Basel Committee, the risk weight for government debt is 0%, that of loan to banks is 20%, for mortgages it is 50%, and for all claims of private sector, it is 100%. Our constraint (13.17) is to solvency goal.

One of the major aims of commercial banks is to manage its liquidity and more precisely the measurement of needs that are directly related to the movement of deposits and loans. So, a major policy of bank is that the ratio of liquid assets to current liability should maintain a certain level. This is a liquidity risk measure. Constraint (13.18) is related to liquidity goal.

The constraint (13.19) is predicated on managing the total duration gap.

The convexity measures are used to create constraint (13.20).

The two limitations mentioned above are utilised to correctly control interest rate risk.

Entire assets must match entire liabilities on the bank's balance sheet and shareholder capital. (constraint 13.21).

The non-negativity condition on both the assets and liability sides is the final constraint (13.22).

13.4 MATHEMATICAL ANALYSIS

In this part, we argue about the solution techniques used to solve this mathematical model.

13.4.1 GOAL PROGRAMMING APPROACH

Several researches have been reported in this field since the pioneering work of this field had been done by Charnes and Cooper (1977). The key factor at the back of the goal programming technique is to minimise the distance between $Z = (Z_1, Z_2, \ldots, Z_k)$ and aspiration levels $\bar{Z} = (z_1, z_2, \ldots, z_k)$, as set by the decision maker. In order to perform this, we first need to introduce the negative and positive deviational variables as:

$$d_r^- = \max(0, \bar{z}_r - Z_r) = \frac{1}{2}\{(\bar{z}_r - Z_r) + |\bar{z}_r - Z_r|\}, \quad r = 1, 2, \ldots, k. \tag{13.23}$$

and

$$d_r^+ = \max(0, Z_r - \bar{z}_r) = \frac{1}{2}\{(Z_r - \bar{z}_r) + |Z_r - \bar{z}_r|\}, \quad r = 1, 2, \ldots, k. \tag{13.24}$$

In this case, minimisation of distance between Z_r and $\bar{z}_r$ is directed to minimising d_r^+ whenever $Z_r \leq \bar{z}_r$ is required for minimisation problem. Now by using min-max goal programming in this case our proposed model had been converted to the following linear programming model

Model 2:

$$\text{Min } \psi \tag{13.25}$$

Subject to

$$Z_r + d_r^- - d_r^+ = z_r, \quad r = 1, 2, 3.$$

$$\psi \geq d_r^+, \quad r = 1, 2, 3.$$

$$d_r^- \cdot d_r^+ = 0, r = 1, 2, 3.$$

$$d_r^-, d_r^+ \geq 0, \quad r = 1, 2, 3.$$

and set of constraints (13.9)–(13.22) of our proposed model.

13.4.2 HYPERBOLIC MEMBERSHIP FUNCTION

Based on the fuzzy decision-making process, a multi-objective linear programming problem can be transformed into an identical convex programming problem by employing various types of linear and non-linear membership functions. While linear membership functions are widely used due to their simplicity, they are not always suitable for practical situations. Linear membership functions are typically defined using two points, representing the lower and upper levels of acceptability. However, in many cases, a linear membership function does not adequately capture the complexity of practical scenarios. In situations where the membership function is interpreted as the decision makers' fuzzy utility, which describes their preferences, indifference, or aversion towards uncertainty, a non-linear membership function provides a better representation. Non-linear membership functions offer a more flexible and nuanced approach to modelling decision makers' subjective perceptions and attitudes towards uncertainty. Therefore, the adoption of non-linear membership functions is considered more appropriate in these cases.

In particular, we have considered a hyperbolic membership function because it is a convex function over the outstanding part and over a section of the objective function with a concave function. The concave portion of the membership function is used when the decision maker has a smaller marginal rate of satisfaction and the convex portion of the membership function is used when the decision maker has a higher marginal rate of satisfaction.

Let us consider for r-th objective function, $\mathcal{U}_r$ is highest acceptable level of achievement and $\mathcal{L}_r$ be the aspired level of achievement. Then for the r-th objective function, the hyperbolic membership function is defined as

$$\mu_r^H\left(Z_r(X)\right) = \frac{1}{2} + \frac{1}{2} \frac{e^{\left\{\frac{\mathcal{U}_r+\mathcal{L}_r}{2}-Z_r(X)\right\}\alpha_r} - e^{-\left\{\frac{\mathcal{U}_r+\mathcal{L}_r}{2}-Z_r(X)\right\}\alpha_r}}{e^{\left\{\frac{\mathcal{U}_r+\mathcal{L}_r}{2}-Z_r(X)\right\}\alpha_r} + e^{-\left\{\frac{\mathcal{U}_r+\mathcal{L}_r}{2}-Z_r(X)\right\}\alpha_r}}, \quad \text{where} \quad \alpha_r = \frac{6}{\mathcal{U}_r - \mathcal{L}_r}. \quad (13.26)$$

This membership function bears the below mentioned properties (Figure 13.1).

I. With respect to $Z_r(X)$, $\mu_r^H\left(Z_r(X)\right)$ is a strictly monotone decreasing function.

II. $Z_r(X) = \dfrac{\mathcal{U}_r + \mathcal{L}_r}{2} \Leftrightarrow \mu_r^H\left(Z_r(X)\right) = \dfrac{1}{2}$;

III. For $Z_r(X) \geq \dfrac{\mathcal{U}_r + \mathcal{L}_r}{2}$, $\mu_r^H\left(Z_r(X)\right)$ is strictly convex and concave for $Z_r(X) \leq \dfrac{\mathcal{U}_r + \mathcal{L}_r}{2}$.

IV. $0 < \mu_r^H\left(Z_r(X)\right) < 1$ for $\mathcal{L}_r < Z_r(X) < \mathcal{U}_r$ and asymptotically it approaches $\mu_r^H\left(Z_r(X)\right) = 0$ and $\mu_r^H\left(Z_r(X)\right) = 1$ as $Z_r(X) \to \infty$ and $-\infty$ respectively.

13.4.3 FGP APPROACH

Few authors had used linear membership functions to solve a multi-objective linear programming problem using the FGP method in the past. In this chapter, we adopt the FGP technique with non-linear membership function just as an approach for solving our proposed multi-objective ALM model. Obviously 1 is the highest degree of membership function. Now for the r-th hyperbolic membership function as given above, considering deviational variables $d_r^+, d_r^- \geq 0$, with aspired level 1 the flexible membership goal can be presented as

$$\frac{1}{2} + \frac{1}{2} \frac{e^{\left\{\frac{\mathcal{U}_r+\mathcal{L}_r}{2}-Z_r(X)\right\}\alpha_r} - e^{-\left\{\frac{\mathcal{U}_r+\mathcal{L}_r}{2}-Z_r(X)\right\}\alpha_r}}{e^{\left\{\frac{\mathcal{U}_r+\mathcal{L}_r}{2}-Z_r(X)\right\}\alpha_r} + e^{-\left\{\frac{\mathcal{U}_r+\mathcal{L}_r}{2}-Z_r(X)\right\}\alpha_r}} + d_r^- - d_r^+ = 1, \quad \text{where} \quad d_r^+ d_r^- = 0. \quad (13.27)$$

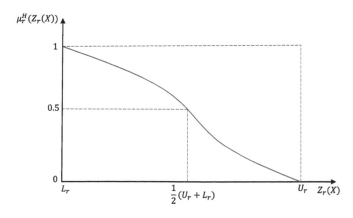

FIGURE 13.1 Graphical representation of hyperbolic membership function.

Any divergence from 1 indicates that the membership value has been fully realised. All that is necessary to achieve the desired level of the fuzzy objective is to minimise its negative deviational variable from 1.

The following model is obtained by applying the $min - max$ goal programming to a fuzzy model of a multi-objective ALM model with a hyperbolic membership function.

Model 3:

$$\text{Min } \varphi \tag{13.28}$$

$$subject\ to,$$

$$\frac{1}{2}+\frac{1}{2}\frac{e^{\left\{\frac{\mathcal{U}_r+\mathcal{L}_r}{2}-Z_r(X)\right\}\alpha_r}-e^{-\left\{\frac{\mathcal{U}_r+\mathcal{L}_r}{2}-Z_r(X)\right\}\alpha_r}}{e^{\left\{\frac{\mathcal{U}_r+\mathcal{L}_r}{2}-Z_r(X)\right\}\alpha_r}+e^{-\left\{\frac{\mathcal{U}_r+\mathcal{L}_r}{2}-Z_r(X)\right\}\alpha_r}}+d_r^- -d_r^+ = 1,$$

$$\varphi \geq d_r^-, \quad r = 1,2,3.$$

$$d_r^- d_r^+ = 0$$

$$\varphi \leq 1$$

$$\varphi \geq 0$$

and set of constraints (13.9)–(13.22) of our proposed model.

13.4.4 Steps of the FGP Approach to Solve Proposed Multi-Objective ALM Model

   i. To solve the multi-objective ALM as a single-objective ALM model, use one objective as the objective function each time and ignore the others.
   ii. Calculate the value of each of the objective functions at each of the previous steps' solutions.
   iii. Now from step ii calculate for each of the objectives the worst value ($\mathcal{U}_r$) and the best value ($\mathcal{L}_r$). For r-th objective function $\mathcal{U}_r$ be the highest acceptable level of achievement, $\mathcal{L}_r$ be the aspired level of achievement.
   iv. Now develop Model 3 and hence solve it.

We have designed a flowchart for the solution of our proposed ALM model using the FGP approach which is given below (Figure 13.2):

13.5 NUMERICAL ILLUSTRATIONS

Here we have considered a theoretical bank financial statement of one-year time frame to verify the corroboration of our model. For each calculation, we have considered the balance sheet based on a total amount of Rupees one lakh for assets and also for liabilities. The supposed data of asset and liability side both is provided below. In our hypothetical bank balance sheet, we have considered some items from assets side and some items from liabilities side, such as cash in hand, balance with

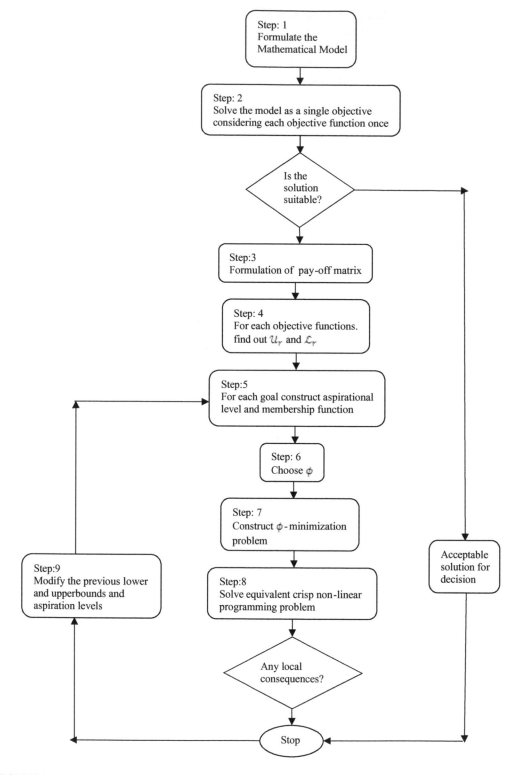

FIGURE 13.2   The entire procedure of the proposed model.

central bank, fixed assets, other assets, reserve and surplus, other liability as known item. Since at beginning of a financial year these items are known to bank's managing persons.

13.5.1 Duration and Convexity of the Balance Sheet Items

To calculate the duration and convexity of all the assets and liabilities of a bank, the formula needed is discussed below.

Duration of interest free bond $= n$

Duration of common bond $= \dfrac{1+r}{r}\left[1-\dfrac{1}{(1+r)^n}\right]$

Duration of annuity bond $= \dfrac{1+r}{r}-\dfrac{n}{(1+r)^n-1}$

Duration of permanent annuity bond $= \dfrac{1+r}{r}$

The duration for assets and liabilities for assets or liabilities without interest rates is 0.

Now for the assets like fixed deposits, at the end of the time period, the principle and interest had both been paid. Therefore, these types of assets/liabilities are just like zero-coupon bond. As a result, duration may be simply calculated via the interest-free bond formula.

Now for the assets like loan and liabilities like borrowings are just like common bond, the interest is being paid at the end of every month.

For example, for a loan for three years we have assumed the rate of interest $r=7.14\%$ per annum.

Then its duration is $D = \dfrac{1+\dfrac{5.95\%}{12}}{\dfrac{5.95\%}{12}}\left[1-\dfrac{1}{\left(1+\dfrac{5.95\%}{12}\right)^{36}}\right] = 32.53$

Similarly for borrowings for two years we have assumed its interest$=9.06\%$ per annum. Then its

duration is $D = \dfrac{1+\dfrac{9.06\%}{12}}{\dfrac{9.06\%}{12}}\left[1-\dfrac{1}{\left(1+\dfrac{9.06\%}{12}\right)^{24}}\right] = 22.04 \approx 22$

In this manner, we have computed the duration of all the assets and the liabilities.

Also using this rate of interest for each of the assets as well as the liabilities using the formula for convexity for assets and liabilities, we have computed convexity for each of the assets and the liabilities.

The Table 13.1 below contains the duration and convexity that correspond to the provided assets.

The Table 13.2 below contains the duration and convexity for the specified assets.

The optimal solutions of liability and asset distribution by solving the above model using FGP technique, which controls both interest rate risk and liquidity risk is shown in the Table 13.3 below and the corresponding Pareto optimal solutions are as follows.

As we know that the liabilities and asset's market value in real situation may alter simultaneously as an effect of changing interest rates, but for simplicity of validation of our proposed model we have directly provided the liabilities and the asset's market value.

In commercial bank's asset liability management, the fluctuations of the rate of interest in future need to be forecasted. With the condition of duration, since it is an immunisation condition when planning, interest rate risk may be avoided. But we have considered the concept of convexity along with the condition of duration since these two in together will assume the positive change in net worth of a commercial bank, whatever and whenever the interest rate changes.

TABLE 13.1

Balance Sheet of the Asset Side of Hypothetical Bank along with Their Duration and Convexities

Assets		Amount	Duration	Convexity
Cash in hand		1583	0	0
Balance with RBI		3223	0	0
Balance with Banks		752	0	0
Money at call and short notice		485	5.1311	36.4992
Securities	Less than one year		11.2674	151.262
	One to two years		57.653	4522.24
	Greater than two years		64.26	5112.84
Loans	One month		1.3441	2.6788
	Six months		5.1294	36.5259
	One year		10.5329	144.6332
	Three years		32.5305	1415.117
	Five years		53.8316	4221.574
Fixed assets		1064		
Other assets		7235		

TABLE 13.2

Balance Sheet of the Liability Side of Hypothetical Bank along with Their Duration and Convexities

Liabilities		Amount	Duration	Convexity
Authorised and issued capital		273	0	0
Subscribed and paid up capital		172	0	0
Statutory and capital reserves		1029	0	0
Share premium			0	0
Current deposits			2.4	8.1466
Fixed deposits	Three month		3	11.9616
	Six months		6	41.8492
	One year		12	155.4166
	Three years		36	1326.026
	Five years		60	3642.495
Borrowings	Less than one year		8.92	81.1664
	One to two years		22	487.88
	Greater than two years		48.56	2368.074
Other liabilities		3955	0	0
Retained earning		379		
Net earnings for the period		71		

As we know if we assumed duration gap to be equal to zero then the situation will be fully immunised. But in practice we know that if the bank is able to take more risk, then the bank will consider $DGAP>0$. We have considered $DGAP>0$ as a constraint and simultaneously minimisation of DGAP in our model because the formula for deriving net value of the bank had been utilised in advance to estimate the risk of loss. But if $DGAP<0$, then the policy for management will be changed. In addition to reducing risk, we have also employed $DGAP$ for speculating.

TABLE 13.3
The Pareto Optimal Solutions of Liability and Asset Distribution

Assets		Amount	Liabilities		Amount
Cash in hand		1582			
Balance with RBI		3223	Authorised and issued capital		273
Balance with banks		752	Subscribed and paid up capital		172
Money at call and short notice		485	Statutory and capital reserves		1029
			Share premium		4527
Securities	Less than one year	8072.55	Current deposits		1072
	One to two years	4785.66	Fixed deposits	Three month	1451.26
	Greater than two years	8072.55			
Loans	One month	1612.27			
	Six months	1822.53		Six months	2794.91
	One year	13,741.3		One year	17,342
	Three years	19,076.2		Three years	21,582.5
	Five years	23,131.7		Five years	35,923.4
Fixed assets		1064	Borrowings	Less than one year	3713.63
Other assets		7235		One to two years	1488.3
				Greater than two years	4226.07
			Other liabilities		3955
			Retained earning		379
			Net earnings for the period		71

13.6 CONCLUSIONS

In this chapter, the proposed mathematical model controls both liquidity risk and interest rate risk, which optimises the profitability of the bank and simultaneously diversify the distribution of the assets. So, it is just like "Hitting multiple targets with one shot".

A satisfying solution can be found using the FGP technique. The decision maker also assesses level of aspiration. The use of FGP to solve the multi-objective ALM problem is investigated in this chapter. The Multi-objective ALM problem is solved using the hyperbolic membership function as well as the non-linear optimisation model.

Finally, we can conclude that the designed quantitative model for the optimal management of the liabilities and assets of commercial banks is an effective model. Our model can also be used in commercial banks level for the determination of appropriate balance sheet structure and managing its assets elements and diversifying the distribution of assets.

REFERENCES

Chambers D., & Charnes A. (1961), Inter-temporal analysis and optimization of bank portfolios. *Management Science*, 7(11), 393–409. https://pubsonline.informs.org/doi/epdf/10.1287/mnsc.7.4.393.

Charnes A., & Cooper W. W. (1977), Goal Programming and multiple objective optimizations: part 1. *European Journal of Operational Research* 1(1), 39–54. https://www.sciencedirect.com/science/article/abs/pii/S0377221777810072.

Cohen K. J., & Hammer F. S. (1967), Linear programming and optimal bank asset management decision. *Journal of Finance*, 22, 42–61. https://onlinelibrary.wiley.com/doi/10.1111/j.1540-6261.1967.tb00002.x.

Eatman L., & Sealey J. (1979), A multi-objective linear programming model for commercial bank balance sheet management. *Journal of Bank Research* 9, 227–236.

Fang S. C., Rajasekera J. R., & Tsao H. S. (1997), *Entropy Optimization and Mathematical Programming*. Kluwer Academic Publisheres, Boston. https://link.springer.com/book/10.1007/978-1-4615-6131-6.

Fielitz D., & Loeffler A. (1979), A linear programming model for commercial bank liquidity management. *Financial Management* 8(3), 44–50. https://www.jstor.org/stable/3665037.

Giokas D., & Vassiloglou M. (1991), A goal programming model for bank assets and liabilities. *European Journal of Operations Research* 50, 48–60. https://www.sciencedirect.com/science/article/abs/pii/037722179190038W.

Guotai C. H. I., & Feng C. H. I. (2007), Optimization model of asset-liability portfolio considering duration perfect matching. IEEE International Conference on Control and Automation, IEEE, 1-4244-0818. https://ieeexplore.ieee.org/document/4376572.

https://www.sciencedirect.com/science/article/abs/pii/0165011481900026.

Hannan E. L. (1981b), On fuzzy goal programming. *Decision Sciences* 12(3), 522–531. https://onlinelibrary.wiley.com/doi/abs/10.1111/j.1540-5915.1981.tb00102.x.

Ignizio J. P. (1983), Generalized goal programming an overview. *Computers & Operations Research* 10(4), 277–289. https://www.sciencedirect.com/science/article/abs/pii/0305054883900035.

Jana P., Roy T. K., & Mazumder S. K. (2007), Multi-objective mean-variance-skewness model for portfolio optimization. *Advanced Modeling and Optimization* 9(1), 2007. https://camo.ici.ro/journal/vol9/v9a13.pdf.

Kapur J. N. (1993), *Maximum Entropy Models in Science and Engineering*. Wiley Eastern Limited, New Delhi. https://searchworks.stanford.edu/view/154524.

Kapur J. N., & Kesavan H. K. (1992), *Entropy Optimization Principles with Application*. Academic Press, Boston. https://www.scirp.org/(S(lz5mqp453edsnp55rrgjct55))/reference/ReferencesPapers.aspx?ReferenceID=1401812.

Kosmidou K., & Zopounidis C. (2002), An optimization scenario methodology for bank ALM. *Operational Research* 2(2), 279–287. https://link.springer.com/article/10.1007/BF02936331.

Lifson K. A., & Blackman B. R. (1973), Simulation and optimization models for asset deployment and funds sources balancing profit liquidity and growth. *Journal of Bank Research* 4(3), 239–255.

Narashiman R. (1980), Goal programming in a fuzzy environment. *Decision Sciences* 11(2), 325–336. https://onlinelibrary.wiley.com/doi/10.1111/j.1540-5915.1980.tb01142.x.

Robertson M. (1972), A Bank Asset Management Model. In: S. Eilon and T. R. Fowkes (Eds.). *Applications of Management Science in Banking and Finance*. Gower Press, Epping, Essex, 149–158.

Tamiz M., Jones D. F., & Romero C. (1998), Goal programming for decision making an overview of the current state-of-the-art. *European Journal of Operational Research* 111(3), 569–581. https://www.sciencedirect.com/science/article/abs/pii/S0377221797003172.

Wu H. & Chi G. (2009), *Bank Assets and Liabilities Portfolio Optimization Model Based on the Dual-gap Immunity of the Directional Duration and Directional Convexity*. IEEE, 1978-1-4244-4639. https://ieeexplore.ieee.org/document/5301499, IEEE Xplore, USA.

Yan D., Chi G., & Wu H. (2009), Asset and Liabilities Management optimal model based on VaR controlled prepared duration gap. International Joint Conference on Computational Sciences and Optimization. IEEE, 978-0-7695-3605. https://ieeexplore.ieee.org/document/5193855.

Yang Z., & Xu W. (2009a), Optimization Model of Asset-Liability Portfolio Based on Controlling Liquidity Risk. IEEE, 978-1-4244-4639. https://ieeexplore.ieee.org/document/5303021, IEEE Xplore, USA.

Yang Z., & Xu W. (2009b), *Optimization Model of Asset-Liabilities Management Considering Interest Rate Risk and Time Structure Risk*. IEEE, 978-0-7695-3887. https://ieeexplore.ieee.org/document/5455614 IEEE Computer Society, United States.

Zangiabadi M., & Maleki H. R. (2007), Fuzzy goal programming for multi-objective transportation problem. *Journal Of Applied Mathematics and Computing* 24(1–2), 449–460. https://link.springer.com/article/10.1007/BF02832333.

14 A Qualitative Mathematical Analysis of Pandemic SARS-Cov-2 with Special Emphasis on Uncertain Environments

Kalyan Das
National Institute of Food Technology
Entrepreneurship and Management

M. N. Srinivas
Vellore Institute of Technology

Md Humayun Kabir and Md Osman Gani
Jahangirnagar University

Md Haider Ali Biswas
Khulna University

14.1 INTRODUCTION

Human pandemics and epidemics have wreaked havoc on humanity before, and these pandemics have often resulted in profound changes in human life. Similarly, the new coronavirus has once again exposed the entire continent to a lethal encounter with the biggest impact on human life [1]. The WHO proclaimed corona a universal virus on March 11, 2020 [2]. As of July 6, 2020, the new coronavirus pandemic had caused 11,301,850 confirmed cases and 531,806 fatalities worldwide, according to WHO [2]. As of July 6, 2020, there were 19,721 fatalities and 700,728 confirmed cases in India [3]. The Indian government declared it a pandemic on March 23, 2020, and ordered a statewide lockdown. The majority of people have been placed under quarantine, and numerous precautionary methods have been put in place, including sanitizing containment areas, identifying close friends, isolating infected people, and encouraging social consensus on personal protection measures like donning a facemask, using hand sanitizer, and regularly washing one's hands, among others. Despite this, there are still new coronavirus infections emerging, and the no. of established cases has reached an extraordinary record. Comparing COVID-19 to prior coronavirus epidemics (like SARS and MERS), unexpected traits have been discovered [4]. COVID-19 is spread through direct contact between people who have no or only minor ciphers of the illness [5]. The presence of SARS-Cov-2 in patients with mild or no symptoms suggests that the virus has a high infectious potential [6]. As a result, the persistence of the epidemic may be aided by subclinical infection.

DOI: 10.1201/9781003387459-14

Modeling is one of the most suitable techniques for effectively controlling disease spread. In the last few decades, several effective mathematical models have been developed to research infectious diseases and design beneficial techniques for the well-organized abolition of infection [38–44]. Compartmental representations and real-world examples are more useful in presenting pertinent data regarding a disease epidemic. To evaluate the intricate COVID-19 epidemic transmission pattern, a number of mathematical models [45–47], DDEs [48], SDEs [29], and FOCD [49–54] have already been created in various nations.

Mathematical modeling is one of the most extensively utilized strategies for forecasting and managing coronavirus spread [7–10]. To represent the spread of infection, the famous SIR model [11] uses prone, contaminated, and removed compartments. To acquire more relevant data, new variables are frequently included in the SIR model. As a result of improving the SIR model, other scientific simulations have been presented to depict the dynamics of COVID-19. A notional SEIR model that includes both private and public answers was created by Lin et al. [12]. The SIDARTHE model, created by Giordano et al. [4], includes both affected individuals who have not been recognized and those who have been recognized. The SEIR model was used by Prem et al. [13] to investigate the effects of control measures. To account for COVID-19 transmission during the latent period, Peng et al. [14] established a widespread S-E-I-R model. During the latent period, the new coronavirus seems to spread from person to person [15]. There is presently no effective vaccine or treatment for the illness. As a result, the only way to monitor the pandemic's spread is to make an educated guess as to how many people are affected, which enables authorities to better formulate control strategies. Models [16–19] are ineffective at predicting the outcomes of an outbreak because they only take into account a small number of variables and leave out important ones like asymptomatic cases, quarantined cases, and so on. LSTM and RNN models are frequently reliant on the number of connections. The influence of confined cases, asymptomatic cases, safe populations, and other factors are ignored by LSTM-based models.

As a result, we feel compelled to present a model that incorporates the missed variables to accurately estimate the number of infected patients. A substantial number of asymptomatic instances have been discovered in India. As a result, asymptomatic cases must be included in the mathematical model.

By enhancing the widespread S-E-I-R model proposed by Peng et al. [14], we suggested a novel mathematical delayed disease model (SVIR) and its significantly afflicted states in this study. Non-quarantined susceptible, quarantined susceptible, infected, and recovered are all factors in the suggested four compartmental delayed models. When compared to other models, the suggested model's simulated outcomes are very close to the actual data.

There are five sections to this study. Section 14.1 provides an outline of the linked works as well as an introduction. Section 14.2 discusses the recently created mathematical delay model's parameters and values. In Section 14.3, we explore mathematical analysis in the absence of delay, such as boundedness, positivity, and equilibrium analysis. In Section 14.4, the model's stability at various equilibriums was discussed in the absence of delay. In Section 14.5, we covered delay analysis using bifurcation analysis. Numerical simulations have been supplied in Section 14.6 in the form of figures with the appropriate attribute using MATLAB. Finally, in Section 14.7, there are conclusions.

14.2 MODEL OF SARS-COV-2 WITH TIME DELAY

We consider $N(t)$: non-vaccinated s.p, $V(t)$: vaccinated s.p, $I(t)$: i.p, and $R(t)$: healthier or invulnerable population. We suggest a model that takes into account the following flowchart and incorporates the time delay impact for infected persons comprehend the COVID-19 outburst. The conclusion is that there should be a length of time for the disease to incubate in both vulnerable non-vaccinated individuals and susceptible individuals when they come into connection with those who have the disease.

$$
\left.\begin{aligned}
N'(t) &= \mu - \alpha NV - \beta NI - \upsilon N \\
V'(t) &= \alpha NV - \gamma VI \\
I'(t) &= \beta NI(t - \tau_1) + \gamma VI(t - \tau_2) - (\alpha + \delta)I(t) \\
R'(t) &= \sigma I(t)
\end{aligned}\right\} \tag{14.1}
$$

with i.c's $N(0) \geq 0$, $V(0) \geq 0$, $I(0) \geq 0$, $R(0) \geq 0$. The list of compartmental parameters and variables that are regarded as non-negative is shown below, along with their corresponding physical explanations.

N: Non-vaccinated s.p; V: vaccinated s.p; I: I.p; R: Recovered or I.p; α: Rate of vaccination; β: 'Rate of nvp having corona positive'; μ: Recruitment rate of the nvsp; υ: Rate of loss of immunity for non-vaccinated population; γ: Rate of vaccinated population having corona positive; σ: "Retrieval rate of dp; δ: corona induced expiry rate of infected individual"; τ: The incubation period of non-quarantined population to be infected and quarantine population to be infected; τ_1 and τ_2 represent the time delays to confirm the infection of corona for non-vaccinated and vaccination individuals, respectively. For mathematical simplicity, we consider the case $\tau_1 = \tau_2 = \tau$ (say) so that the model (14.1) takes the following form

$$
\left.\begin{aligned}
N'(t) &= \mu - \alpha NV - \beta NI - \upsilon N \\
V'(t) &= \alpha NV - \gamma VI \\
I'(t) &= \beta NI(t - \tau) + \gamma VI(t - \tau) - \alpha I - \delta I \\
R'(t) &= \sigma I
\end{aligned}\right\} \tag{14.2}
$$

14.3　MATHEMATICAL ANALYSIS OF SYSTEM (14.2) WITHOUT TIME DELAY

To investigate the system's local dynamics, we first solve the algebraic system to get the non-negative equilibria listed below. The following system algebraic equations can be used to find the non-negative stable states of the system (14.2).

$$
\left.\begin{aligned}
\mu - \alpha NV - \beta NI - \upsilon N &= 0 \\
\alpha NV - \gamma VI &= 0 \\
\beta NI + \gamma VI - \alpha I - \delta I &= 0 \\
\sigma I &= 0
\end{aligned}\right\} \tag{14.3}
$$

The steady states of the system (14.2) are given by

$$
E_0 = (N,V,I,R) = \left(\frac{\mu}{\upsilon}, 0, 0, 0\right); \quad E_1 = (N,V,I,R) = \left(\frac{\sigma + \delta}{\beta}, 0, \frac{\mu\beta - \upsilon(\sigma + \delta)}{\beta(\sigma + \delta)}, R_1\right)
$$

$$
E_2 = (N^*, V^*, I^*, R^*) = \left(\frac{\gamma\mu}{\alpha\delta + \gamma\upsilon + \alpha\sigma}, \frac{\alpha(\sigma + \delta) + \gamma(\upsilon\sigma + \delta\upsilon - \beta\mu)}{\gamma(\alpha\delta + \gamma\upsilon + \alpha\sigma)}, \frac{\alpha\mu}{\gamma(\alpha\delta + \gamma\upsilon + \alpha\sigma)}, R^*\right)
$$

where $N^* = \dfrac{\gamma\mu}{\alpha\delta + \gamma\upsilon + \alpha\sigma}; V^* = \dfrac{\alpha(\sigma + \delta) + \gamma(\upsilon\sigma + \delta\upsilon - \beta\mu)}{\gamma(\alpha\delta + \gamma\upsilon + \alpha\sigma)}; I^* = \dfrac{\alpha\mu}{\gamma(\alpha\delta + \gamma\upsilon + \alpha\sigma)}$

The model (14.3) is subjected to mathematical examination [20]. The following sections cover boundedness and non-negativity analysis, as well as calculating the model's fundamental reproduction number.

14.3.1 Boundedness of the Model

The boundedness and non-negativity [21] of system solutions (14.2) are proved in this part using the following Lemmas.

Lemma 14.1

A positively invariant set $\Omega = \{(N(t), V(t), I(t), R(t)) \in \mathbb{R}^4_+\}$ of the model (14.2) makes up the region.

Proof: Assume that there are $N(t)$ people living there overall $N_1(t) = N(t) + V(t) + I(t) + R(t)$. Then $N_1'(t) = N'(t) + V'(t) + I'(t) + R'(t)$

From (14.2),

$$N_1'(t) = \mu - \upsilon N + (-\alpha - \delta + \sigma)I \tag{14.4}$$

Over an extended length of time 't', both the sickly and the confined populations go extinct. In the absence of a s-d populace ($V = 0; I = 0$) that has received vaccinations, we can extrapolate from equation (14.4) that

$$N_1'(t) = \mu - \upsilon N \tag{14.5}$$

This is comparable to a LDE with an IF $\exp\left(\int \upsilon \, dt\right)$. As a result, we may solve (14.5) and arrive at

$$N_1(t) = \frac{\mu}{\upsilon} + \left(N_0 - \frac{\mu}{\upsilon}\right)\exp(-\upsilon t) \tag{14.6}$$

As 't' approaches infinity, we write limit $(N_1(t))$ is equal to (μ / υ), which shows that $N_1(t)$ is smaller than or equal to (μ / υ), i.e., (μ / υ) is the UB of $N_1(t)$, as a result, the solutions asymptotically approach Ω. Now Lemma 3.1's proof is finished.

Lemma 14.2

If $N(t) \geq 0, V(t) \geq 0, I(t) \geq 0, R(t) \geq 0$, consequently, system (14.2)'s solutions are non-negative.

Proof: We must first assess the system's initial equation (14.2) in order to demonstrate Lemma 3.2.

$$N'(t) = \mu - \alpha NV - \beta NI - \upsilon N \tag{14.7}$$

Now we utilize the following to establish the solution to equation (14.7)'s non-negativity.

$$N'(t) + \rho N \geq \mu \tag{14.8}$$

Therefore,

$$N(t) \geq (\mu / \upsilon) + c \exp(-\upsilon t) \tag{14.9}$$

where c is constant of integration. We have $N(0) \geq (\mu / \upsilon) + c$ by using at $t=0$.

$$N(t) \geq (\mu / \upsilon) + \big(N(0) - (\mu / \upsilon)\big) \exp(-\upsilon t) \tag{14.10}$$

Hence (14.10) provides that '$N(t) \geq 0$ at $t = 0$ and $t \to \infty$'.

BRN: The fundamental reproduction number (BRN) is crucial to the disease epidemic model because it allows for forecasting the spread of illness. We use the symbol to signify the fundamental reproduction number, which is the proportion of newly infected people to all people who are infected. Because it guarantees whether the disease is still present or has disappeared, it is very frequently employed in epidemiology. In the proposed model, the susceptible populations who have not received vaccinations, who have received vaccinations but are still susceptible, and the infected population all help to spread the infection among the susceptible populations who have not been exposed to it. The population that has recovered or is immune cannot accomplish this. To get R_0 of the model, we therefore analyze the system (14.2) as follows.

$$\left. \begin{aligned} N'(t) &= \mu - \alpha NV - \beta NI - \upsilon N \\ V'(t) &= \alpha NV - \gamma VI \\ I'(t) &= \beta NI + \gamma VI - \alpha I - \delta I \end{aligned} \right\} \tag{14.10a}$$

The below can be shaped from (14.10a).

$$F = \begin{bmatrix} \mu & 0 & 0 \\ \alpha V & \alpha N & 0 \\ \beta I & \gamma I & \beta N + \gamma V \end{bmatrix} \quad \text{and} \quad V = \begin{bmatrix} \alpha V + \beta I + \upsilon & \alpha N & \beta N \\ 0 & \gamma I - \alpha N & \gamma V \\ 0 & 0 & \alpha + \delta \end{bmatrix}$$

At   DFE $E_0 = (N, V, I, R) = \left(\dfrac{\mu}{\upsilon}, 0, 0, 0 \right)$, $F = \begin{bmatrix} \mu & 0 & 0 \\ 0 & \alpha\mu/\upsilon & 0 \\ 0 & 0 & \beta\mu/\upsilon \end{bmatrix}$ and

$$V = \begin{bmatrix} \upsilon & \alpha\mu/\upsilon & \beta\mu/\upsilon \\ 0 & \alpha\mu/\upsilon & 0 \\ 0 & 0 & \alpha+\delta \end{bmatrix}; \quad FV^{-1} = \left(\frac{\mu}{\upsilon} \right)^2 \begin{bmatrix} 1 & 1 & \beta\mu/\upsilon(\alpha+\delta) \\ 0 & -1 & 0 \\ 0 & 0 & \beta(\alpha+\delta) \end{bmatrix}$$

Therefore, system (14.2)'s fundamental reproduction number is $R_0 = \left(\dfrac{\mu}{\upsilon} \right)^2 (\alpha+\delta)\beta$

14.4 INVESTIGATION OF THE IDEAL'S STABILITY AT STEADINESS WITHOUT TIME DELAY

System (14.2) is examined as

$$x'(t) = f(t,x); \ x(0) = x_0 \tag{14.11}$$

the immovability examination of the ideal be carried out at steady state where $x = (N(t), V(t), I(t), R(t)); \ f = (f_1, f_2, f_3, f_4); \ x_0 = (N_0, V_0, I_0, R_0)$ with

$$f_1(N,V,I,R) = \mu - \alpha NV - \beta NI - \upsilon N$$

$$f_2(N,V,I,R) = \alpha NV - \gamma VI$$

$$f_3(N,V,I,R) = \beta NI + \gamma VI - \alpha I - \delta I$$

$$f_4(N,V,I,R) = \sigma I$$

For steadiness, we linearize scheme (14.11) at x^*, resulting in the below structure.

$$J = \begin{bmatrix} -\alpha V - \beta I - \upsilon & -\alpha N & -\beta N & 0 \\ \alpha V & \alpha N - \gamma I & -\gamma V & 0 \\ \beta I & \gamma I & \beta N + \gamma V - \alpha - \delta & 0 \\ 0 & 0 & \sigma & 0 \end{bmatrix} \tag{14.12}$$

14.4.1 STABILITY ANALYSIS OF THE MODEL DFE $E_0 = (N,V,I,R) = \left(\dfrac{\mu}{\upsilon}, 0, 0, 0\right)$

We suggest Theorem 4.1 to examine the steadiness of (14.2) at the DFE $E_0 = (N,V,I,R) = \left(\dfrac{\mu}{\upsilon}, 0, 0, 0\right)$.

Theorem 14.1

"The dfe point of system (14.2) is locally asymptotically stable if $R_0 < 1$ and $\dfrac{\beta\mu}{\upsilon} < 1 + \alpha + \gamma$ and unstable otherwise".

Proof: The jacobian matrix can be evaluated at $E_0 = (N,V,I,R) = \left(\dfrac{\mu}{\upsilon}, 0, 0, 0\right)$ is in the form

of $J_1 = \begin{bmatrix} a_1 & -b_1 & c_1 & 0 \\ 0 & b_1 & 0 & 0 \\ 0 & 0 & d_1 & 0 \\ 0 & 0 & e_1 & 0 \end{bmatrix}$

where $a_1 = -\upsilon; b_1 = \dfrac{\alpha\mu}{\upsilon}; c_1 = -\dfrac{\beta\mu}{\upsilon}; d_1 = \dfrac{\beta\mu}{\upsilon} - \alpha - \gamma; e_1 = \sigma;$ The eigenvalues of J_1 can be obtained as follows $0, a_1, b_1, d_1$. That is $\lambda_1 = 0; \lambda_2 = -\upsilon; \lambda_3 = \dfrac{\alpha\mu}{\upsilon}; \lambda_4 = \dfrac{\beta\mu}{\upsilon} - \alpha - \gamma;$. In that case, the DFE is LSS if $R_0 < 1$, $\alpha\mu < \upsilon$ and $\dfrac{\beta\mu}{\upsilon} < 1 + \alpha + \gamma$ this disease-free steady state is unstable otherwise. Finally verified as DFE is unsteady.

14.4.2 Immovability Examination of the vpf- Free Point

For free stable state $E_1 = (N,V,I,R) = \left(\dfrac{\sigma+\delta}{\beta}, 0, \dfrac{\mu\beta - \upsilon(\sigma+\delta)}{\beta(\sigma+\delta)}, R_1 \right)$ is necessary for the infected population's stability, we suggest the subsequent statement.

Theorem 14.2

From (14.2), the ifp steady state is LAS if $R_0 < 1$ and unstable if $R_0 > 1$.

Proof: The matrix can be assessed at $E_1 = (N,V,I,R) = \left(\dfrac{\sigma+\delta}{\beta}, 0, \dfrac{\mu\beta - \upsilon(\sigma+\delta)}{\beta(\sigma+\delta)}, R_1 \right)$ is in

the form of $J_2 = \begin{bmatrix} a_{11} & b_{11} & c_{11} & 0 \\ 0 & d_{11} & 0 & 0 \\ e_{11} & f_{11} & g_{11} & 0 \\ 0 & 0 & h_{11} & 0 \end{bmatrix}$

where $a_{11} = -\beta I - \upsilon - \rho; b_{11} = -\alpha N; c_{11} = -\beta N; d_{11} = \alpha N - \gamma I; e_{11} = \beta I; f_{11} = \gamma I; g_{11} = \beta N - \alpha - \delta; h_{11} = \sigma$ The eigenvalues of J_2 can be obtained as follows:

$$\lambda_1 = 0, \lambda_2 = d_{11}, \lambda_3 = (a_{11}/2) + (g_{11}/2) - \frac{1}{2}\sqrt{a_{11}^2 - 2a_{11}g_{11} + g_{11}^2 + 4c_{11}e_{11}},$$

$$\lambda_4 = (a_{11}/2) + (g_{11}/2) - \frac{1}{2}\sqrt{a_{11}^2 - 2a_{11}g_{11} + g_{11}^2 + 4c_{11}e_{11}}.$$

It is found that the eigenvalues have a convoluted form preventing us from using Routh-Hurwitz criteria to determine their nature. We can demonstrate numerically that in the absence of infection, the model is unstable if $R_0 > 1$ and only if $R_0 < 1$, it is locally asymptotically stable and relating to the values of the parameters provided in the table.

14.4.3 Analysis of the Endemic Stable State's Stability

The below examines the study of the stability of the ESS $E_3 = \left(N^*, V^*, I^*, R^* \right)$.

Theorem 14.3

The EEP of (14.2) is LAS if $R_0 > 1$ and unstable if $R_0 < 1$.

Proof: The matrix can be assessed at $E_2 = \left(N^*, V^*, I^*, R^* \right)$, is in the form of

$$J_4 = \begin{bmatrix} e_{11} & e_{22} & e_{33} & 0 \\ e_{44} & e_{55} & e_{66} & 0 \\ e_{77} & e_{88} & e_{99} & 0 \\ 0 & 0 & e_{10} & 0 \end{bmatrix} \quad J = \begin{bmatrix} -\alpha V^* - \beta I^* - \upsilon & -\alpha N^* & -\beta N^* & 0 \\ \alpha V^* & \alpha N^* - \gamma I^* & -\gamma V^* & 0 \\ \beta I^* & \gamma I^* & \beta N^* + \gamma V^* - \alpha - \delta & 0 \\ 0 & 0 & \sigma & 0 \end{bmatrix}$$

where $E_2 = \left(\dfrac{\gamma\mu}{\alpha\delta + \gamma\upsilon + \alpha\sigma}, \dfrac{\alpha(\sigma+\delta) + \gamma(\upsilon\sigma + \delta\upsilon - \beta\mu)}{\gamma(\alpha\delta + \gamma\upsilon + \alpha\sigma)}, \dfrac{\alpha\mu}{\gamma(\alpha\delta + \gamma\upsilon + \alpha\sigma)}, R^* \right)$ and where $e_{11} = -\alpha V^* - \beta I^* - \upsilon$; $e_{22} = -\alpha N^*$; $e_{33} = -\beta N^*$; $e_{44} = \alpha V^*$; $e_{55} = \alpha N^* - \gamma I^*$; $e_{66} = -\gamma V^*$

$$e_{77} = \beta I^*; e_{88} = \gamma I^*; e_{99} = \beta N^* + \gamma V^* - \alpha - \delta; e_{10} = \sigma;$$

With additional complexity, the eigenvalues of can be found. Due to the intricacy of the eigenvalues' unambiguous form, the nature of the eigenvalues cannot be analytically compared using the R-H criterion. However, we show mathematically that the widespread steady state is unstable ($R_0 < 1$) for the parameters shown in the table, but is asymptotically stable when α, A, ρ are changed. So there we have $R_0 > 1$. Finally, the stability of steady states is thought to be dependent on R_0 and can also play an important function in epidemiological infection control.

14.5   ANALYSIS OF THE DELAYED NVIR MODEL

In view of an epidemiological system, consider the interior equilibrium point of the system (14.2) as $E(N^*, V^*, I^*, R^*) = (f^*, g^*, h^*, k^*)$

Let $f = N - f^*$; $g = V - g^*$; $h = I - h^*$; $k = R - k^*$ be the perturbed variables. The derived linearized system corresponds to (14.2) after the nonlinear terms have been eliminated.

$$\begin{cases} \dfrac{df}{dt} = \left[-\alpha g^* - \beta h^* - \upsilon\right]f + \left[-\alpha f^*\right]g - \left[\beta f^*\right]h \\[2mm] \dfrac{dg}{dt} = \left[\alpha g^*\right]f + \left[\alpha f^* - \gamma h^*\right]g - \left[\gamma g^*\right]h \\[2mm] \dfrac{dh}{dt} = \left[\left(\beta f^* + \gamma g^*\right)e^{-\lambda \tau}h(t)\right] - \left[\sigma + \delta\right]h(t) \\[2mm] \dfrac{dk}{dt} = \sigma h \end{cases} \qquad (14.13)$$

The characteristic equation of the system (14.13) is

$$\lambda^3 + A_1\lambda^2 + A_2\lambda + A_3 + e^{-\lambda t}\left[B_2\lambda + B_3\right] = 0 \qquad (14.14)$$

here $A_1 = -(J_{11} + J_{22} + J_{33})$; $A_2 = (J_{11} + J_{22})(-\sigma - \delta)$; $A_3 = J_{21}J_{22}J_{23} + J_{11}(\sigma + \delta)$;

$$B_2 = \left(\beta f^* + \gamma g^*\right)\{J_{11} + J_{22}\}; B_3 = -\left(\beta f^* + \gamma g^*\right)J_{11}J_{22};$$

where $J_{11} = -\alpha g^* - \beta h^* - \upsilon$; $J_{21} = \alpha g^*$; $J_{22} = \alpha f^* - \gamma h^*$;

$$J_{33} = \left[\beta f^* + \gamma g^*\right]e^{-\lambda \tau} - (\sigma + \delta); \quad J_{23} = -\gamma g^*;$$

14.5.1   STABILITY ANALYSIS IN THE PRESENCE OF TIME DELAY

For $\tau > 0$, assume $\lambda = i\omega$ ($\omega > 0$) is a root of equation (14.14). Then

$$-i\omega^3 + A_1(-\omega^2) + A_2(i\omega) + A_3 + (\cos \omega t - i \sin wt)\left\{B_2(-\omega^2) + B_3\right\} = 0$$

i.e. $\left[\left(A_1(-\omega^2) + A_3\right) + i\left(-\omega^3 + A_2\omega\right)\right] + \left[\left(-B_2\omega^2 + B_3\right)\cos \omega\tau + i\left(B_2\omega^2 - B_3\right)\sin \omega\tau\right] = 0$

By equating real and imaginary parts, we get

$$\left(B_2\omega^2 - B_3 \right)\cos \omega t = -A_1\omega^2 + A_3 \tag{14.15}$$

$$\left(B_3 - B_2\omega^2 \right)\sin \omega t = -\omega^3 + A_2\omega \tag{14.16}$$

Squaring and adding of (14.15) and (14.16), we get,

$$\omega^6 + P_1\omega^4 + P_2\omega^2 + P_3 = 0 \tag{14.17}$$

where

$$P_1 = \left(A_1^2 - 2A_2 + B_2^2 \right); \quad P_2 = \left(A_1^2 - 2A_1A_3 + 2B_2B_3 \right);$$

$$P_3 = \left(A_3^2 - B_3^2 \right); \quad P_4 = \left(A_4^2 - B_4^2 \right);$$

Let $\omega^2 = U$ then we get

$$\tau \in [0,\tau_0); \tau = \tau_0 \tag{14.18}$$

We may acquire all the roots of equation (14.18) based on the discussion of the distribution of the roots of equation (14.18) and the fact that all the values of parameters in system (14.1) are known (14.18). As a result, the following assumptions are made: (i) equation (14.18) has at least one positive root U_0 If condition (i) holds, then there exists $u_0 > 0 \ni$ (14.18) has a pair of purely imagined roots $\pm i\omega_0 = \pm i\sqrt{U_0}$. Solving (14.15) and (14.16), we get $\cos \omega t = \dfrac{\left[A_3 - A_1\omega^2 \right]}{\left[B_2\omega^2 - B_3 \right]}$

So corresponding to $\lambda = i\omega_0$, there exists,

$$\tau_0 = \frac{1}{\omega_0}\cos^{-1}\left[\frac{A_3 - A_1\omega^2}{B_2\omega^2 - B_3} \right] \tag{14.19}$$

14.5.2 HOPF-BIFURCATION ANALYSIS

Differentiating (14.14) w.r.t τ, we get

$$3\lambda^2 \frac{d\lambda}{d\tau} + A_1 2\lambda \frac{d\lambda}{d\tau} + A_2 \frac{d\lambda}{d\tau} + e^{-\lambda\tau}\left[B_2 \frac{d\lambda}{d\tau} \right] + \left[B_2\lambda + B_3 \right]e^{-\lambda\tau}\left[-\lambda - \tau \frac{d\lambda}{d\tau} \right] = 0$$

$$\left(\frac{d\lambda}{d\tau} \right)^{-1} = \frac{3\lambda^2 + 2A_1\lambda + A_2}{\lambda e^{-\lambda\tau}\left(B_2\lambda + B_3 \right)} - \frac{\tau}{\lambda} + \frac{B_2}{\lambda\left(B_2\lambda + B_3 \right)} \tag{14.20}$$

$$\left(\frac{d\lambda}{d\tau} \right)^{-1} = \frac{3\lambda^2 + 2A_1\lambda + A_2}{-\lambda\left(\lambda^3 + A_1\lambda^2 + A_2\lambda + A_3 \right)} + \frac{B_2}{\lambda\left(B_2\lambda + B_3 \right)} - \frac{\tau}{\lambda} \text{ (Using equation (14.14))}$$

Put $\lambda = i\omega_0$ in (14.20), we get,

$$\left(\frac{d\lambda}{d\tau} \right)^{-1} = \frac{(-3\omega_0^2 + A_2) + i(2A_1\omega_0)}{(-\omega_0^4 + A_2\omega_0^2) + i(A_1\omega_0^2 - A_3\omega_0)} + \frac{i\tau}{\omega_0} + \frac{B_2}{i(B_3\omega_0) - B_2\omega_0^2}$$

$$\text{Re}\left(\frac{d\lambda}{d\tau}\right)^{-1} = \frac{3\omega_0^6 - 3A_2\omega_0^4 - A_2\omega_0^4 + A_2^2\omega_0^2 + 2A_1^2\omega_0^3 - 2A_1A_3\omega_0^6}{\omega_0^2\left(\omega_0^6 - 2A_2\omega_0^4 + A_1^2\omega_0^2 + A_2^2\omega_0^2 - 2A_1A_3\omega_0\right)} - \frac{B_2\omega_0^2}{\omega_0^2\left(B_2\omega_0^2 + B_3^2\right)}$$

$$\text{Re}\left(\frac{d\lambda}{d\tau}\right)^{-1} = \frac{3\omega_0^4 - 4A_2\omega_0^2 + 2A_1^2\omega_0 + A_2 - 2A_1A_3}{\omega_0^6 - 2A_2\omega_0^4 + (A_1^2 + A_2^2)\omega_0^2 - 2A_1A_3\omega_0 + A_3^2} - \frac{B_2}{\left(B_2\omega_0^2 + B_3^2\right)}$$

$$\text{Re}\left[\frac{d\lambda}{d\tau}\right]_{\tau=\tau_0}^{-1} = \frac{f^1(U_0)}{\omega_0^6 - 2A_2\omega_0^4 + (A_1^2 + A_1^2)\omega_0^2 - 2A_1A_3\omega_0 + A_3^2}$$

where $U_0 = \omega_0^2$ and $f(U_0) = U^3 + P_1U^2 + P_2U + P_3$. Therefore, if condition (ii): $f^1(U_0) \neq 0$ holds, then $\text{Re}\left[\frac{d\lambda}{d\tau}\right]_{\tau=\tau_0}^{-1} \neq 0$. Based on the previous discussion and the Hopf bifurcation theorem in [37], we have the following

Theorem 14.4

Let (i), (ii) hold for system (14.1). The point $E\left(N^*, V^*, I^*, R^*\right)$ is LAS when $\tau \in [0, \tau_0)$; a H.bif. occurs at $E\left(N^*, V^*, I^*, R^*\right)$ when $\tau = \tau_0$ and a domestic of periodic resolutions bifurcate from $E\left(N^*, V^*, I^*, R^*\right)$ near $\tau = \tau_0$.

14.6 NUMERICAL SIMULATIONS

For this study, we accomplish the subsequent mathematical replications of the ideal as a regular IVP by introducing a relevant initial condition.

14.6.1 NUMERICAL OBSERVATIONS

We run mathematical replications of the ideal as a conventional IVP by introducing a relevant beginning condition. We employ the RK fourth-order technique for the mathematical arrangement of the suggested model with initial conditions. The start circumstances are chosen from the identical dataset [56]:

Moreover, we take parameter values as $\mu = 2$, $\alpha = 0.747$, $\beta = 0.583$, $\upsilon = 0.2$, $\gamma = 0.583$, $\delta = 0.0752$, $\sigma = 0.153$ $\delta = 0.0752$, $\sigma = 0.153$. Our primary field of research is on analyzing how dispersal has affected the Corona infection in Bangladesh. In our ideal, the attributes may be used to describe how frequently people move across lockdown areas in terms of how the coronavirus infection spreads. Also, the values of β and υ represent the rate of non-vaccinated and rate of loss immunity for non-vaccinated populations, respectively. We emphasize these three factors in order to comprehend how well the model fits the actual COVID-19 circumstance.

We start by concentrating on the parameter, which, despite having little effect on the population that is affected, is in charge of promoting immunological development through vitamin intake and physical activity. Individuals should boost their immunity during this pandemic to prevent the emergence of COVID-19 symptoms and, as a result, the need for vaccination.

Figure 14.1 exhibits the stable solutions of all populations along with time and the attributes $\mu = 2$, $\alpha = 0.747$, $\beta = 0.583$, $\upsilon = 0.2$, $\gamma = 0.583$, $\delta = 0.0752$, $\sigma = 0.153$, $\sigma = 0.153$ $\delta = 0.0752$. Time series assessment population classes $N(t)$, $V(t)$, $I(t)$, and $R(t)$ in separate subplots with the characteristics of Figure 14.1 is shown in grouped form in Figure 14.2.

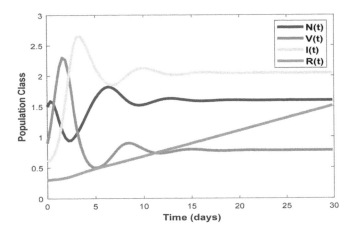

FIGURE 14.1 Time series evaluation of population classes with the attributes $\mu = 2$, $\alpha = 0.747$, $\beta = 0.583, \upsilon = 0.2, \gamma = 0.583, \delta = 0.0752, \sigma = 0.153$.

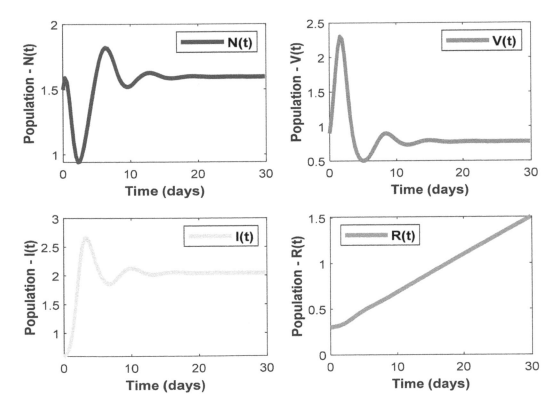

FIGURE 14.2 Time series evaluation of individual populations with the attributes $\mu = 2$, $\alpha = 0.747$, $\beta = 0.583$, $\upsilon = 0.2$, $\gamma = 0.583$, $\delta = 0.0752$, $\sigma = 0.153$.

The projections for the population classes "$N(t)$, $V(t)$, $I(t)$, and $R(t)$" are shown in Figures 14.3–14.6.

Figures 14.7–14.10 show the discrepancy in population classes "$N(t)$, $V(t)$, $I(t)$, and $R(t)$" for different values of α along $\mu = 2$, $\alpha = 0.747$, $\beta = 0.583$, $\upsilon = 0.2$, $\gamma = 0.583$, $\delta = 0.0752$, $\sigma = 0.153$, $\sigma = 0.153$ $\delta = 0.0752$.

As the rate of vaccination (α) increases, population class $N(t)$ i.e. non-vaccinated individuals reduced which is shown in Figure 14.4a. As the rate of vaccination (α) increases, population

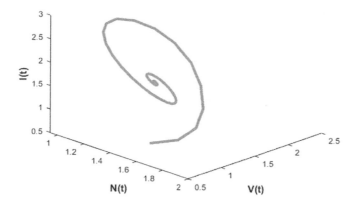

FIGURE 14.3 Phase portraits of the populations of non-vaccinated susceptible-vaccinated susceptible-infected, vaccinated-infected-recovered, non-vaccinated-infected and recovered and non-vaccinated-vaccinated-recovered for the values of attributes $\mu = 2$, $\alpha = 0.747$, $\beta = 0.583$, $\upsilon = 0.2$, $\gamma = 0.583$, $\delta = 0.0752$, $\sigma = 0.153$.

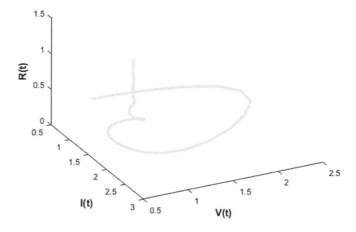

FIGURE 14.4 Phase portraits of the populations of non-vaccinated susceptible-vaccinated susceptible-infected, vaccinated-infected-recovered, non-vaccinated-infected and recovered and non-vaccinated-vaccinated-recovered for the values of attributes $\mu = 2$, $\alpha = 0.747$, $\beta = 0.583$, $\upsilon = 0.2$, $\gamma = 0.583$, $\delta = 0.0752$, $\sigma = 0.153$.

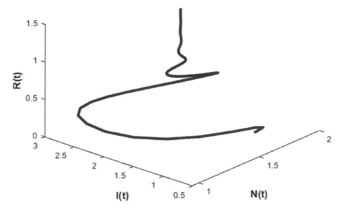

FIGURE 14.5 Phase portraits of the populations of non-vaccinated susceptible-vaccinated susceptible-infected, vaccinated-infected-recovered, non-vaccinated-infected and recovered and non-vaccinated-vaccinated-recovered for the values of attributes $\mu = 2$, $\alpha = 0.747$, $\beta = 0.583$, $\upsilon = 0.2$, $\gamma = 0.583$, $\delta = 0.0752$, $\sigma = 0.153$.

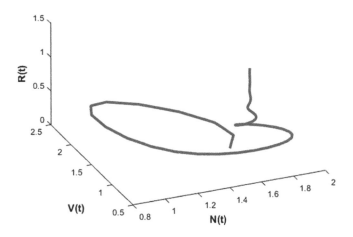

FIGURE 14.6 Phase portraits of the populations of non-vaccinated susceptible-vaccinated susceptible-infected, vaccinated-infected-recovered, non-vaccinated-infected and recovered and non-vaccinated-vaccinated-recovered for the values of attributes $\mu = 2$, $\alpha = 0.747$, $\beta = 0.583$, $\upsilon = 0.2$, $\gamma = 0.583$, $\delta = 0.0752$, $\sigma = 0.153$.

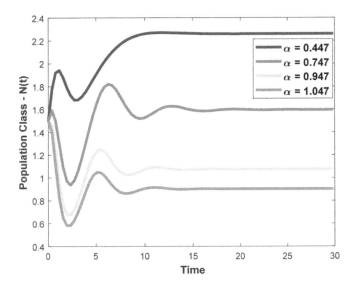

FIGURE 14.7 Time series evaluation of the population classes N(t) with the attributes as the rate of vaccination (β) increases for $\mu = 2$, $\alpha = 0.747$, $\beta = 0.583$, $\upsilon = 0.2$, $\gamma = 0.583$, $\delta = 0.0752$, $\sigma = 0.153$.

class $V(t)$ i.e. vaccinated individuals increases which is shown in Figure 14.8. As the rate of vaccination (α) increases, population class $I(t)$ i.e. infected individuals reduced which is shown in Figure 14.9.

Figures 14.11–14.14 show the variations of "$N(t)$, $V(t)$, $I(t)$, and $R(t)$" for different β along with $\mu = 2$, $\alpha = 0.747$, $\beta = 0.583$, $\upsilon = 0.2$, $\gamma = 0.583$, $\delta = 0.0752$, $\sigma = 0.153$, $\sigma = 0.153$ $\delta = 0.0752$.

As the rate of nvp having corona positive (β) increases, population class $N(t)$ i.e. non-vac. susceptible individuals increased which is shown in Figure 14.11. As the rate of nvp having corona positive (β) increases, population class $V(t)$ i.e. vac. individuals decreases which is shown in Figure 14.12. As the rate of nvp having corona positive (β) increases, population class $I(t)$ i.e. infected individuals increased which is shown in Figure 14.13. Rate of non-vac. individuals having COVID-19 positive (β) increases, correspondingly the susceptible and infected are increased gradually.

Figures 14.15–14.18 shows the variations in "$N(t)$, $V(t)$, $I(t)$, and $R(t)$" for different δ along with $\mu = 2$, $\alpha = 0.747$, $\beta = 0.583$, $\upsilon = 0.2$, $\gamma = 0.583$, $\delta = 0.0752$, $\sigma = 0.153$, $\sigma = 0.153$ $\delta = 0.0752$.

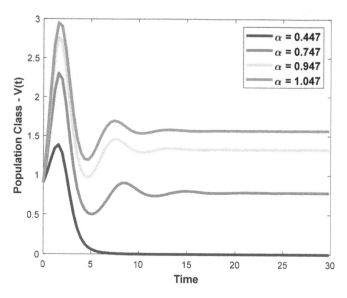

FIGURE 14.8 Time series evaluation of the population classes V(t) with the attributes as the rate of vaccination (β) increases for $\mu = 2$, $\alpha = 0.747$, $\beta = 0.583$, $\upsilon = 0.2$, $\gamma = 0.583$, $\delta = 0.0752$, $\sigma = 0.153$.

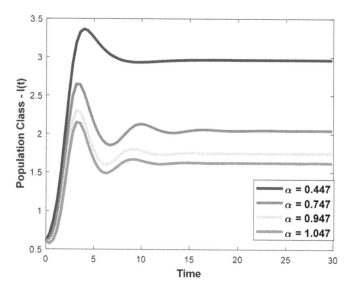

FIGURE 14.9 Time series evaluation of the population classes I(t) with the attributes as the rate of vaccination (β) increases for $\mu = 2$, $\alpha = 0.747$, $\beta = 0.583$, $\upsilon = 0.2$, $\gamma = 0.583$, $\delta = 0.0752$, $\sigma = 0.153$.

As the induced death rate of infected individuals (δ) increases, population class $N(t)$ i.e non vacc. individuals increased which is shown in Figure 14.15. As the induced death rate of infected individuals (δ) increases, population class $V(t)$ i.e. vac. individuals decreases which is shown in Figure 14.16. As the induced death rate of infected individuals (δ) increases, population class $I(t)$ i.e. infected individuals increased which is shown in Figure 14.17. Induced death rate of infected increases correspondingly the susceptible and infected are increased gradually, as infection spreading is increasing rapidly due to the non-vaccinated population class.

Figures 14.19–14.22 show the variations in "$N(t)$, $V(t)$, $I(t)$, and $R(t)$" for different γ along with the attributes $\mu = 2$, $\alpha = 0.747$, $\beta = 0.583$, $\upsilon = 0.2$, $\gamma = 0.583$, $\delta = 0.0752$, $\sigma = 0.153$, $\delta = 0.0752$.

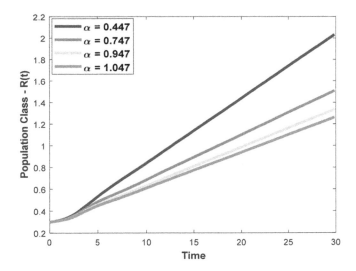

FIGURE 14.10 Time series evaluation of the population classes R(t) with the attributes as the rate of vaccination (β) increases for $\mu = 2$, $\alpha = 0.747$, $\beta = 0.583$, $\upsilon = 0.2$, $\gamma = 0.583$, $\delta = 0.0752$, $\sigma = 0.153$.

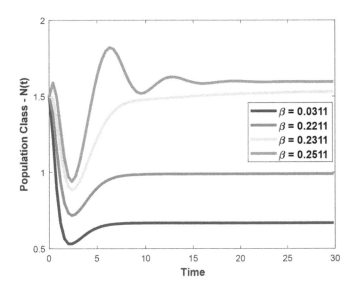

FIGURE 14.11 Time series evaluation of populations classes N(t) with the attributes of non-vaccinated, vaccinated, infected and recovered when the death rate (δ) for $\mu = 2$, $\alpha = 0.747$, $\beta = 0.583$, $\upsilon = 0.2$, $\gamma = 0.583$, $\delta = 0.0752$, $\sigma = 0.153$.

As rate of vac. population having COVID-19 positive (γ) increases, population class $N(t)$ i.e non-vac. individuals decreased which is shown in Figure 14.19. As rate of vac. population having COVID-19 positive (γ) increases, population class $V(t)$ i.e vac. individuals increases which is shown in Figure 14.20. As the rate of vac. population having COVID-19 positive (γ) increases, population class $I(t)$ i.e infected individuals increased which is shown in Figure 14.21. As the rate of vac. population having COVID-19 positive (γ) increases correspondingly the non-vac. susceptible decreasing and infected are increased gradually, as infection spreading is increasing rapidly due to lack of immunity in all population classes.

Figures 14.23–14.26 show the variations in "$N(t)$, $V(t)$, $I(t)$, and $R(t)$" for various values of μ along with $\mu = 2$, $\alpha = 0.747$, $\beta = 0.583$, $\upsilon = 0.2$, $\gamma = 0.583$, $\delta = 0.0752$, $\sigma = 0.153$, $\sigma = 0.153$ $\delta = 0.0752$.

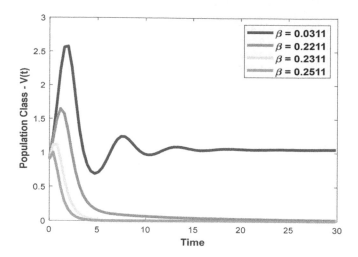

FIGURE 14.12 Time series evaluation of populations of non-vaccinated, vaccinated, infected and recovered when the rate of non-vaccinated (β) is increasing for the values of $\mu = 2$, $\alpha = 0.747$, $\beta = 0.583$, $\upsilon = 0.2$, $\gamma = 0.583$, $\delta = 0.0752$, $\sigma = 0.153$.

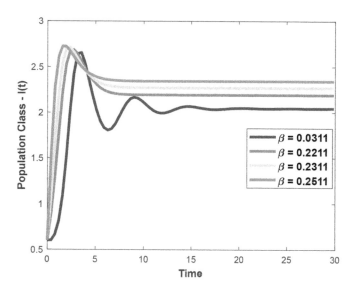

FIGURE 14.13 Time series evaluation of populations of non-vaccinated, vaccinated, infected and recovered when the rate of non-vaccinated (β) is increasing for the values of $\mu = 2$, $\alpha = 0.747$, $\beta = 0.583$, $\upsilon = 0.2$, $\gamma = 0.583$, $\delta = 0.0752$, $\sigma = 0.153$.

Recruitment rate of the non-vac.susceptible population (μ) increases, population class $N(t)$ i.e non vac. individuals decreased which is shown in Figure 14.23. Recruitment rate of the non-vac.susceptible population (μ) increases, population class $V(t)$ i.e vac. individuals increases which is shown in Figure 14.24. Recruitment rate of the non-vac. susceptible population (μ) increases, population class $I(t)$ i.e infected individuals increased which is shown in Figure 14.25. Recruitment rate of the non-vac.susceptible population (μ) increases, population class $R(t)$ i.e Recovered individuals decreased as infected are increased (shown in the previous figure) which is shown in Figure 14.26. Recruitment rate of the non-vac. susceptible population (μ) increases correspondingly the non-vac. susceptible and infected are increased gradually, as infection spreading is increasing rapidly due to lack of immunity, not wearing masks and not following social distancing. So in this scenario, recovered class decreases correspondingly.

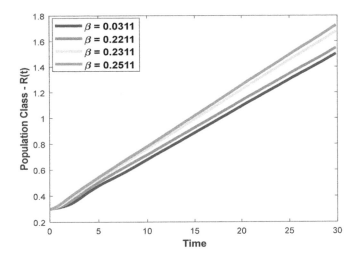

FIGURE 14.14   Time series evaluation of populations of non-vaccinated, vaccinated, infected and recovered when the rate of non-vaccinated (β) is increasing for the values of $\mu = 2$, $\alpha = 0.747$, $\beta = 0.583$, $v = 0.2$, $\gamma = 0.583$, $\delta = 0.0752$, $\sigma = 0.153$.

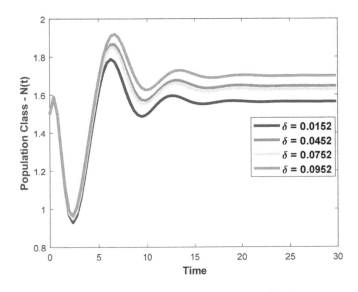

FIGURE 14.15   Time series evaluation of populations classes N(t) with the attributes of non-vaccinated, vaccinated, infected and recovered when the death rate (δ) for $\mu = 2$, $\alpha = 0.747$, $\beta = 0.583$, $v = 0.2$, $\gamma = 0.583$, $\delta = 0.0752$, $\sigma = 0.153$.

Figure 14.27 is a grouped figure of "$N(t)$, $V(t)$, $I(t)$, and $R(t)$" in individual subplots with a delay $\tau = 10.5$ along with $\mu = 2$, $\alpha = 0.747$, $\beta = 0.583$, $v = 0.2$, $\gamma = 0.583$, $\delta = 0.0752$, $\sigma = 0.153$, $\sigma = 0.153$ $\delta = 0.0752$. Figure 14.10a–d represents the projections of "$N(t)$, $V(t)$, $I(t)$, and $R(t)$" with the values of Figure 14.27 with a delay $\tau = 10.5$

Figures 14.28–14.31 are grouped figures of '$N(t)$, $V(t)$, $I(t)$, and $R(t)$' in individual subplots with a delay $\tau = 20.5$ along with $\mu = 2$, $\alpha = 0.747$, $\beta = 0.583$, $v = 0.2$, $\gamma = 0.583$, $\delta = 0.0752$, $\sigma = 0.153$, $\sigma = 0.153$ $\delta = 0.0752$. Figure 14.32 represents the phase portrait projections among populations '$N(t)$, $V(t)$, $I(t)$, and $R(t)$' with the values of Figures 14.28–14.31 with a delay $\tau = 20.5$.

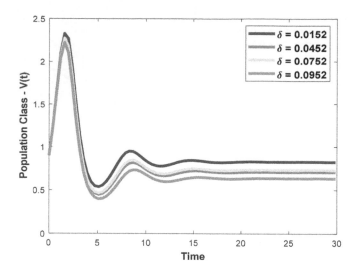

FIGURE 14.16 Time series evaluation of populations of non-vaccinated, vaccinated, infected and recovered when the death rate (δ) for the values of $\mu = 2, \alpha = 0.747, \beta = 0.583, \upsilon = 0.2, \gamma = 0.583, \delta = 0.0752, \sigma = 0.153$.

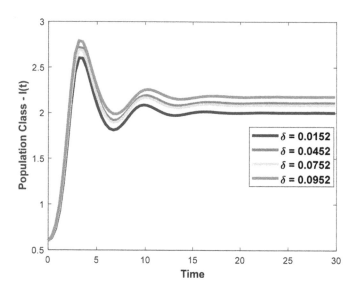

FIGURE 14.17 Time series evaluation of populations of non-vaccinated, vaccinated, infected and recovered when the death rate (δ) for the values of $\mu = 2, \alpha = 0.747, \beta = 0.583, \upsilon = 0.2, \gamma = 0.583, \delta = 0.0752, \sigma = 0.153$.

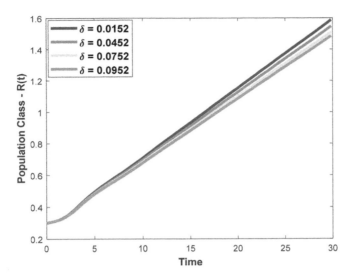

FIGURE 14.18   Time series evaluation of populations classes R(t) with the attributes of non-vaccinated, vaccinated, infected and recovered when the death rate (δ) for $\mu = 2, \alpha = 0.747, \beta = 0.583, \upsilon = 0.2, \gamma = 0.583, \delta = 0.0752, \sigma = 0.153$.

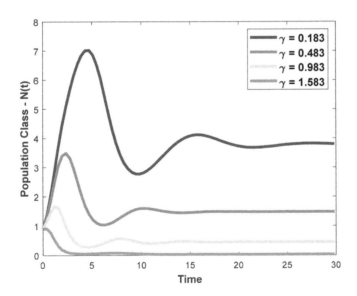

FIGURE 14.19   Time series evaluation of population Classes N(t) of non-vaccinated, vaccinated, infected and recovered when the rate of loss of immunity for non-vaccinated population (γ) for the values of $\mu = 2, \alpha = 0.747, \beta = 0.583, \upsilon = 0.2, \gamma = 0.583, \delta = 0.0752, \sigma = 0.153$.

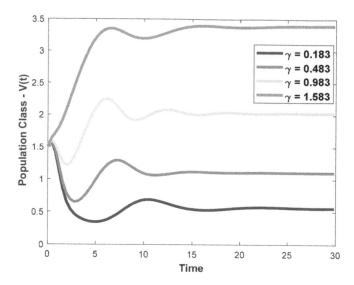

FIGURE 14.20   Time series evaluation of populations of non-vaccinated, vaccinated, infected and recovered when the rate of loss of immunity for non-vaccinated population (γ) for the values of $\mu = 2$, $\alpha = 0.747$, $\beta = 0.583$, $\upsilon = 0.2$, $\gamma = 0.583$, $\delta = 0.0752$, $\sigma = 0.153$.

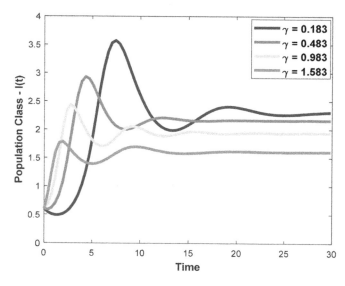

FIGURE 14.21   Time series evaluation of populations of non-vaccinated, vaccinated, infected and recovered when the rate of loss of immunity for non-vaccinated population (γ) for the values of $\mu = 2$, $\alpha = 0.747$, $\beta = 0.583$, $\upsilon = 0.2$, $\gamma = 0.583$, $\delta = 0.0752$, $\sigma = 0.153$.

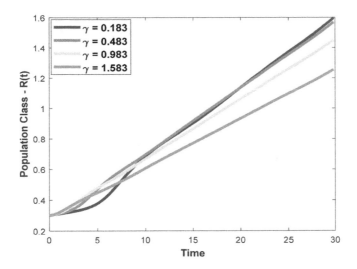

FIGURE 14.22   Time series evaluation of populations of non-vaccinated, vaccinated, infected and recovered when the rate of loss of immunity for non-vaccinated population (γ) for the values of $\mu = 2$, $\alpha = 0.747$, $\beta = 0.583$, $v = 0.2$, $\gamma = 0.583$, $\delta = 0.0752$, $\sigma = 0.153$.

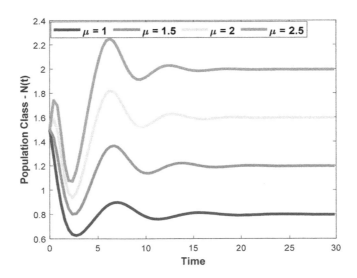

FIGURE 14.23   Time series evaluation of populations of non-vaccinated, vaccinated, infected and recovered for various values of (μ) for the values of $\mu = 2$, $\alpha = 0.747$, $\beta = 0.583$, $v = 0.2$, $\gamma = 0.583$, $\delta = 0.0752$, $\sigma = 0.153$.

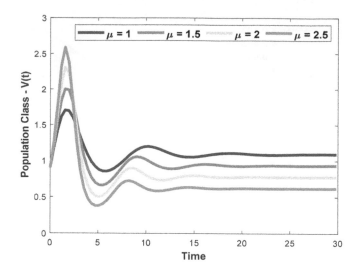

FIGURE 14.24   Time series evaluation of populations of non-vaccinated, vaccinated, infected and recovered for various values of (μ) for the values of $\mu = 2$, $\alpha = 0.747$, $\beta = 0.583$, $\upsilon = 0.2$, $\gamma = 0.583$, $\delta = 0.0752$, $\sigma = 0.153$.

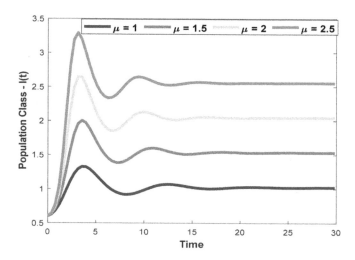

FIGURE 14.25   Time series evaluation of populations of non-vaccinated, vaccinated, infected and recovered for various values of (μ) for the values of $\mu = 2$, $\alpha = 0.747$, $\alpha = 0.747$, $\beta = 0.583$, $\upsilon = 0.2$, $\gamma = 0.583$, $\delta = 0.0752$, $\sigma = 0.153$.

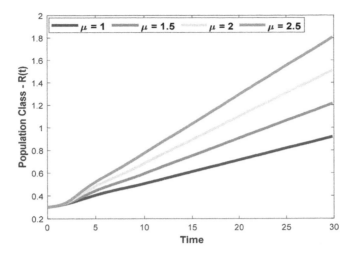

FIGURE 14.26 Time series evaluation of population Classes R(t) of non-vaccinated, vaccinated, infected and recovered when the rate of loss of immunity for non-vaccinated population (μ) for the various values of as given by $\mu = 2, \alpha = 0.747, \beta = 0.583, \upsilon = 0.2, \gamma = 0.583, \delta = 0.0752, \sigma = 0.153$.

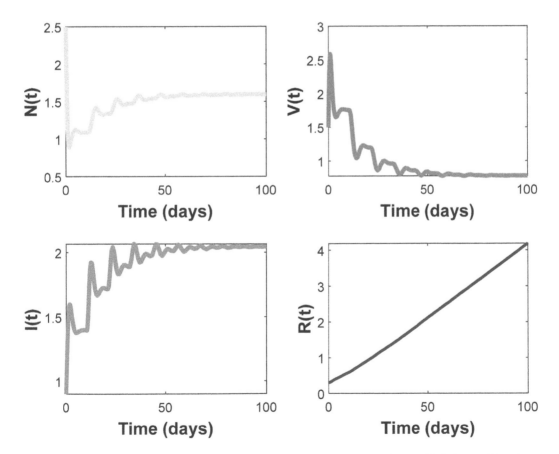

FIGURE 14.27 Time series evaluation of individual populations with time delay $\tau = 10.5$ along with attributes of $\mu = 2, \alpha = 0.747, \beta = 0.583, \upsilon = 0.2, \gamma = 0.583, \delta = 0.0752, \sigma = 0.153$.

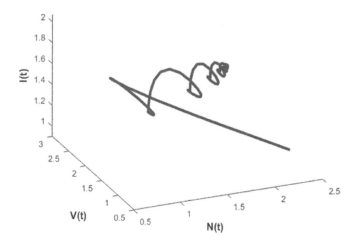

FIGURE 14.28 Phase portraits of populations of non-vaccinated-vaccinated-infected, vaccinated-infected-recovered, non-vaccinated-infected-recovered and non-vaccinated-vaccinated-recovered with time delay $\tau = 10.5$ along with $\mu = 2$, $\alpha = 0.747$, $\beta = 0.583$, $\upsilon = 0.2$, $\gamma = 0.583$, $\delta = 0.0752$, $\sigma = 0.153$.

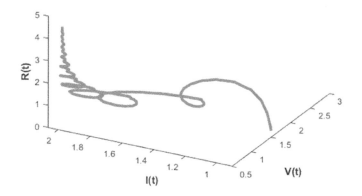

FIGURE 14.29 Phase portraits of populations of non-vaccinated-vaccinated-infected, vaccinated-infected-recovered, non-vaccinated-infected-recovered and non-vaccinated-vaccinated-recovered with time delay $\tau = 10.5$ along with $\mu = 2$, $\alpha = 0.747$, $\beta = 0.583$, $\upsilon = 0.2$, $\gamma = 0.583$, $\delta = 0.0752$, $\sigma = 0.153$.

14.7 DISCUSSION AND CONCLUDING REMARKS

COVID-19 is the biggest pandemic with more variations and stages taken so many lives and still exists in many countries including India. To examine the dynamics of such a pandemic illness COVID-19, we considered and analyzed a compartmental epidemic model that consists of four divisions: non-vaccinated susceptible (N), vaccinated susceptible (V), infected (I), and recovered or immune (R) populations. We calculate the model's fundamental reproduction number analytically to divide the pandemic into epidemic and endemic cases. We perform a stability analysis and a Hopf bifurcation analysis of the suggested model in order to better understand the dynamics of Novel Coronavirus with a time delay. Parameter analysis is carried out through numerical simulation with best fitted values which can validate and justify the considered model. Finally, numerical simulations and discussions are used to present, demonstrate the analytical findings and validate with graphical findings. Simulations helped us to draw some remarkable conclusions in a real-world situation of COVID-19 transmission (Figures 14.33–14.36).

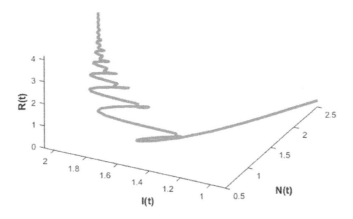

FIGURE 14.30 Phase portraits of populations of non-vaccinated-vaccinated-infected, vaccinated-infected-recovered, non-vaccinated-infected-recovered and non-vaccinated-vaccinated-recovered with time delay $\tau = 10.5$ along with $\mu = 2$, $\alpha = 0.747$, $\beta = 0.583$, $\upsilon = 0.2$, $\gamma = 0.583$, $\delta = 0.0752$, $\sigma = 0.153$.

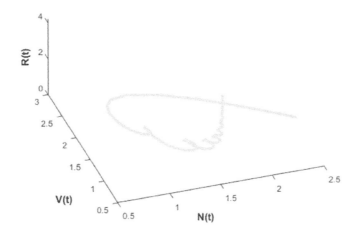

FIGURE 14.31 Phase portraits of populations of non-vaccinated-vaccinated-infected, vaccinated-infected-recovered, non-vaccinated-infected-recovered and non-vaccinated-vaccinated-recovered with time delay $\tau = 10.5$ along with $\mu = 2$, $\alpha = 0.747$, $\beta = 0.583$, $\upsilon = 0.2$, $\gamma = 0.583$, $\delta = 0.0752$, $\sigma = 0.153$.

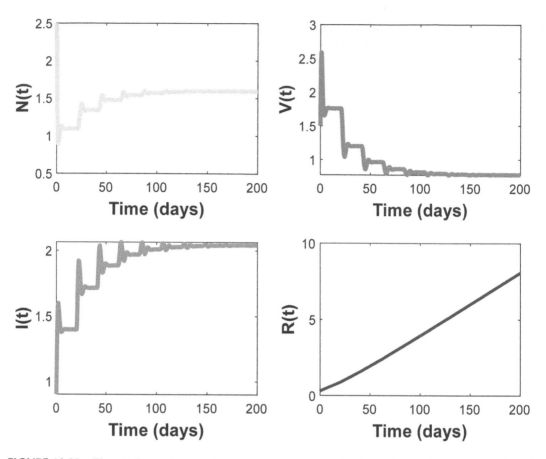

FIGURE 14.32 Time series evaluation of individual populations with time delay $\tau = 20.5$ along with attributes of $\mu = 2, \alpha = 0.747, \beta = 0.583, \upsilon = 0.2, \gamma = 0.583, \delta = 0.0752, \sigma = 0.153$.

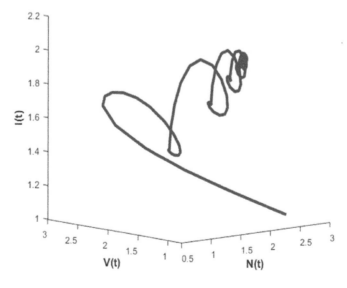

FIGURE 14.33 Phase portraits of populations of non-vaccinated-vaccinated-infected, vaccinated-infected-recovered, non-vaccinated-infected-recovered and non-vaccinated-vaccinated-recovered with time delay $\tau = 20.5$ along with attributes of $\mu = 2, \alpha = 0.747, \beta = 0.583, \upsilon = 0.2, \gamma = 0.583, \delta = 0.0752, \sigma = 0.153$.

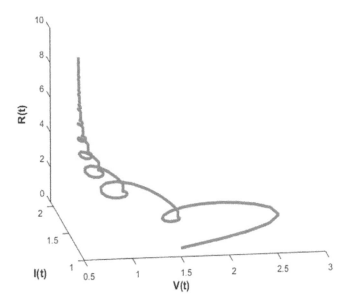

FIGURE 14.34 Phase portraits of populations of non-vaccinated-vaccinated-infected, vaccinated-infected-recovered, non-vaccinated-infected-recovered and non-vaccinated-vaccinated-recovered with time delay $\tau = 20.5$ along with attributes of $\mu = 2$, $\alpha = 0.747$, $\beta = 0.583$, $\upsilon = 0.2$, $\gamma = 0.583$, $\delta = 0.0752$, $\sigma = 0.153$.

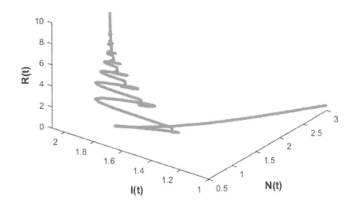

FIGURE 14.35 Phase portraits of populations of non-vaccinated-vaccinated-infected, vaccinated-infected-recovered, non-vaccinated-infected-recovered and non-vaccinated-vaccinated-recovered with time delay $\tau = 20.5$ along with attributes of $\mu = 2$, $\alpha = 0.747$, $\beta = 0.583$, $\upsilon = 0.2$, $\gamma = 0.583$, $\delta = 0.0752$, $\sigma = 0.153$.

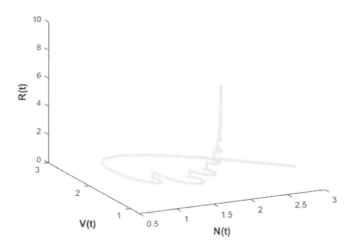

FIGURE 14.36 Phase portraits of populations of non-vaccinated-vaccinated-infected, vaccinated-infected-recovered, non-vaccinated-infected-recovered and non-vaccinated-vaccinated-recovered with time delay $\tau = 20.5$ along with attributes of $\mu = 2$, $\alpha = 0.747$, $\beta = 0.583$, $\upsilon = 0.2$, $\gamma = 0.583$, $\delta = 0.0752$, $\sigma = 0.153$.

CONTRIBUTIONS OF AUTHORS

To qualify as co-authors and corresponding authors, all authors must have made an equal contribution to the article.

CONFLICT OF INTEREST

The authors and others do not have any conflicts of interest.

ACKNOWLEDGMENT

The Department of Basic and Applied Sciences, NIFTEM Knowledge Centre, NIFTEM and Department of Mathematics, School of Advanced Sciences, Vellore Institute of Technology have all provided invaluable assistance.

REFERENCES

1. Kamrujjaman M, Mahmud MS, Islam MS (2020) Coronavirus outbreak and the mathematical growth map of Covid-19. *Annu Res Rev Biol* 35:72–78. https://doi.org/10.9734/arrb/2020/v35i130182.
2. WHO. Coronavirus disease (COVID 19) pandemic. Available from: https://www.who.int/emergencies/diseases/novelcoronavirus-2019. Accessed 6 July 2020.
3. Covid19 India. Available from: https://www.covid19india.org/. Accessed 6 July 2020.
4. Giordano G, Blanchini F, Bruno R, Colaneri P, Di Filippo A, Di Matteo A, Colaneri M (2020) Modelling the COVID-19 epidemic and implementation of population-wide interventions in Italy. *Nat Med* 26(6):855–860. https://doi.org/10.1038/s41591-020-0883-7.
5. Wang Y, Wang Y, Chen Y, Qin Q (2020) Unique epidemiological and clinical features of the emerging 2019 novel coronavirus pneumonia (COVID19) implicate special control measures. *J Med Virol* 92(6):568–576.
6. Zou L, Ruan F, Huang M, Liang L, Huang H, Hong Z, Yu J, Kang M, Song Y, Xia J, Guo Q, Song T, He J, Yen HL, Peiris M, Wu J (2020) SARS-CoV-2 viral load in upper respiratory specimens of infected patients. *N Engl J Med* 382(12):1177–1179.
7. Anderson RM, May RM (1992) *Infectious diseases of humans: dynamics and control*. Oxford University Press Inc., New York.
8. Diekmann O, Heesterbeek JAP (2000) *Mathematical epidemiology of infectious diseases: model building, analysis and interpretation*. John Wiley & Sons, Chichester.

9. Hethcote H (2000) The mathematics of infectious diseases. *SIAM Rev* 42(4):599–653.
10. Brauer F, Chavez CC (2012) *Mathematical models in population biology and epidemiology.* Springer, New York. https://doi. org/10.1007/978-1-4614-1686-9.
11. Kermack WO, McKendrick AG (1927) A contribution to the mathematical theory of epidemics. *Proc Roy Soc Lond Ser A Contain Pap Math Phys Charact* 115(772):700–721.
12. Lin Q, Zhao S, Gao D, Lou Y, Yang S, Musa S, Wang M, Cai Y, Wang W, Yang L, He D (2020) A conceptual model for the outbreak of Coronavirus disease 2019 (COVID-19) in Wuhan, China with individual reaction and governmental action. *Int J Infect Dis* 93:211–216.
13. Prem K, Liu Y, Russell TW, Kucharski AJ, Eggo RM, Davies N, Flasche S, Clifford S, Pearson CAB, Munday JD, Abbott S, Gibbs H, Rosello A, Quilty BJ, Jombart T, Sun F, Diamond C, Gimma A, Zandvoort KV, Funk S, Jarvis CI, Edmunds WJ, Bosse NI, Hellewell J, Jit M, Klepac P (2020) The effect of control strategies to reduce social mixing on outcomes of the COVID-19 epidemic in Wuhan, China: a modelling study. *Lancet Public Health* 5(5):e261–e270. https://doi.org/10.1016/S2468-2667(20)30073-6.
14. Peng L, Yang W, Zhang D, Zhuge C, Hong L (2020) Epidemic analysis of COVID-19 in China by dynamical modeling. arXiv preprint arXiv:.06563, [Submitted on 16 Feb 2020 (v1), last revised 25 Jun 2020 (this version, v2)].
15. López L, Rodo X (2020) A modified SEIR model to predict the COVID-19 outbreak in Spain and Italy: simulating control scenarios and multi-scale epidemics. Results Phys. 2021 Feb;21:103746. doi: 10.1016/j.rinp.2020.103746. Epub 2020 Dec 25. PMID: 33391984; PMCID: PMC7759445. Available at SSRN: https://doi.org/10.2139/ssrn.3576802.
16. Cantó B, Coll C, Sánchez E (2017) Estimation of parameters in a structured SIR model. *Adv Diff Eqs* 2017(1):33.
17. Chen Y, Cheng J, Jiang Y, Liu K (2020) A time delay dynamical model for outbreak of 2019-nCoV and the parameter identification. *J Inverse Ill-Posed Prob* 28(2):243–250.
18. Ma S, Xia Y (2008) Mathematical understanding of infectious disease dynamics, lecture notes series, Institute for Mathematical Sciences, National University of Singapore. *World Sci* 16:240. https://doi. org/10.1142/7020.
19. Liu C, Ding G, Gong J, Wang L, Cheng K, Zhang D (2004) Studies on mathematical models for SARS outbreak prediction and warning. *Chin Sci Bull* 49(21):2245–2251.
20. Khatun MS, Biswas MHA (2020) Mathematical analysis and optimal control applied to the treatment of leukemia. *J Appl Math Comput* 64:331–353.
21. Khatun MS, Biswas MHA (2020) Modeling the effect of adoptive T cell therapy for the treatment of leukemia. *Comput Math Methods* 2(2):e106.
22. Ferguson NM, Cummings Derek AT, Fraser C, Cajka James C, Cooley PC, Burke DS (2006) Strategies for mitigating an influenza pandemic. *Nature* 442(7101):448–452.
23. Khatun MS, Biswas MHA (2020) Optimal control strategies for preventing hepatitis B infection and reducing chronic liver cirrhosis incidence. *Infect Dis Model* 5:91–110.
24. Khatun MS, Biswas MHA (2020) Mathematical analysis and optimal control applied to the treatment of leukemia. *J Appl Math Comput* 64:331–353.
25. Khatun MS, Biswas MHA (2020) Modeling the effect of adoptive T cell therapy for the treatment of leukemia. *Comput Math Methods* 2(2):e106.
26. Khatun MS, Biswas MHA (2020) Optimal control strategies for preventing hepatitis B infection and reducing chronic liver cirrhosis incidence. *Infect Dis Model* 5:91–110.
27. Koltsova EM, Elena SK, Vasetsky AM (2020) Mathematical modeling of the spread of the coronavirus disease 2019 (COVID-19) taking into account the undetected infections. The case of China. Commun Nonlinear Sci Numer Simul. 2020 Sep;88:105303. doi: 10.1016/j.cnsns.2020.105303. Epub 2020 Apr 30. PMID: 32355435; PMCID: PMC7190554. *Comput Nanotechnol* (1):99–105.
28. Kucharski AJ, Russell TW, Diamond C, Liu Y, Edmunds J, Funk S, Eggo RM (2020) Early dynamics of transmission and control of COVID-19: a mathematical modelling study. *Lancet Infect Dis* 20(5):553–558.
29. Lau JTF, Tsui H, Lau M, Yang X (2004) SARS transmission, risk factors, and prevention in Hong Kong. *Emerg Infect Dis* 10(4):587.
30. Mandal M, Jana S, Nandi SK, Khatua A, Adak S, Kar TK (2020) A model based study on the dynamics of COVID-19: prediction and control. *Chaos Solitons Fractals* 2020:109889.
31. May RM (1991) *Infectious diseases of humans: dynamics and control.* Oxford University Press, New York.
32. Anderson RM, May RM (1979) Population biology of infectious diseases: part I. *Nature* 280(5721): 361–367.
33. May RM, Anderson RM (2019) Coronavirus Disease 2019 (COVID-19)-Symptoms and Causes, Mayo Clinic, Retrieved 14 April 2020.

34. Mehra MR, Desai SS, Kuy SR, Henry TD, Patel AN (2020) Cardiovascular disease, drug therapy, and mortality in Covid-19. *New Engl J Med* 382(25):e102.

35. Mondal MK, Hanif M, Biswas MHA (2018) A mathematical analysis of the transmission dynamics of ebola virus diseases. *J Nonlinear Anal Optim Theory Appl* 7(2):57–66.

36. Kabir MH, Gani MO, Mandal S, Biswas MHA (2020) Modeling the dispersal effect to reduce the infection of COVID-19 in Bangladesh. *Sensors Int* 1:100043.

37. Kuang Y, ed. (1993) *Delay differential equations: with applications in population dynamics.* Academic Press, Boston.

38. Egonmwan AO, Okuonghae D (2019) Mathematical analysis of a tuberculosis model with imperfect vaccine. *Int J Biomath* 12(07):1950073.

39. Kermack WO, McKendrick AG (1927) A contribution to the mathematical theory of epidemics. *Proc Roy Soc Lond Ser A Contain Pap Math Phys Character* 115(772):700–721.

40. Nwankwo A, Okuonghae D (2019) A mathematical model for the population dynamics of malaria with a temperature dependent control. *Differ Equ Dyn Syst* 2019:1–30.

41. Okuonghae D (2019) Backward bifurcation of an epidemiological model with saturated incidence, isolation and treatment functions. *Qual Theory Dyn Syst* 18:413–440.

42. Omame A, Okuonghae D, Umana RA, Inyama SC (2020) Analysis of a co-infection model for HPV-TB. *Appl Math Model* 77:881–901.

43. Omame A, Okuonghae D, Inyama SC (2020) A mathematical study of a model for HPV with two high-risk strains. *Math Model Health Soc Appl Sci* 2020:107–149.

44. Sene N (2020) SIR epidemic model with Mittag-Leffler fractional derivative. *Chaos Solitons Fractals* 137:109833.

45. Iboi E, Sharomi OO, Ngonghala C, Gumel AB (2020) Mathematical modeling and analysis of COVID-19 pandemic in Nigeria. Math Biosci Eng. 2020 Oct 22;17(6):7192-7220. doi: 10.3934/mbe.2020369. PMID: 33378893. medRxiv. *Preprint posted online* July 31.

46. Aslan İH, Demir M, Wise MM, Lenhart S (2020) Forecasting and analyzing the dynamics of the outbreak in Hubei and Turkey. *Math Methods Appl Sci* 45:6481–6494.

47. Alqarni MS, Alghamdi M, Muhammad T, Alshomrani AS, Khan MA (2022) Mathematical modeling for novel coronavirus (COVID-19) and control. *Numer Methods Partial Differ Equ* 38(4):760–776.

48. Zhao S, Chen H (2020) Modeling the epidemic dynamics and control of COVID-19 outbreak in China. *Quant Biol* 8:11–19.

49. Atangana A (2020) Modelling the spread of COVID-19 with new fractal-fractional operators: can the lockdown save mankind before vaccination? *Chaos Solitons Fractals* 136:109860.

50. Khan MA, Atangana A (2020) Modeling the dynamics of novel coronavirus (2019-nCov) with fractional derivative. *Alex Eng J* 59(4):2379–2389.

51. Awais M, Alshammari FS, Ullah S, Khan MA, Islam S (2020) Modeling and simulation of the novel coronavirus in Caputo derivative. *Res Phys* 19:103588.

52. Khan MA, Atangana A, Alzahrani E (2020) The dynamics of COVID-19 with quarantined and isolation. *Adv Differ Equ* 2020(1):425.

53. Chu Y-M, Ali A, Khan MA, Islam S, Ullah S (2021) Dynamics of fractional order COVID-19 model with a case study of Saudi Arabia. *Res Phys* 21:103787.

54. Ali A, Alshammari FS, Islam S, Khan MA, Ullah S (2021). Modeling and analysis of the dynamics of novel coronavirus (COVID-19) with Caputo fractional derivative. *Res Phys* 20:103669.

55. Lu Z, Yu Y, Chen Y, Ren G, Xu C, Wang S, Yin Z (2020) A fractional-order SEIHDR model for COVID-19 with inter-city networked coupling effects. *Nonlinear Dyn* 101(3):1717–1730.

56. World Health Organization (WHO). Worldometer. COVID-19 coronavirus pandemic. 2020. [cited 2020 April 6].

15 A Game Theory Model to Analyze Business Strategies for Increasing Profits

Analytical and Computational Approaches

Wong Wai Peng
[1]Monash University, Malaysia Campus, Malaysia

Sardar M N Islam
Victoria University, Australia

Daniel Christopher Schoch
American University of Ras Al Khaimah, UAE

15.1 INTRODUCTION: BACKGROUND AND DRIVING FORCES

Game theory can be deployed to aid business decision-making at the strategic management level in all industries, including automobile companies. The results of applied game theory models can provide useful information for companies as to which strategy they should take in maintaining market competitiveness. In addition, game theory could offer valuable insights to decision-makers in strategic business operations and development decisions. In this study, game theory models will be developed to address strategic business issues for automobile companies in a developing economy and resolve these issues by utilizing game theory to select the best strategy.

In Malaysia, UMW Holdings Berhad and its competitor, DRB-HICOM Berhad are two big automobile companies with strategic relationships in marketing and business development. Therefore, the game theory model can be developed for these two companies to determine their strategic market share, business development, and operations.

The objectives of this study are threefold: firstly, analyze the sales data for the UMW industry and the county to increase the market share of UMW Holding Berhad. Secondly, determine whether UMW Holding Berhad is entitled to any compensation for excess sales, financial cost and depreciation reduction, and inventory control. In addition, it would have earned ordinary sales after implementing the findings in game theory. Finally, give recommendations to the automotive industry.

This is the first time that a two-person, zero-sum game as an analysis approach is applied in Malaysia's automotive market. Maximin and minimax strategies are also examined in this paper for the first time to find out the best strategy for the two players in the game in Malaysia's automotive market. This study will explore some hitherto unexplored problems in Malaysia's automotive market. The game theory model of this study will provide practical strategy choices for the players in Malaysia's automotive market.

This chapter is organized as follows: Section 15.2 briefly reviews the company context, and Section 15.3 discusses game theory, i.e. minimax theorem. In Section 15.4, we consider a two-person game in which data are analyzed. The recommendation is provided in Section 15.5, and concluding comments are given in Section 15.6.

15.2   THE COMPANY CONTEXT

UMW Holdings Berhad is a big industrial enterprise in Malaysia and the Asia-Pacific region (this Company Context is prepared from the company websites and other publicly available materials). It has around 13,000 employees worldwide. UMW Holdings Berhad is a major public-listed company. UMW Holdings Berhad has four strategic business units which are the following: automotive business, equipment, manufacturing industrial business, engineering, and gas and oil.

The company has different operations in the following areas:
manufactures and trades lubricant products,
import and assembly markets,
spare parts,
markets agency lines in light and heavy industrial,
passenger and commercial vehicles,
material handling equipment,
original or replacement automotive parts,
and offshore O&G operations.

The company's main problem is the drastic decrease in profit in 2015. The profit for the year in 2015 was RM 2,192,000, while in 2014 was RM 1,213,005,000. It has dropped more than 99.8% over the year. We found that the drop in profit was due to the company's decreasing revenue. Moreover, the increase in depreciation and financial costs played a role. Lastly, it was caused by the changes in inventories integrative figure.

In Malaysia, DRB-HICOM Berhad is a big conglomerate. Through a merger between Diversified Resources Berhad (DRB) and Heavy Industries Corporation of Malaysia Berhad (HICOM), this company was established in 2000. DRB-HICOM Berhad is a competitor of UMW Holdings Berhad. UMW Holdings Berhad assembles and distributes customized vehicles such as ambulances, commercial vehicles and motorcycles. Audi, Honda, Isuzu, Volkswagen, Mitsubishi, Suzuki and Mercedes-Benz are the marques assembled or distributed by DRB-HICOM Berhad. It has more than 80 operating companies. It has more than 60,000 employees. The diversified business portfolio of DRB-HICOM Berhad is an advantage for the company. However, the profit of this company decreased from RM 650,270,000 to RM 385,148,000 in a year.

According to the 2015 annual report, the sales and revenue of the company in 2015 and 2014 was RM 14,441,583,000 and RM 14,932,490,000, respectively. It showed a decrease of about 3.29%. DRB-HICOM Berhad's revenue also declined 3.61%, from RM 14,200,742,000 to RM 13,687,839,000.

Moreover, the depreciation and amortization last year was RM 510,711,000, while in 2014, were RM 378,744 million. Thus, it increased by about RM 131,917,000, which is 34.84%. DRB-HICOM Berhad's depreciation decreased in 2015.

Besides that, the increase in the financial cost of UMW Holding Berhad in 2015 is also a factor that causes the decrease in the profit of UMW Holding Berhad. One of the categories of financial cost is bank borrowing increase of 61.04%, from RM 67,502,000 in 2014 to RM 108,705,000 in 2015. The borrowing of DRB-HICOM Berhad also increased by 7.69% from 2014 to 2015.

The change in inventory of UMW Holding Berhad is a negative figure of – RM 199,210,000 in 2015. On the other hand, in 2014, the change in inventory was a positive figure of RM 81,816,000. This issue is a problem for UMW Holding Berhad and should be solved immediately.

15.3 GAME THEORY AS AN ANALYTICAL APPROACH

Game theory is the mathematical model for strategic decision-making in a multi-agent environment. It is an analytical and mathematical method for specifying and analyzing the strategic relationships among agents in the areas of competition and cooperation. In game theory, there can be multiple decision-makers and they are called players. These players can compete against each other or cooperate among themselves. Each player chooses one strategy from multiple strategies, often without knowing the strategy selected by other players. The outcomes of the strategies selected by players provide the value or payoff of the game to the players. Game theory has been applied extensively in real-world multi-agent situations where strategic relationships exist, such as the economy, organizations, companies, political parties, teams, etc.

One player's maximin strategy is to maximize its objective function, which minimizes the objective function of other players. On the other hand, the minimax strategy for a player is to minimize its objective function that maximizes the objective function of other players.

The starting point of game theory is the minimax theorem (see Ben-El-Mechaiekh and Dimand (2010) for a review of literature in this area stated below). von Neumann (1928) provided the first proof of the minimax theorem. Later Ville (1938) made substantial contributions to this area. He established a connection between the max-min theorems and the concept of convexity. He also developed the mathematical connection between the existence of a minimax solution and the solvability of a system of linear inequalities. Ville's contributions have initiated many significant developments in some areas of mathematics and some areas close to game theory. See also Satoh and Tanka (2017) and Kjeldsen (2001) for other developments of the minimax theorem in mathematics and game theory.

In this study, two-person, zero-sum games will be used. We examine the maximin and minimax strategies for two players: UMW Holdings Berhad and DRB-HICOM Berhad. Zero-sum implies that the gain or loss for one player in a two-person zero-sum game will be equal to the loss or gain of another player. As a result, the gain or loss balances out for the game, which means that one player wins and the other player loses.

15.4 THE GAME MODEL

Suppose that there are two players in the automotive market in Malaysia, UMW Holdings Berhad ($P1$) and DRB-HICOM Berhad ($P2$). Let us consider a matrix game with four rows and four columns. Let Γ^1 denote the strategy space of $P1's$ pure strategies and Γ^2 denote the strategy space of $P2's$ pure strategies, we have $\Gamma^1 = \Gamma^2 =$ {Restructuring organization; Control the volume of production; Reduce the borrowing from the bank; Extend warranties to the customers}.

The strategy of restructuring the organization can reduce costs such as employee salaries and increase the profit of UMW Holdings Berhad. Besides that, UMW Holdings Berhad did not have a marketing department in their organization to form a marketing department after the restructuring of the organization. The number of employees of DRB-HICOM Berhad is around 15,000 people. DRB-HICOM Berhad can restructure its organization to reduce costs.

In 2015, the changes in inventories were negative figures, which means UMW Holdings Berhad has a problem controlling its inventories. If the organization chooses to control the volume of production, then it can avoid an oversupply of the inventories or lack of inventories.

Moreover, the bank borrowing of UMW Holdings Berhad increased by 61.04% in 015 compared with the year 2014. The borrowing of DRB-HICOM Berhad also increased by 7.69%. UMW Holdings Berhad and DRB-HICOM Berhad can choose to reduce the financial cost and manage the company's financial activities to increase profit in the future.

UMW Holdings Berhad can choose strategy 4 to extend the automotive warranties to attract the public's buying intention. In 2015, the revenue of UMW Holdings Berhad decreased by 3.29%.

DRB-HICOM Berhad's revenue also decreased by 3.61% from 2014 to 2015. Therefore, this strategy can increase the sales and revenue of UMW Holdings Berhad and DRB-HICOM Berhad.

Let the probability distribution of $P1's$ pure strategies space as

$$p = \{p_1, p_2, p_3, p_4\} \quad \text{and} \quad \sum_{k=1}^{4} p_k = 1,$$

where $p_k \in [0,1]$, $k \in \{1,2,3,4\}$, is the probability that $P1$ would use strategy k; and the probability distribution on the space of $P2's$ pure strategies as

$$q = \{q_1, q_2, q_3, q_4\} \quad \text{and} \quad \sum_{h=1}^{4} q_h = 1,$$

where $q_h \in [0,1]$, $h \in \{1,2,3,4\}$, is the probability that $P2$ would use strategy h.

Let π_k^1 and π_h^1 denote the strategy that $P1$ and $P2$ would adopt if DRB-HICOM Berhad chooses π_1^2, the market share of UMW Berhad will increase by 2% with a probability p_1, increase 1% with probability p_2, increase 3% with probability p_3 and not change with probability p_4. If DRB-HICOM Berhad chooses π_2^2, the market share of UMW Berhad will increase by 1% with a probability p_1, increase 0% with probability p_2, increase 2% with probability p_3 and a decrease of 1% with the probability p_4. If DRB-HICOM Berhad chooses π_3^2, the market share of UMW Berhad will reduce by 1% with a probability p_1, decrease 2 by % with probability p_2, no change in probability p_3 and increase by 1% with the probability p_4. If DRB-HICOM Berhad chooses π_4^2, the market share of UMW Berhad will increase by 3% with a probability p_1, increase by 2% with probability p_2, decrease by 1% with probability p_3 and decrease by 2% with the probability p_4.

Let a_{kh} denote the payoff to $P1$ when he uses strategy k while $P2$ uses strategy h; b_{kh} denote the payoff to $P2$ if $P1$ uses strategy k, and $P2$ uses strategy h. The payoff is present in the table below.

The objective functions (or expected payoffs) of $P1$ and $P2$ are (Table 15.1)

$$E^1(p,q) = \sum_{k=1}^{4} \sum_{h=1}^{4} p_k a_{kh} q_h; \quad \text{and}$$

$$E^2(p,q) = \sum_{k=1}^{4} \sum_{h=1}^{4} p_k b_{kh} q_h.$$

TABLE 15.1
Payoff Matrix

		DRB-HICOM			
		π_1^2	π_2^2	π_3^2	π_4^2
	π_1^1	2, −2	1, −1	−1, 1	3, −3
UMW	π_2^1	1, −1	0, 0	−2, 2	2, −2
	π_3^1	3, −3	2, −2	0, 0	−1, 1
	π_4^1	0, 0	−1, 1	1, −1	−2, 2

As strategy π_1^1 of UMW strictly dominates strategy π_2^1, the payoff matrix reduces to

		DRB-HICOM			
		π_1^2	π_2^2	π_3^2	π_4^2
	π_1^1	2, −2	1, −1	−1, 1	3, −3
UMW	π_3^1	3, −3	2, −2	0, 0	−1, 1
	π_4^1	0, 0	−1, 1	1, −1	−2, 2

Similarly, strategy π_2^2 of DRB-HICOM strictly dominates the strategy π_1^2. Hence the payoff matrix is reduced to

		DRB-HICOM		
		π_2^2	π_3^2	π_4^2
	π_1^1	1, −1	−1, 1	3, −3
UMW	π_3^1	2, −2	0, 0	−1, 1
	π_4^1	−1, 1	1, −1	−2, 2

It is easy to verify that the game has no equilibrium in pure strategies. As $q_h \in [0,1]$ and $q_1 = 0$, we write the expected payoffs for UMW when it chooses a different strategy as:

$$E_1^1\left(\pi_1^1, \pi_h^2\right) = q_2 - q_3 + 3q_4,$$

$$E_3^1\left(\pi_3^1, \pi_h^2\right) = 2q_2 - q_4,$$

$$E_4^1\left(\pi_4^1, \pi_h^2\right) = -q_2 + q_3 - 2q_4.$$

With $\sum_{h=1}^{4} q_h = 1$ and $q_1 = 0$, the above equations become:

$$E_1^1\left(\pi_1^1, \pi_h^2\right) = -2q_2 - 4q_3 + 3,$$

$$E_3^1\left(\pi_3^1, \pi_h^2\right) = 3q_2 + q_3 - 1,$$

$$E_4^1\left(\pi_4^1, \pi_h^2\right) = q_2 + 3q_3 - 2.$$

The following opportunities for mixed strategies of DRB-HICOM make UMW indifferent to two of its strategies:

$$E_1^1\left(\pi_1^1, \pi_h^2\right) = E_3^1\left(\pi_3^1, \pi_h^2\right) \langle = \rangle 5q_2 + 5q_3 = 4,$$

$$E_3^1\left(\pi_3^1,\pi_h^2\right)=E_4^1\left(\pi_4^1,\pi_h^2\right)\langle=\rangle 2q_2-2q_3=-1,$$

$$E_1^1\left(\pi_1^1,\pi_h^2\right)=E_4^1\left(\pi_4^1,\pi_h^2\right)\langle=\rangle 3q_2+7q_3=5.$$

Solve the above equations, we have $q_2=\dfrac{3}{20}$, $q_3=\dfrac{13}{20}$ and $q_4=\dfrac{1}{5}$. The expected outcome at the best response for UMW is $E_4^1\left(\pi_4^1,\pi_h^2\right)=E_3^1\left(\pi_3^1,\pi_h^2\right)=E_4^1\left(\pi_4^1,\pi_h^2\right)=0.1$. As $p_k\in[0,1]$ and $p_2=0$, the expected outcomes of DRB-HICOM when it chooses a different strategy are:

$$E_2^2\left(\pi_k^1,\pi_2^2\right)=-p_1-2p_3+p_4,$$

$$E_3^2\left(\pi_k^1,\pi_3^2\right)=p_1-p_4,$$

$$E_4^2\left(\pi_k^1,\pi_4^2\right)=-3p_1+p_3+2p_4.$$

With $\sum\limits_{k=1}^{4}p_k=1$ and $p_2=0$, the above equations become:

$$E_2^2\left(\pi_k^1,\pi_2^2\right)=-2p_1-3p_3+1,$$

$$E_3^2\left(\pi_k^1,\pi_3^2\right)=2p_1+p_3-1,$$

$$E_4^2\left(\pi_k^1,\pi_4^2\right)=-5p_1-p_3+2.$$

The following opportunities for mixed strategies of UMW make DRB-HICOM indifferent to two of its strategies:

$$E_2^2\left(\pi_k^1,\pi_2^2\right)=E_3^2\left(\pi_k^1,\pi_3^2\right)\langle=\rangle 2PA_1+2PA_3=1,$$

$$E_3^2\left(\pi_k^1,\pi_3^2\right)=E_4^2\left(\pi_k^1,\pi_4^2\right)\langle=\rangle 7PA_1+2PA_3=3,$$

$$E_2^2\left(\pi_k^1,\pi_2^2\right)=E_4^2\left(\pi_k^1,\pi_4^2\right)\langle=\rangle 3PA_1-2PA_3=1.$$

Solve the above equations, we have $p_1=\dfrac{2}{5}$, $p_3=\dfrac{1}{10}$ and $p_4=\dfrac{1}{2}$. The expected outcome at the best response for

$$E_2^2\left(\pi_k^1,\pi_2^2\right)=E_3^2\left(\pi_k^1,\pi_3^2\right)=E_4^2\left(\pi_k^1,\pi_4^2\right)=-0.1.$$

Therefore, a pair of vectors

$$\left\{p^*=(0.4,\ 0,\ 0.1,\ 0.5),q^*=(0,\ 0.15,\ 0.65,\ 0.2)\right\}$$

constitutes an equilibrium in mixed strategies.

15.5   VALUE OF FUELS AND LIGNOCELLULOSE AS RAW MATERIAL

Since the players in the market do not know the other player's strategies, we will investigate two strategies: maximin strategies and minimax strategies for two players in this section.

UMW holdings Berhad: Consider the following payoff matrix for UMW:

		DRB-HICOM			
		π_1^2	π_2^2	π_3^2	π_4^2
	π_1^1	2	1	−1	3
UMW	π_2^1	1	0	−2	2
	π_3^1	3	2	0	−1
	π_4^1	0	−1	1	−2

Here four strategies are available to both players to choose from. In such a payoff matrix, from UMW's perspective, the largest of the smallest values in each row is −1 (maximin), and the smallest of the largest values in each column is 1 (minimax).

The minimax choice for UMW is the strategy π_1^1 and strategy π_3^1, and the minimax choice for the DRB-HICOM is the strategy π_3^2. But these strategies do not lead to a Nash equilibrium. In this case, either player would choose to change their strategy given the knowledge of the other player's strategies. Therefore, we will investigate the mixed minimax strategies.

We assume that if UMW Holdings Berhad uses a mixed strategy $p = (p_1, p_2, p_3, p_4)$, DRB-HICOM Berhad selects the following strategy as it minimizes UMW Holdings Berhad's expected gain:

$$\min_{\pi_h^2}\left[E_1^1\left(\pi_1^1,\pi_h^2\right), E_2^1\left(\pi_2^1,\pi_h^2\right), E_3^1\left(\pi_3^1,\pi_h^2\right), E_4^1\left(\pi_4^1,\pi_h^2\right)\right].$$

UMW Holdings Berhad will choose its optimal mixed strategy using the maximin strategy. The maximin strategy is to maximize the minimum expected gain. The objective can be written as follows:

$$\max_{\pi_k^1}\min_{\pi_h^2}\left[E_1^1\left(\pi_1^1,\pi_h^2\right), E_2^1\left(\pi_2^1,\pi_h^2\right), E_3^1\left(\pi_3^1,\pi_h^2\right), E_4^1\left(\pi_4^1,\pi_h^2\right)\right].$$

The individual expected gain of DRB-HICOM Berhad, $E_1^2\left(\pi_k^1,\pi_1^2\right)$, $E_2^2\left(\pi_k^1,\pi_2^2\right)$, $E_3^2\left(\pi_k^1,\pi_3^2\right)$, $E_4^2\left(\pi_k^1,\pi_4^2\right)$, must equal or greater than the expected gain of UMW Holdings Berhad:

$$E_1^2\left(\pi_k^1,\pi_1^2\right) \geq E^1\left(p,q\right),$$

$$E_2^2\left(\pi_k^1,\pi_2^2\right) \geq E^1\left(p,q\right),$$

$$E_3^2\left(\pi_k^1,\pi_3^2\right) \geq E^1\left(p,q\right),$$

$$E_4^2\left(\pi_k^1,\pi_4^2\right) \geq E^1\left(p,q\right).$$

Moreover, since

$$E_1^2\left(\pi_k^1, \pi_1^2\right) = 2p_1 + p_2 + 3p_3 + 0p_4,$$

$$E_2^2\left(\pi_k^1, \pi_2^2\right) = p_1 + 0p_2 + 2p_3 - p_4,$$

$$E_3^2\left(\pi_k^1, \pi_3^2\right) = -p_1 - 2p_2 + 0p_3 + p_4,$$

$$E_4^2\left(\pi_k^1, \pi_4^2\right) = 3p_1 + 2p_2 - p_3 - 2p_4,$$

and the sum of the mixed strategy probabilities for UMW Holdings Berhad must equal 1:

$$\sum_{k=1}^{4} p_k = 1.$$

The linear program below can give UMW Holdings Berhad an optimal mixed strategy to maximize its expected gain $E^1\left(p,q\right)$:

$$2p_1 + p_2 + 3p_3 - 0p_4 - E^1\left(p,q\right) \geq 0,$$

$$p_1 + 0p_2 + 2p_3 - p_4 - E^1\left(p,q\right) \geq 0,$$

$$-p_1 - 2p_2 + 0p_3 + p_4 - E^1\left(p,q\right) \geq 0,$$

$$3p_1 + 2p_2 - p_3 - 2p_4 - E^1\left(p,q\right) \geq 0.$$

By using LINGO software, we solve the above linear program and have $p_1 = 0.4$, $p_2 = 0$, $p_3 = 0.1$, $p_4 = 0.5$, and $E^1\left(p,q\right) = 0.1$.

The results showed that UMW Holdings Berhad's optimal mixed strategy is to restructure the organization with a probability of 0.40, reduce the borrowing from the bank with a probability of 0.10 and extend warranties to the customers with a probability of 0.50. UMW Holdings Berhad should never control the volume of production because $p_2 = 0$. The expected value of this mixed strategy is a 0.1% increase in market share for UMW Holdings Berhad.

15.5.1   DRB-HICOM Berhad

If UMW chooses π_1^1, DRB-HICOM will decrease in market share by 2%, with q_1, loss 1% with q_2, but DRB- HICOM will increase by 1% with q_3, and decrease by 3% with q_4. If UMW Holdings select π_2^1, DRB-HICOM will decrease 1% with q_1, no loss happens in q_2, DRB-HICOM will increase 2% with q_3, in q_4 DRB-HICOM lost 2% of the market share. While in π_3^1, DRB-HICOM will lose 3% of its market share with q_1, and a loss 2% with q_2, but do not have any decreases in q_3, but then will increase 1% with q_4. In π_4^1, DRB-HICOM gain no loss of market share with q_1, and it will increase 1% with q_2, but with q_3 will decrease 1% of share, and with q_4 DRB-HICOM will increase 2%.

Supposed that DRB-HICOM will select a strategy that would maximize its expected gain:

$$\max_{\pi_h^1}\left[E_1^2\left(\pi_k^1,\pi_1^2\right),E_1^2\left(\pi_k^1,\pi_2^2\right),E_1^2\left(\pi_k^1,\pi_3^2\right),E_1^2\left(\pi_k^1,\pi_4^2\right)\right].$$

Meanwhile, UMW will select its optimal mixed strategy by using a minimax strategy to minimize the expected gain of DRB-HICOM. This objective is written as:

$$\min_{\pi_k^1}\max_{\pi_h^2}\left[E_1^2\left(\pi_k^1,\pi_1^2\right),E_1^2\left(\pi_k^1,\pi_2^2\right),E_1^2\left(\pi_k^1,\pi_3^2\right),E_1^2\left(\pi_k^1,\pi_4^2\right)\right].$$

Therefore, all of the individual expected gains of UMW, $E_1^1\left(\pi_1^1,\pi_h^2\right)$, $E_2^1\left(\pi_2^1,\pi_h^2\right)$, $E_3^2\left(\pi_3^1,\pi_h^2\right)$, $E_4^2\left(\pi_4^1,\pi_h^2\right)$ must be less than or equal to the expected gain of DRB-HICOM:

$$E_1^1\left(\pi_1^1,\pi_h^2\right)\le E^2,$$

$$E_2^1\left(\pi_2^1,\pi_h^2\right)\le E^2,$$

$$E_3^2\left(\pi_3^1,\pi_h^2\right)\le E^2,$$

$$E_4^2\left(\pi_4^1,\pi_h^2\right)\le E^2.$$

Furthermore, the sum of the DRB-HICOM's mixed strategy probabilities must equal to 1: $\sum_{h=1}^{4}q_h=1$. By solving the linear program below

$$2q_1+q_2-q_3+3q_4-E^2\le 0,$$

$$q_1+0q_2-2q_3+2q_4-E^2\le 0,$$

$$3q_1+2q_2+0q_3-3q_4-E^2\le 0,$$

$$0q_1-q_2+q_3-2q_4-E^2\le 0,$$

we have $q_1=0$, $q_2=0.15$, $q_3=0.65$, $q_4=0.2$, and $E^2\left(p,q\right)=-0.1$.

DRB-HICOM Berhad's optimal mixed strategy is to control the production volume with a probability of 0.15, reduce the borrowing from the bank with a probability of 0.65 and extend warranties to the customers with a probability of 0.20. DRB-HICOM Berhad should not restructure the organization because $q_1=0$. The expected loss of this mixed strategy is 0.1% in the market share of DRB-HICOM Berhad.

15.6   RECOMMENDATIONS

DRB-HICOM Berhad will minimize UMW Holdings Berhad's expected gain by selecting a mixed strategy from the strategy space with a probability distribution {0, 0.15, 0.65, 0.2}. However, UMW Holdings has chosen its optimal mixed strategy by maximizing this minimum expected gain. UMW Holdings Berhad obtains an expected gain in market share of 0.1% regardless of the strategy selected by DRB-HICOM Berhad.

Therefore, the optimal strategy for UMW Holdings Berhad is the mixed strategy with a probability distribution {0.4, 0,0.1, 0.5}. The expected gain, which is 0.1% is better than UMW Holdings Berhad's best pure strategy, which is π_1^1 and π_3^1. These two strategies provide a 1% decrease in the market share.

UMW Holdings Berhad will maximize DRB-HICOM Berhad's expected loss by selecting either π_2^1 or π_3^1 or π_4^1. However, DBR-HICOM Beerhad has chosen its optimal mixed strategy by minimizing this maximum expected loss. DBR-HICOM Berhad obtains an expected loss in market share of 0.1% regardless of the strategy selected by UMW Holdings Berhad.

Therefore, the optimal strategy for DRB-HICOM Berhad is the mixed strategy with $q_1 = 0.0$, $q_2 = 0.15$, $q_3 = 0.65$ and $q_4 = 0.2$. The expected loss, which is 0.1% is better than DRB-HICOM Berhad's best pure strategy, which is π_3^2. This strategy provides a 1% loss in the market share.

The optimal mixed strategy solution with a value of 0.1% is an equilibrium solution. Given UMW Holdings Berhad's mixed strategy probabilities, DBR-HICOM Berhad cannot improve the value of the game by changing q_1, q_2, q_3 or q_4. Given DBR-HICOM Berhad's mixed strategy probabilities, UMW Holdings Berhad cannot improve the value of the game by changing p_1, p_2, p_3 or p_4. The solution to the linear program will give an optimal equilibrium mixed strategy solution for the game.

The expected gain of 0.1% of the market share for UMW Holdings Berhad is the same as the expected loss of 0.1% of the market share for DRB-HICOM Berhad. This showed that the mixed strategy is zero-sum for the expected payoffs.

UMW Holdings Berhad can choose to restructure the organization, reduce the borrowing from the bank and extend warranties to the customers. DRB-HICOM Berhad can want to control production volume, reduce borrowing from the bank and extend warranties to the customers.

15.7   IMPLICATIONS AND CONCLUSION

The above application of game theory aids business decision-making at the strategic management level for automobile companies. The results have provided useful information for the two companies to formulate strategies for maintaining market competitiveness. In addition, this study revealed that game theory could provide helpful insight to business decision-makers in making decisions in strategy formulation for business development and marketing for solving their market share problems in the automobile industry in a developing economy. This study contributes to business and strategy knowledge by addressing strategic business issues for automobile companies in a developing economy context and providing guidance about how to resolve these issues by utilizing game theory to select the best strategy for automobile companies.

We have used game theory methods (both analytical and computational) to find and compete for the market share from this business problem with UMW Holdings Berhad and DRB-HICOM Berhad. We are using four decision strategies to choose the best strategy. Hence, we will get a better result by using zero-sum games involving two players participating in the game, and the result comes out with the gained.

We use an analytical approach to determine the best strategy for entitlement to any compensation for excess sales, reduce financial cost and depreciation, and inventory control and LINGO are also applied to reconfirm the game results and data analysis. Interestingly, both the analytical and computational approaches generate the same results and outcomes for this game.

The results showed that UMW Holdings Berhad's optimal mixed strategy is to restructure the organization with a probability of 0.40, reduce the borrowing from the bank with a probability of 0.10

and extend warranties to the customers with a probability of 0.50. UMW Holdings Berhad should never control the volume of production because $p_2=0$. The expected value of this mixed strategy is a 0.1% increase in market share for UMW Holdings Berhad.

DRB-HICOM Berhad's optimal mixed strategy is to control the production volume with a probability of 0.15, reduce the borrowing from the bank with a probability of 0.65 and extend warranties to the customers with a probability of 0.20. DRB-HICOM Berhad should not restructure the organization because $q_1=0$. The expected loss of this mixed strategy is 0.1% in the market share of DRB-HICOM Berhad.

Overall, we can identify that UMW Holdings Berhad is entitled to improve its comprehensive service, such as extending the warranties to improve its market share.

For future work, it is suggested to focus on incorporating multiple objectives into the model. In particular, to investigate whether collusion can cause unfair market advantage and the effect of using different game theory models need further analysis.

ACKNOWLEDGMENT

The authors would like to thank Dr. Yingxuan Zhang for her extensive contribution to this article.

REFERENCES

Ben-El-Mechaiekh, H., Dimand, R. W. (2010) Von Neumann, Ville, and the minimax theorem. *International Game Theory Review* 12(2), 115–137.

Kjeldsen, T. H. (2001). John von Neumann's conception of the minimax theorem: A journey through different mathematical contexts. *Archive for History of Exact Sciences* 56, 39–68.

Satoh, A., Tanaka, Y. (2017). Maximin and minimax strategies in two-players game with two strategic variables. *International Game Theory Review* 20, 1750030. doi:10.1142/S021919891750030X.

Ville, J. (1938). Sur la Théorie génerale des jeux oú intervient l'habileté des joueurs. In Gus Gutoski and John Watrous. 2007. Toward a general theory of quantum games. In Proceedings of the thirty-ninth annual ACM symposium on Theory of computing (STOC '07). Association for Computing Machinery, New York, NY, USA, 565–574. https://doi.org/10.1145/1250790.1250873

Von Neumann, J. (1928). Zur Theorie der Gesellschaftsspiele, Mathematische Annalen 100, 295–320, trans. S. Bargmann as on the Theory of Games of Strategy, in *Contributions to the Theory of Games*, 4, (eds.) A. W. Tucker and R. D. Luce, Annals of Mathematics Studies, 40 (Princeton, NJ: Princeton University Press, 1959).

16 An Efficient Course Assignment Technique Based on Teachers Rating to Support Higher Education Systems

Chittaranjan Mallick, Sourav Kumar Bhoi,
Kalyan Kumar Jena, and Debasis Mohapatra
Parala Maharaja Engineering College

16.1 INTRODUCTION

Education is the focal point of a country's financial, political, mechanical, technological, and logical improvement of public advancement. Education is supposed to increment individual information, and further develop social and financial life which means increasing Public advancement. No nation can accomplish economic improvement without focusing on the mental ability of its residents. Work on the way of life and get everybody in the country from murkiness to light that can be conveyed to battle against destitution, which is a strong weapon of the Country. Public improvement begins with the person; that is, public improvement is an element of individual advancement in the nation whereas individual improvement is the degree of education that secures a person. Each Instructive establishment ought to ensure that a gathering of Teacher individuals are playing out the tasks they are impeccably fit to or not. The Top of the Association or Scholastic Facilitator must allocate courses to teachers given their skill and their degree of viability toward the start of every semester or scholarly meeting. The vast majority of the top of the Association or Scholastic Facilitators don't know that the task model which is an exceptional device of task exploration can assist them with deciding the ideal task that will expand teacher's viability and limit Teacher planning time. Rather, they settle on the designation of teachers to the course founded on their instinct, teachers' insight, and their comprehension of teachers' ability with no respect to logical methods of occupation tasks. In this issue, a task is required. There are a few strategies for tackling the task issue like the identification strategy, transportation technique, Hungarian technique, and the proposed technique for task. In this work, we have utilized the Hungarian and proposed strategy for the task to take care of our concern.

The major contributions in this work are stated as follows.

1. In this work, we have used the Hungarian method and the proposed method assignment techniques to solve the educational course assignment problem, and the results are compared for performance evaluation.
2. From the analysis of the two methods, it is observed that both methods show the same optimal solution of 166 hours for common random data taken, however, the proposed method can solve the assignment in fewer steps.
3. The simulation is performed using MATLAB. From the simulation, it is observed that the Proposed method shows lesser computation time (seconds) than the Hungarian method.

DOI: 10.1201/9781003387459-16

The rest of the work is organized into different parts as follows. Section 16.2 presents the related works. Section 16.3 presents the materials and methods. Section 16.4 presents the proposed method of assignment for course assignment. Section 16.5 presents the case study. Section 16.6 presents the results. Section 16.7 presents the conclusion part.

16.2 RELATED WORKS

Many examination works have been finished in the space obviously assignment. Some of them are examined as follows. At this stage, people in Instructive foundations should be prepared by council part in their course of study. This board part choice of educators to influence their understudies with their insight to expand their future for superior asspects. Cheung, furthermore, Jesús [1], concentrated on the ideal and stable outcomes by utilizing task issues, related Hungarian calculations and novel outcomes. Fenster [2] stated that the level of these experts' effectiveness for the nature of the school system for advantage of understudies conceded into a superior organization. Frimpong and Owusu [3], used to decide direct programming issues to address under-distribution and over-allotment of the study hall issues. Idris also, Hussein [4] applied the task model to Alhram Court Center in Saudi Arabia in the portion of laborers to an alternate part of the store which has practical experience in the deals of garments. Kabiru et al. [5], brought up that task issues assume a huge part in tackling genuine issues in doling out educators to science subjects in Nigeria. Konig [6] proposed a strategy for assignment to track down an ideal answer for a task issue. Mansi [7], fostered a calculation for itself and furthermore demonstrated with a mathematical model that his technique yields a comparative outcome to that of Hungarian however with less advances which makes it simpler. Zavlanos et al. [8] zeroed in on straight task issues in the exploration work. Omo [9] contends that the effect of these experts called educators on understudies is undisputable jobs in the general public. Robert [10], discussed the task of laborers to occupations that the model shows balance and should be stretched out to a powerful system. Simon [11], utilized task issues to take care of staff-subject portion issue to expand the nature of information on instructors' influence on understudies' lives. Srinivas, what's more, Ganesan [12] accepts task issue is to accomplish enhancement in both assembling and administration framework. Thongsanit [13], fostered a numerical model to take care obviously homeroom task issue. Xian-Ying [14], utilized a task model in tackling educators' allotment issues to limit time to be spent in planning for instructors. Four instructors who are fit to take four distinct courses were chosen for the review. The ideal arrangement was found with the assistance of the Hungarian strategy utilized to tackle the task issue. Numerous connected exploration works are found in references [15–22]. Mallick Chittaranjan et al. [23] concentrated on course speaker assignment issues in (TURCOMAT) by task strategy.

The above works addressed the course assignment utilizing numerous task strategies. Nonetheless, as far as anyone is concerned, very little work has been finished in the space of a proposed strategy for task. In this work, we have involved Hungarian as well as a proposed technique for the task for looking at the time taken by the two strategies to tackle the course assignment issue.

16.3 MATERIALS AND METHODS

In this section, a case has been taken where n teachers are to be assigned with n subjects, and the main objective is to optimally assign these subjects to different teachers attached, based on the capability of the teachers, who will complete the task in a different time. Then, different subjects are assigned to different teachers to find the optimum assignment. To perform this, five subjects are divided into six teachers that students are admitted in the semester, five (5) are Fundamental courses that are compulsory for students in the departmental workload while one (1) course is optional. All of them are specialists in their subjects to take any five subjects that are included in simulation. Each teacher is to rate himself 100% efficiency on their level of proficiency in taking any of five (5) subjects in simulation. This problem is solved using the Hungarian method [6,7,11] and the Proposed method of assignment. The proposed method of assignment is discussed as follows.

16.3.1 ASSIGNMENT MODEL

This Assignment model is a part of linear programming that requires n teachers to perform m subjects:

Where;

n=Number of teachers to take (teach) the subjects

m=Number of subjects to perform (teach)

C=Teacher's efficiency

i=representing the subject

j=representing teachers

X=1 if the subject is assigned to a Teacher, 0 if not assigned

C_{ij}=Teacher i efficiency taking subject j

X_{ij}=1 if Teacher i will be taking subject j (0 if Teacher i will not be taking subject j)

Z=Objective Function (Maximize)

$$Z = C_{11}X_{11} + C_{12}X_{12} \tag{16.1}$$

The problem can be formulated in this canonical form:

$$Z = \sum_{i=1}^{n} \sum_{j=1}^{m} C_{ij}X_{ij} \tag{16.2}$$

with the following constraints:

$$\sum_{i=1}^{n} X_{ij} = 1 \quad i = 1,2,3,\ldots,n \left(\text{A Teacher takes a subject} \right)$$

$$\sum_{j=1}^{m} X_{ij} = 1 \quad j = 1,2,3,\ldots,m \left(\text{A subject must be taken by a Teacher} \right)$$

$$X_{ij} = 1 \quad \text{or} \quad 0 \quad \left(1 = \text{Subject assigned}; 0 = \text{Subject not assigned} \right)$$

16.4 PROPOSED METHOD OF ASSIGNMENT FOR COURSE ASSIGNMENT

The steps of the proposed method are discussed as follows:

Stage 1: Think about the given expense matrix. If the number of teachers is not equivalent to the number of subjects then making it a square matrix of given rows and columns is added with zero expense.

Stage 2: Find the littlest component in each line and afterward deduct that component from each row. Consequently, the principal diminished cost framework is created where each row has precisely one zero.

Stage 3: Find the littlest component in every section of the row and afterward deduct that component from every column segment. Subsequently, the main diminished cost grid is created where every column segment has precisely one zero.

Stage 4: Examine each row in the new framework table to distinguish a row with a zero, (leave any row with more than a zero and move to the following rows) when precisely one zero is found then relegate it to the related row and erase the comparing row and column line segment after designation. Generally tracked down the area of zero beneath for further interaction.

Stage 5: On the off chance that there is more than one zero, track down the replacement of nothing and analyze the greatest worth and appoint zero.

Stage 6: Rehash steps (4), and (5) and track down the optimal solutions.

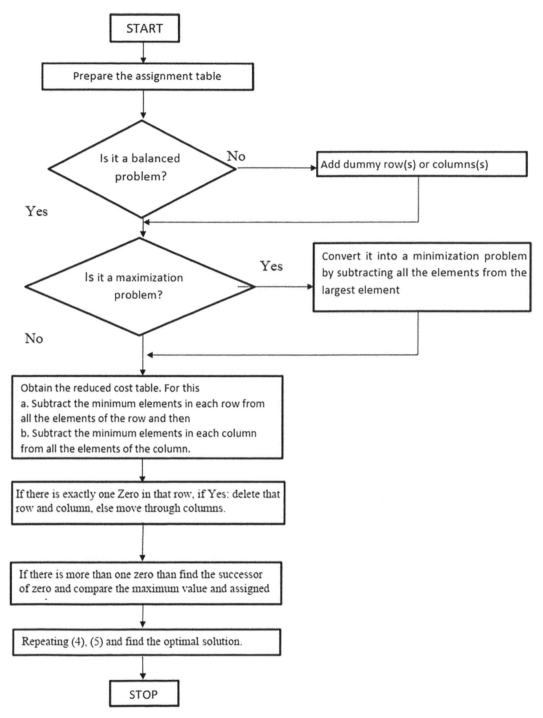

FIGURE 16.1 Flowchart for the proposed method of assignment for course assignment.

Flowchart for the proposed method of assignment for course assignment is mentioned in Figure 16.1.

16.5 CASE STUDY

In this study, the objective is to assign the merit of five teachers from six teachers to teach five different subjects, so that minimization can be done for the total number of class hours. The following

TABLE 16.1
Teacher Efficiency Rating

Course Title	Course Code	Rating (100%)
Teacher X		
Course-101	Th-1	30
Course-102	Th-2	39
Course-103	Th-3	31
Course-104	Th-4	38
Course-105	Th-5	40
Teacher Y		
Course-101	Th-1	43
Course-102	Th-2	37
Course-103	Th-3	32
Course-104	Th-4	35
Course-105	Th-5	38
Teacher Z		
Course-101	Th-1	34
Course-102	Th-2	41
Course-103	Th-3	33
Course-104	Th-4	41
Course-105	Th-5	34
Teacher P		
Course-101	Th-1	39
Course-102	Th-2	36
Course-103	Th-3	43
Course-104	Th-4	32
Course-105	Th-5	36
Teacher Q		
Course-101	Th-1	32
Course-102	Th-2	49
Course-103	Th-3	35
Course-104	Th-4	40
Course-105	Th-5	37
Teacher R		
Course-101	Th-1	36
Course-102	Th-2	42
Course-103	Th-3	35
Course-104	Th-4	44
Course-105	Th-5	42

list in Table 16.1 shows their competence level based on the Efficiency Rating measures. This is random data taken for performance evaluation. Entries in Table 16.1 show teachers self-rating on a 100% efficiency and the entries in the first column are the subject-titles to be allocated. The second column displays the segmentation of the topics.

16.6   RESULTS

In this section, we have analyzed the performance of the two methods (Hungarian and Proposed method) on random data taken in Table 16.2 and Figure 16.2. Table 16.2 shows the ratings of

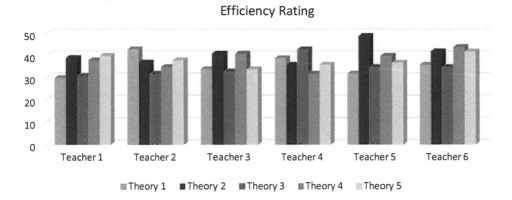

FIGURE 16.2 Efficiency ratings of Teacher's theory wise.

TABLE 16.2

Assignment Model Table with Ratings of Teachers Theory Wise (Theory Is Represented as Th)

Courses/Teachers	Th-1	Th-2	Th-3	Th-4	Th-5
Teacher X	30	39	31	38	40
Teacher Y	43	37	32	35	38
Teacher Z	34	41	33	41	34
Teacher P	39	36	43	32	36
Teacher Q	32	49	35	40	37
Teacher R	36	42	35	44	42

---

teacher's theory (Th) wise. The two methods are also simulated on a random dataset generated using MATLAB to evaluate the computation time taken by the methods to find the efficiency.

Efficiency ratings of teacher's theory wise are mentioned in Figure 16.2.

16.6.1 HUNGARIAN METHOD

In the given problem (Table 16.2), the number of rows is not equal to the number of columns. Hence, it is an unbalanced assignment problem. So, this problem should be converted into a balanced assignment problem by introducing a dummy column with all zero cell entries as shown in Table 16.3.

The row minimum is 0 in every row. Row reduction is carried out in Table 16.3. Table 16.3 describes the conversion mechanism for the minimization problem. Table 16.4 shows the column minimum of each column.

The column reduction is carried out as shown in Table 16.5 by subtracting the elements from the column minimum. The matrix Table 16.5 is the input for the next iteration.

Table 16.6 shows the minimum required several lines which are drawn to cover all the zeros. The number of squares marked in Table 16.6 is not equal to the number of rows. Hence go to the next iteration.

The minimum among the undeleted entries in Table 16.6 is 1. The entries in Table 16.6 are obtained from Table 16.5 by applying step 5. Table 16.5 also shows the minimum required several lines which are drawn to cover all the zeros. In Table 16.7, the total number of cells marked with squares is 5 which is not equal to the number of rows of the matrix. Hence, go to the next iteration.

TABLE 16.3
Balancing the Rows and Columns by Adding Dummy Columns

Courses/Teachers	Th-1	Th-2	Th-3	Th-4	Th-5	Th-6
Teacher X	30	39	31	38	40	0
Teacher Y	43	37	32	35	38	0
Teacher Z	34	41	33	41	34	0
Teacher P	39	36	43	32	36	0
Teacher Q	32	49	35	40	37	0
Teacher R	36	42	35	44	42	0

TABLE 16.4
Matrix after Row Reduction

Courses/Teachers	Th-1	Th-2	Th-3	Th-4	Th-5	Th-6
Teacher X	30	39	31	38	40	0
Teacher Y	43	37	32	35	38	0
Teacher Z	34	41	33	41	34	0
Teacher P	39	36	43	32	36	0
Teacher Q	32	49	35	40	37	0
Teacher R	36	42	35	44	42	0
Column minimum	30	36	31	32	34	0

TABLE 16.5
Matrix after Column Reduction

Courses/Teachers	Th-1	Th-2	Th-3	Th-4	Th-5	Th-6
Teacher X	0	3	0	6	6	0
Teacher Y	13	1	1	3	4	0
Teacher Z	4	5	2	9	0	0
Teacher P	9	0	12	0	2	0
Teacher Q	2	13	4	8	3	0
Teacher R	6	6	4	12	8	0

TABLE 16.6
Row Wise Allocation

Courses/Teachers	Th-1	Th-2	Th-3	Th-4	Th-5	Th-6
Teacher X	0	3	0	6	6	0
Teacher Y	13	1	1	3	4	0
Teacher Z	4	5	2	9	0	0
Teacher P	9	0	12	0	2	0
Teacher Q	2	13	4	8	3	0
Teacher R	6	6	4	12	8	0

TABLE 16.7
Column Wise Allocation

Courses/Teachers	Th-1	Th-2	Th-3	Th-4	Th-5	Th-6
Teacher X	0	3	0	6	7	1
Teacher Y	12	0	0	2	4	0
Teacher Z	3	4	1	8	0	0
Teacher P	9	0	12	0	3	1
Teacher Q	1	12	3	7	3	0
Teacher R	5	5	3	11	8	0

TABLE 16.8
Final Allocation for a Course Assignment

Courses/Teachers	Th-1	Th-2	Th-3	Th-4	Th-5	Th-6
Teacher X	0	3	0	6	7	2
Teacher Y	12	0	0	2	4	1
Teacher Z	3	4	1	8	0	1
Teacher P	9	0	12	0	3	2
Teacher Q	0	11	2	6	2	0
Teacher R	4	4	2	10	7	0

TABLE 16.9
Optimum Allocation Table

Topic	Theory	Teacher	Efficiency Rating
Course-101	Th-3	Teacher X	31
Course-102	Th-2	Teacher Y	37
Course-103	Th-5	Teacher Z	34
Course-104	Th-4	Teacher P	32
Course-105	Th-1	Teacher Q	32
	Th-6	Teacher R	0
Total efficiency			166 hours

Table 16.8 also shows the minimum required several lines which are drawn to cover all zeros.

In Table 16.8, the total number of cells marked with squares is 6, which is equal to the number of rows of the square matrix. So, the solution of this iteration is feasible and optimal and the corresponding results are given below in Table 16.9.

A total number of allocations=the Total number of row orders of the matrix, hence the assignment is optimal. Since the result is optimal, we can allocate teachers to the topics from the assignment model. Allocation will be made to each cell with a squared zero.

Table 16.9 above shows the person and course assignment results obtained from the computation algorithm mentioned in the Hungarian method. The result showed that the Institutions should assign Course-101 (Th-3) to Teacher X to obtain 31% efficiency in the knowledge of Course-101, Course-102 (Th-2) should be assigned to Teacher Y to get 37% efficiency; Teacher Z should take Course-103 (Th-5) to achieve 34% efficiency. Course-104 (Th-4) should be assigned to Teacher P to

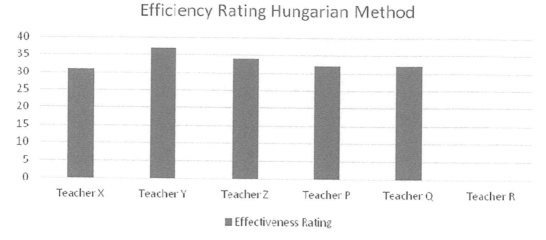

FIGURE 16.3 Efficiency ratings of Teacher's theory wise after applying the Hungarian method; Teacher X: Th-3, Teacher Y: Th-2, Teacher Z: Th-5, Teacher P: Th-4, Teacher Q: Th-1, Teacher R: Th-6.

derive 32% of efficiency; Course-105 (Th-1) should be assigned to Teacher Q to get 32% efficiency: finally, Teacher R in (Th-6) to achieve 0% efficiency i.e, no class has been assigned to Teacher R in Subject 6. Presently, Course-101 (Th-1) is allocated to Teacher X who is 30% effective in the teaching of that topic, Course-102 (Theory2) is allocated to Teacher Y with a 37% level of efficiency, Course-103 (Th-3) is given to Teacher Z with 33% efficiency while Course-104 (Theory4) is allocated to Teacher P who is 32% effective in teaching that topic and lastly, Course-105 (Th-5) is allocated to Teacher Q with 37% effective in taking the topic, finally, no subject is assigned to Teacher R in (Th-6), because the efficiency of Teacher R is 0, leaving the department to achieve 166 efficiencies based on heuristic approach employed by the Head of Department on the five topics which are effective in analyzing decision taken by the department of the College. The efficiency is also mentioned in Figure 16.3.

16.6.2 PROPOSED METHOD

In this section, the data in Table 16.2 is solved using the Proposed method of assignment. The steps are discussed as follows:

Table 16.10 shows the balancing of the rows and columns by adding a dummy column (column 6) as the number of teachers is 6 and the Theory is 5.

The row minimum is 0 in every row. Row reduction is carried out in Table 16.11.

The column reduction is carried out as shown in Table 16.12. The matrix Table is the input for the next iteration.

Table 16.13 shows the assignment of Teacher R to Th-6 and deleting required rows and columns of the above matrix, as shown in Table 16.14.

From Table 16.14, Teacher Y and Teacher Q's rows do not contain any zeros, by assigning the smallest element of that row and subtracting it from the required elements of that row. Row reduction is carried out in Table 16.15.

From Table 16.16, Assign Teacher Q to assign Th-1 and delete the obtained rows and columns of the above matrix as shown in Table 16.17.

From Table 16.18, Assign Teacher Z in Th-5 and delete obtained rows and columns of the above matrix as shown in Table 16.19. The above process continues from Tables 16.19–16.22 to find the optimum allocation table in Table 16.23.

TABLE 16.10

Balancing the Rows and Columns by Adding Dummy Columns

Courses/Teachers	Th-1	Th-2	Th-3	Th-4	Th-5	Th-6
Teacher X	30	39	31	38	40	0
Teacher Y	43	37	32	35	38	0
Teacher Z	34	41	33	41	34	0
Teacher P	39	36	43	32	36	0
Teacher Q	32	49	35	40	37	0
Teacher R	36	42	35	44	42	0

TABLE 16.11

Matrix after Row Reduction

Courses/Teachers	Th-1	Th-2	Th-3	Th-4	Th-5	Th-6
Teacher X	30	39	31	38	40	0
Teacher Y	43	37	32	35	38	0
Teacher Z	34	41	33	41	34	0
Teacher P	39	36	43	32	36	0
Teacher Q	32	49	35	40	37	0
Teacher R	36	42	35	44	42	0
Column minimum	30	36	31	32	34	0

TABLE 16.12

Matrix after Column Reduction

Courses/Teachers	Th-1	Th-2	Th-3	Th-4	Th-5	Th-6
Teacher X	0	3	0	6	6	0
Teacher Y	13	1	1	3	4	0
Teacher Z	4	5	2	9	0	0
Teacher P	9	0	12	0	2	0
Teacher Q	2	13	4	8	3	0
Teacher R	6	6	4	12	8	0

TABLE 16.13

Assigning Teacher with Different Subjects

Rows	Columns
Teacher X	Th-1, Th-3, Th-6
Teacher Y	Th-6
Teacher Z	Th-5, Th-6
Teacher P	Th-2, Th-4
Teacher Q	Th-6
Teacher R	Th-6

TABLE 16.14
Assigning after Deletion of Teacher R and Th-6

Courses/Teachers	Th-1	Th-2	Th-3	Th-4	Th-5
Teacher X	0	3	0	6	6
Teacher Y	13	1	1	3	4
Teacher Z	4	5	2	9	0
Teacher P	9	0	12	0	2
Teacher Q	2	13	4	8	3

TABLE 16.15
Row Reduction after Subtracting Minimum Element (1)

Courses/Teachers	Th-1	Th-2	Th-3	Th-4	Theory5
Teacher X	0	3	0	6	6
Teacher Y	12	0	0	2	3
Teacher Z	4	5	2	9	0
Teacher P	9	0	12	0	2
Teacher Q	0	11	2	6	1

TABLE 16.16
Teacher Assigned with Different Subjects

Rows	Columns
Teacher X	Th-1, Th-3,
Teacher Y	Th-2, Th-3
Teacher Z	Th-5
Teacher P	Th-4
Teacher Q	Th-1

TABLE 16.17
Deletion of Th-1 and Teacher Q

Courses/Teachers	Th-2	Th-3	Th-4	Th-5
Teacher X	3	0	6	6
Teacher Y	0	2	3	3
Teacher Z	5	2	9	0
Teacher P	0	12	0	0

TABLE 16.18
Assigning Teachers to Different Subjects

Rows	Columns
Teacher X	Th-3
Teacher Y	Th-2
Teacher Z	Th-5
Teacher P	Th-1, Th-4, Th-5

TABLE 16.19
Deletion of Teacher Z and Th-5

Courses/Teachers	Th-2	Th-3	Th-4
Teacher X	3	0	6
Teacher Y	0	2	3
Teacher P	0	12	0

TABLE 16.20
Assigning Teachers with Different Subjects

Rows	Columns
Teacher X	Th-3
Teacher Y	Th-2
Teacher P	Th-2, Th-4

TABLE 16.21
Deletion of Teacher Y and Th-2

Courses/Teachers	Th-3	Th-4
Teacher X	0	0
Teacher P	2	8

TABLE 16.22
Subtracting Minimum Element (2)

Courses/Teachers	Th-3	Th-4
Teacher X	0	0
Teacher P	0	6

TABLE 16.23
Optimum Allocation Table

Topic	Theory	Teacher	Efficiency
Course-101	Th-3	Teacher X	31
Course-102	Th-2	Teacher Y	37
Course-103	Th-5	Teacher Z	34
Course-104	Th-4	Teacher P	32
Course-105	Th-1	Teacher Q	32
	Th-6 (Dummy)*	Teacher R	0
Total efficiency			166 hours

So minimal assignment $31+37+34+32+32+0=166$ hours. The total time is 166 hours, and Teacher 6 is not assigned to any subject.

Efficiency ratings of teacher's theory wise after applying the Proposed method are mentioned in Figure 16.4.

To find the computation time of the two methods, we have simulated the two methods using MATLAB programming. For that, we have varied the cases such as 10 teachers with 5 subjects, 20 teachers with 15 subjects, 30 teachers with 25 subjects, 40 teachers with 35 subjects, 50 teachers with 45 subjects, 60 teachers with 55 subjects, 70 teachers with 65 subjects, 80 teachers with 75 subjects, 90 teachers with 85 subjects, and 100 teachers with 95 subjects. The results are shown in Figure 16.5 as follows. From the two methods, it is shown that the proposed method shows lesser

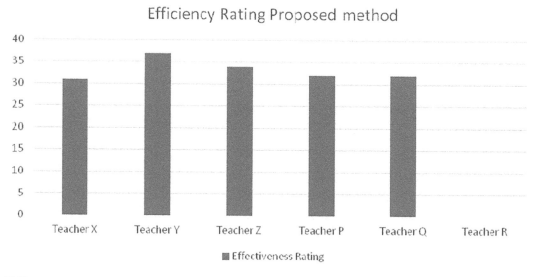

FIGURE 16.4   Efficiency ratings of Teacher's theory wise after applying the Proposed method; Teacher X: Th-3, Teacher Y: Th-2, Teacher Z: Th-5, Teacher P: Th-4, Teacher Q: Th-1, Teacher R: Th-6.

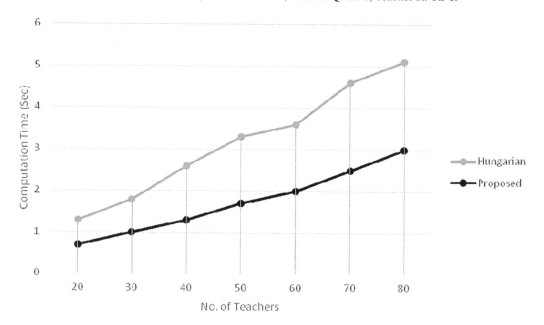

FIGURE 16.5   Computation time (seconds) calculated in MATLAB for the Hungarian method and Proposed method when the no. of teachers and number of subjects varies.

time than the Hungarian method in all the cases for solving the assignment problem. Computation time (seconds) calculated in MATLAB for the Hungarian method and Proposed method when the number of teachers and number of subjects varies is mentioned in Figure 16.5.

16.6.3   LIMITATIONS OF THE STUDY

The limitations of the study are:

1. This work considers only one educational institute and one department for analysis.
2. The size of the number of teachers and courses taken are also small (Teachers=06, Courses=05).
3. It is only compared with one standard assignment approach (Hungarian method).
4. The proposed method gives a systematic and transparent solution as compared to the Hungarian method, researchers may follow this method.

16.7   CONCLUSION

In this work, the assignment problem of course assignment is solved using the Hungarian method and the proposed method of assignment, and the results are compared for the performance of evaluation. If the solution suggested by the above discussion by the Head of the Organization will experience 166 hours of maximum efficiency on the five subjects in Analysis for Business Decision to be undertaken for the five best teachers. From the analysis of the two methods, it is observed that both methods show the same optimal solution of 166 hours, however, the proposed method can solve the problem in fewer steps. The simulation is also performed using MATLAB by varying the number of subjects and teachers. It is observed that the Proposed method shows lesser computation time than the Hungarian method. The use of the Proposed method of solving assignment problems gives a systematic and transparent solution as compared to the Hungarian method. Therefore, the researchers are recommended to adopt the Proposed method of solving assignment problems in other areas of research. Also, the limitations discussed above can be further explored for better research work.

REFERENCES

[1] Cheung, R., & De Loera, J. A. (2011). The Geometry of the Simplex Method and Applications to the Assignment Problems.
[2] Fenster, D. E. (2014). Implications of teacher tenure on teacher quality and student performance in North Carolina (Doctoral dissertation, Duke University Durham).
[3] Frimpong, F. O., & Owusu, A. (2015). Allocation of classroom space using linear programming (a case study: premier nurses training college, Kumasi). *Journal of Economics and Sustainable Development*, 6(2), 12–20.
[4] Idriss, E. M., & Hussein, E. M. (2015). Application of linear programming (assignment model). *International Journal of Science and Research (IJSR)*, 4(3), 1446–1449.
[5] Kabiru, S., Saidu, B. M., Abdul, A. Z., & Ali, U. A. (2017). An optimal assignment schedule of staff-subject allocation. *Journal of Mathematical Finance*, 7(04), 805.
[6] Konig, D. (1931). Graphok es matrixok (Hungarian)[Graphs and matrices]. *Matematikai és Fizikai Lapok*, 38, 116–119.
[7] Gaglani, M. S. (2011). A study on transportation problems, transshipment problems, assignment problems, and supply chain management (Doctoral dissertation, Saurashtra University).
[8] Michael, N., Zavlanos, M. M., Kumar, V., & Pappas, G. J. (2008, May). Distributed multi-robot task assignment and formation control. *2008 IEEE International Conference on Robotics and Automation*, 128–133.
[9] Omo, A. (2011). Quality of teachers and performance: evidence from schools in Ibadan metropolis in Nigeria. *Ozean Journal of Social Science*, 4(3), 163–175.

[10] Shimer, R. (2005). The assignment of workers to jobs in an economy with coordination frictions. *Journal of Political Economy, 113*(5), 996–1025.

[11] Simon, K. (2012). *Staff assignment problem*, https://www.academia.edu/9461669/STAFF_ASSIGNMENT_PROBLEM accessed on April 2021.

[12] Srinivas, B., & Ganesan, G. (2015). A method for solving branch-and-bound techniques for assignment problems using triangular and trapezoidal fuzzy. *International Journal of Management and Social Science, 3*, 7–10.

[13] Thongsanit, K. (2014). Solving the course - classroom assignment problem for a university. *Silpakorn University Science and Technology Journal, 8*, 46–52.

[14] Xian-ying, M. (2012). Application of assignment model in PE human resources allocation. *Energy Procedia, 16*, 1720–1723.

[15] Alsubaie, A., Alaithan, M., Boubaid, M., & Zaman, N. (2018, February). Making learning fun: educational concepts & logics through the game. In *2018 20th International Conference on Advanced Communication Technology (ICACT)* (pp. 454–459). IEEE.

[16] Alamri, M. Z., Jhanjhi, N. Z., & Humayun, M. (2020). Digital curriculum importance for new era education. Advances in Electronic Government, Digital Divide, and Regional Development. In *Employing Recent Technologies for Improved Digital Governance* (pp. 1–18). IGI Global.

[17] Khalil, M. I., Humayun, M., & Jhanjhi, N. Z. (2021). COVID-19 impact on the educational system globally. *Emerging Technologies for Battling Covid-19: Applications and Innovations 324*, (pp. 257–269).

[18] Mallicka, C. (2021). CLAPS: Course and lecture assignment problem solver for educational institution using Hungarian method. *Turkish Journal of Computer and Mathematics Education (TURCOMAT), 12*(10), 3085–3092.

[19] Rezaeipanah, A., Matoori, S. S., & Ahmadi, G. (2021). A hybrid algorithm for the university course assignment problem using the improved parallel genetic algorithm and local search. *Applied Intelligence, 51*(1), 467–492.

[20] Osorio, J. A., & Esquivel, A. M. (2020). A solution to the university course assignment problem using a hybrid method based on genetic algorithms. *DYNA: Revista de la Facultad de Minas. Universidad Nacional de Colombia. Sede Medellín, 87*(215), 47–56.

[21] Tavakoli, M. M., Shirouyehzad, H., Lotfi, F. H., & Najafi, S. E. (2020). Proposing a novel heuristic algorithm for university course assignment problem with the quality of courses rendered approach; a case study. *Alexandria Engineering Journal, 59*(5), 3355–3367.

[22] Thepphakorn, T., & Pongcharoen, P. (2020). Performance improvement strategies on Cuckoo Search algorithms for solving the university course assignment problem. *Expert Systems with Applications, 161*, 113732.

[23] Mallick Chittaranjan et al. (2021). CLAPS: Course and Lecture Assignment Problem Solver for Educational Institution Using Hungarian Method. Turkish Journal of Computer and Mathematics Education (TURCOMAT), 12(10), 3085–3092. Retrieved from https://turcomat.org/index.php/turkbilmat/article/view/4959Studied course lecturer assignment problems in (TURCOMAT) by assignment technique.

Index

algorithms 76–79, 81–85, 92, 93, 103–105, 107, 108, 110, 111, 113–115, 117, 123–126, 152, 153, 155, 161, 164–168, 171, 172, 181
aqueous humor 66–69, 71, 74
artificial intelligence 98, 152, 161
Artificial Neural Network (ANN) 164, 171, 174, 176
asset liability management 187–189, 201
automotive market 235, 237

Channel Equalization 109–115
coefficient of friction 59, 65
conjoint analysis 43–50, 52, 53
conjoint package 48–50
convexity 187–191, 193, 196, 201, 237

deep perceptron 172
drilling 128–130, 132, 133, 135, 137, 138

entropy 23, 24, 188, 189, 191, 192, 195

FIFA world cup 170, 171
financial ratios 22, 24, 25, 29, 30, 41
fish 1, 2, 4–6, 12, 15–17, 66, 84, 123
fuzzy differential equation 140, 141
fuzzy linear programming 76, 90, 91
fuzzy logic 76–78, 85, 93, 96–103, 105–115
fuzzy nonlinear optimization 76–81, 83, 84, 86–93
fuzzy optimization 76, 79, 84, 85, 89, 90, 91–93, 167

game theory 167, 235–237, 244, 245
GFRP 128, 129, 137
glaucoma 67–69, 74
grey relational analysis 138
GWO 123–126

harvesting 1, 2, 5–7, 9, 17
Hopf-bifurcation 6, 16

Hungarian method 246, 247, 253, 259

intraocular pressure (IOP) 66–69, 73, 74

machine learning 100, 104, 113, 114, 152, 170, 171
market research 43–46, 48, 52, 53
mathematical models 141, 164, 179, 206
MOORA 56, 59, 60, 64, 65

nonlinear optimization 76–81, 83, 84, 86–93, 117

optimization 22, 25–27, 60, 65, 76–93, 102, 105, 113, 114, 117, 123, 124, 165–167, 174

plankton 1, 2, 4, 12, 16, 17
PROMETHEE 23, 42, 56, 59, 64, 65
PSO 76, 78–81, 83–85, 87–92, 117, 118, 123–126

reproduction number 208, 209, 228

Schlemm's Canal 67, 68, 69
soccer game 171, 172
stability 1, 2, 4, 5, 9–17, 23, 29, 40, 41, 99, 100, 106, 141, 147–150, 206, 211, 212, 228
steady state 5, 9, 10, 13–15, 17, 119, 122, 207, 210–212
stochastic 1, 2, 9, 10, 12, 16, 17, 161, 167, 188
strategies 24, 43, 91, 93, 100, 167, 180, 181, 184, 187, 188, 206, 235, 237–241, 244, 246, 247
supervised learning 152, 156, 171, 174, 177, 179

Taguchi method 129
time delay 1, 206, 207, 228
trabecular meshwork 66–69, 74

VIKOR 22–28, 40, 41

wireless communications 96, 104, 112

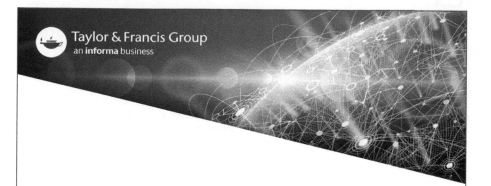

Taylor & Francis eBooks

www.taylorfrancis.com

A single destination for eBooks from Taylor & Francis with increased functionality and an improved user experience to meet the needs of our customers.

90,000+ eBooks of award-winning academic content in Humanities, Social Science, Science, Technology, Engineering, and Medical written by a global network of editors and authors.

TAYLOR & FRANCIS EBOOKS OFFERS:

A streamlined experience for our library customers

A single point of discovery for all of our eBook content

Improved search and discovery of content at both book and chapter level

REQUEST A FREE TRIAL
support@taylorfrancis.com

Milton Keynes UK
Ingram Content Group UK Ltd.
UKHW020822141024
449569UK00008B/520

9 781032 479613